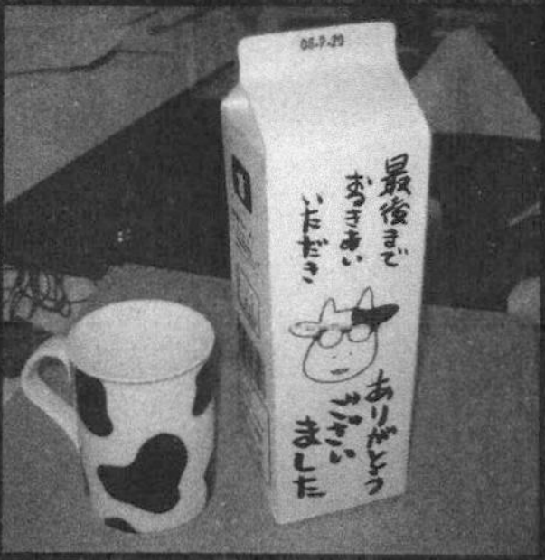
最後まで
おつきあい
いただき
ありがとう
ございました

Thank you very much for staying with me till the end.

I've always tried my best to insert words of greeting and thanks into the characters' dialogue in *Fullmetal Alchemist*. I truly believe that a simple greeting or giving thanks helps us appreciate the fact that we, as human beings, depend on the support of one another to live.

And now, as this journey comes to an end, I'd like say to everyone who was involved, "See you around" and "Thank you very much."

—Hiromu Arakawa, 2010

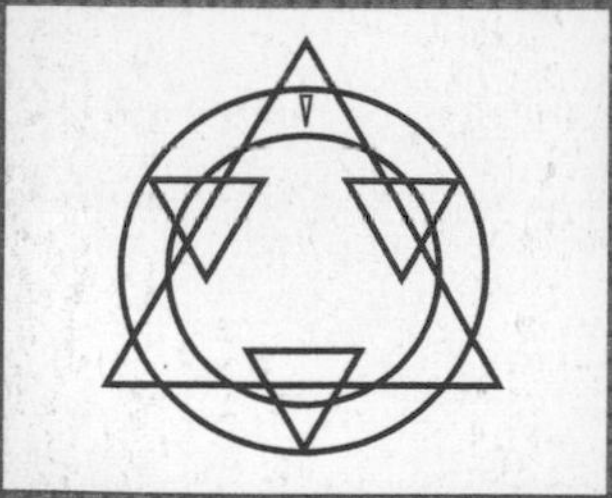

Born in Hokkaido (northern Japan), Hiromu Arakawa first attracted national attention in 1999 with her award-winning manga *Stray Dog*. Her series *Fullmetal Alchemist* debuted in 2001 in Square Enix's monthly manga anthology *Shonen Gangan*.

FULLMETAL ALCHEMIST
VOL. 27

VIZ Media Edition

Story and Art by Hiromu Arakawa

Translation/Akira Watanabe
English Adaptation/Jake Forbes
Touch-up Art & Lettering/Wayne Truman
Cover Design/Julie Behn
Interior Design/Ronnie Casson
Editor/Alexis Kirsch

Hagane no RenkinJutsushi vol. 27 © 2010 Hiromu Arakawa/SQUARE ENIX. First published in Japan in 2010 by SQUARE ENIX CO., LTD. English translation rights arranged with SQUARE ENIX CO., LTD. and VIZ Media, LLC.

The rights of the author(s) of the work(s) in this publication to be so identified have been asserted in accordance with the Copyright, Designs and Patents Act 1988. A CIP catalogue record for this book is available from the British Library.

The stories, characters and incidents mentioned in this publication are entirely fictional.

No portion of this book may be reproduced or transmitted in any form or by any means without written permission from the copyright holders.

Printed in the U.S.A.

Published by VIZ Media, LLC
P.O. Box 77010
San Francisco, CA 94107

10 9 8 7 6 5 4 3 2 1
First printing, December 2011

www.viz.com

RATED
PARENTAL ADVISORY
FULLMETAL ALCHEMIST is rated T for Teen and is recommended for ages 13 and up. Contains mildly strong language, tobacco/alcohol use and fantasy violence.
FOR TEEN
ratings.viz.com

鋼の錬金術師

FULLMETAL ALCHEMIST

27

荒川弘

HIROMU ARAKAWA

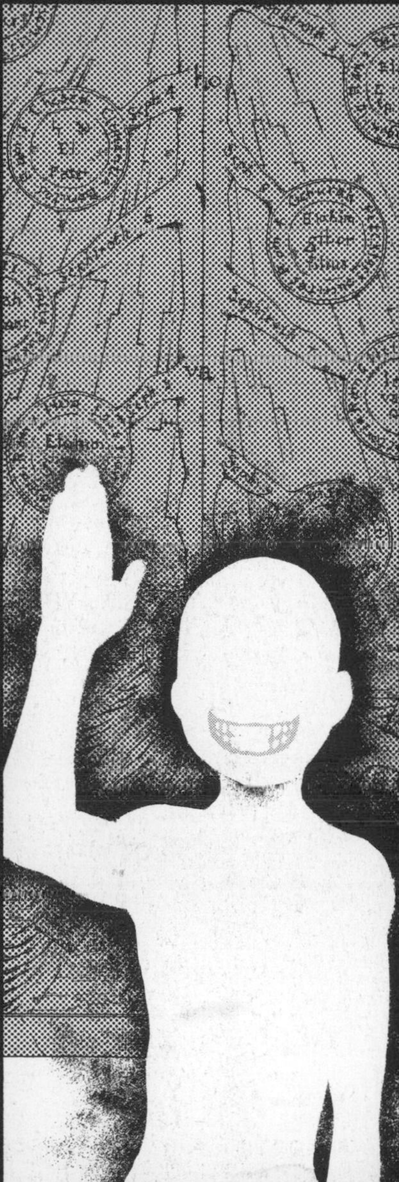

■ アルフォンス・エルリック

Alphonse Elric

■ エドワード・エルリック

Edward Elric

■ アレックス・ルイ・アームストロング

Alex Louis Armstrong

■ ロイ・マスタング

Roy Mustang

OUTLINE
FULLMETAL ALCHEMIST

Using a forbidden alchemical ritual, the Elric brothers attempted to bring their dead mother back to life. But the ritual went wrong, consuming Edward Elric's leg and Alphonse Elric's entire body. At the cost of his arm, Edward was able to graft his brother's soul into a suit of armor. Equipped with mechanical "auto-mail" to replace his missing limbs, Edward becomes a state alchemist in hopes of finding a way to restore their bodies. Their search embroils them in a deadly conspiracy that threatens to take the innocence, if not the lives, of everyone involved.

Now, on the Day of Reckoning, as the original Homunculus reaches for godhood, the Elric brothers and the other alchemists who dared open a portal to the Truth are fighting the battle of their lives, with the fate of the world hanging in the balance.

鋼の錬金術師
FULLMETAL ALCHEMIST

▊CHARACTERS
FULLMETAL ALCHEMIST

□ お父様

Father

□ スカー

Scar

□ オリヴィエ・ミラ・アームストロング

Olivier Mira Armstrong

□ リン・ヤオ（グリード）

Lin Yao (Greed)

□ メイ・チャン

May Chang

□ ヴァン・ホーエンハイム

Van Hohenheim

CONTENTS

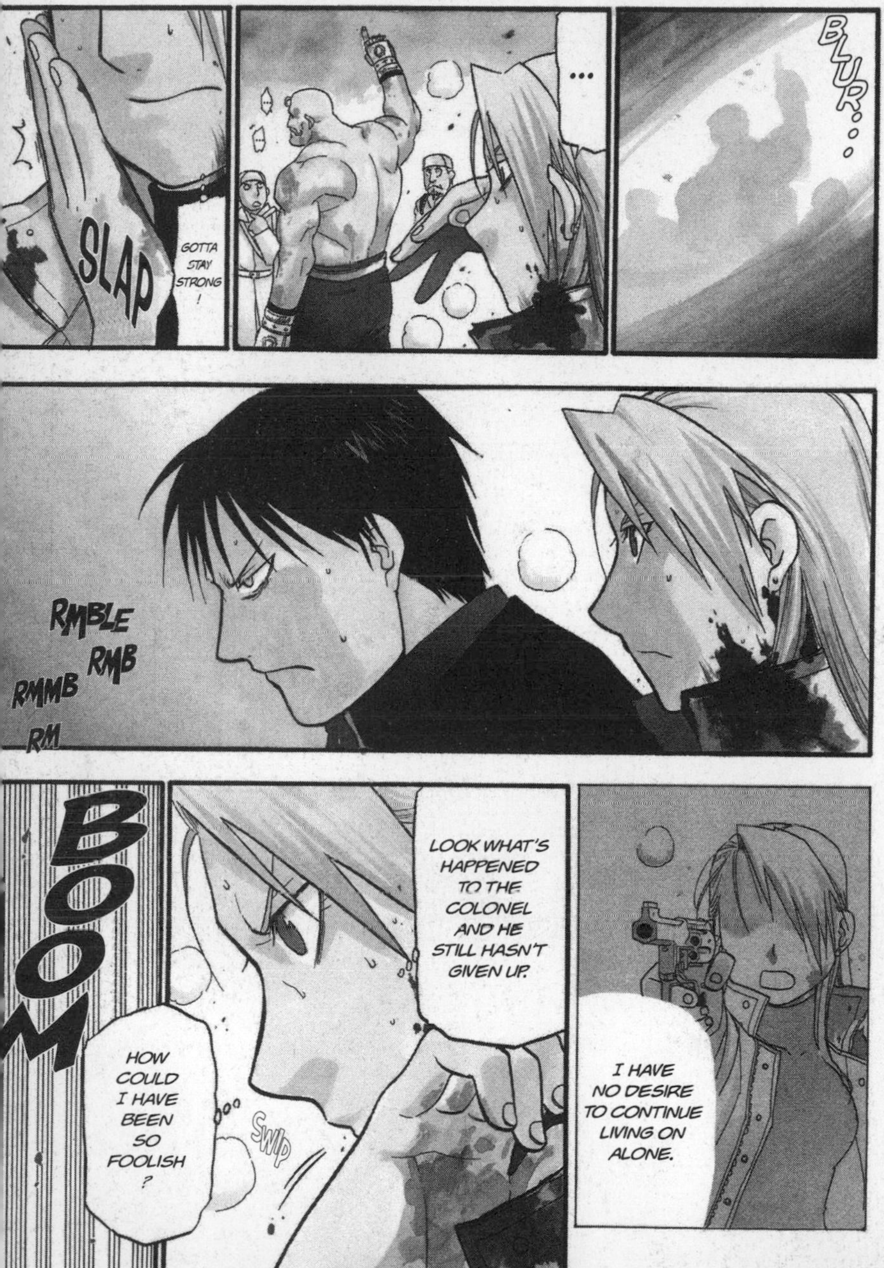
BLUR...
...
GOTTA STAY STRONG!
SLAP
RMBLE RMB
RMMB RM
I HAVE NO DESIRE TO CONTINUE LIVING ON ALONE.
LOOK WHAT'S HAPPENED TO THE COLONEL AND HE STILL HASN'T GIVEN UP.
HOW COULD I HAVE BEEN SO FOOLISH?
SWIP
BOOM

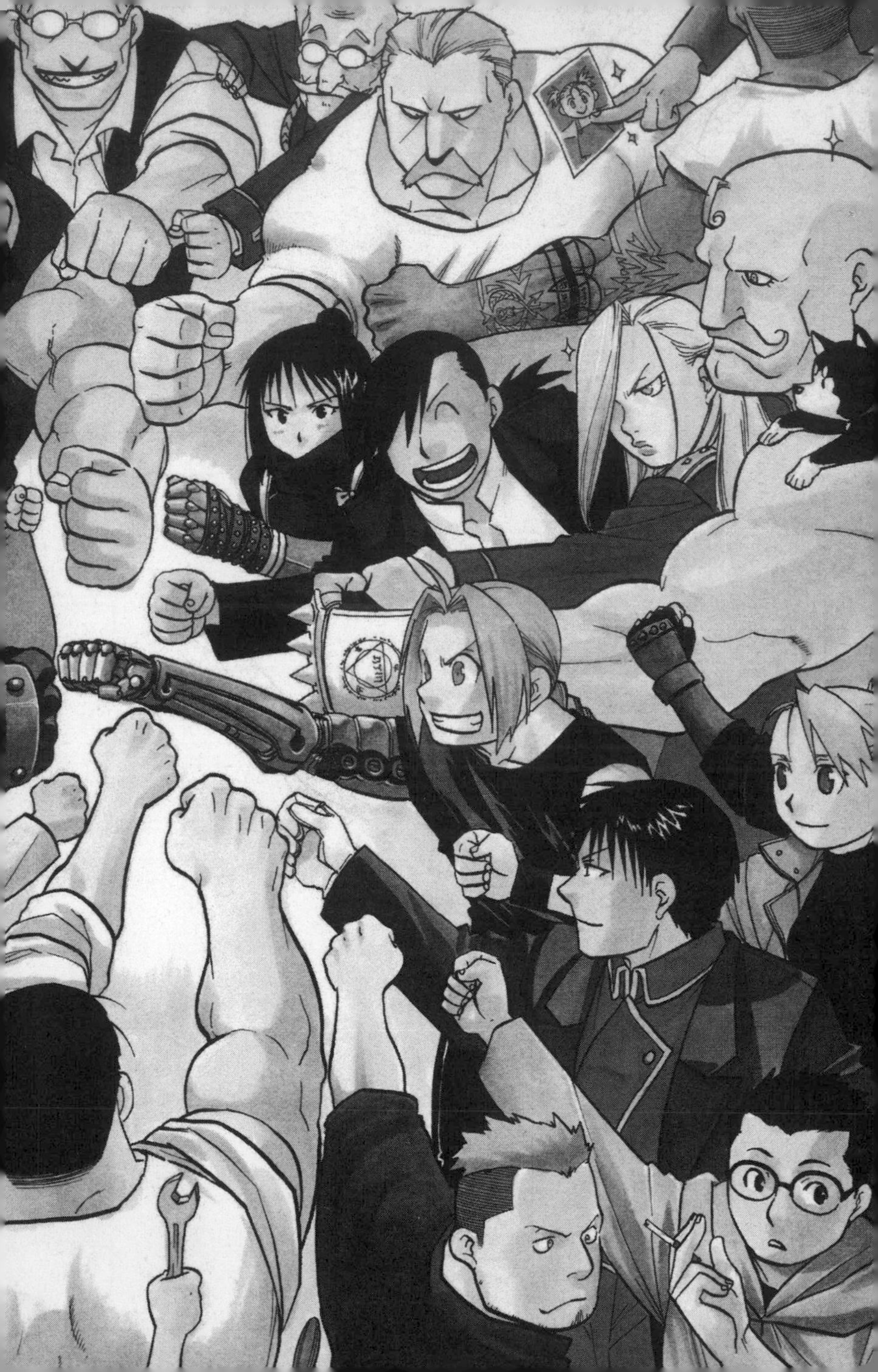

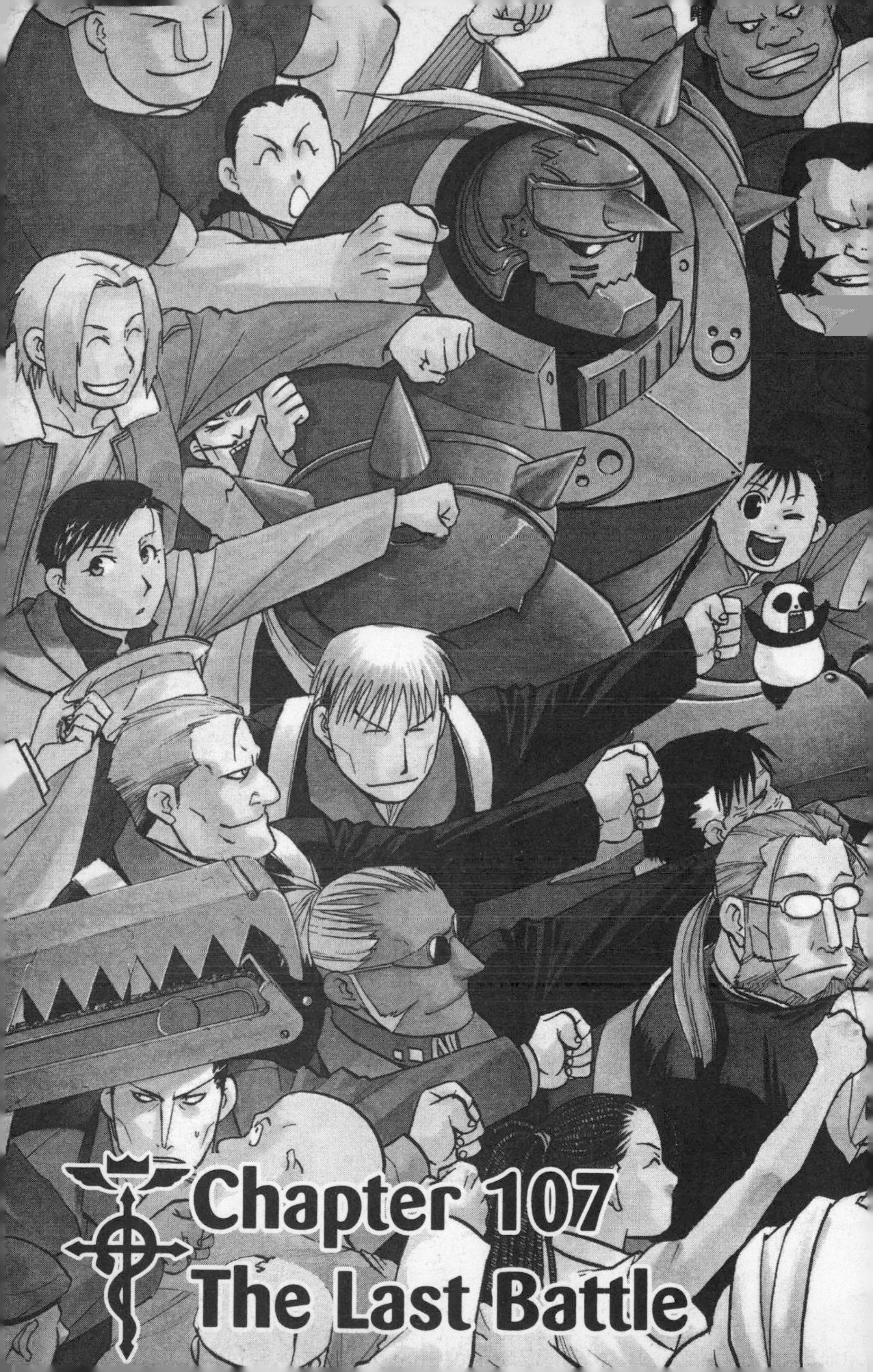

Chapter 107
The Last Battle

FULLMETAL
ALCHEMIST

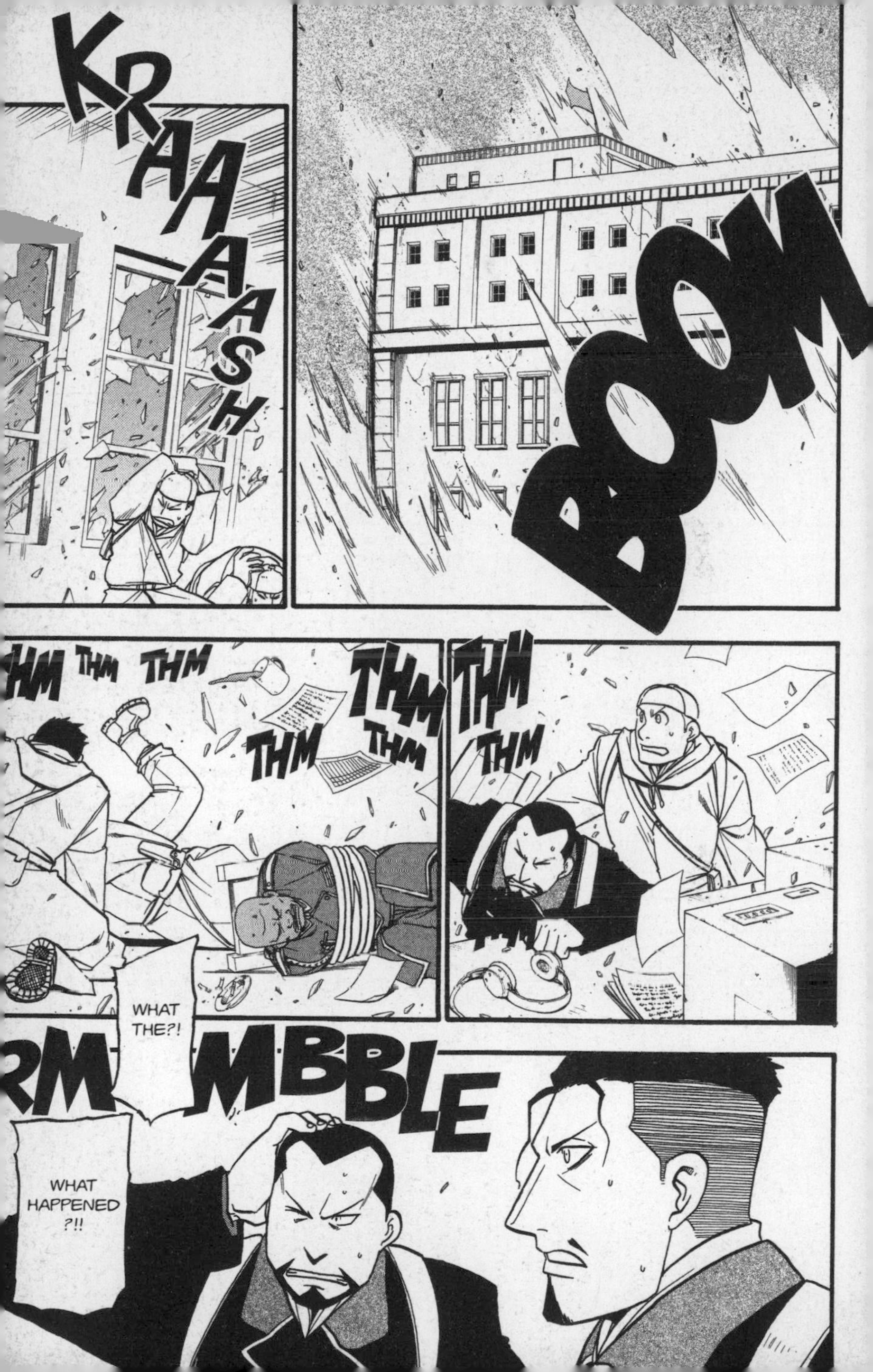
BOOM
KRAAAASH
THM THM
THM THM
THM
THM THM THM
RMMBBLE
WHAT THE?!
WHAT HAPPENED ?!!

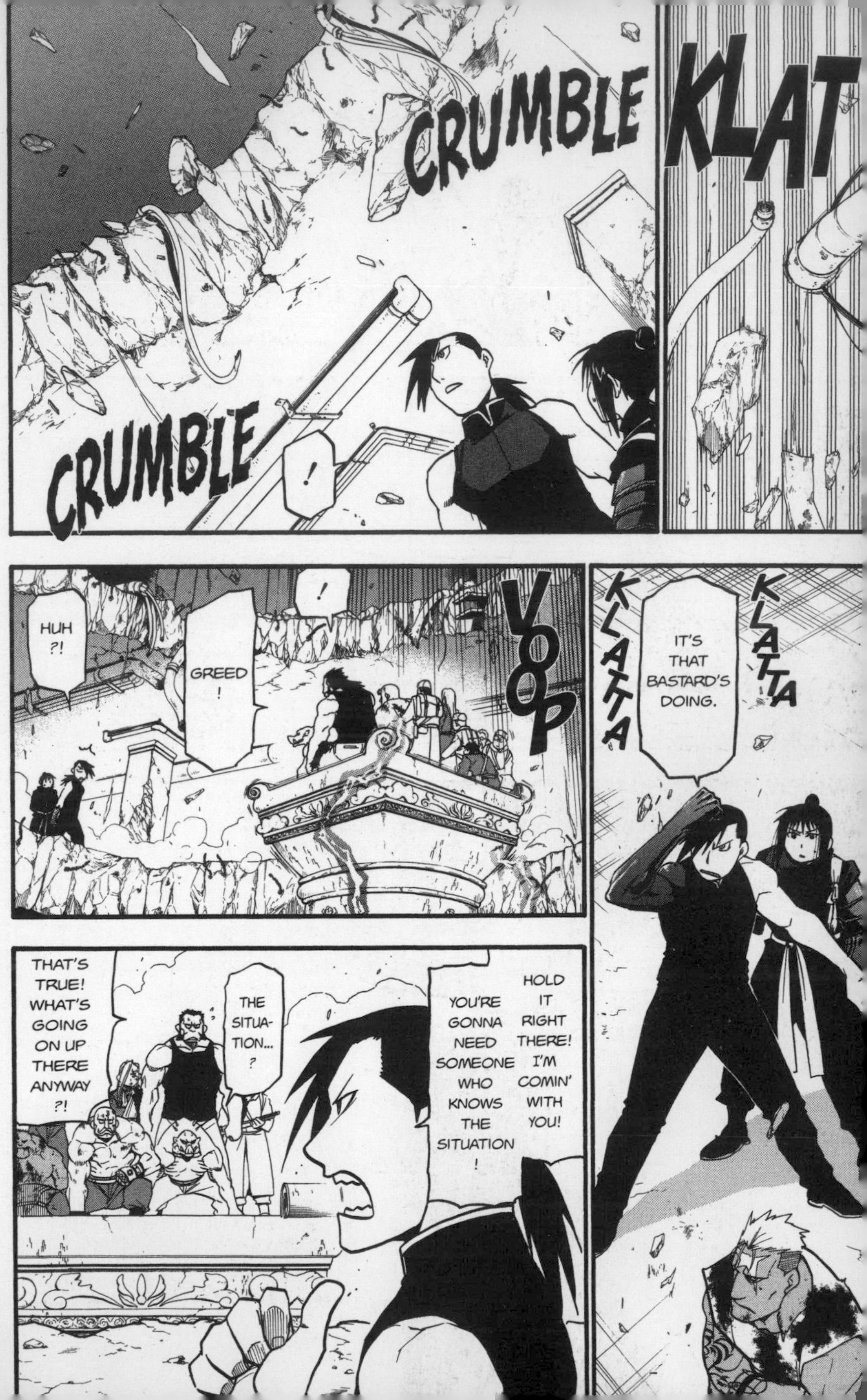
KLAT
CRUMBLE
CRUMBLE
!
KLATTA
KLATTA
IT'S THAT BASTARD'S DOING.
VOOP
!
GREED!
HUH?!
HOLD IT RIGHT THERE! I'M COMIN' WITH YOU!
YOU'RE GONNA NEED SOMEONE WHO KNOWS THE SITUATION!
THE SITUATION...?
THAT'S TRUE! WHAT'S GOING ON UP THERE ANYWAY?!

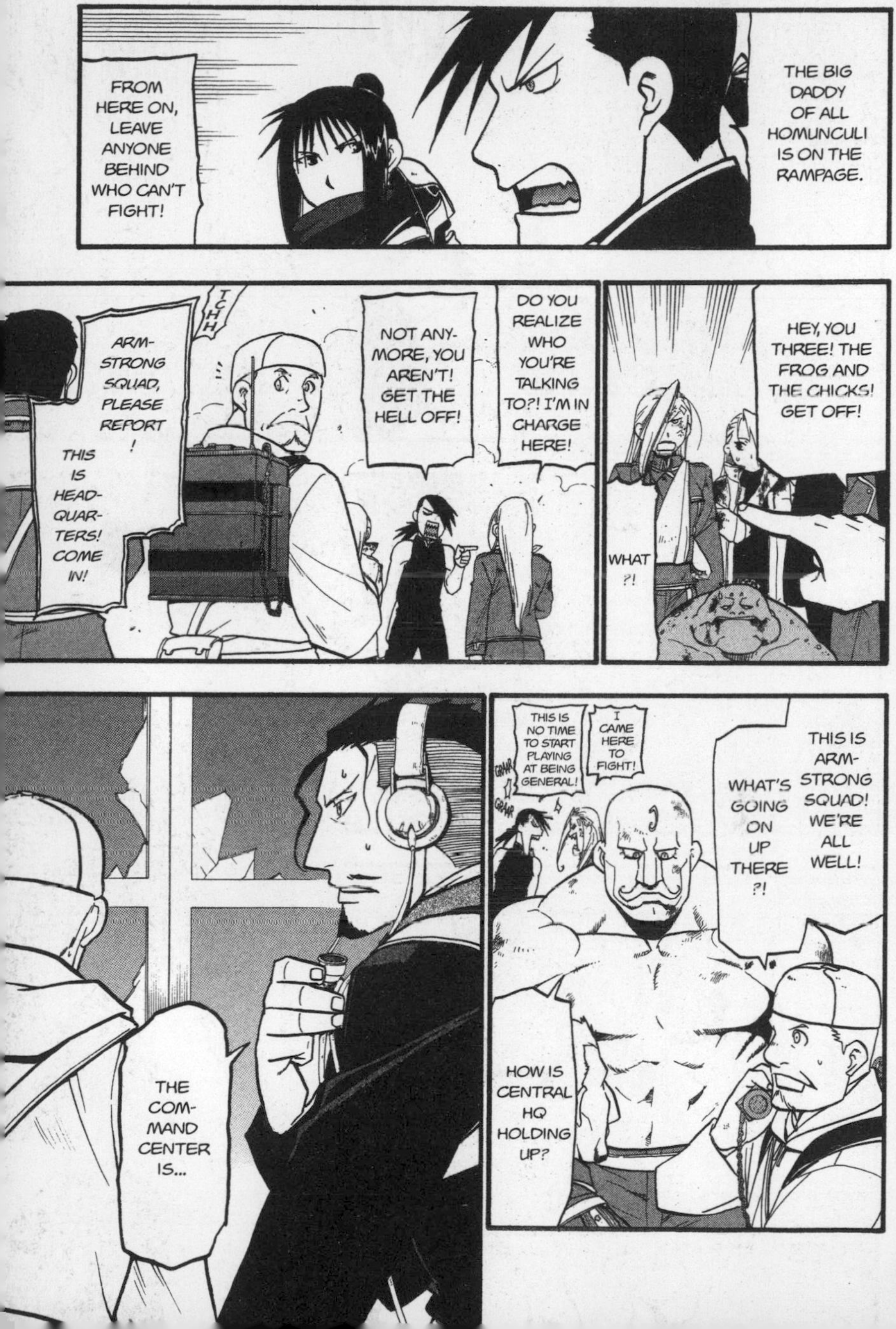
THE BIG DADDY OF ALL HOMUNCULI IS ON THE RAMPAGE.
FROM HERE ON, LEAVE ANYONE BEHIND WHO CAN'T FIGHT!
HEY, YOU THREE! THE FROG AND THE CHICKS! GET OFF!
WHAT?!
DO YOU REALIZE WHO YOU'RE TALKING TO?! I'M IN CHARGE HERE!
NOT ANY-MORE, YOU AREN'T! GET THE HELL OFF!
TCHH
ARM-STRONG SQUAD, PLEASE REPORT!
THIS IS HEAD-QUAR-TERS! COME IN!
THIS IS ARM-STRONG SQUAD! WE'RE ALL WELL!
WHAT'S GOING ON UP THERE?!
I CAME HERE TO FIGHT!
THIS IS NO TIME TO START PLAYING AT BEING GENERAL!
GRAAR
GRAAR
HOW IS CENTRAL HQ HOLDING UP?
THE COM-MAND CENTER IS...

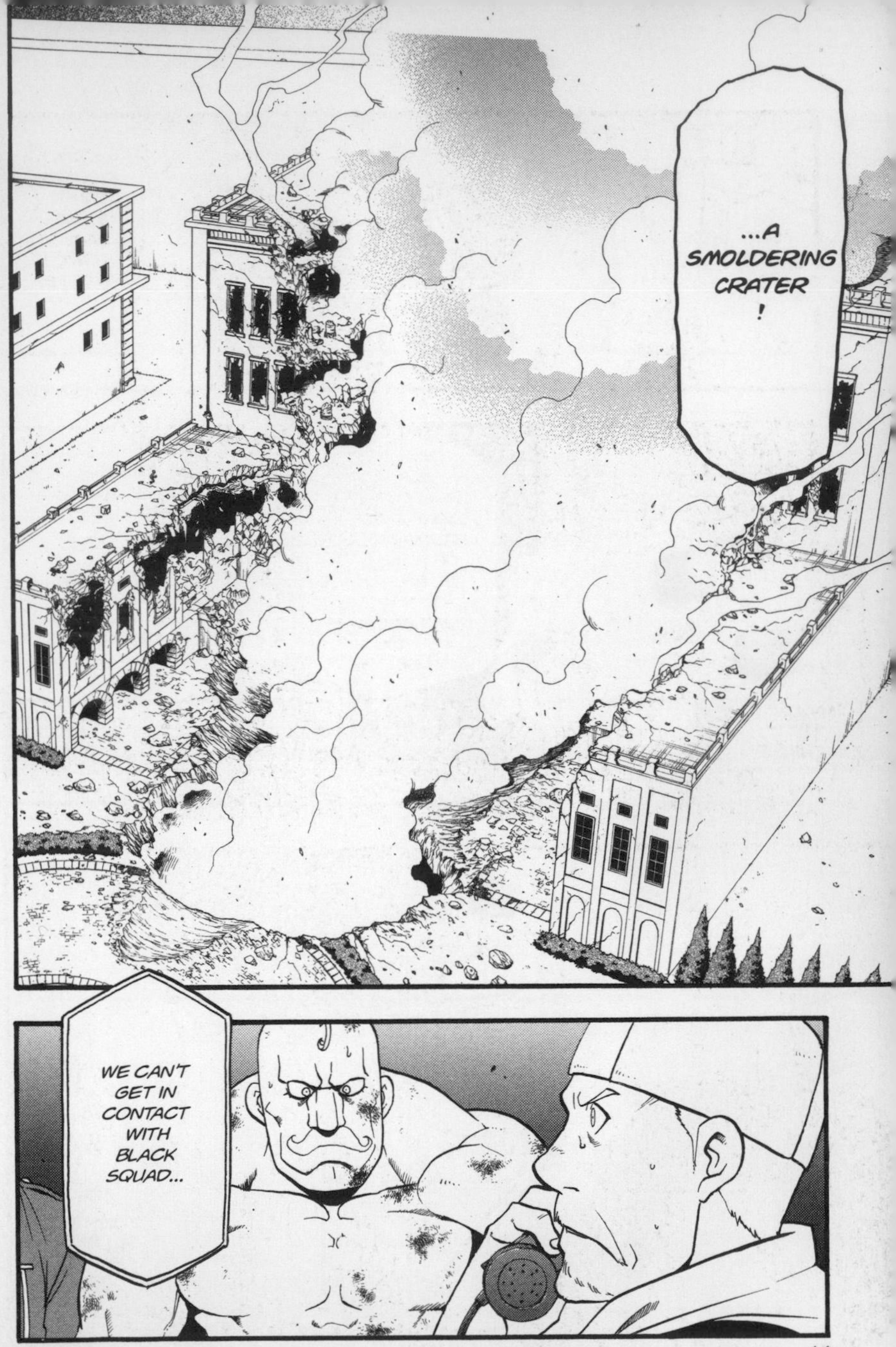
...A SMOLDERING CRATER !
WE CAN'T GET IN CONTACT WITH BLACK SQUAD...

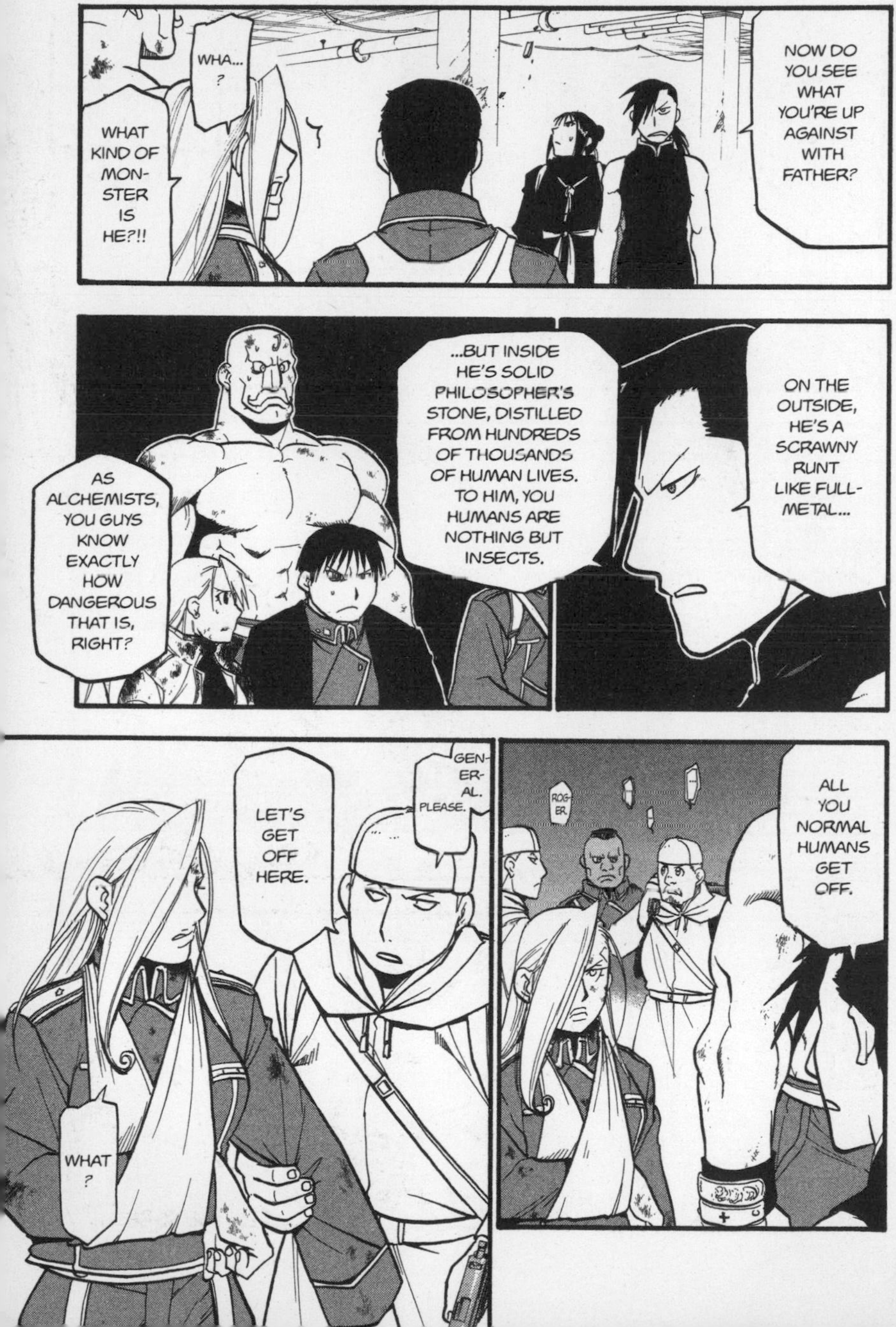
NOW DO YOU SEE WHAT YOU'RE UP AGAINST WITH FATHER?
WHA...?
WHAT KIND OF MONSTER IS HE?!!
ON THE OUTSIDE, HE'S A SCRAWNY RUNT LIKE FULLMETAL...
...BUT INSIDE HE'S SOLID PHILOSOPHER'S STONE, DISTILLED FROM HUNDREDS OF THOUSANDS OF HUMAN LIVES. TO HIM, YOU HUMANS ARE NOTHING BUT INSECTS.
AS ALCHEMISTS, YOU GUYS KNOW EXACTLY HOW DANGEROUS THAT IS, RIGHT?
ALL YOU NORMAL HUMANS GET OFF.
ROGER.
GENERAL.
PLEASE.
LET'S GET OFF HERE.
WHAT?

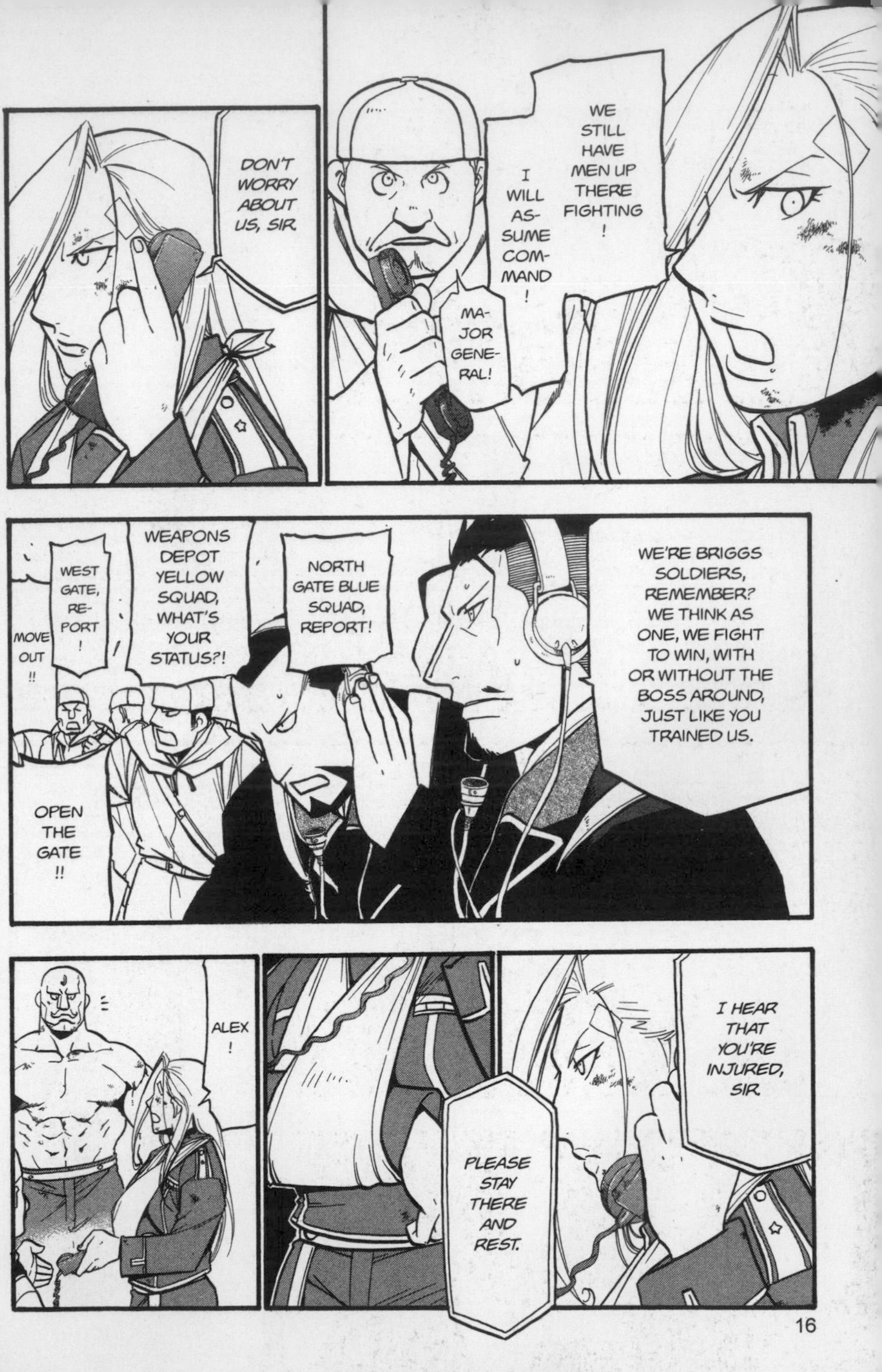
WE STILL HAVE MEN UP THERE FIGHTING!
I WILL ASSUME COMMAND!
MAJOR GENERAL!
DON'T WORRY ABOUT US, SIR.
WE'RE BRIGGS SOLDIERS, REMEMBER? WE THINK AS ONE, WE FIGHT TO WIN, WITH OR WITHOUT THE BOSS AROUND, JUST LIKE YOU TRAINED US.
NORTH GATE BLUE SQUAD, REPORT!
WEAPONS DEPOT YELLOW SQUAD, WHAT'S YOUR STATUS?!
WEST GATE, REPORT!
MOVE OUT!!
OPEN THE GATE!!
I HEAR THAT YOU'RE INJURED, SIR.
PLEASE STAY THERE AND REST.
ALEX!

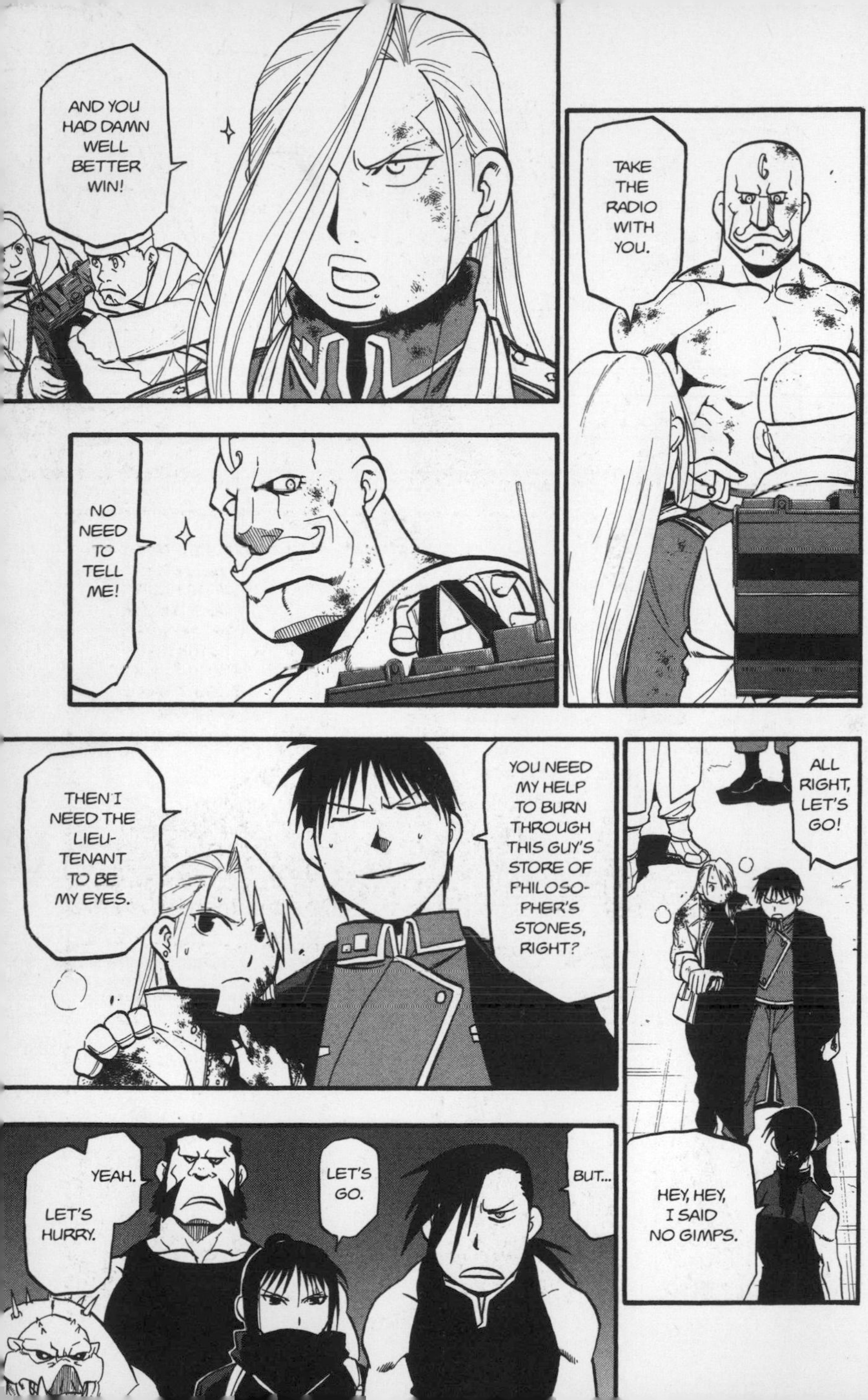
TAKE THE RADIO WITH YOU.
AND YOU HAD DAMN WELL BETTER WIN!
NO NEED TO TELL ME!
ALL RIGHT, LET'S GO!
HEY, HEY, I SAID NO GIMPS.
YOU NEED MY HELP TO BURN THROUGH THIS GUY'S STORE OF PHILOSO-PHER'S STONES, RIGHT?
THEN I NEED THE LIEU-TENANT TO BE MY EYES.
BUT...
LET'S GO.
YEAH.
LET'S HURRY.

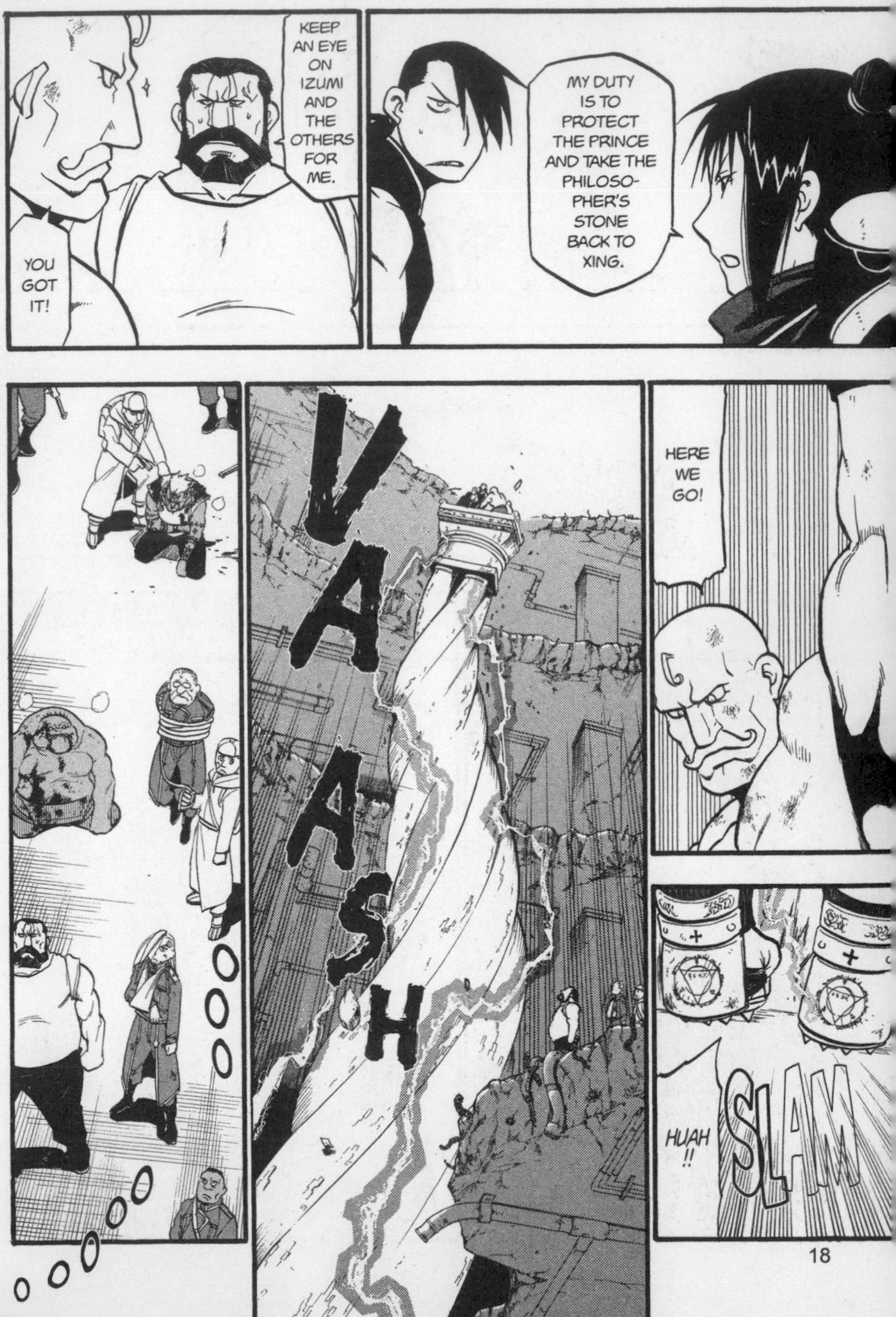
MY DUTY IS TO PROTECT THE PRINCE AND TAKE THE PHILOSO-PHER'S STONE BACK TO XING.
KEEP AN EYE ON IZUMI AND THE OTHERS FOR ME.
YOU GOT IT!
HERE WE GO!
HUAH!!
SLAM
VAASH

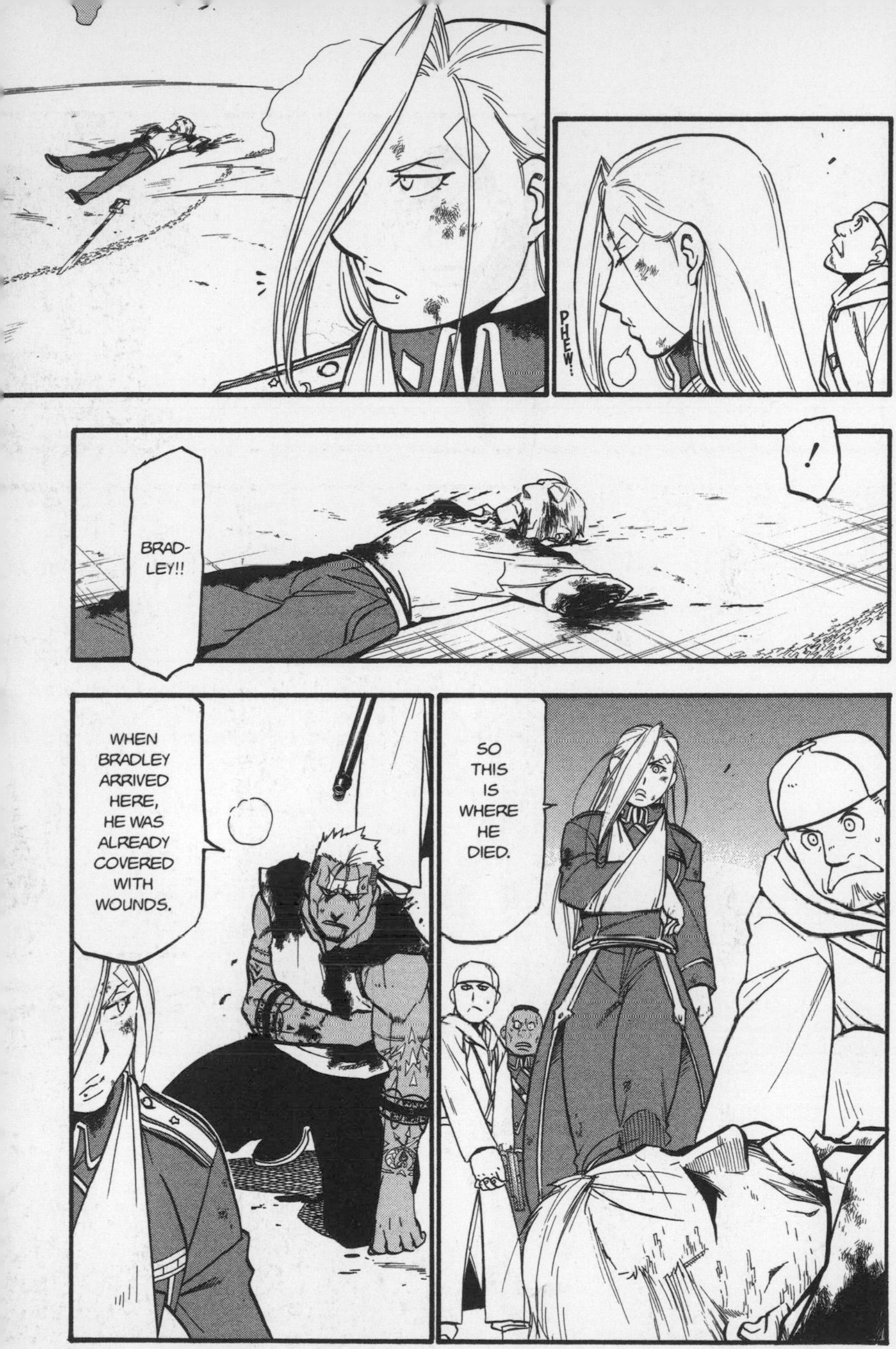
PHEW...
!
BRAD-LEY!!
SO THIS IS WHERE HE DIED.
WHEN BRADLEY ARRIVED HERE, HE WAS ALREADY COVERED WITH WOUNDS.

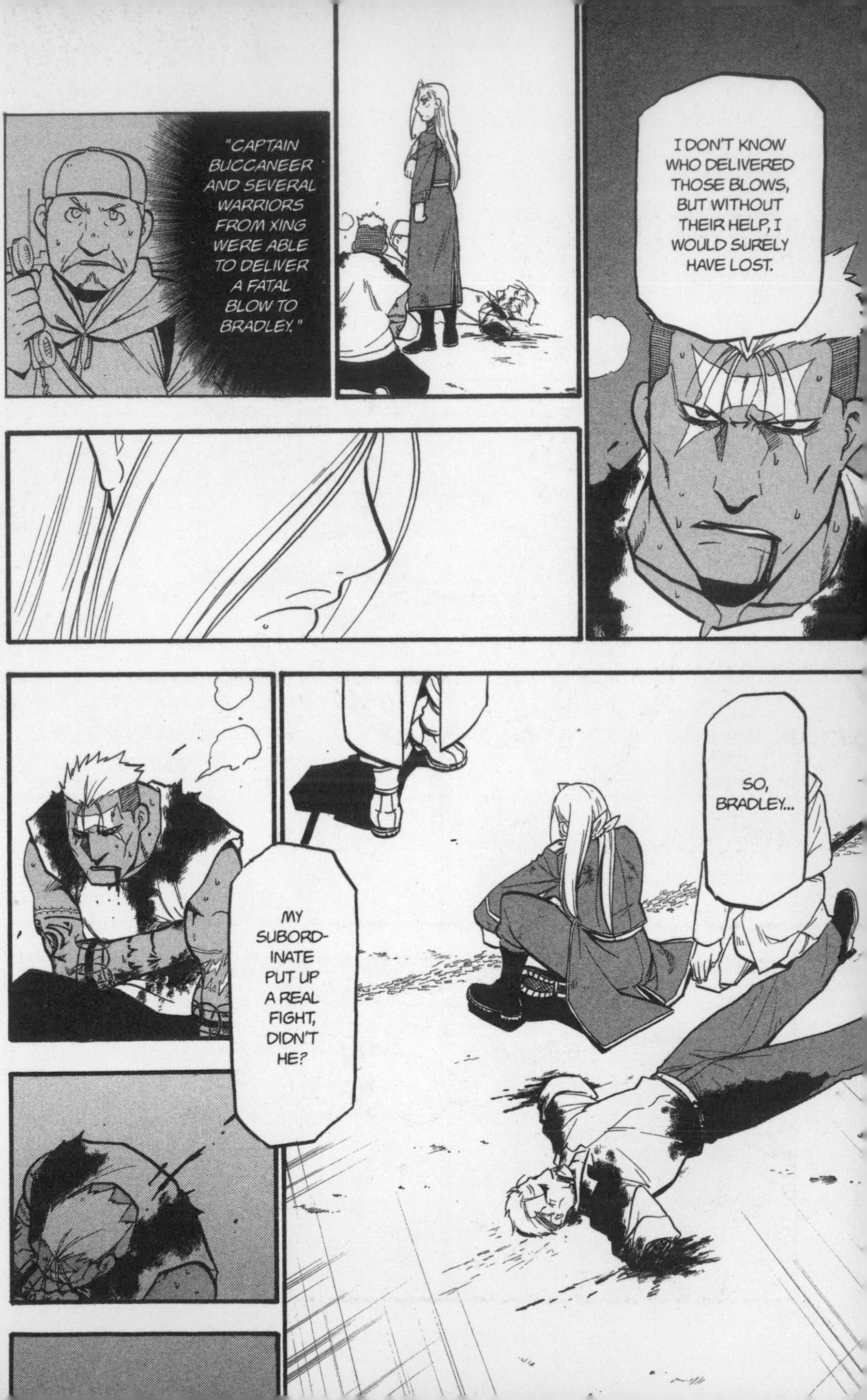
I DON'T KNOW WHO DELIVERED THOSE BLOWS, BUT WITHOUT THEIR HELP, I WOULD SURELY HAVE LOST.
"CAPTAIN BUCCANEER AND SEVERAL WARRIORS FROM XING WERE ABLE TO DELIVER A FATAL BLOW TO BRADLEY."
SO, BRADLEY...
MY SUBORD-INATE PUT UP A REAL FIGHT, DIDN'T HE?

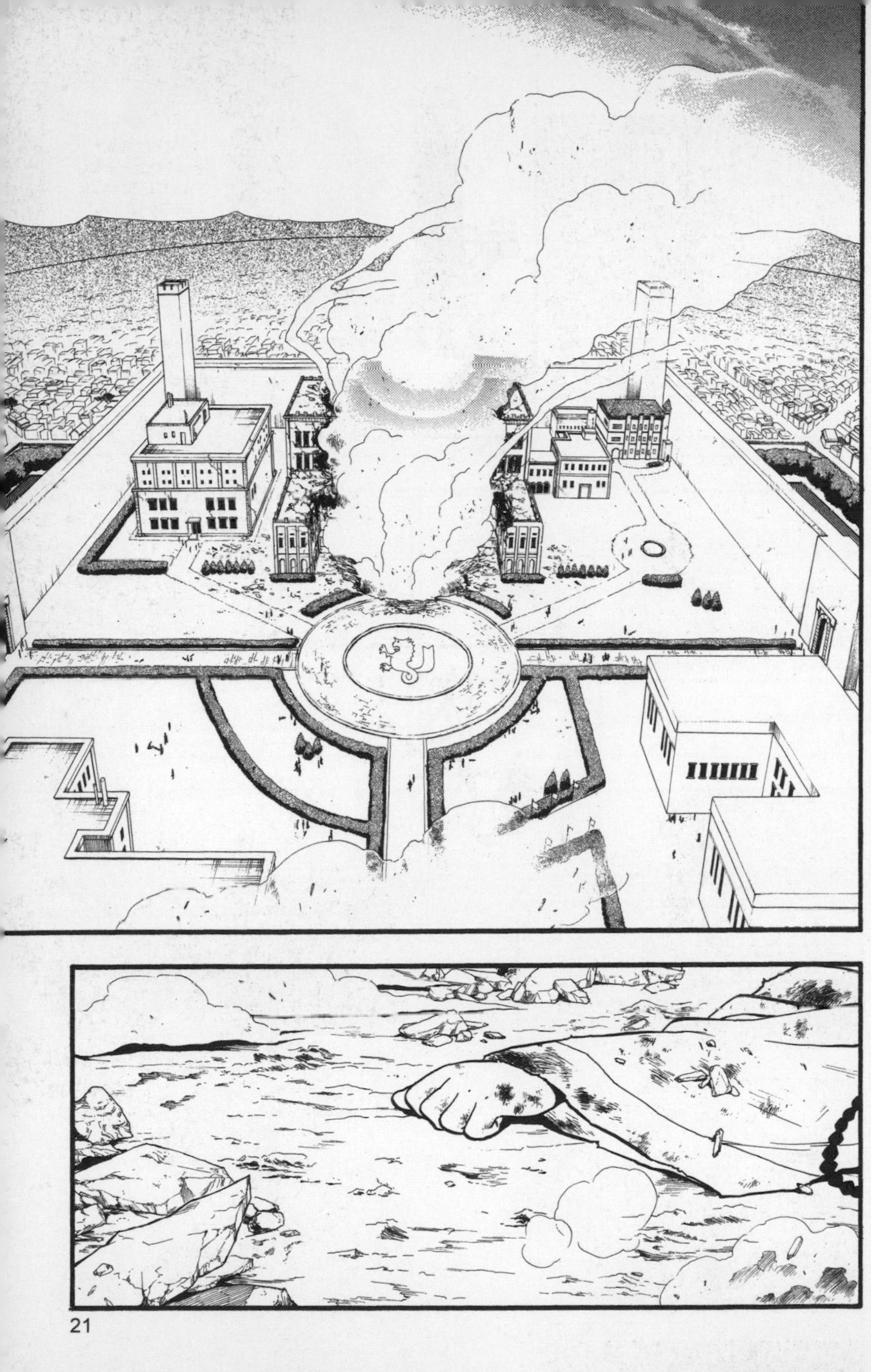

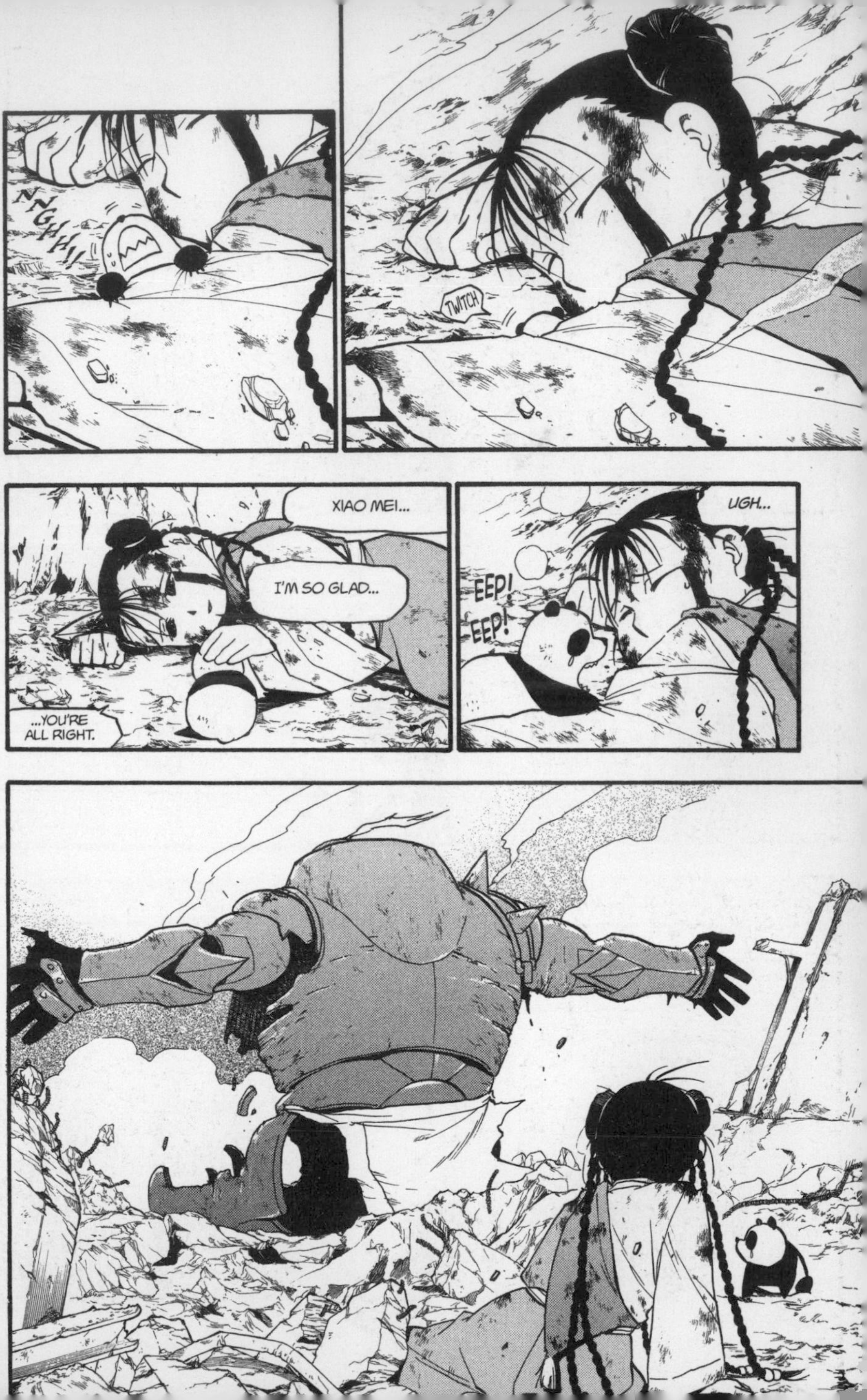
TWITCH
NNGH!!
UGH...
EEP!
EEP!
XIAO MEI...
I'M SO GLAD...
...YOU'RE ALL RIGHT.

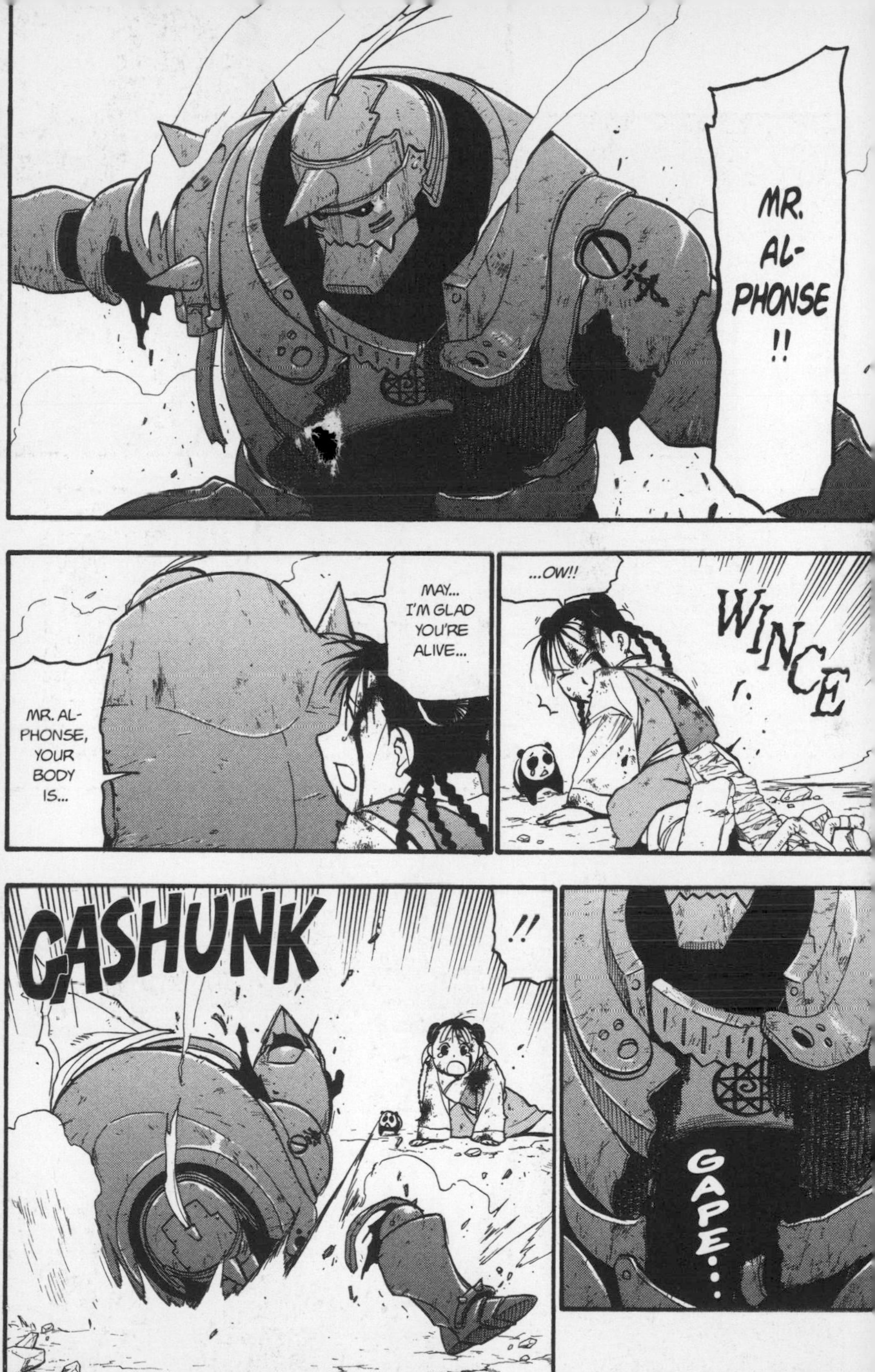
MR. AL-PHONSE !!
...OW!!
WINCE
MAY... I'M GLAD YOU'RE ALIVE...
MR. AL-PHONSE, YOUR BODY IS...
GAPE...
GASHUNK
!!

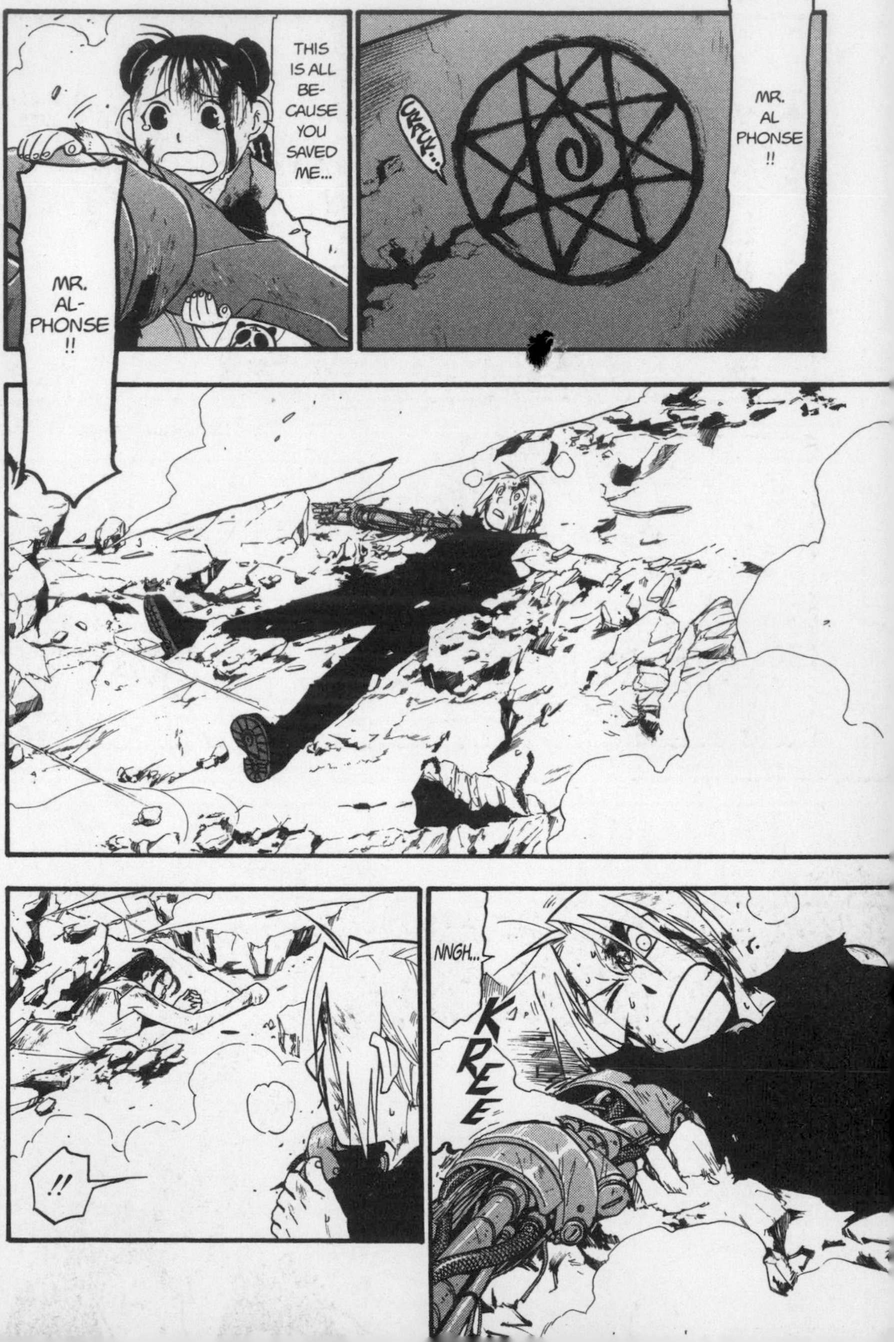
MR. AL PHONSE !!
CRACK...
THIS IS ALL BE-CAUSE YOU SAVED ME...
MR. AL-PHONSE !!
NNGH...
KREE
!!

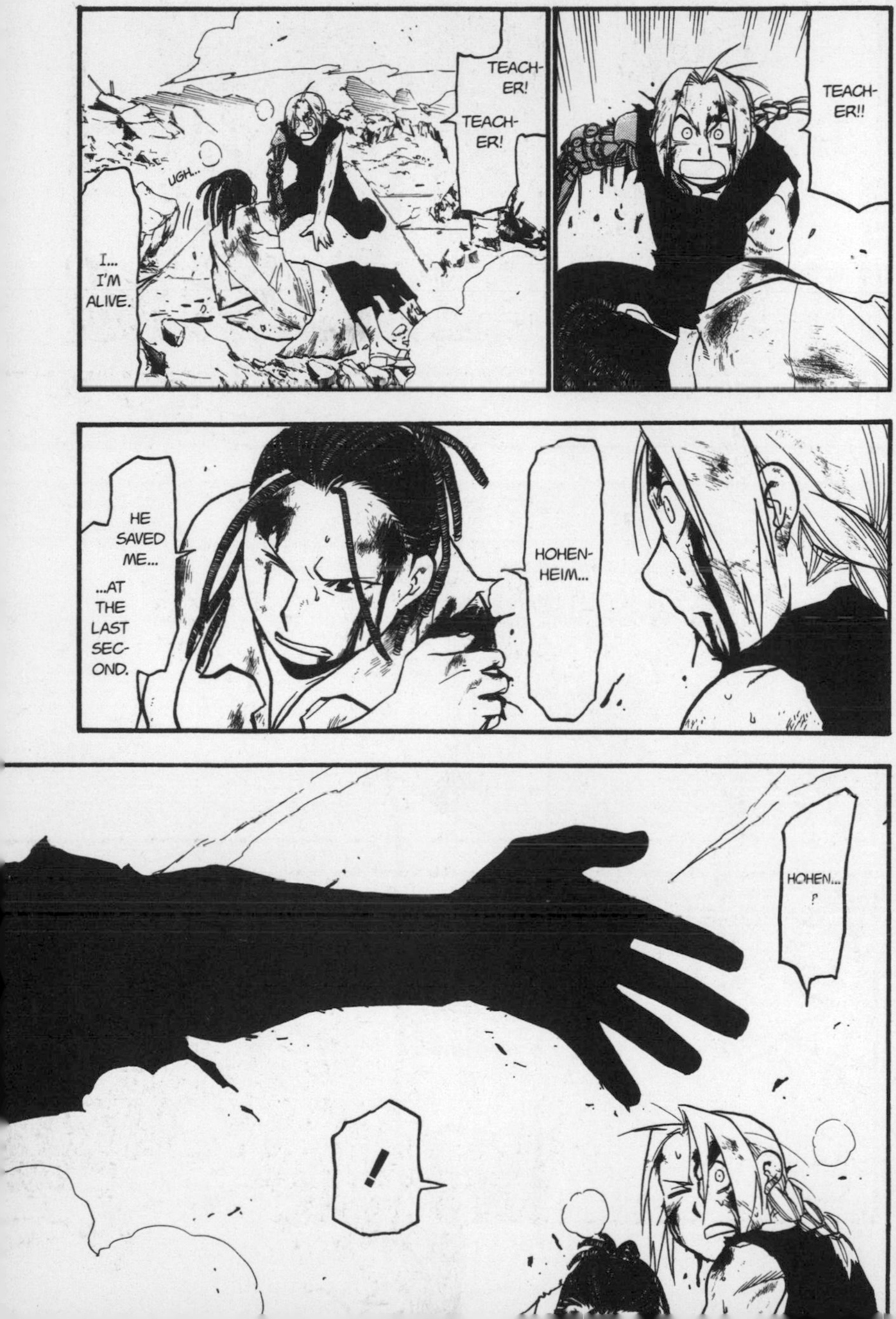
TEACHER!!
TEACHER! TEACHER!
UGH...
I... I'M ALIVE.
HOHENHEIM...
HE SAVED ME... ...AT THE LAST SECOND.
HOHEN...?
!

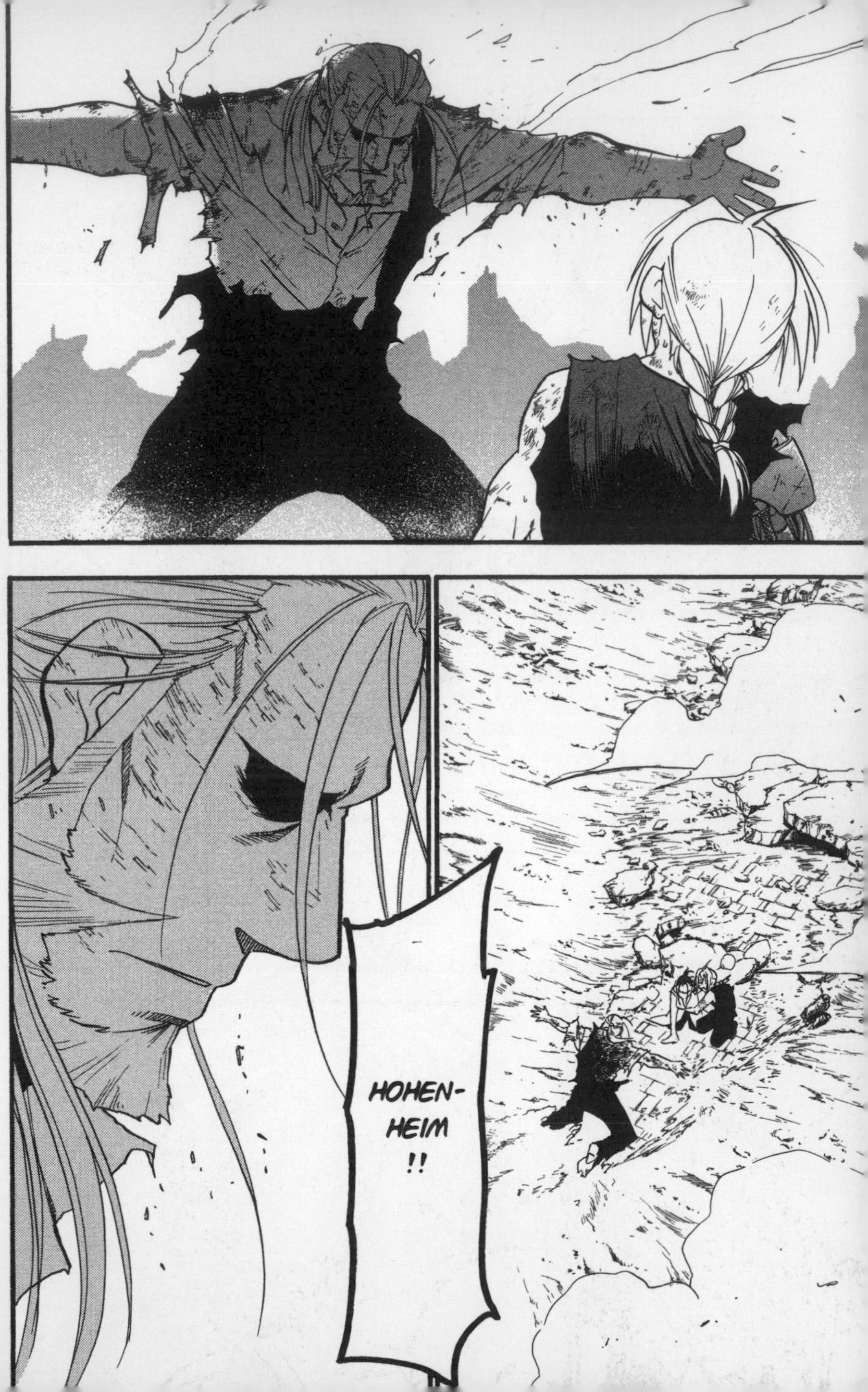
HOHEN- HEIM !!

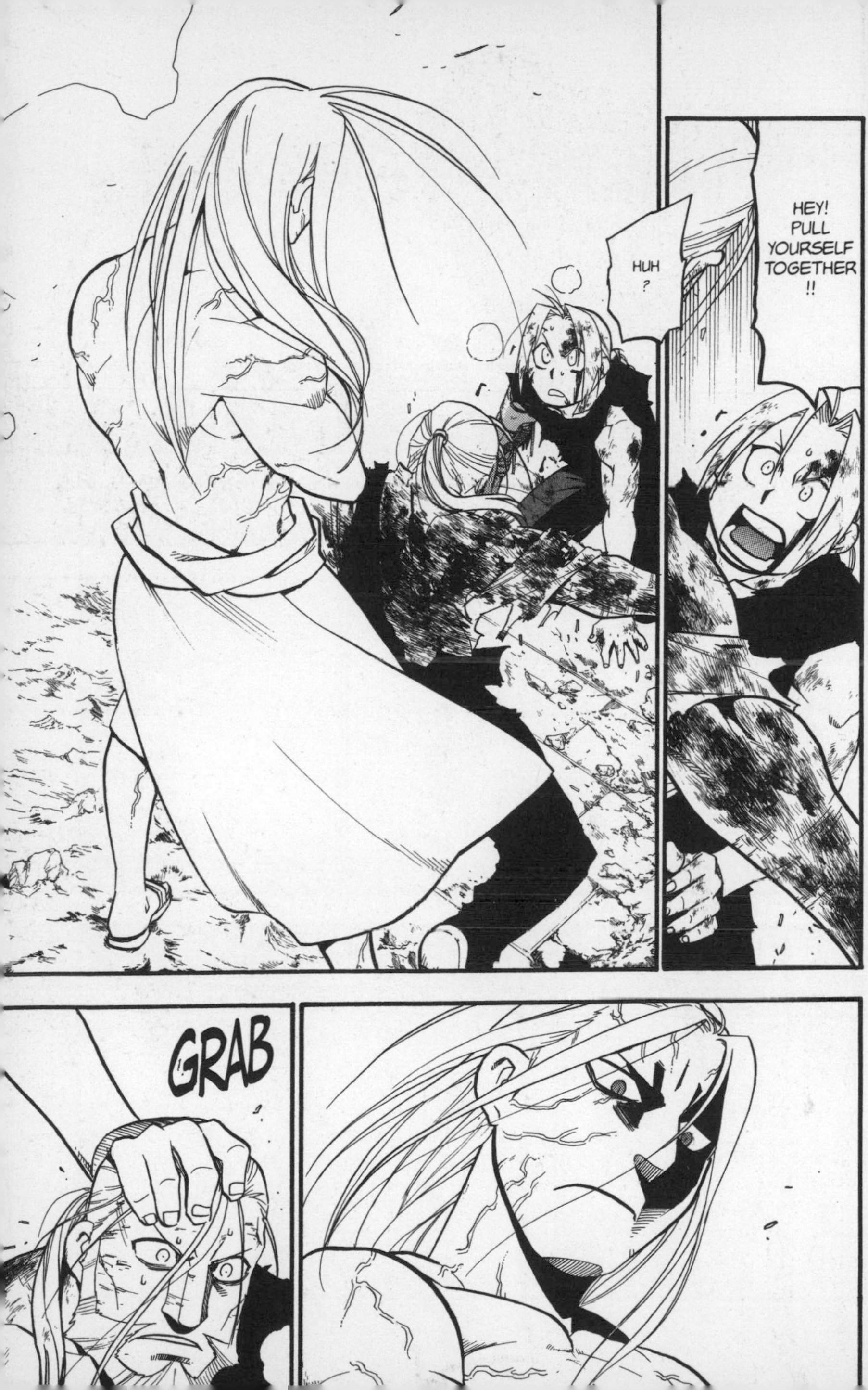
HEY! PULL YOURSELF TOGETHER !!
HUH ?
GRAB

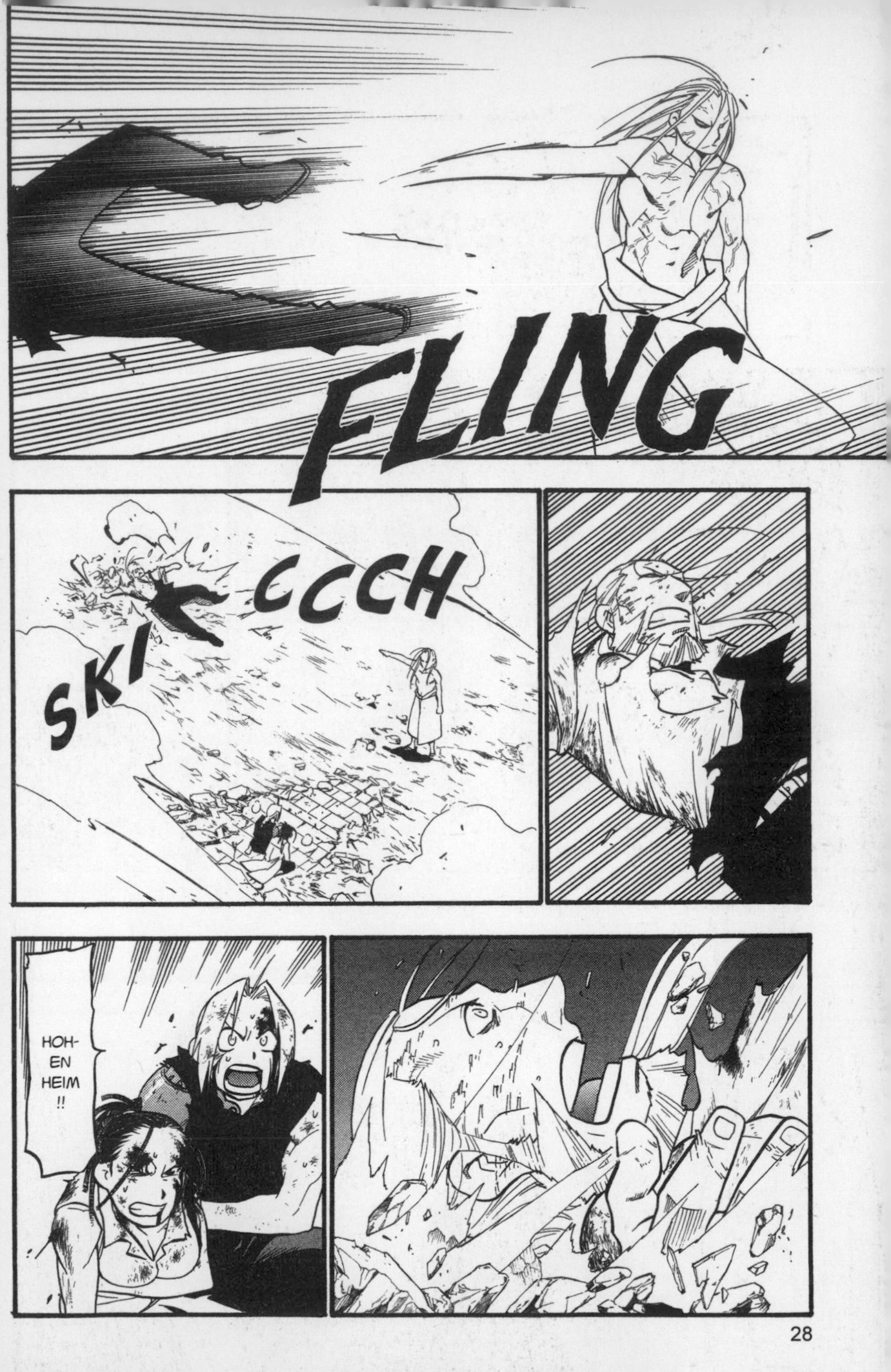
FLING
SKI CCCH
HOH-EN HEIM !!

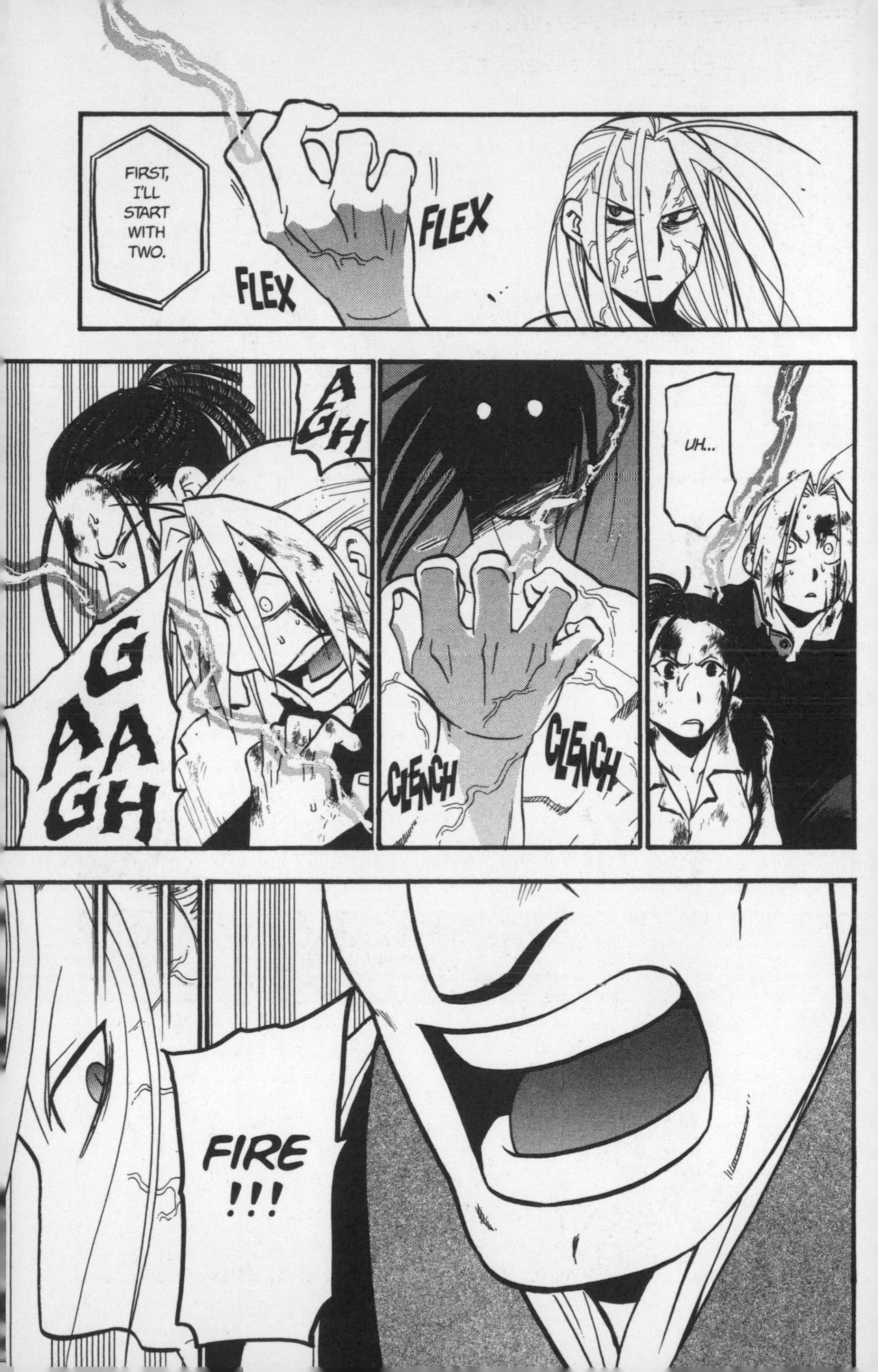
FIRST, I'LL START WITH TWO.
FLEX
FLEX
...
UH...
CLENCH
CLENCH
AGH
GAAGH
FIRE!!!

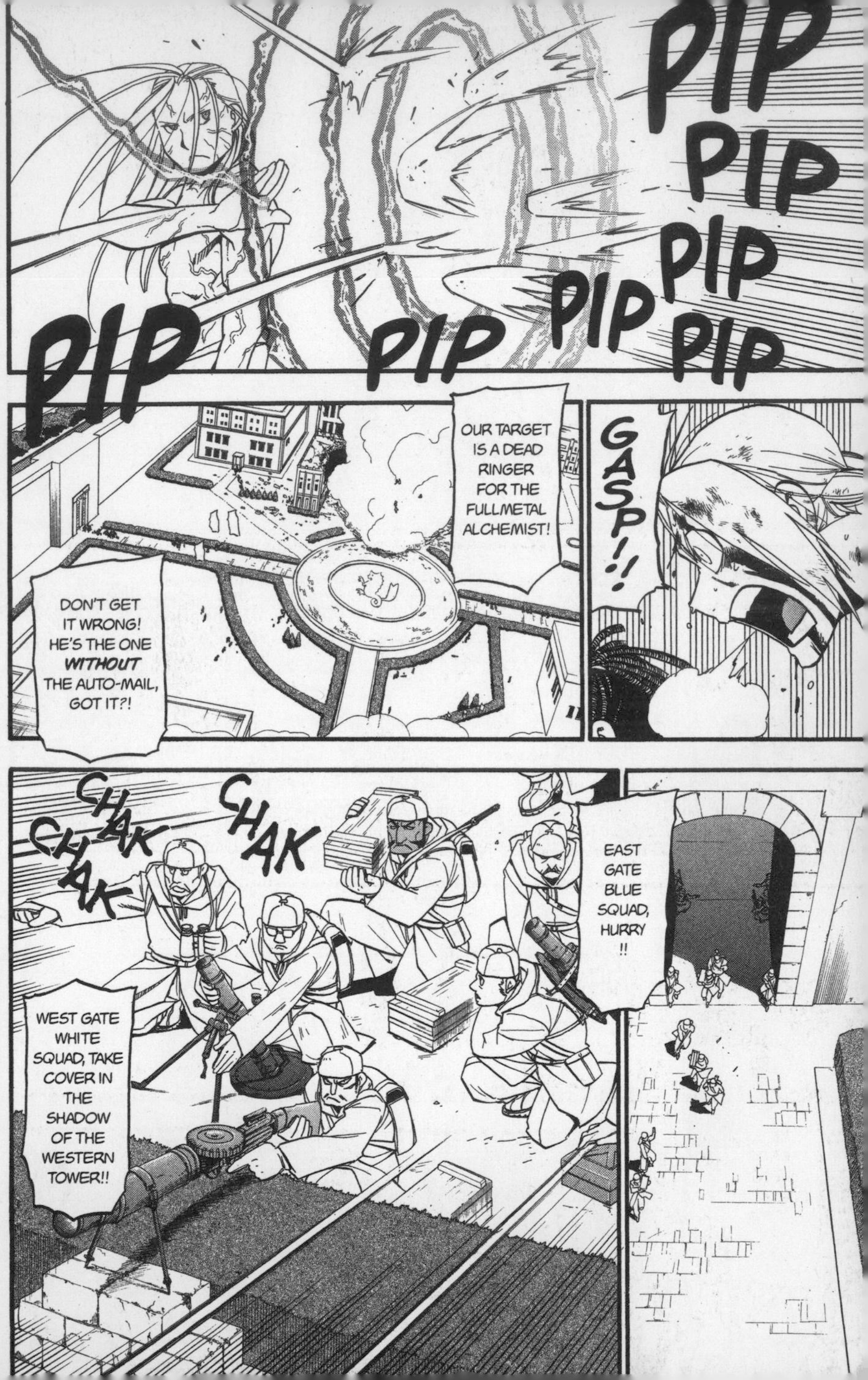
PIP
PIP
PIP
PIP
PIP
PIP
PIP
GASP!!
OUR TARGET IS A DEAD RINGER FOR THE FULLMETAL ALCHEMIST!
DON'T GET IT WRONG! HE'S THE ONE ***WITHOUT*** THE AUTO-MAIL, GOT IT?!
EAST GATE BLUE SQUAD, HURRY !!
CHAK
CHAK
CHAK
WEST GATE WHITE SQUAD, TAKE COVER IN THE SHADOW OF THE WESTERN TOWER!!

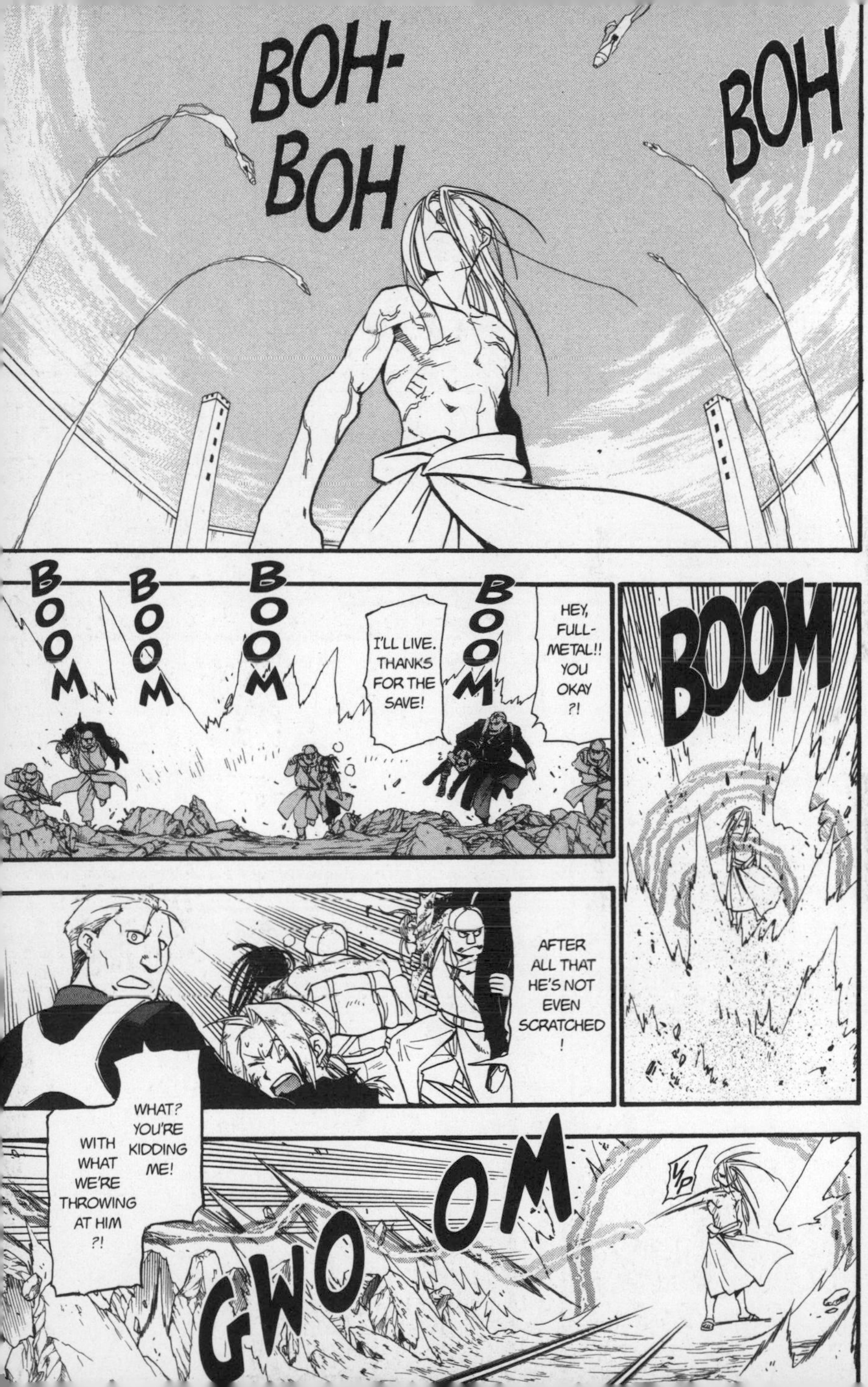
BOH
BOH-BOH
BOOM
HEY, FULL-METAL!! YOU OKAY?!
BOOM
I'LL LIVE. THANKS FOR THE SAVE!
BOOM
BOOM
BOOM
AFTER ALL THAT HE'S NOT EVEN SCRATCHED!
WHAT? YOU'RE KIDDING ME!
WITH WHAT WE'RE THROWING AT HIM?!
GWO-OM

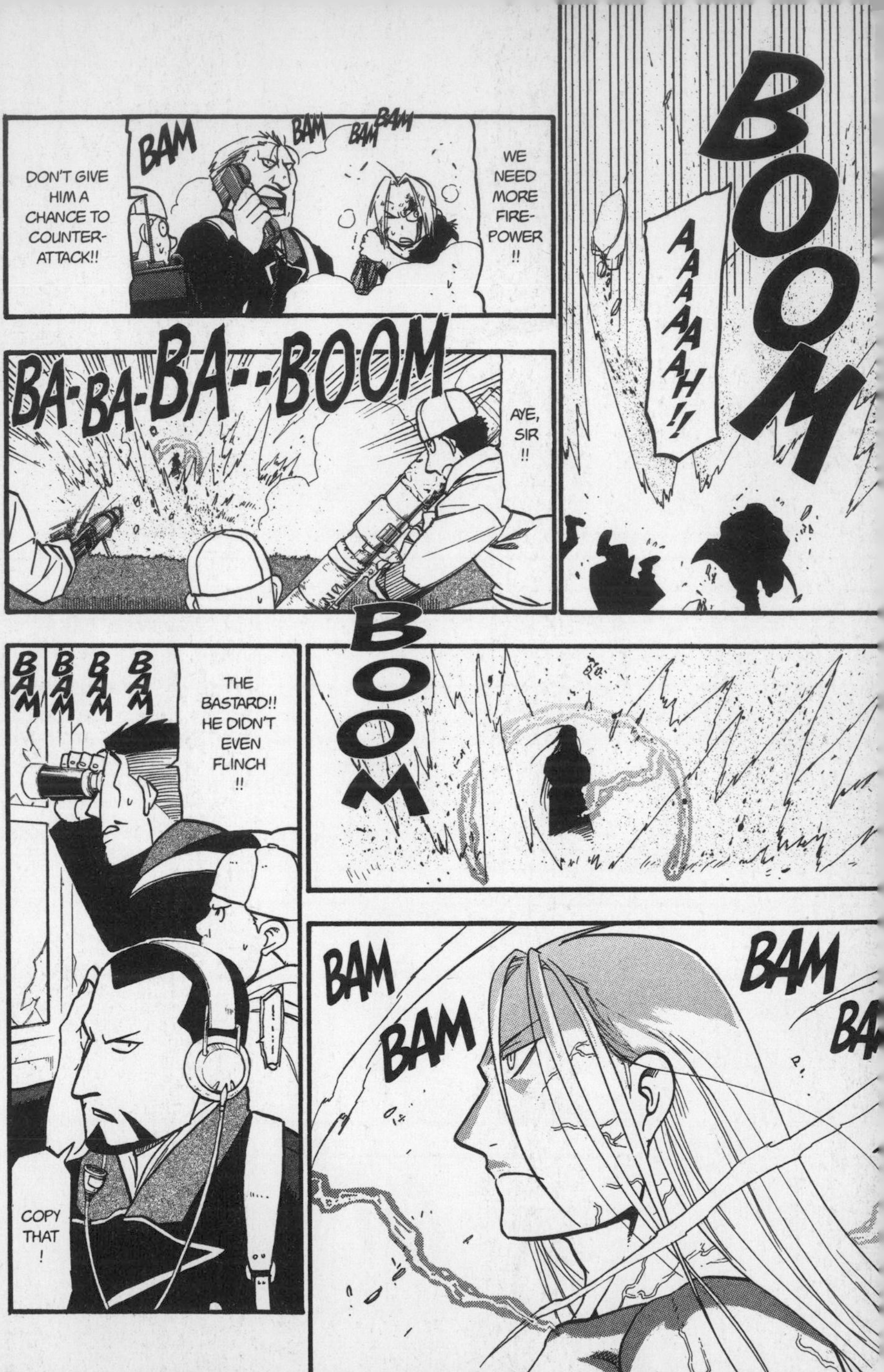
BOOM
AAAAAAH!!
BAM BAM BAM
WE NEED MORE FIRE-POWER!!
BAM
DON'T GIVE HIM A CHANCE TO COUNTER-ATTACK!!
BA-BA-BA--BOOM
AYE, SIR!!
BOOM
BAM
BAM
BAM
BAM BAM BAM BAM
THE BASTARD!! HE DIDN'T EVEN FLINCH!!
COPY THAT!

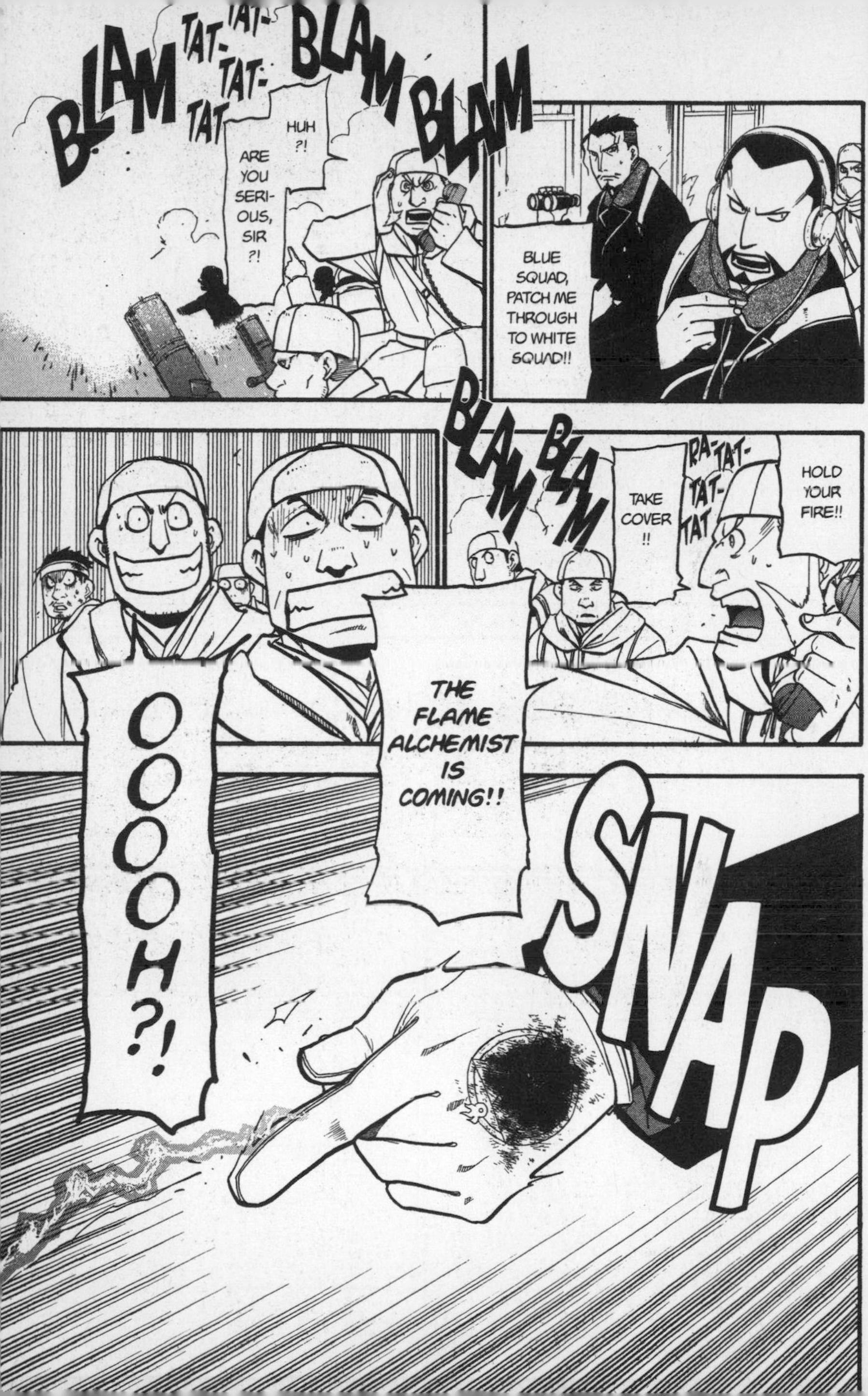
BLUE SQUAD, PATCH ME THROUGH TO WHITE SQUAD!!
BLAM BLAM
BLAM
TAT-TAT-TAT-TAT
BLAM
HUH ?!
ARE YOU SERI- OUS, SIR ?!
BLAM BLAM
HOLD YOUR FIRE!!
RA-TAT-TAT-TAT
TAKE COVER !!
THE FLAME ALCHEMIST IS COMING!!
OOOOH?!
SNAP

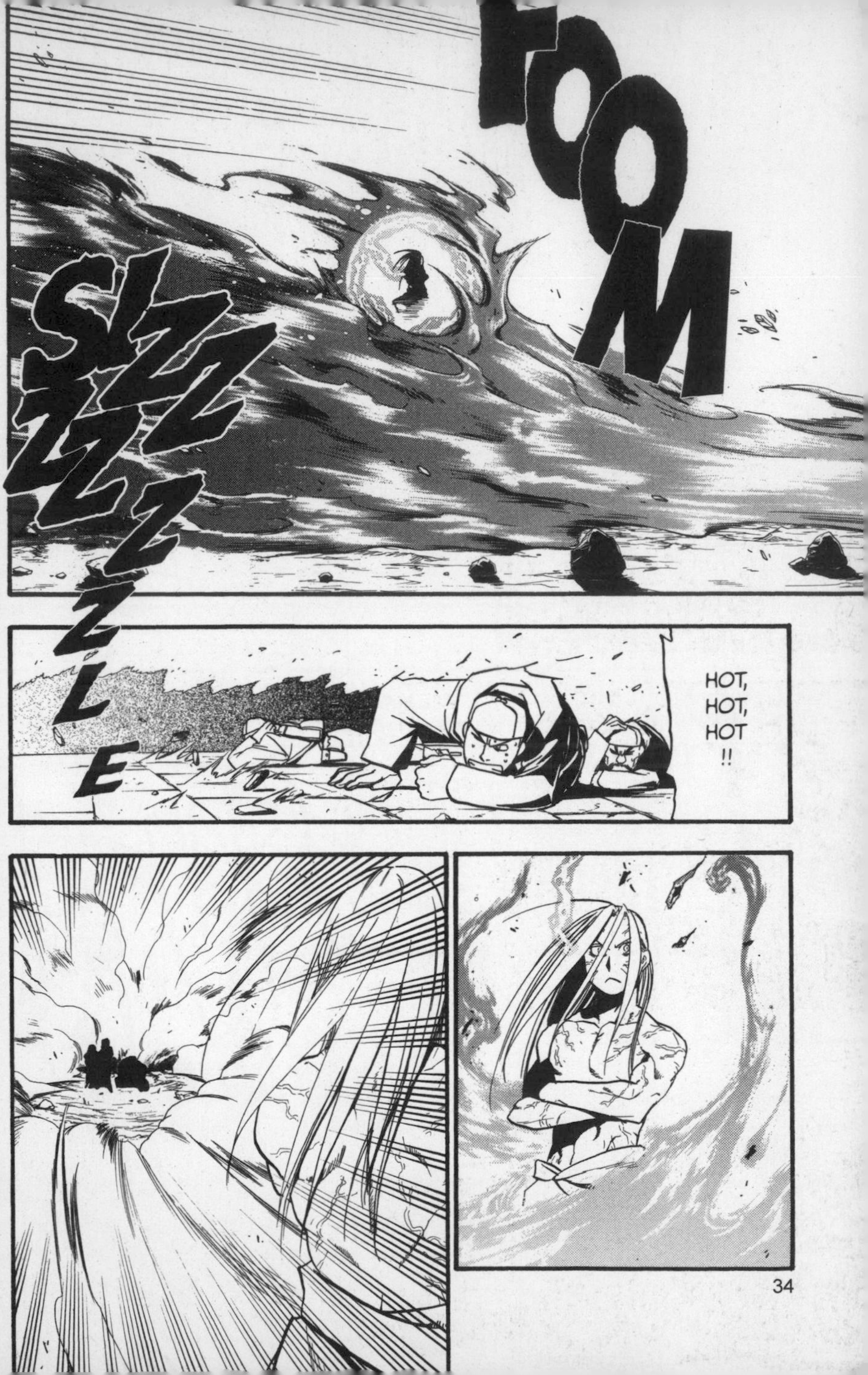
rOOM
SIZZZZZLE
HOT, HOT, HOT!!

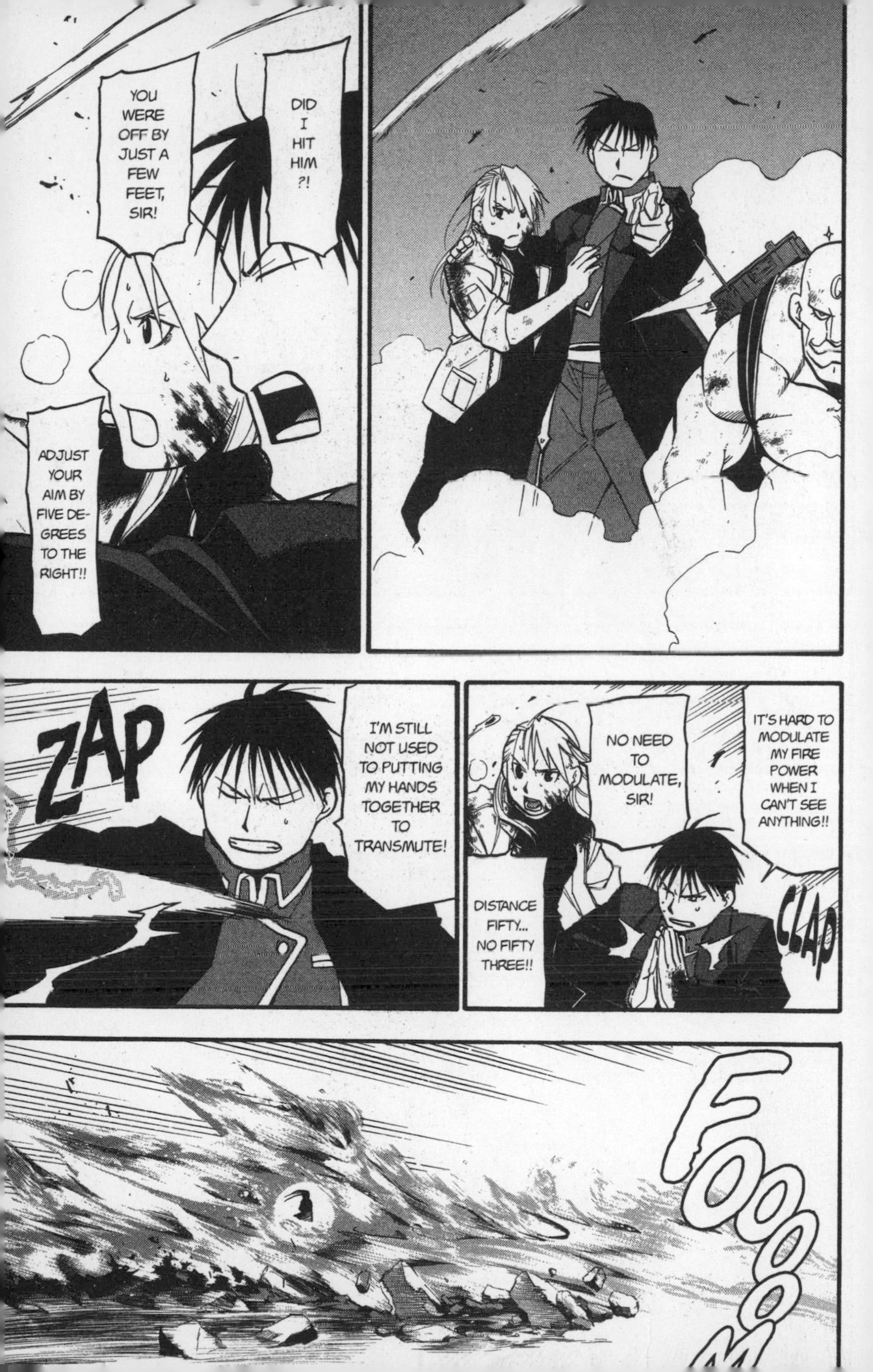
DID I HIT HIM?!
YOU WERE OFF BY JUST A FEW FEET, SIR!
ADJUST YOUR AIM BY FIVE DEGREES TO THE RIGHT!!
IT'S HARD TO MODULATE MY FIRE POWER WHEN I CAN'T SEE ANYTHING!!
NO NEED TO MODULATE, SIR!
DISTANCE FIFTY... NO FIFTY THREE!!
CLAP
I'M STILL NOT USED TO PUTTING MY HANDS TOGETHER TO TRANSMUTE!
ZAP
FOOOOM

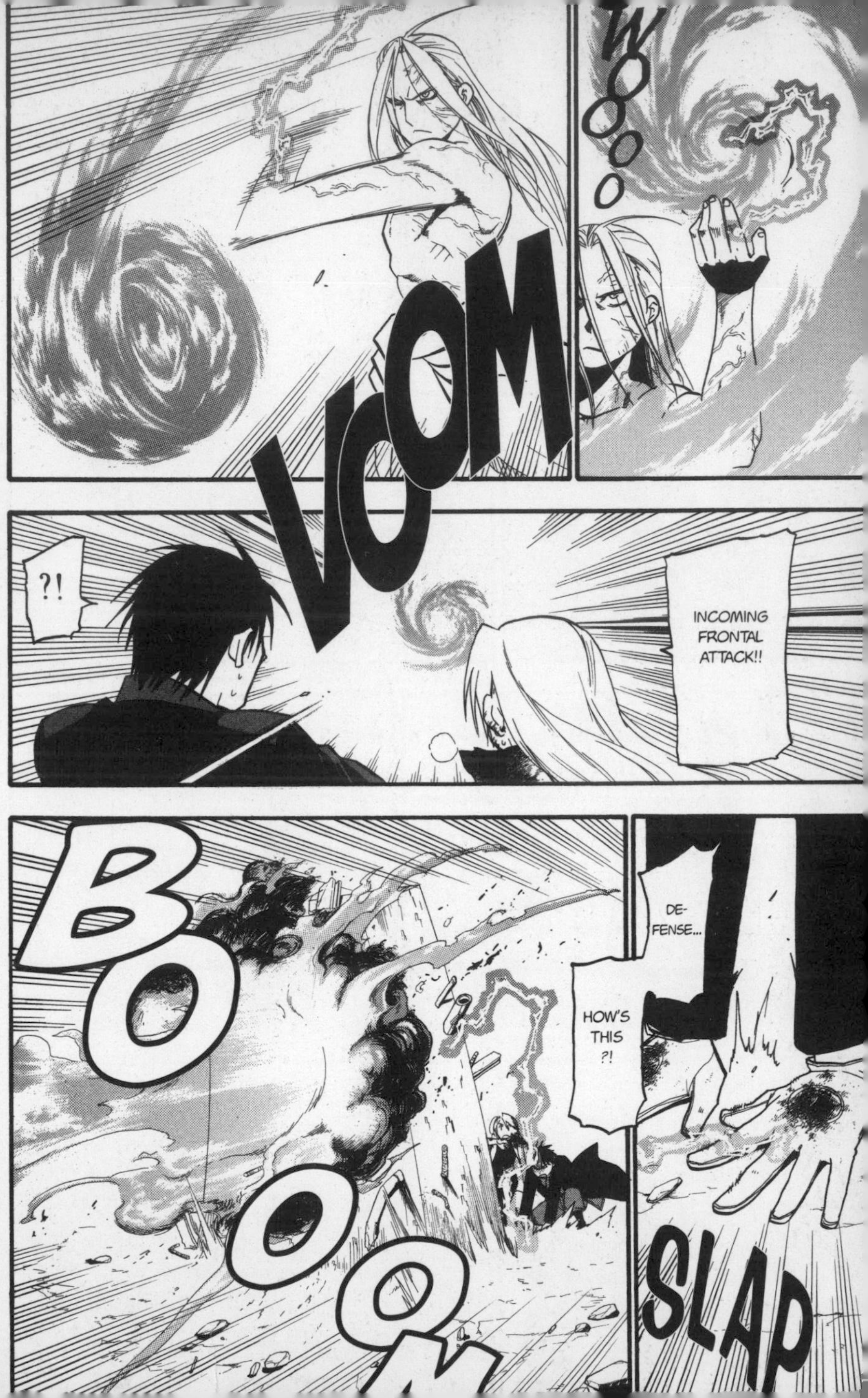
WOOOOO
VOOM
INCOMING FRONTAL ATTACK!!
?!
DE-FENSE...
HOW'S THIS?!
SLAP
BOOOOM

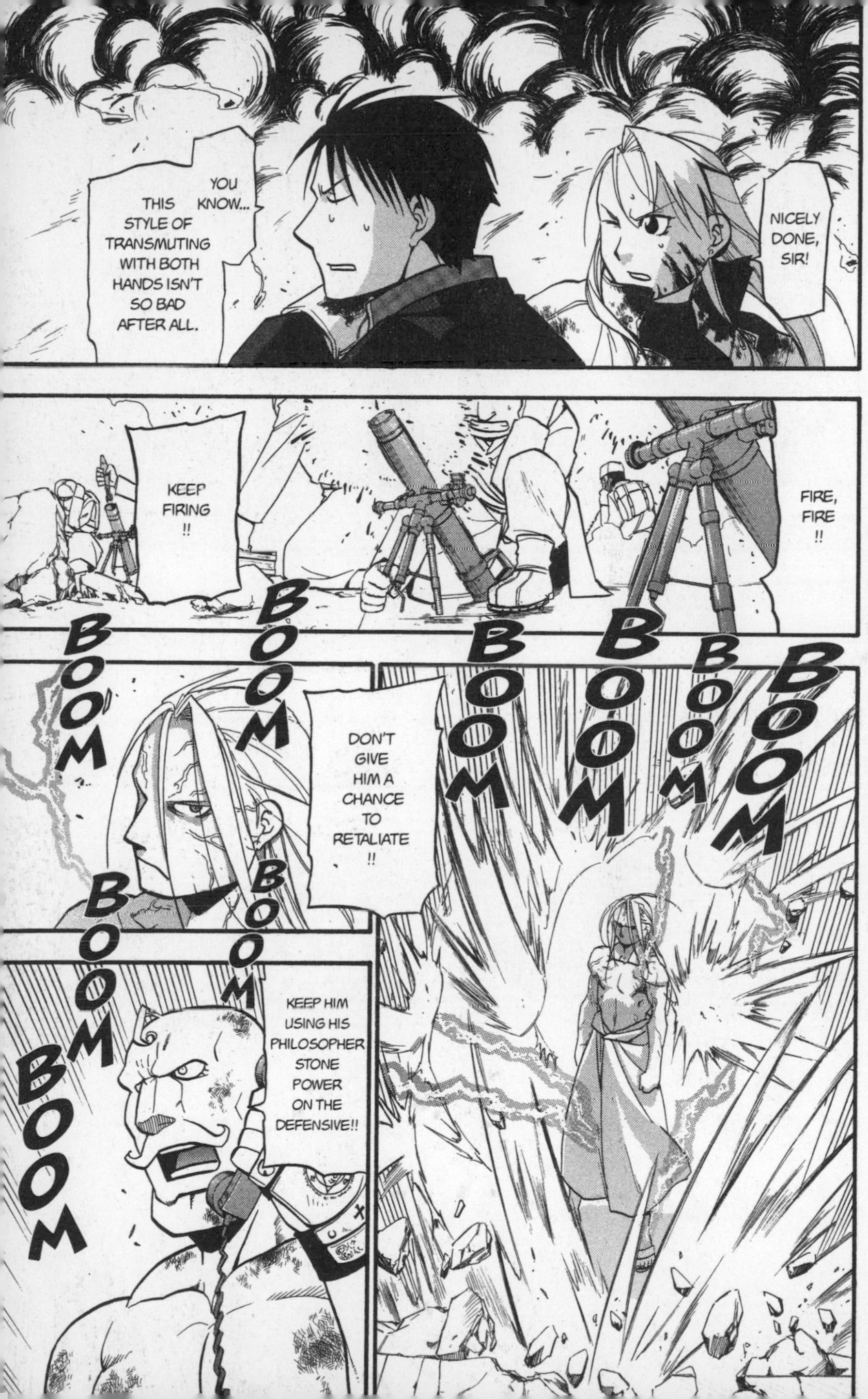
NICELY DONE, SIR!
YOU KNOW... THIS STYLE OF TRANSMUTING WITH BOTH HANDS ISN'T SO BAD AFTER ALL.
FIRE, FIRE !!
KEEP FIRING !!
BOOM
BOOM
BOOM
BOOM
BOOM
BOOM
DON'T GIVE HIM A CHANCE TO RETALIATE !!
BOOM
BOOM
BOOM
KEEP HIM USING HIS PHILOSOPHER STONE POWER ON THE DEFENSIVE!!

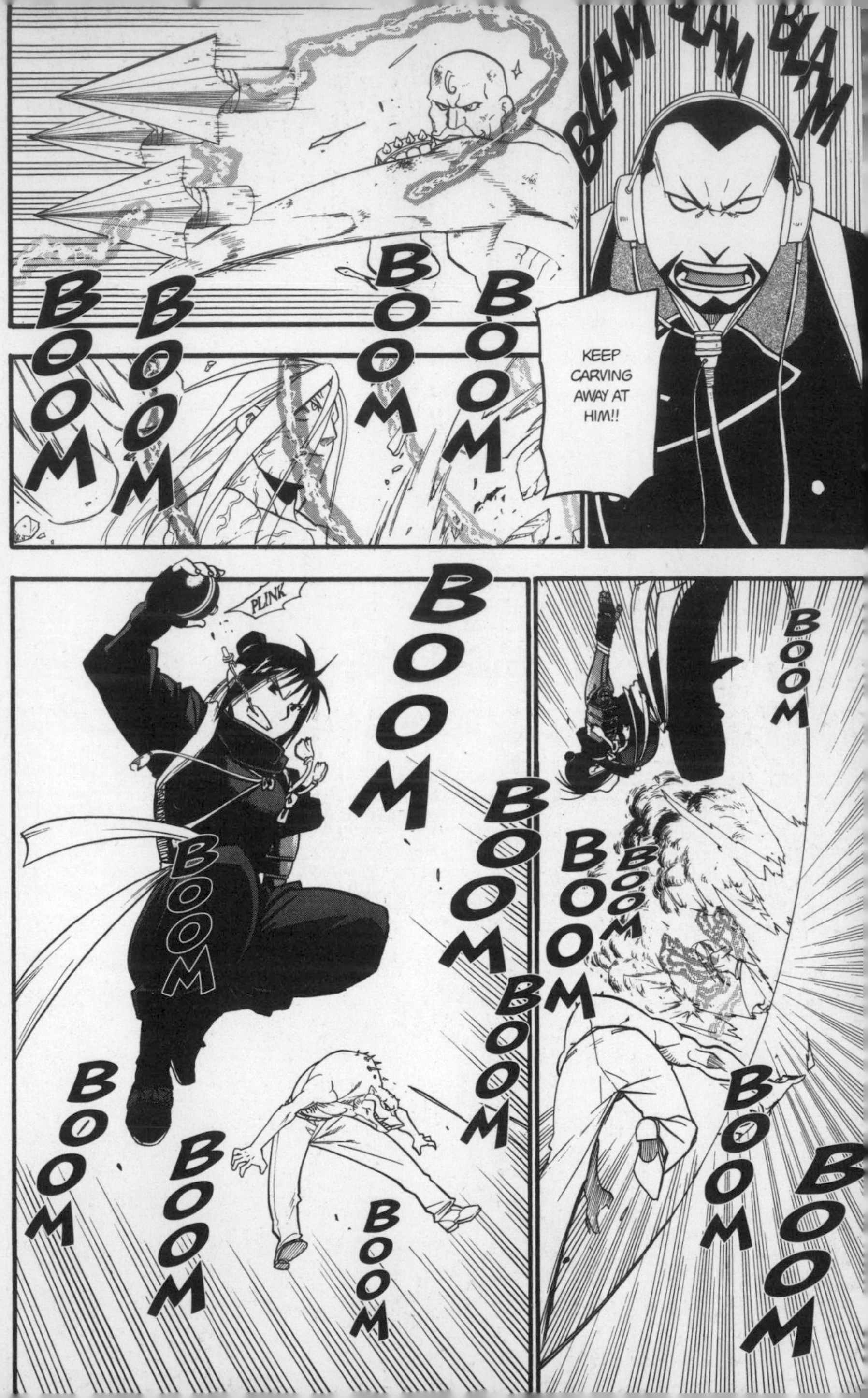
BLAM BLAM BLAM
KEEP CARVING AWAY AT HIM!!
BOOM
BOOM
BOOM
BOOM
BOOM
BOOM
BOOM
BOOM
BOOM
BOOM
BOOM
PLINK
BOOM
BOOM
BOOM
BOOM
BOOM
BOOM
BOOM

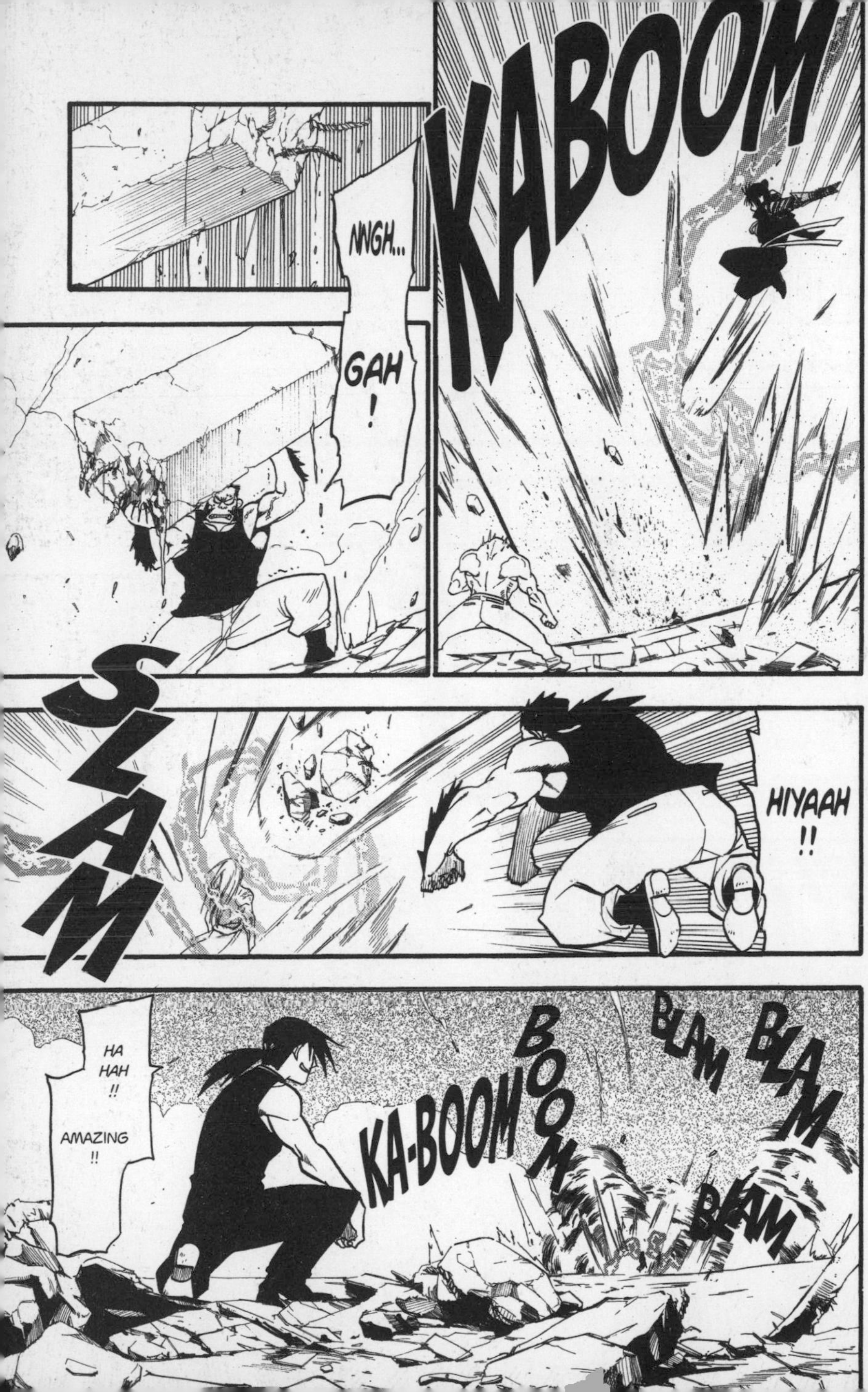
KABOOM
NNGH...
GAH!
HIYAAH!!
SLAM
BLAM
BLAM
BOOM
BLAM
KA-BOOM
HA HAH!!
AMAZING!!

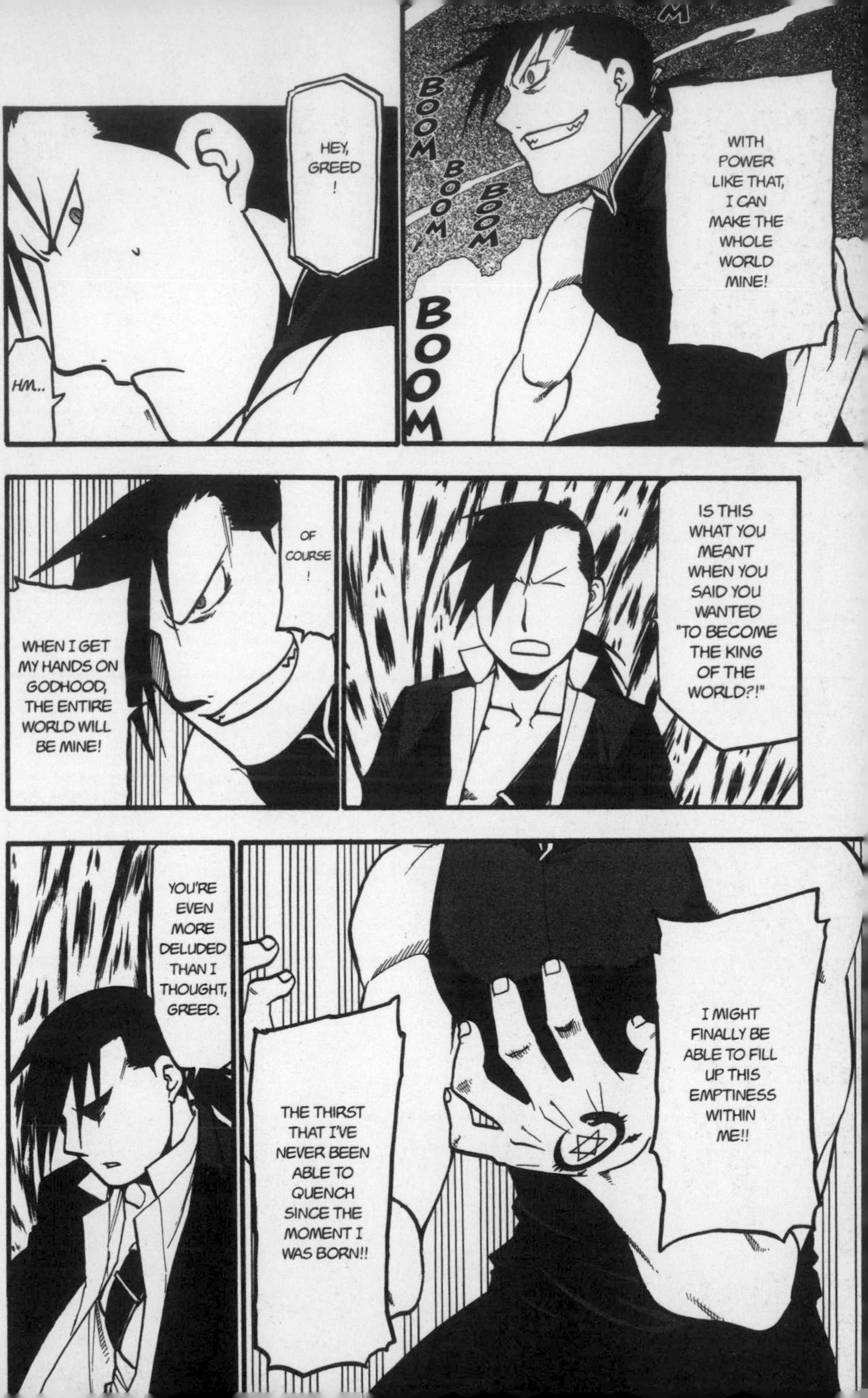
M
WITH POWER LIKE THAT, I CAN MAKE THE WHOLE WORLD MINE!
BOOM BOOM BOOM BOOM
BOOM
HEY, GREED!
HM...
IS THIS WHAT YOU MEANT WHEN YOU SAID YOU WANTED "TO BECOME THE KING OF THE WORLD?!"
OF COURSE!
WHEN I GET MY HANDS ON GODHOOD, THE ENTIRE WORLD WILL BE MINE!
I MIGHT FINALLY BE ABLE TO FILL UP THIS EMPTINESS WITHIN ME!!
THE THIRST THAT I'VE NEVER BEEN ABLE TO QUENCH SINCE THE MOMENT I WAS BORN!!
YOU'RE EVEN MORE DELUDED THAN I THOUGHT, GREED.

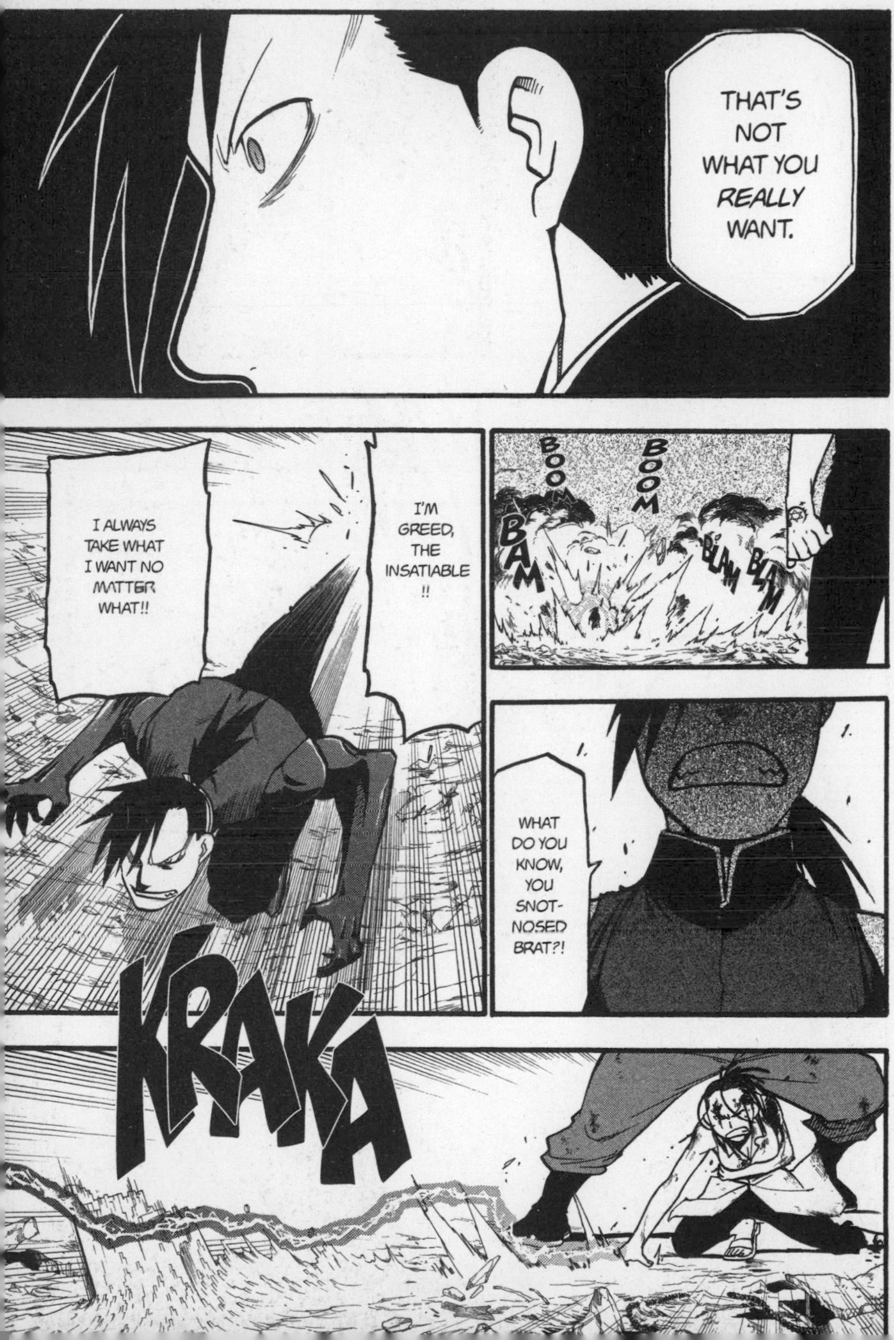
THAT'S NOT WHAT YOU REALLY WANT.
BOOM
BOOM
BAM
BLAM
BLAM
WHAT DO YOU KNOW, YOU SNOT-NOSED BRAT?!
I'M GREED, THE INSATIABLE!!
I ALWAYS TAKE WHAT I WANT NO MATTER WHAT!!
KRAKA

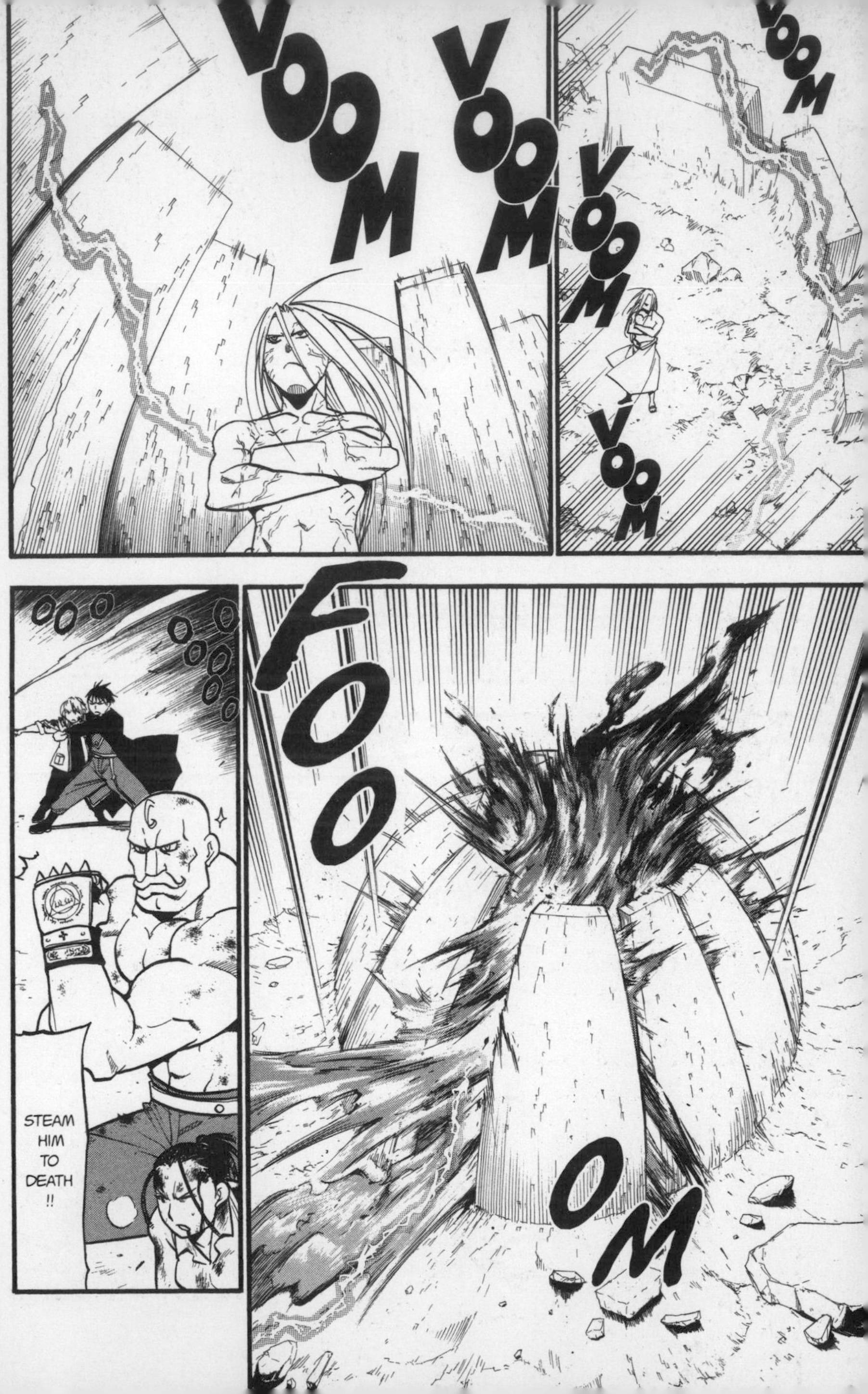
VOOM
VOOM
VOOM
VOOM
VOOM
FOOOOM
STEAM HIM TO DEATH !!

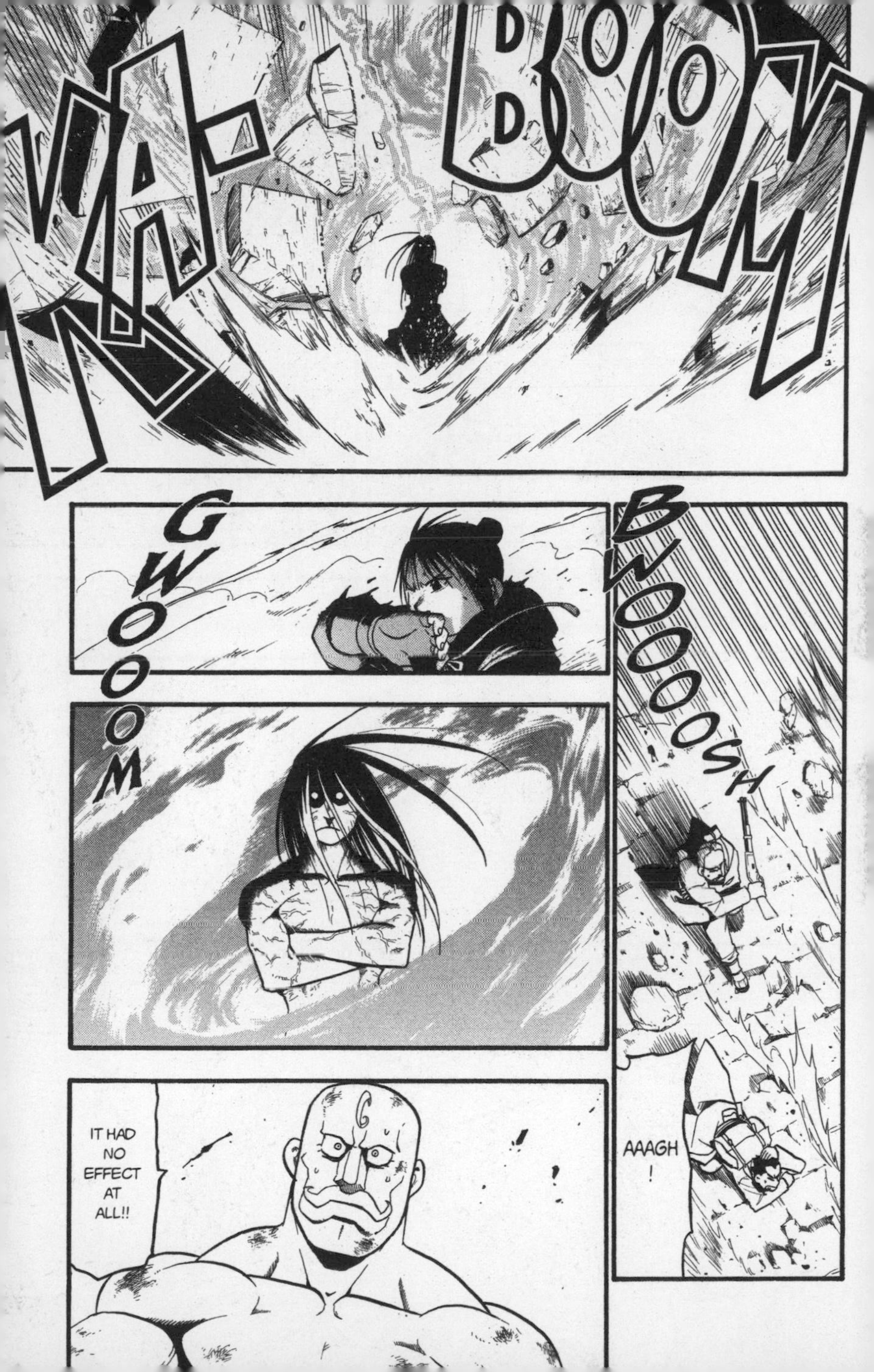
KA-BOOOM
BWOOOOOSH
AAAGH!
GWOOOOM
IT HAD NO EFFECT AT ALL!!

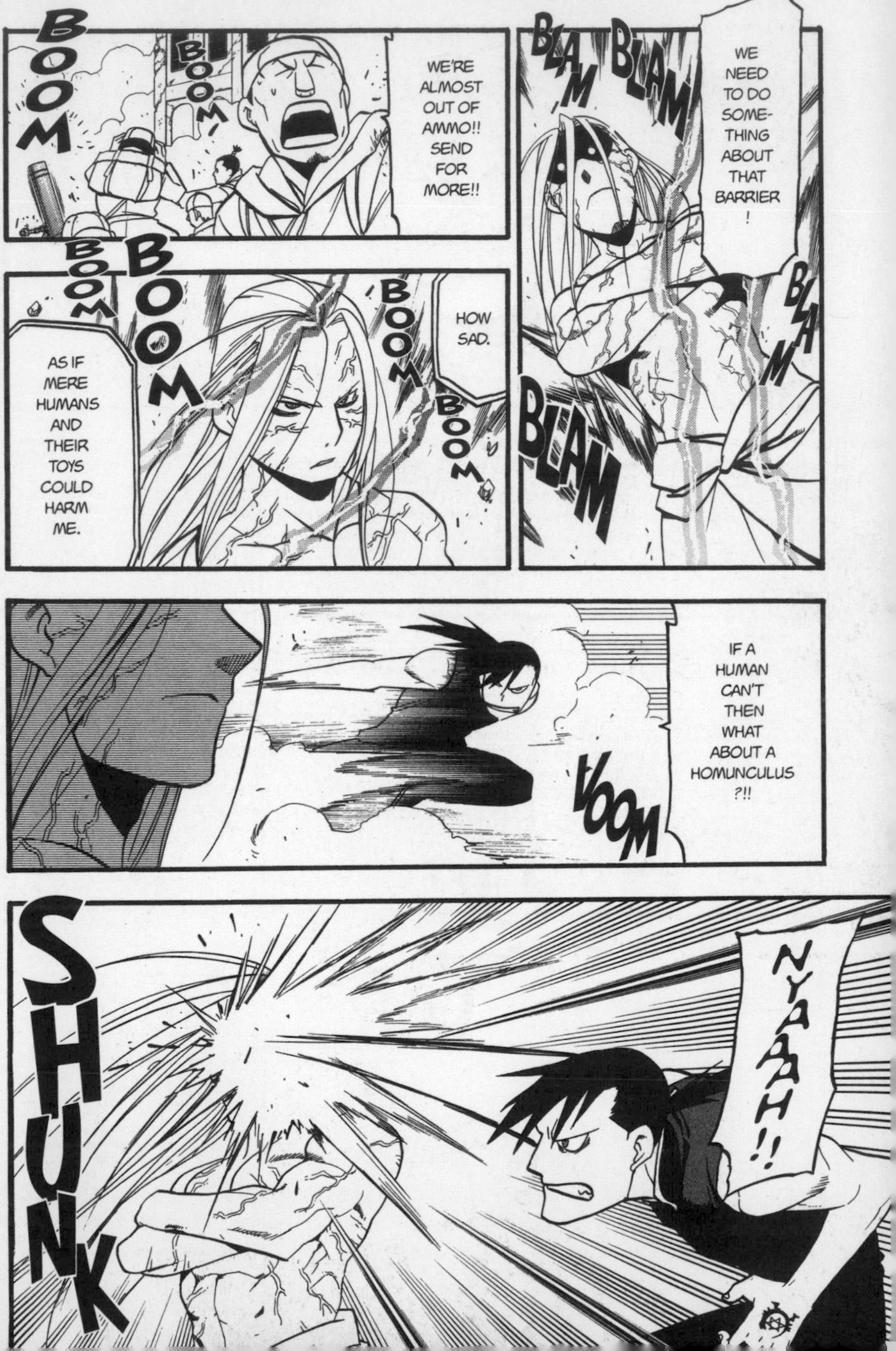
BLAM BLAM
WE NEED TO DO SOMETHING ABOUT THAT BARRIER!
BLAM
BLAM
WE'RE ALMOST OUT OF AMMO!! SEND FOR MORE!!
BOOM BOOM
BOOM
BOOM BOOM
BOOM BOOM
HOW SAD.
AS IF MERE HUMANS AND THEIR TOYS COULD HARM ME.
IF A HUMAN CAN'T THEN WHAT ABOUT A HOMUNCULUS?!!
VOOM
NYAAAH!!
SHUNK

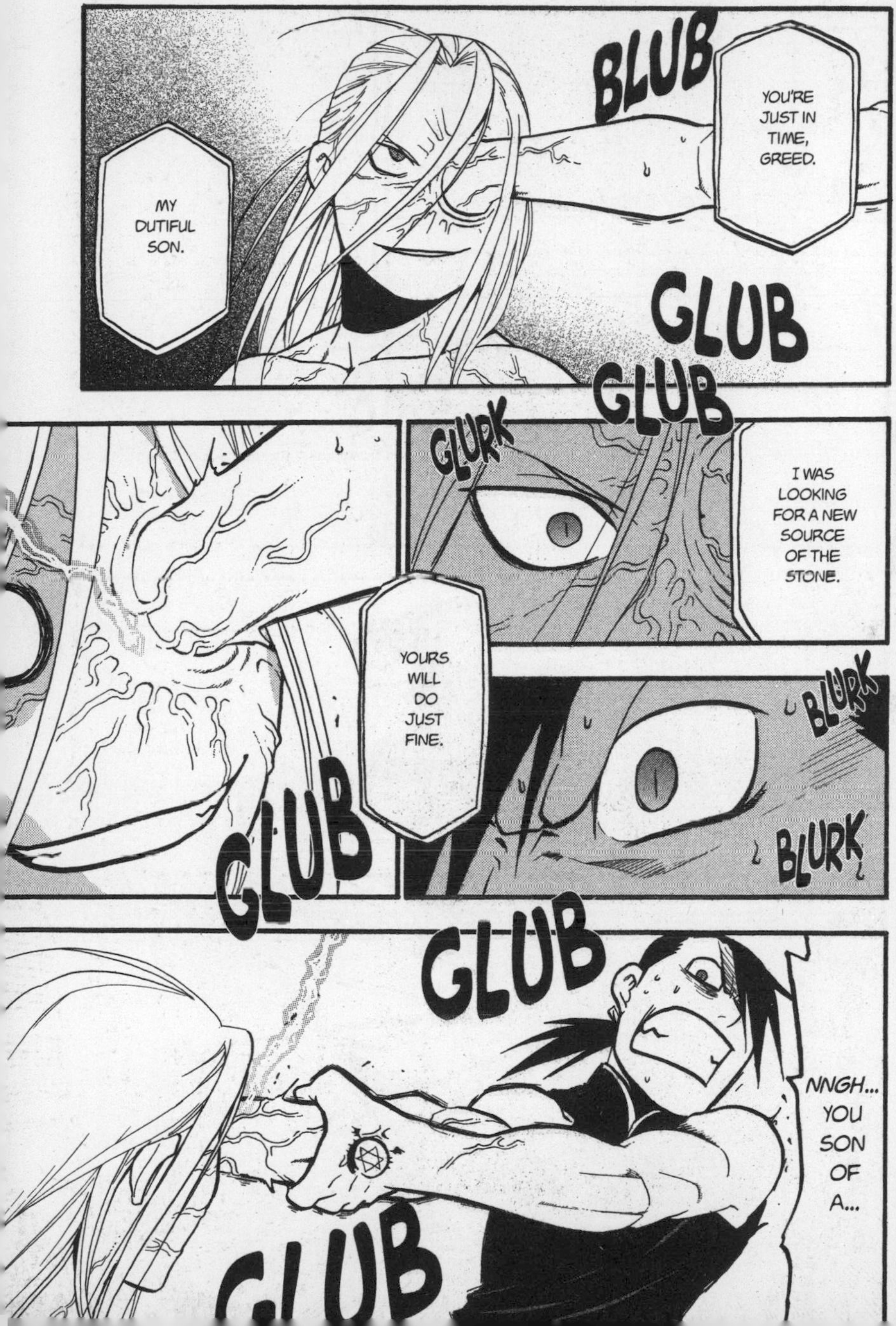
BLUB
YOU'RE JUST IN TIME, GREED.
MY DUTIFUL SON.
GLUB
GLUB
GLURK
I WAS LOOKING FOR A NEW SOURCE OF THE STONE.
BLURK
BLURK
YOURS WILL DO JUST FINE.
GLUB
GLUB
NNGH... YOU SON OF A...
GLUB

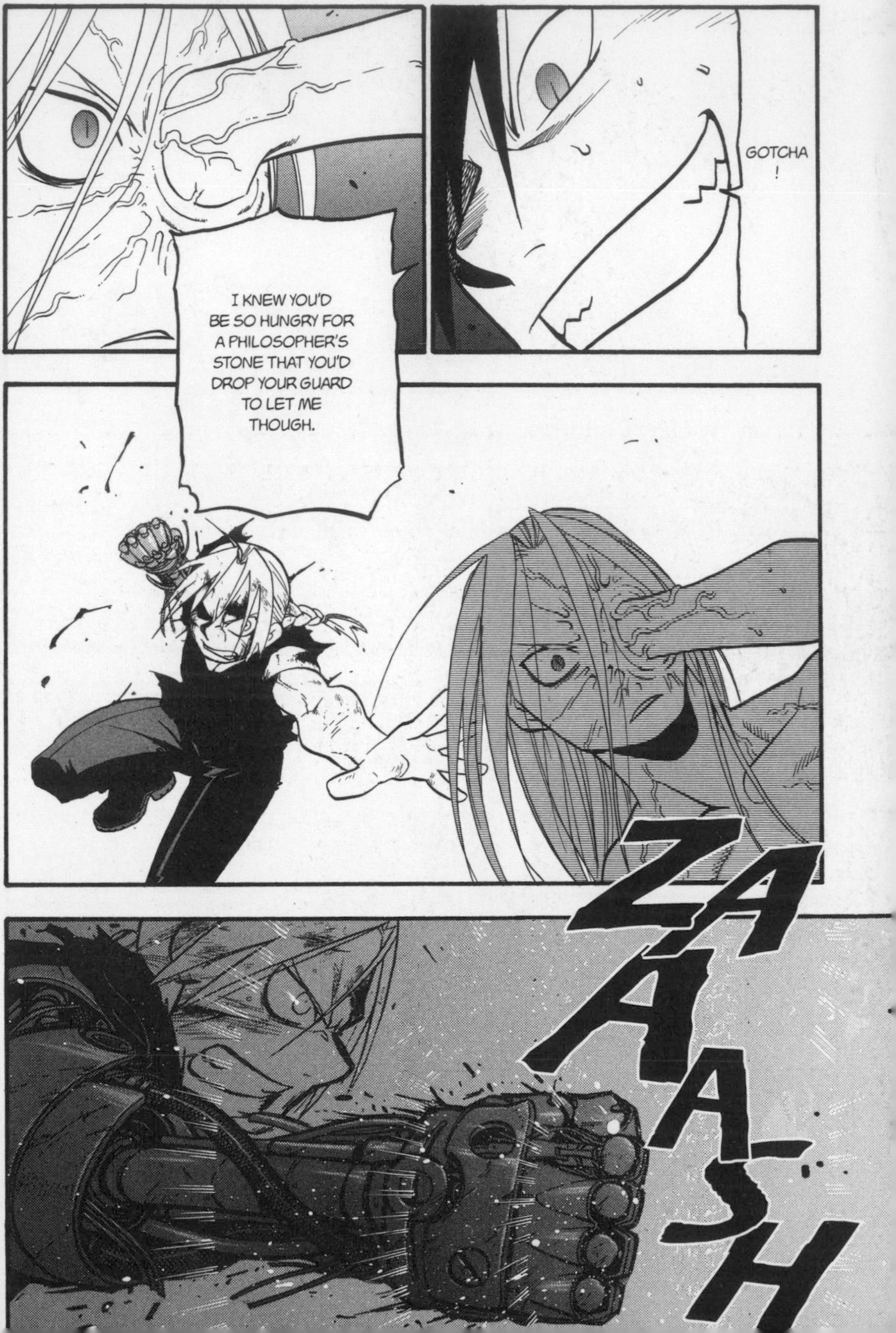
GOTCHA!
I KNEW YOU'D BE SO HUNGRY FOR A PHILOSOPHER'S STONE THAT YOU'D DROP YOUR GUARD TO LET ME THOUGH.
ZAAASH

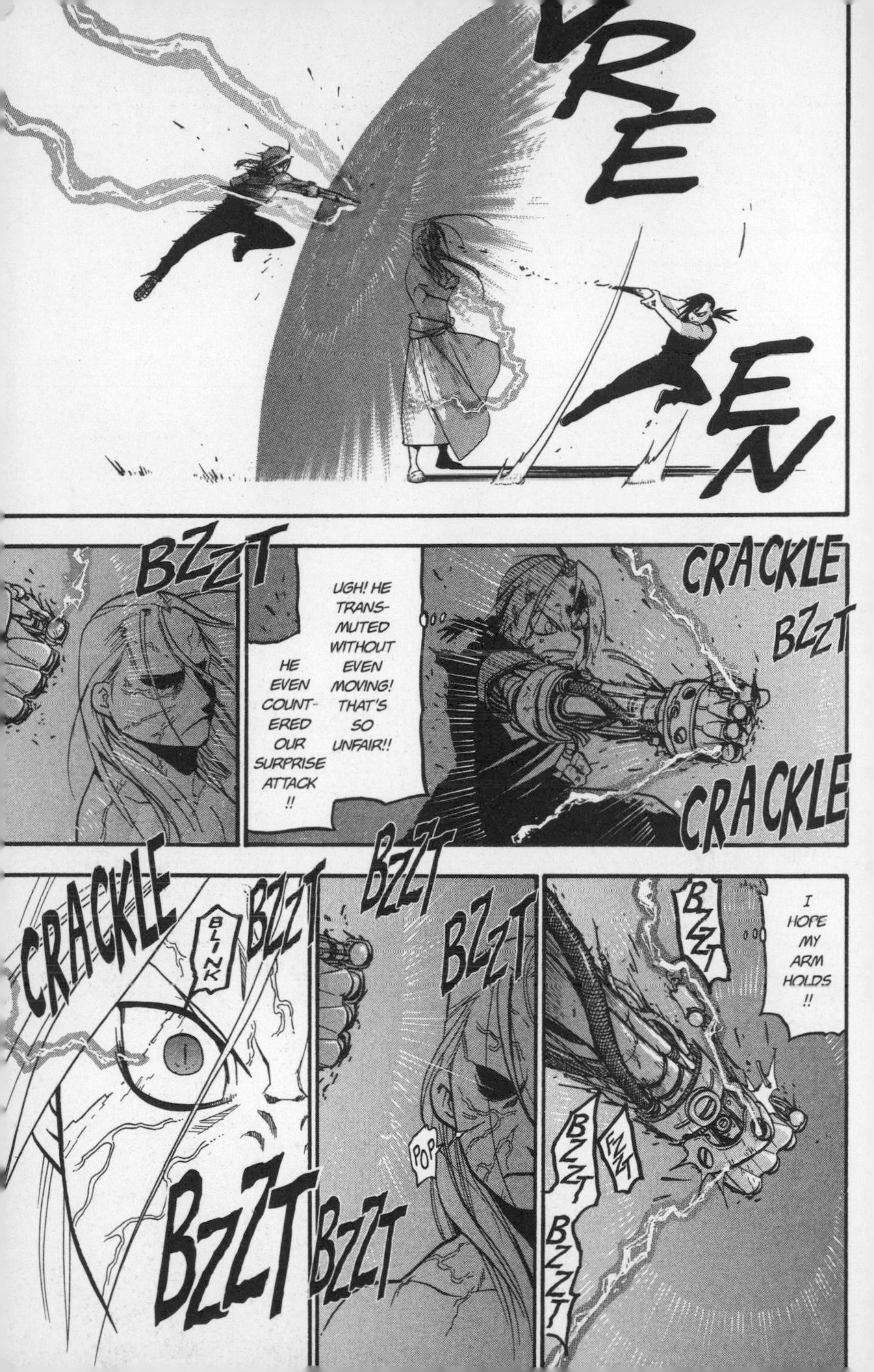
VRE
EN
CRACKLE
BZZT
CRACKLE
UGH! HE TRANSMUTED WITHOUT EVEN MOVING! THAT'S SO UNFAIR!!
HE EVEN COUNTERED OUR SURPRISE ATTACK!!
BZZT
BZZT
I HOPE MY ARM HOLDS!!
BZZT
FZZT
BZZT
BZZT
BZZT
BZZT
POP
BZZT
CRACKLE
BLINK
BZZT
BZZT

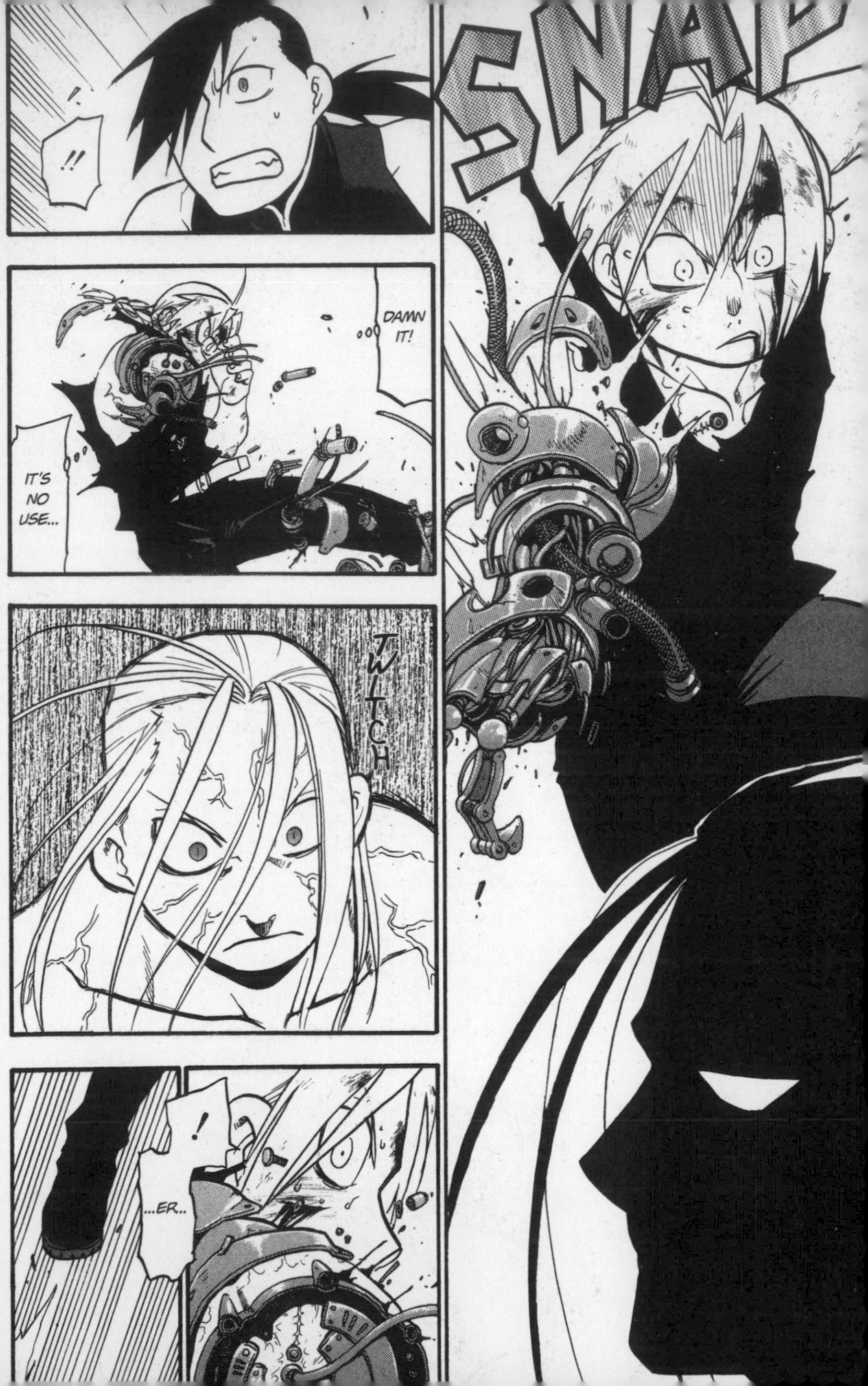
SNAP
!!
DAMN IT!
IT'S NO USE...
TWITCH
!
...ER...

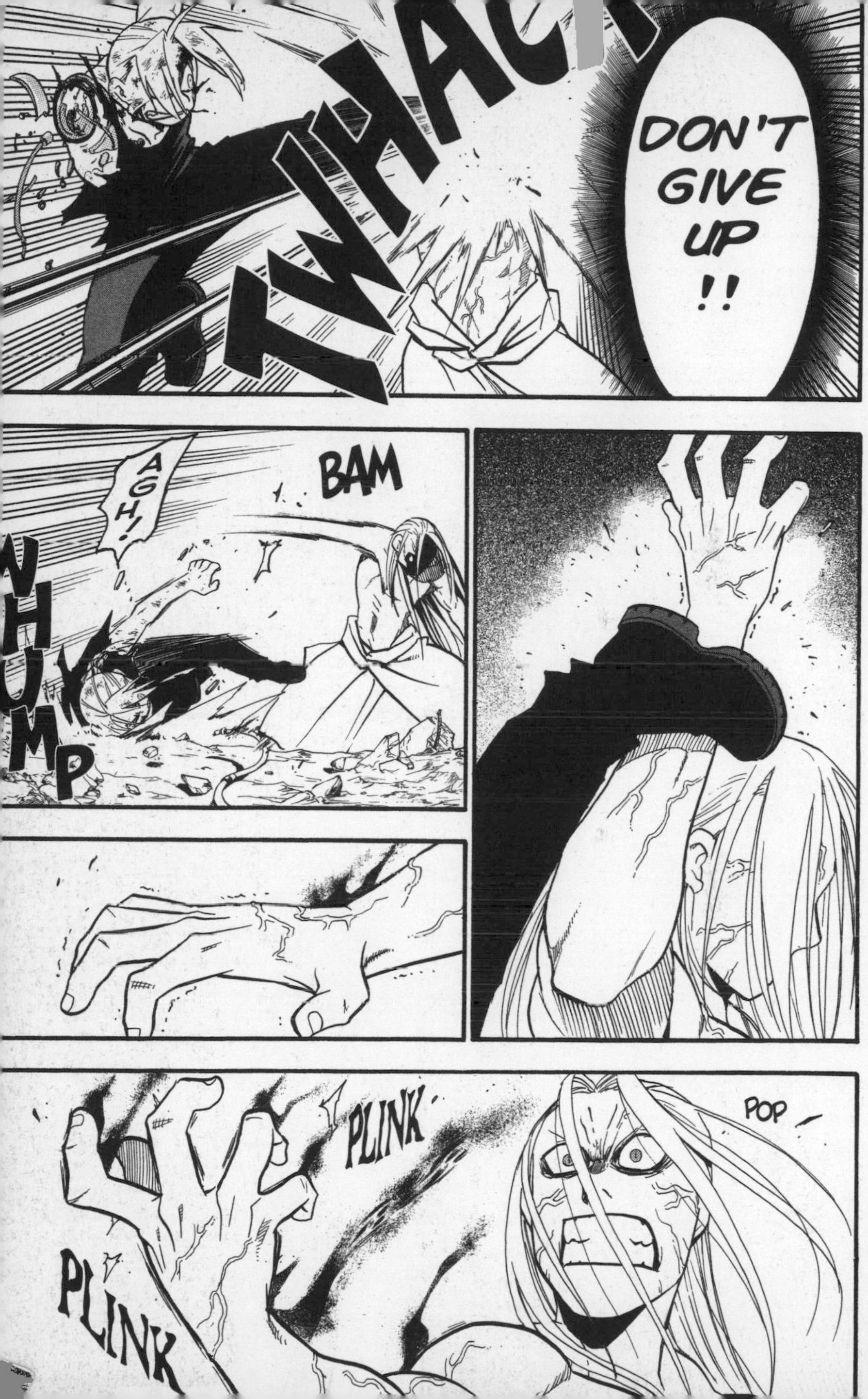

DON'T GIVE UP!!
TWHAC
BAM
AGH!
THUMP
POP
PLINK
PLINK

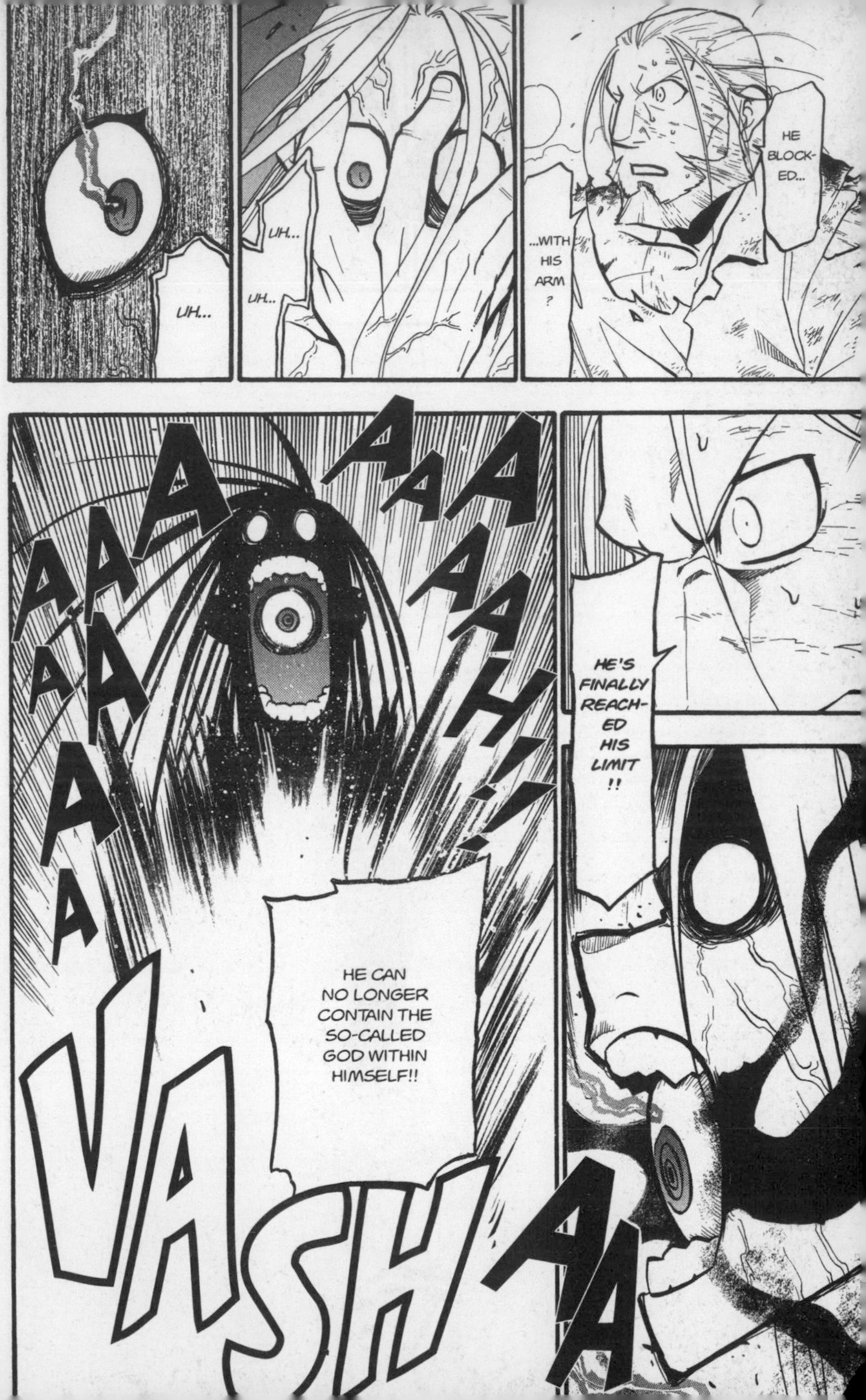
HE BLOCKED...
...WITH HIS ARM?
UH...
UH...
UH...
HE'S FINALLY REACHED HIS LIMIT!!
AAAAAAAAAA
AAAAAH!!!
HE CAN NO LONGER CONTAIN THE SO-CALLED GOD WITHIN HIMSELF!!
VASHAA

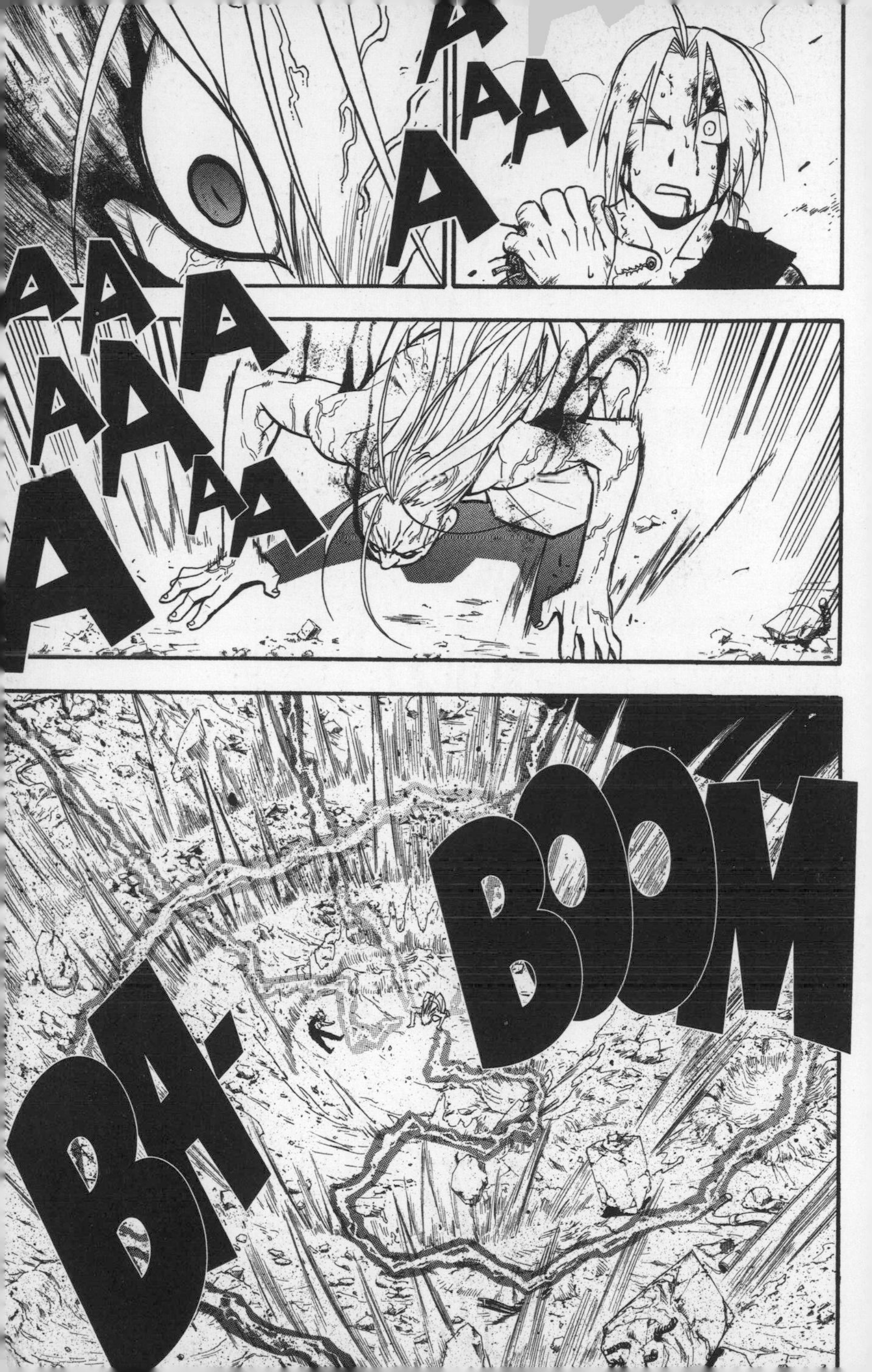
AAAA
AAAAAAAA
BA-BOOM

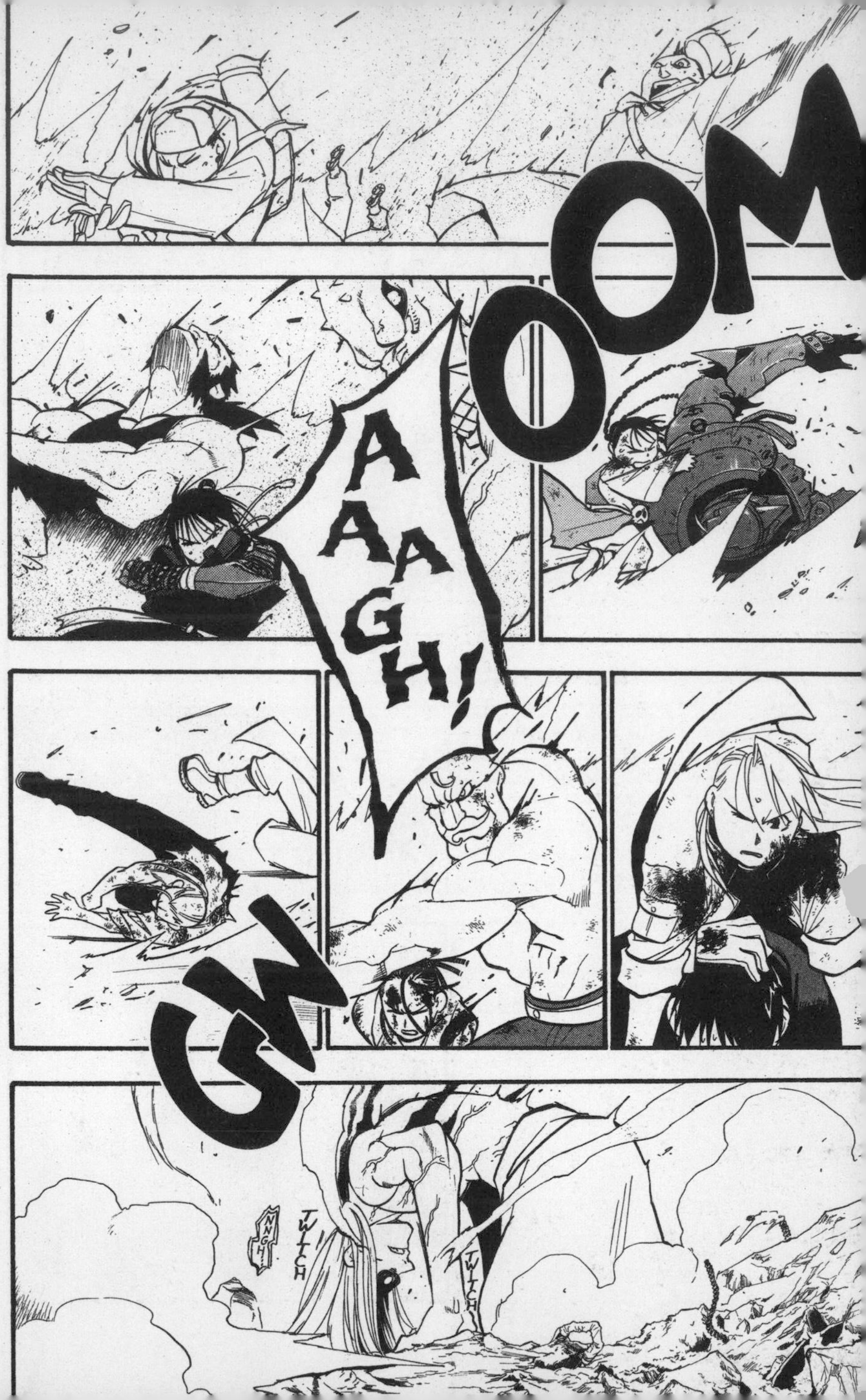
GWOOOM
AAAGH!
TWITCH
TWITCH
NNGH!

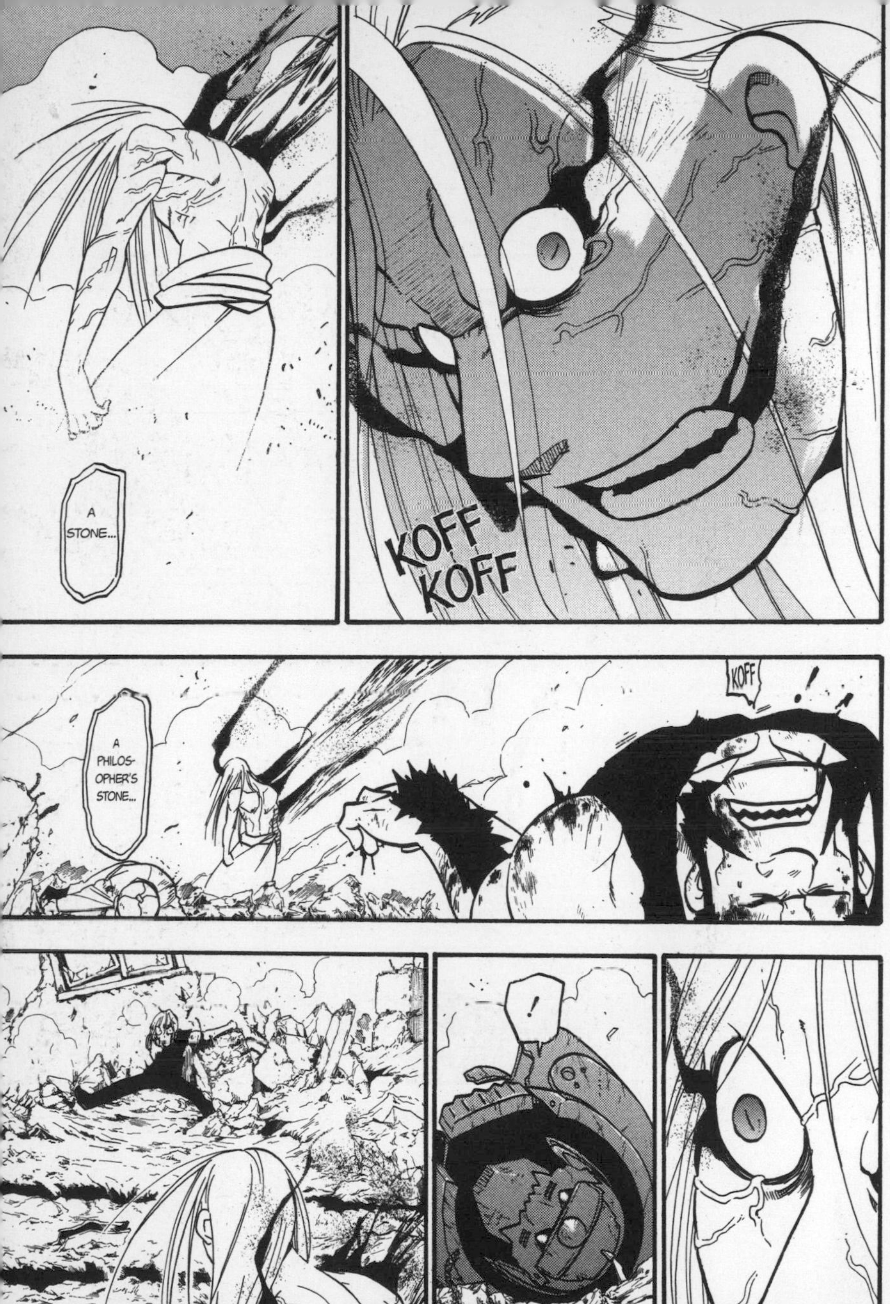
KOFF KOFF
A STONE...
KOFF
A PHILOSOPHER'S STONE...
!

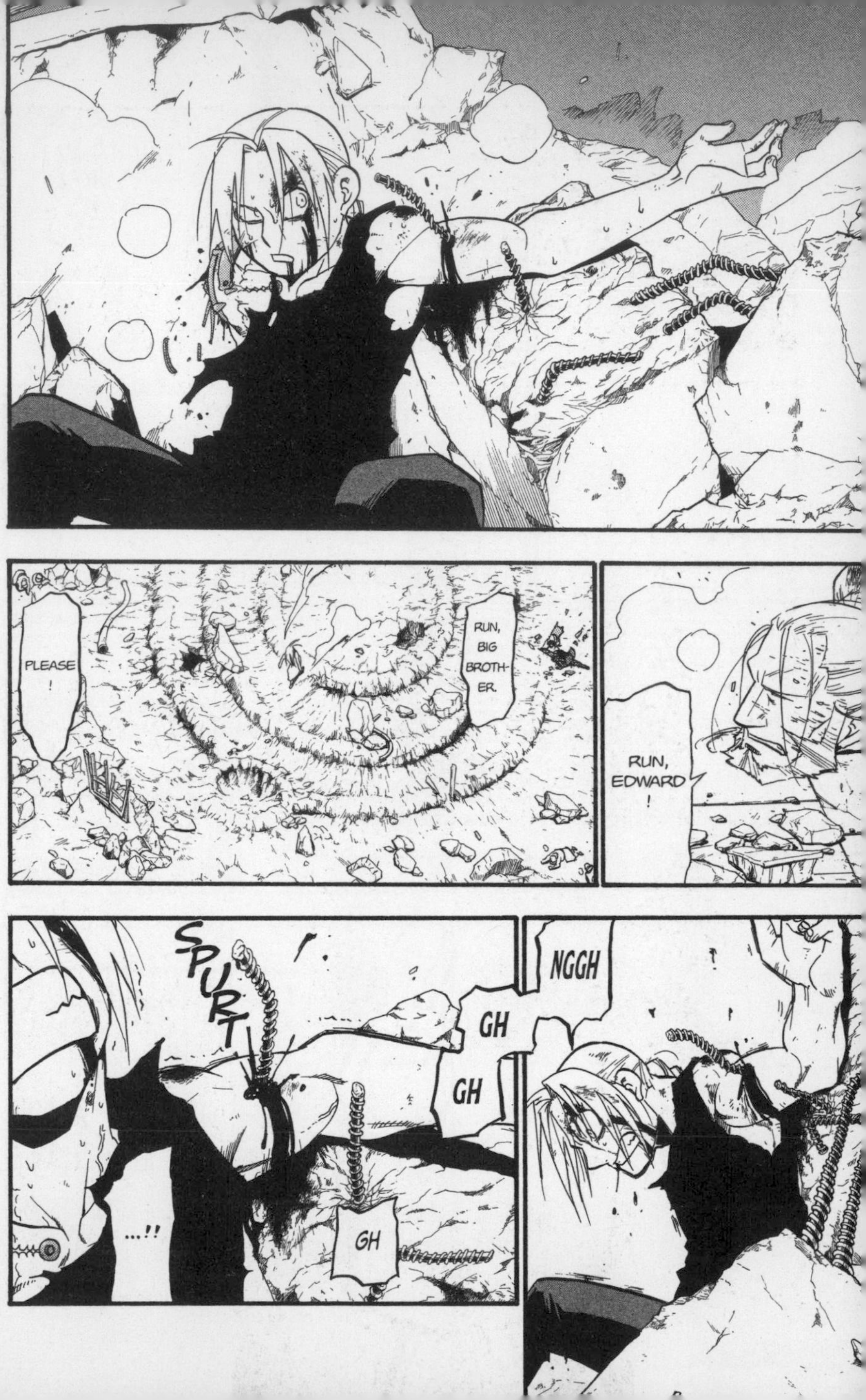
RUN, EDWARD!
RUN, BIG BROTHER.
PLEASE!
NGGH
GH
GH
SPURT
...!!
GH

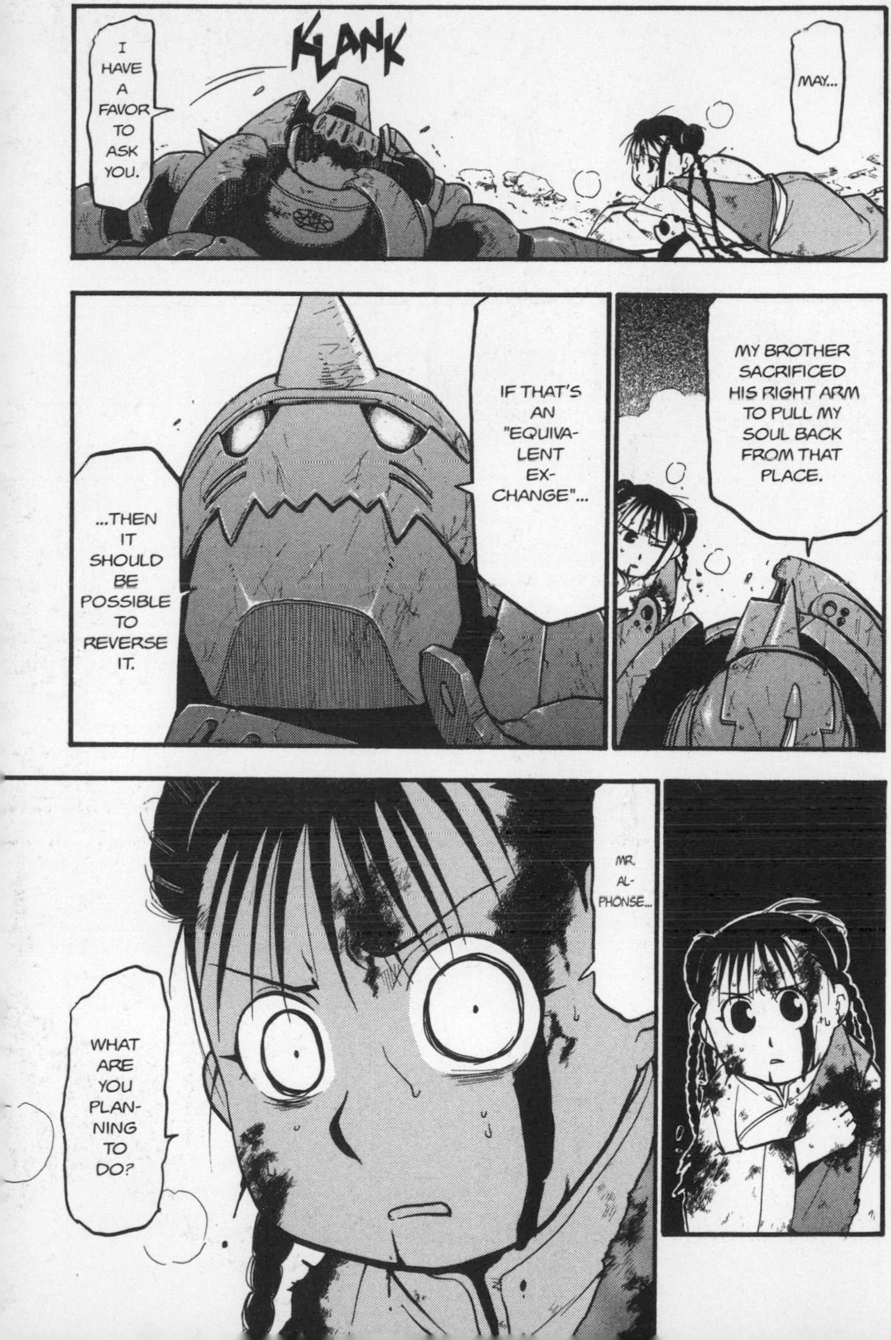
MAY...
KLANK
I HAVE A FAVOR TO ASK YOU.
MY BROTHER SACRIFICED HIS RIGHT ARM TO PULL MY SOUL BACK FROM THAT PLACE.
IF THAT'S AN "EQUIVALENT EXCHANGE"...
...THEN IT SHOULD BE POSSIBLE TO REVERSE IT.
MR. ALPHONSE...
WHAT ARE YOU PLANNING TO DO?

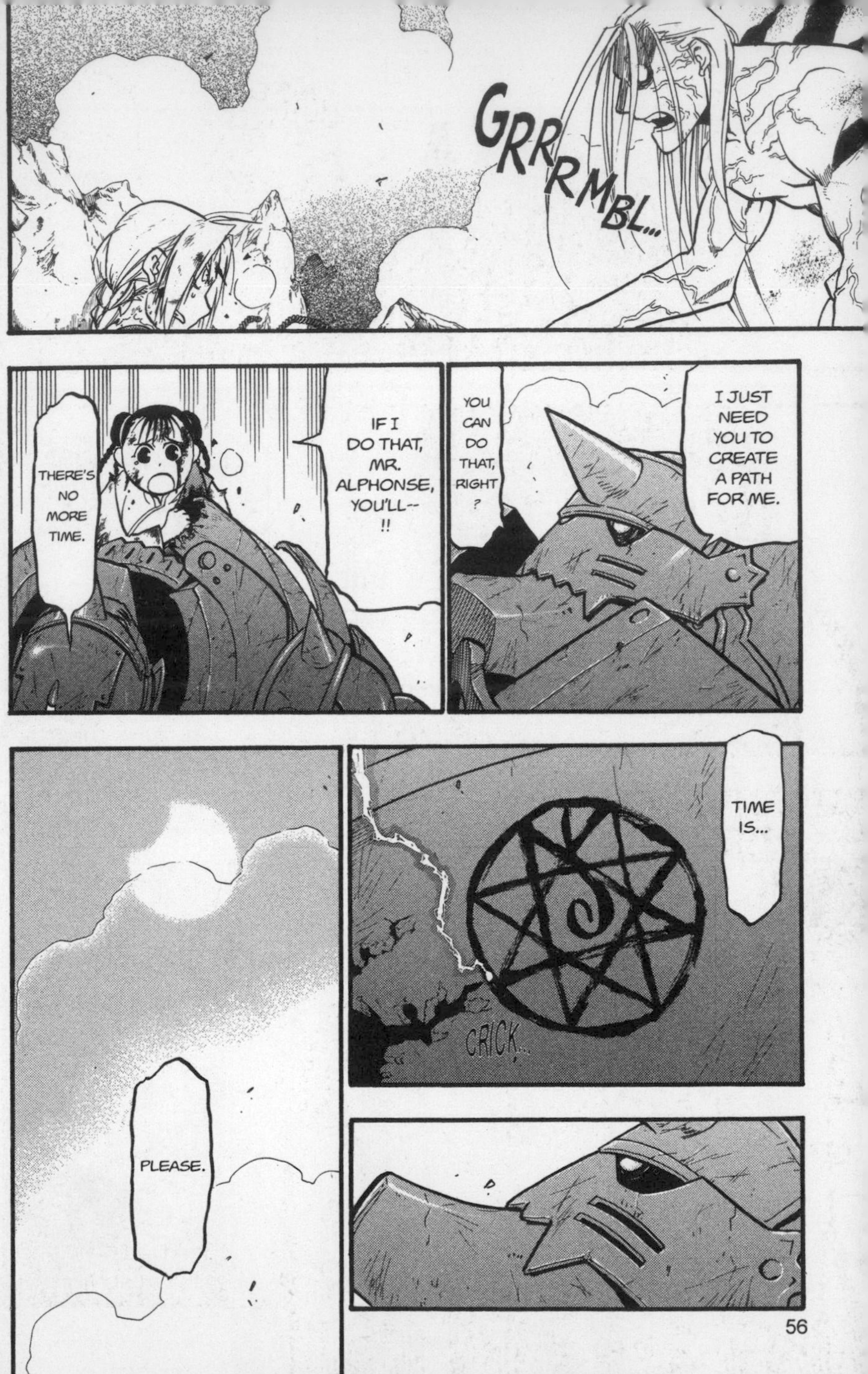
GRRRMBL...
I JUST NEED YOU TO CREATE A PATH FOR ME.
YOU CAN DO THAT, RIGHT?
IF I DO THAT, MR. ALPHONSE, YOU'LL-- !!
THERE'S NO MORE TIME.
TIME IS...
CRICK...
PLEASE.

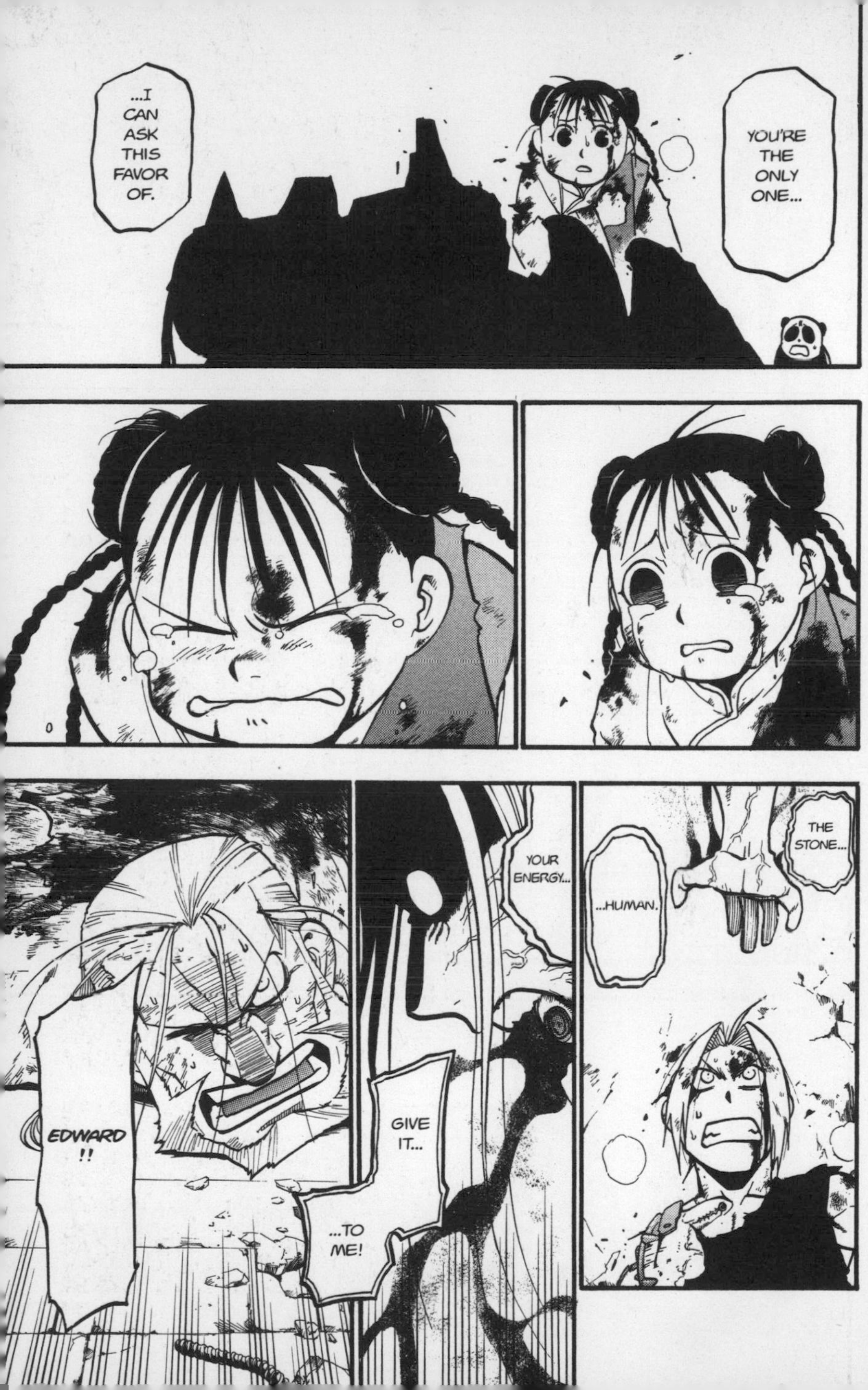
YOU'RE THE ONLY ONE...
...I CAN ASK THIS FAVOR OF.
THE STONE...
...HUMAN.
YOUR ENERGY...
GIVE IT...
...TO ME!
EDWARD !!

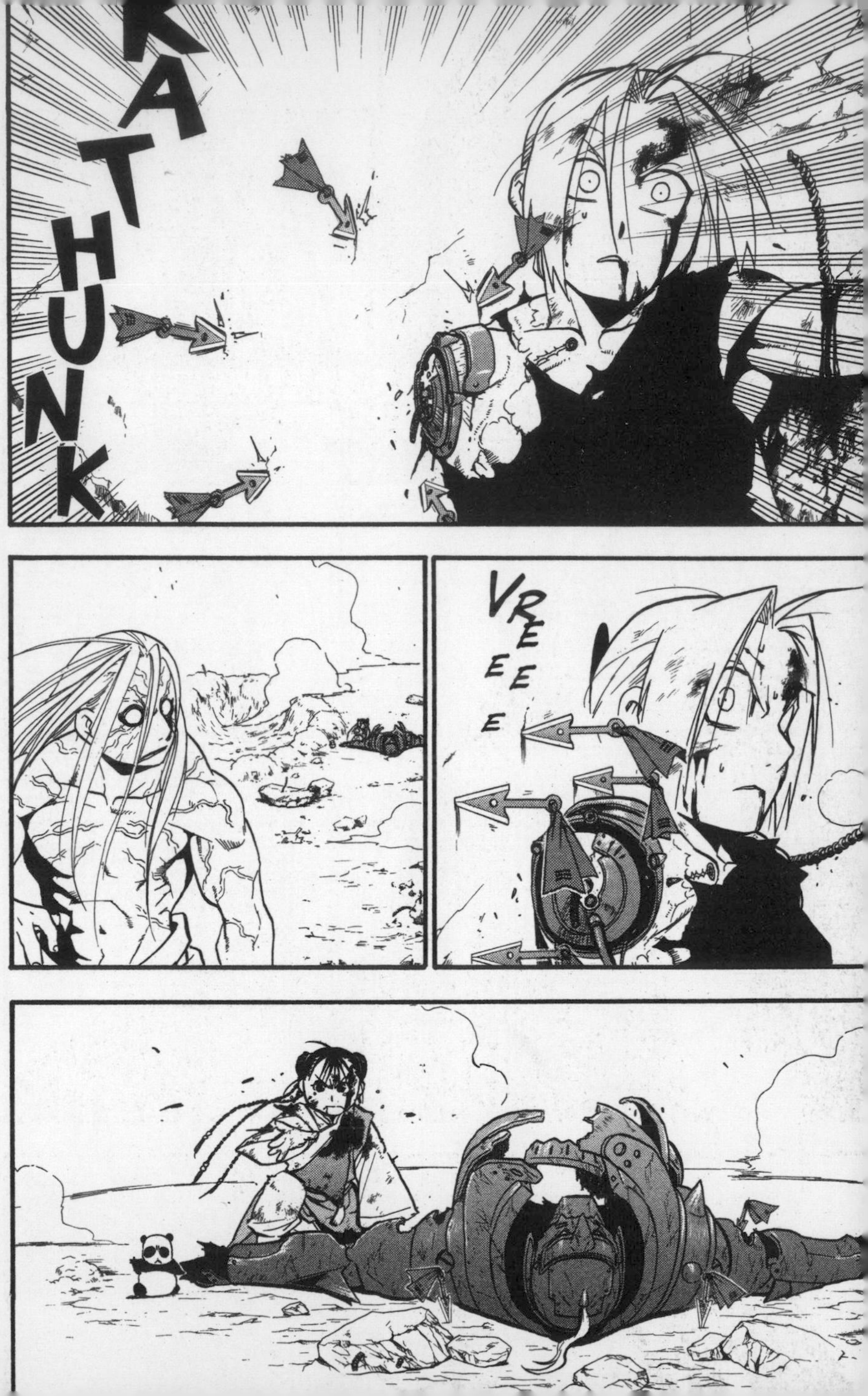
KATHUNK
VREEEEE

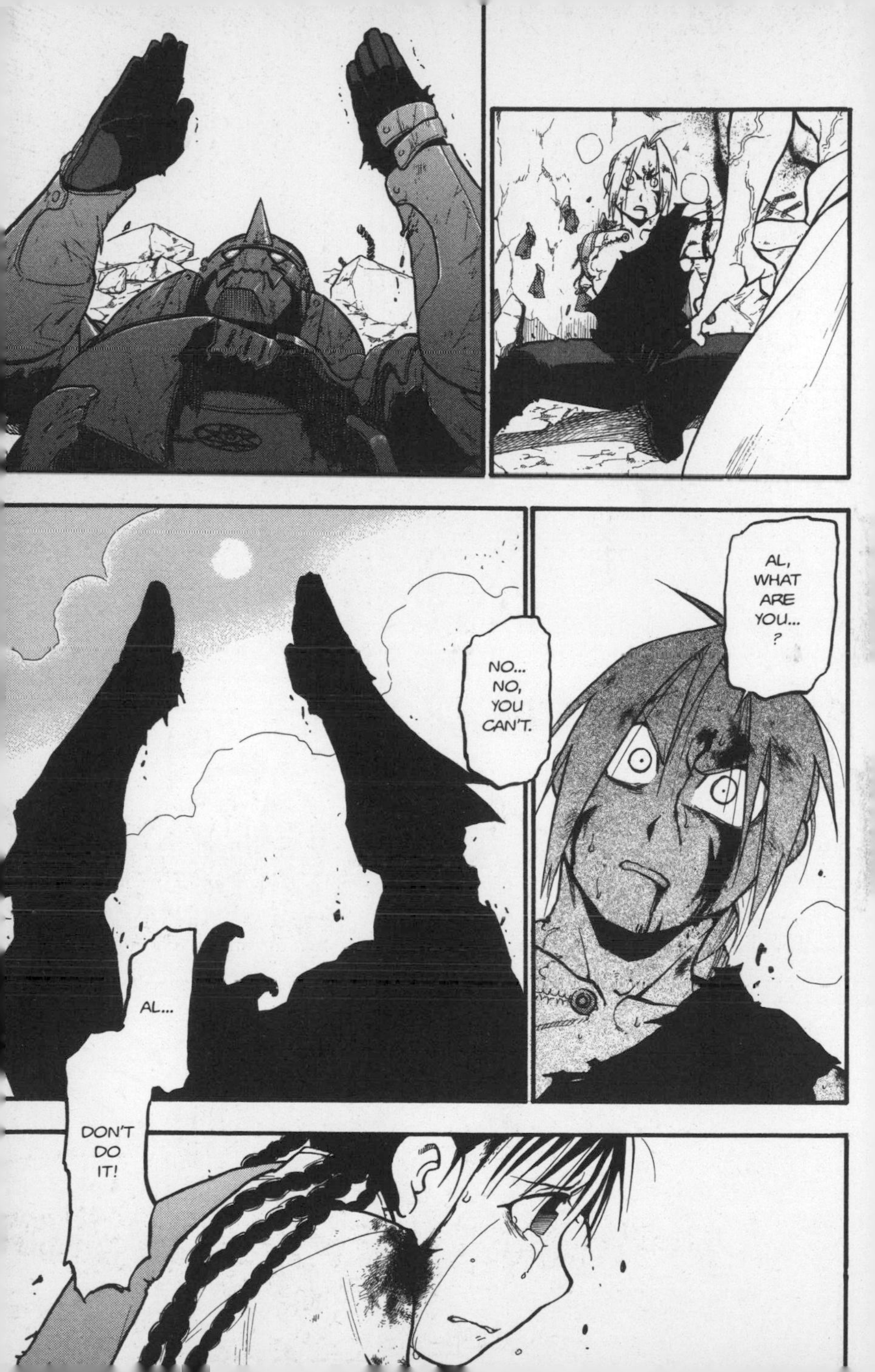
AL, WHAT ARE YOU...?
NO... NO, YOU CAN'T.
AL...
DON'T DO IT!

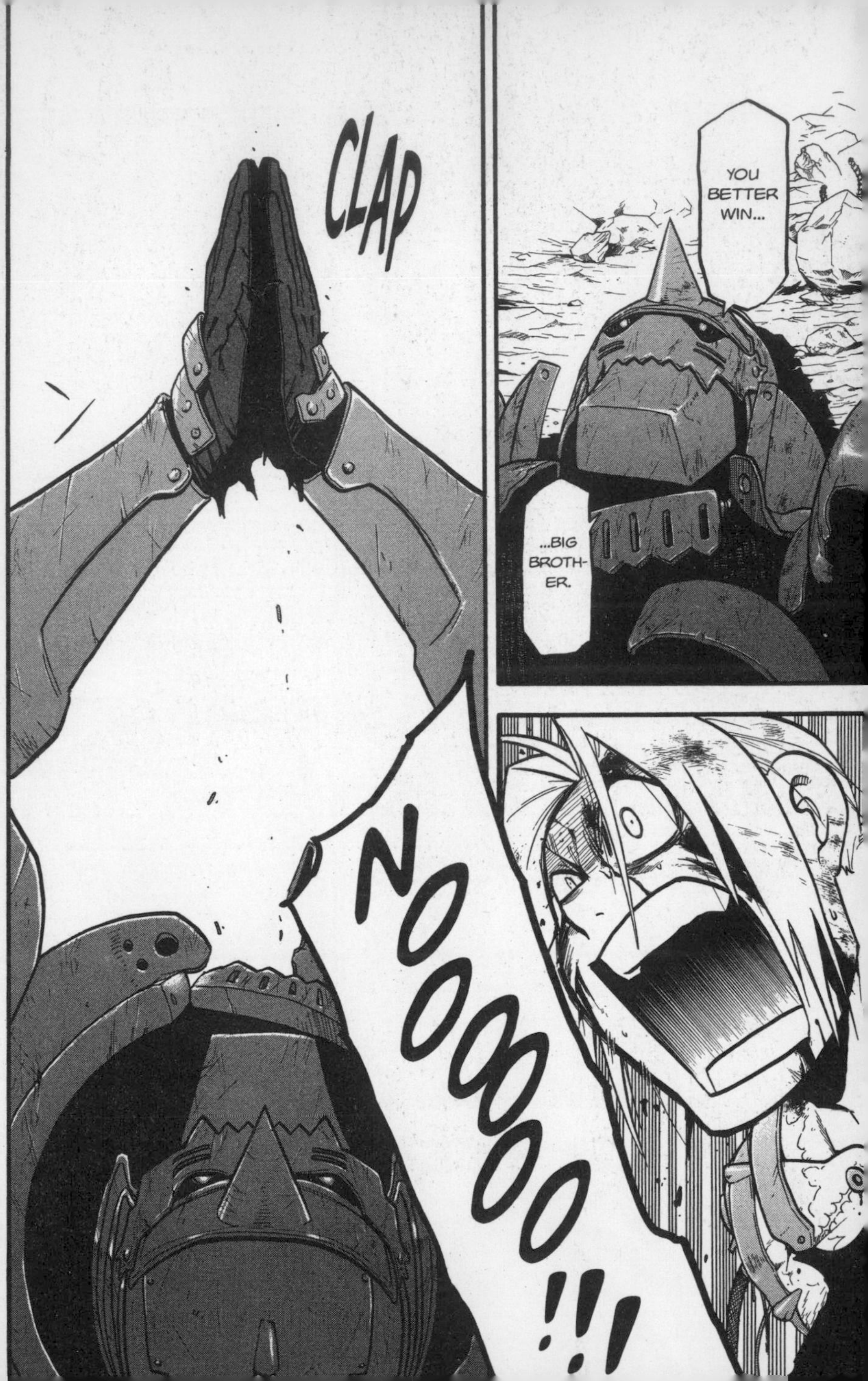

YOU BETTER WIN...
...BIG BROTHER.
NOOOOOO!!!
CLAP

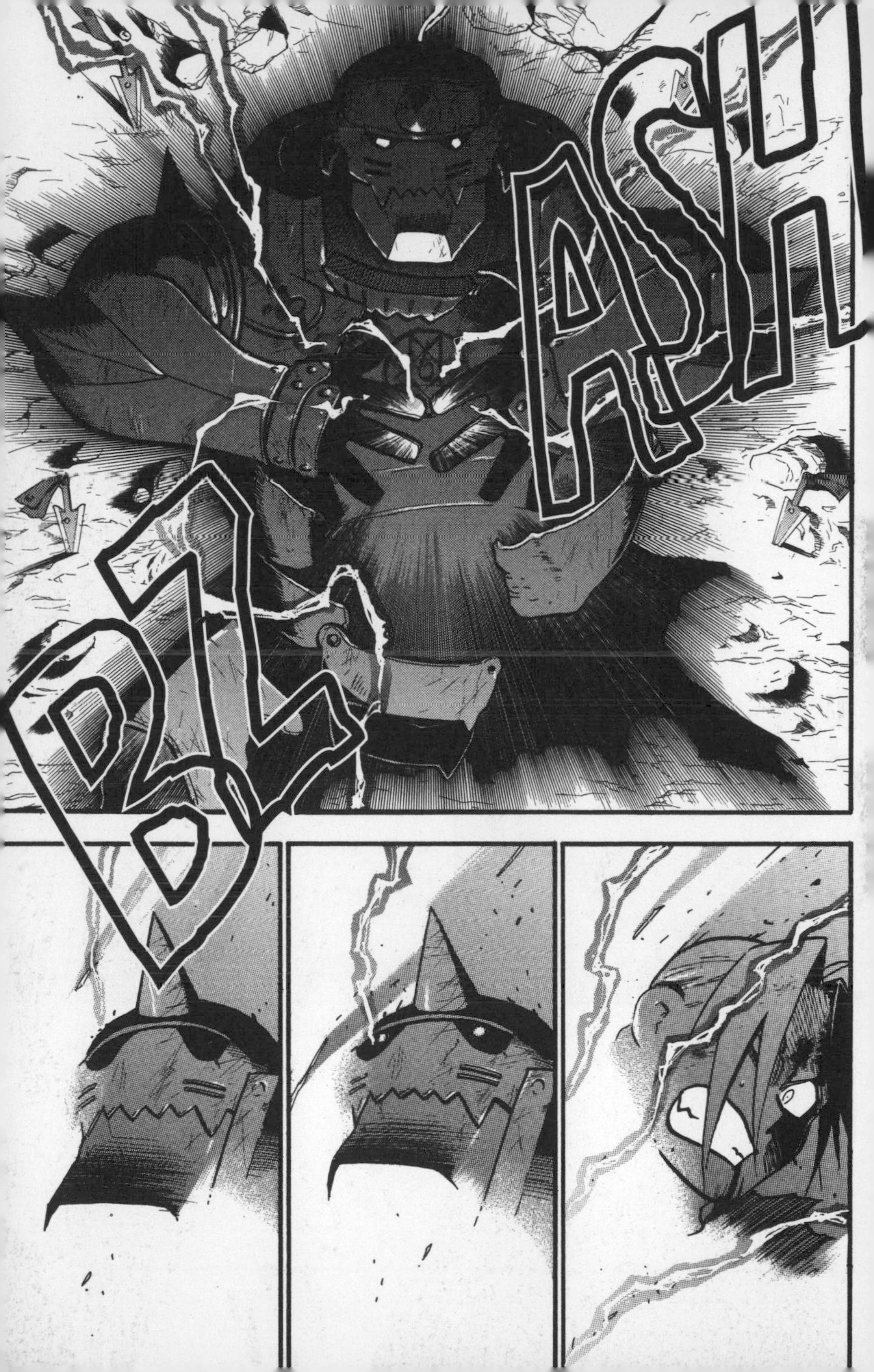

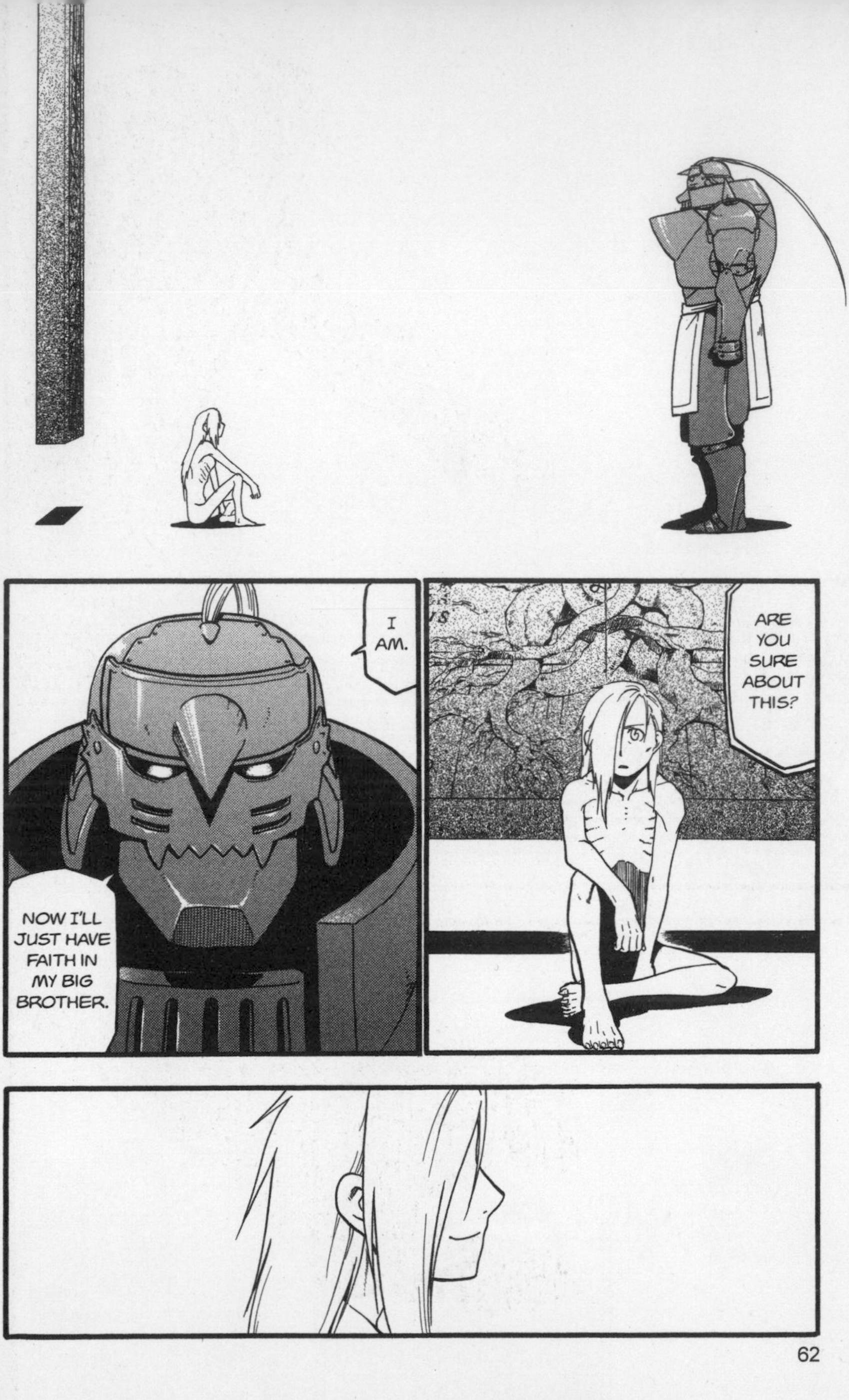
ARE YOU SURE ABOUT THIS?
I AM.
NOW I'LL JUST HAVE FAITH IN MY BIG BROTHER.

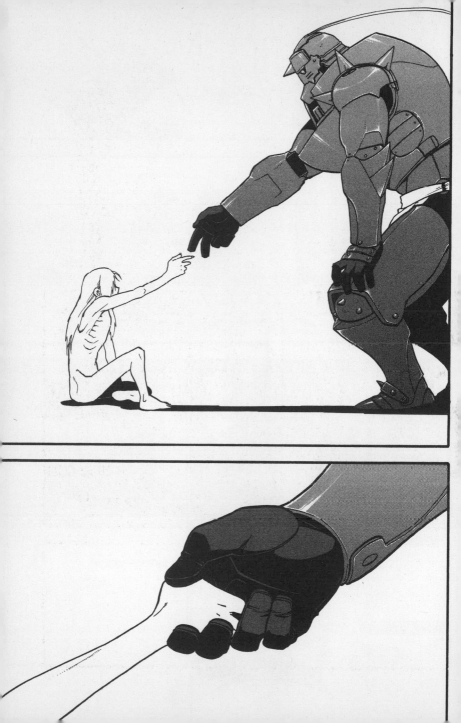

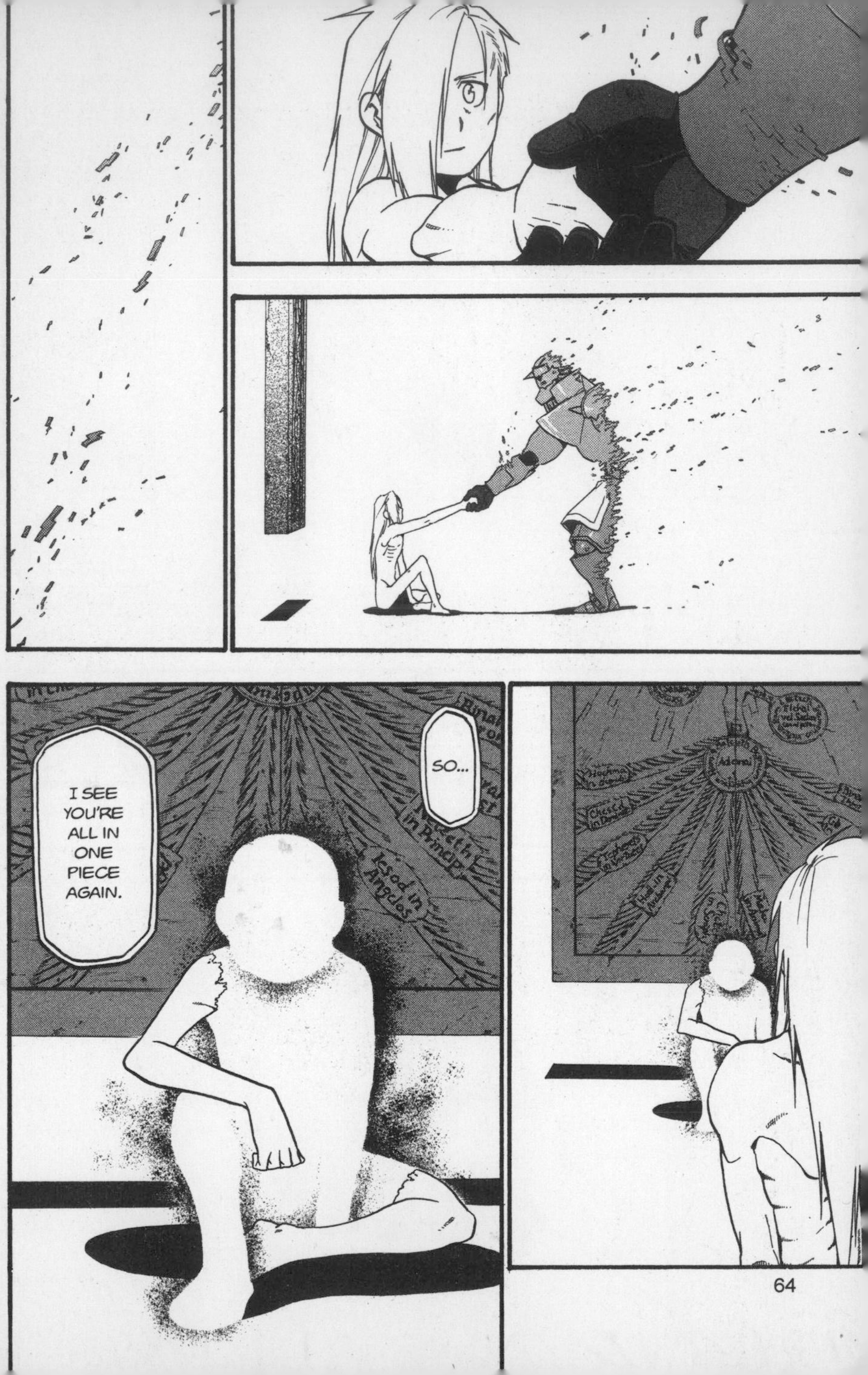
SO...
I SEE YOU'RE ALL IN ONE PIECE AGAIN.

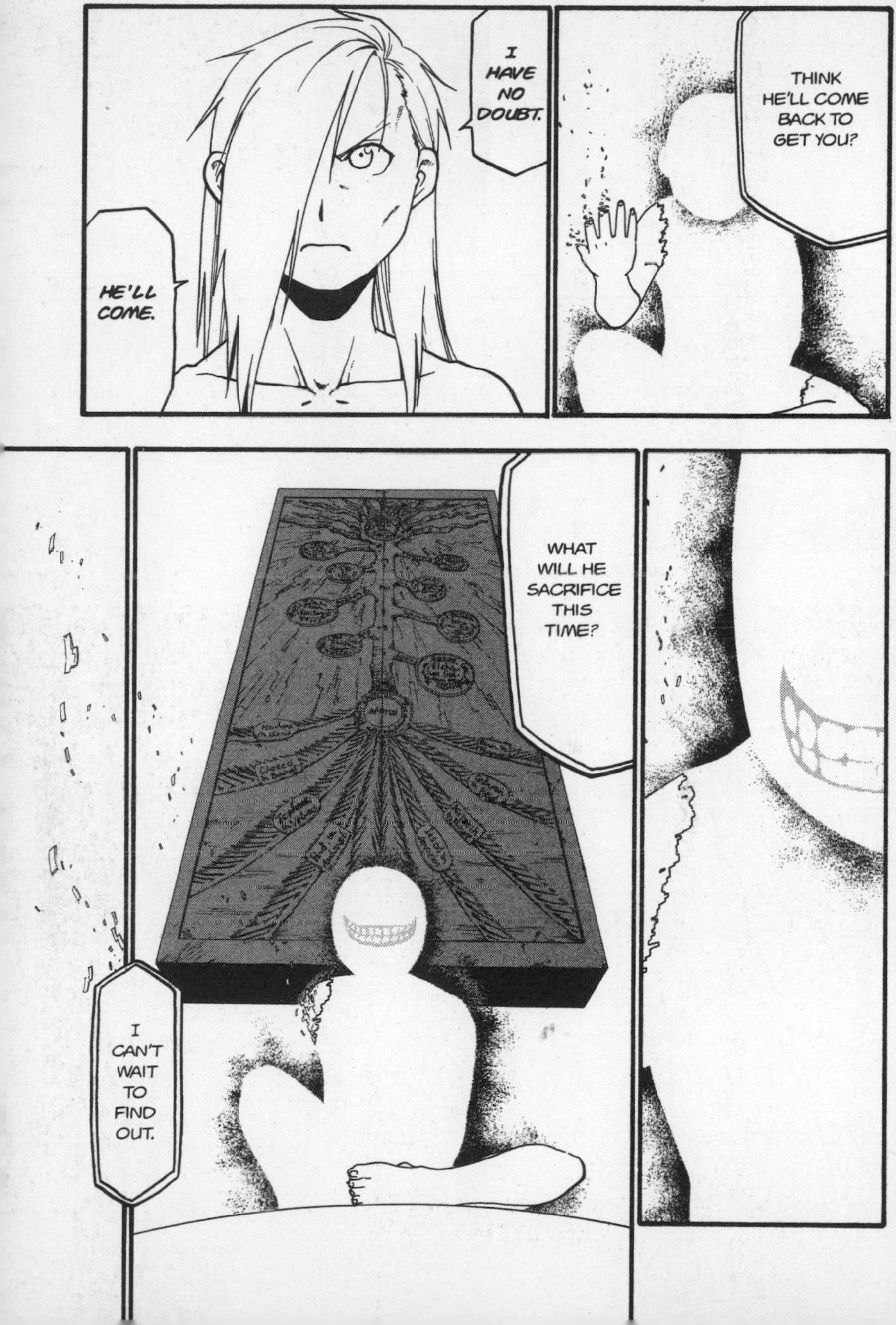
THINK HE'LL COME BACK TO GET YOU?
I HAVE NO DOUBT.
HE'LL COME.
WHAT WILL HE SACRIFICE THIS TIME?
I CAN'T WAIT TO FIND OUT.

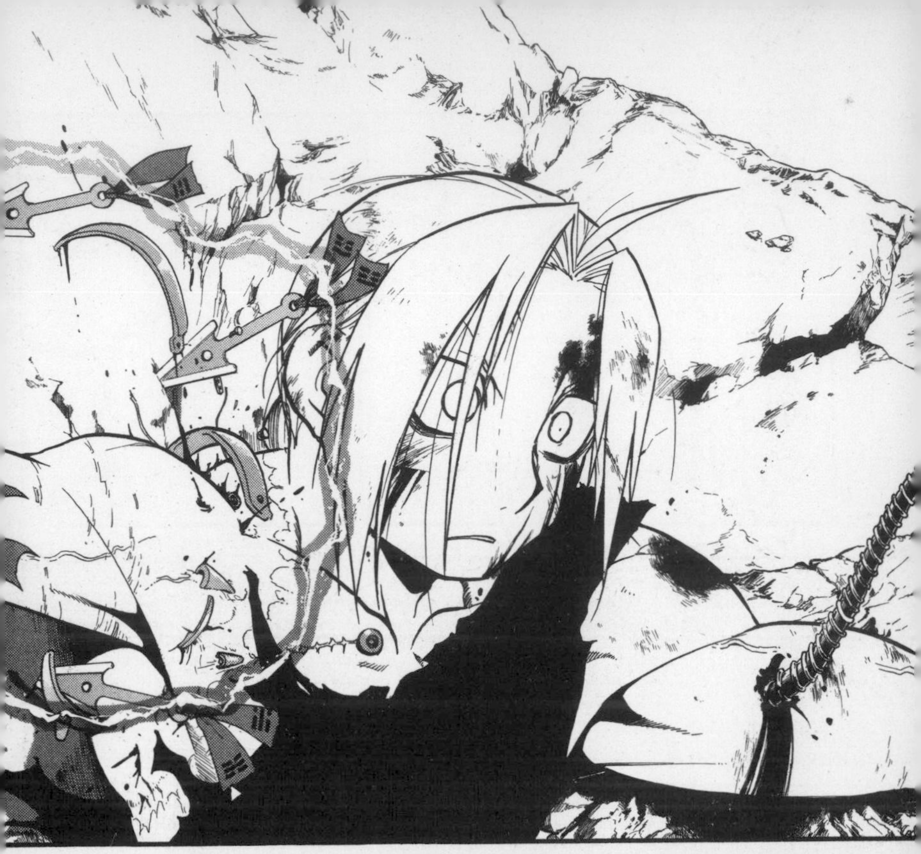

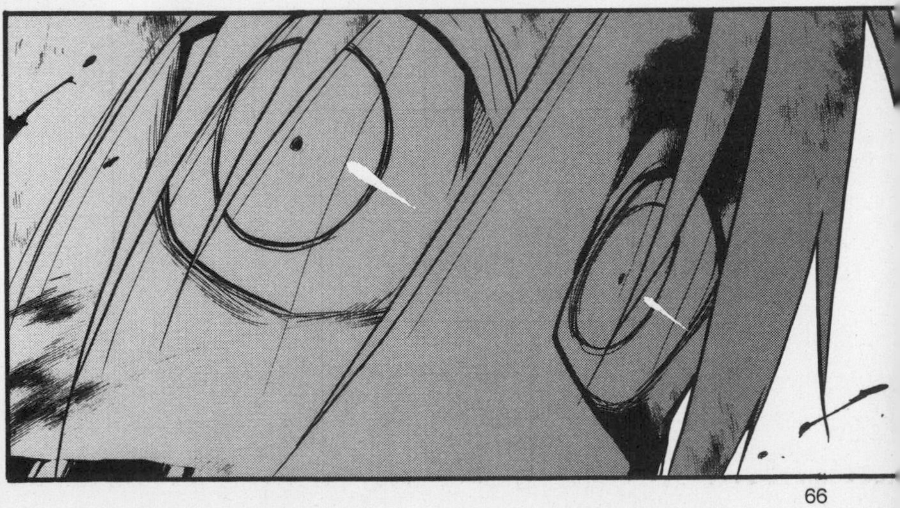

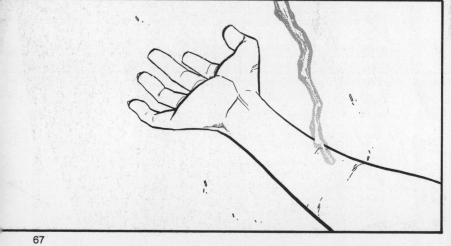

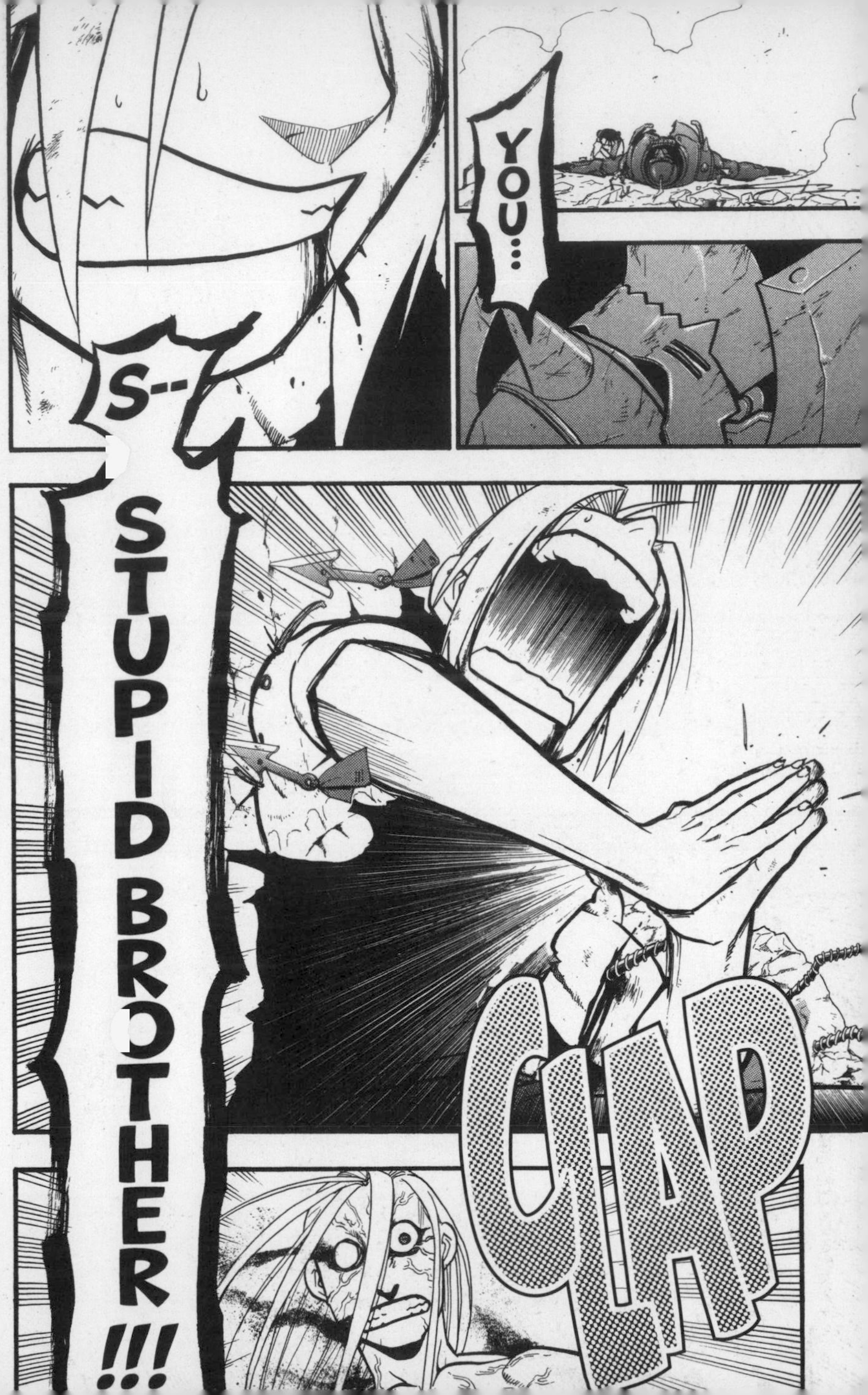
YOU...
S--
STUPID BROTHER!!!
CLAP

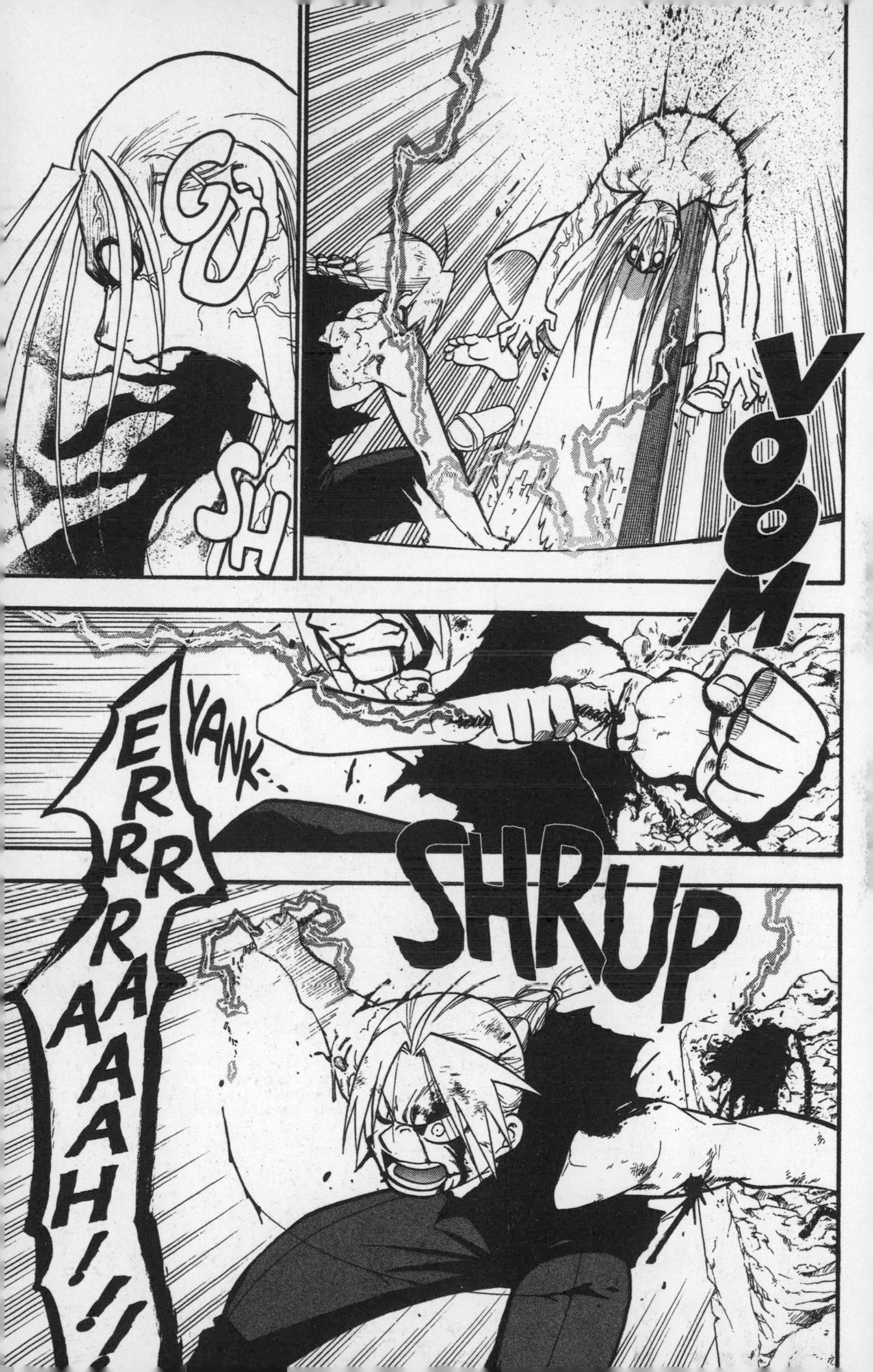
VOOM
GUSH
YANK
SHRUP
ERRRRAAAAH!!!

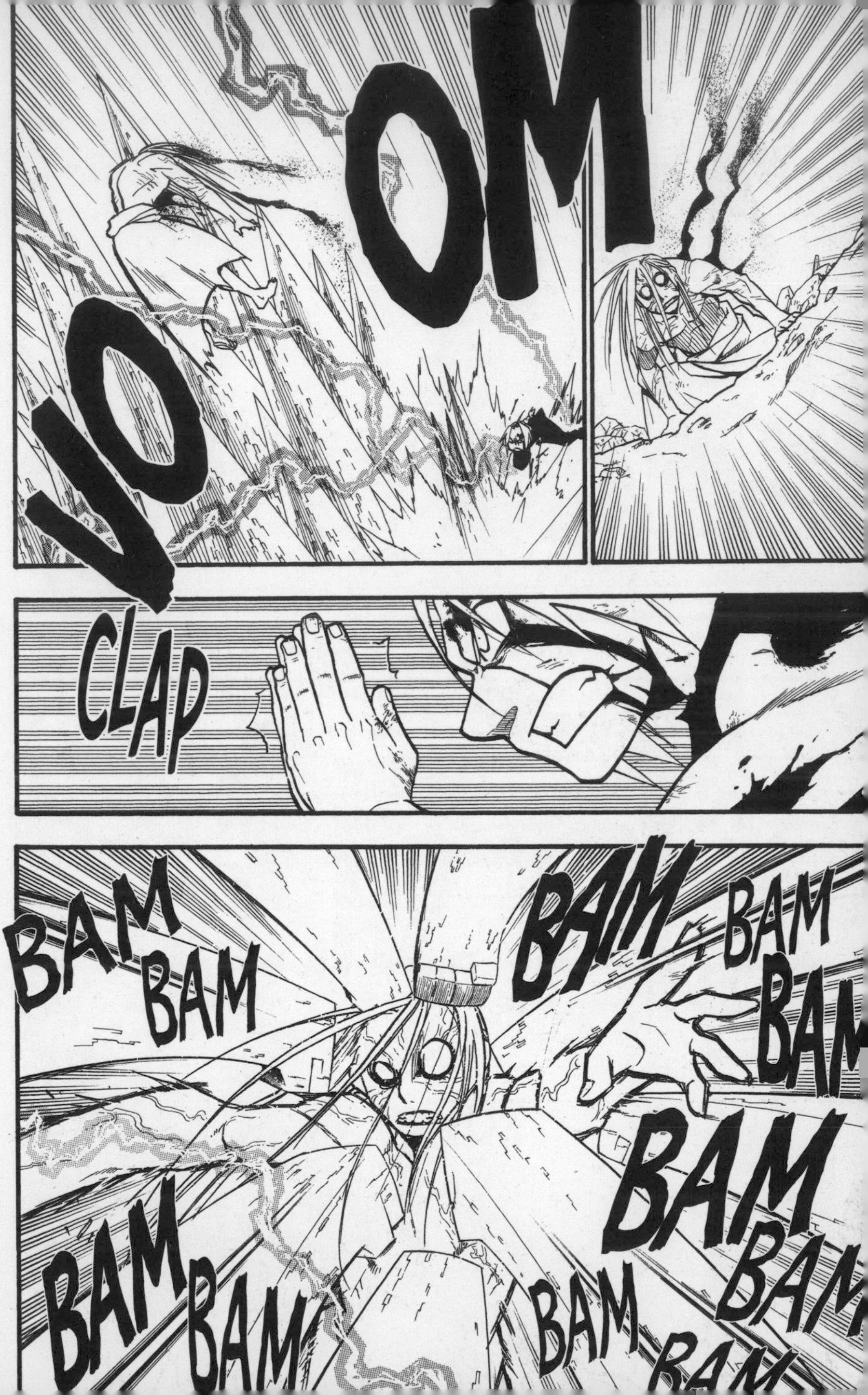
VOOM
CLAP
BAM
BAM
BAM
BAM
BAM
BAM
BAM
BAM

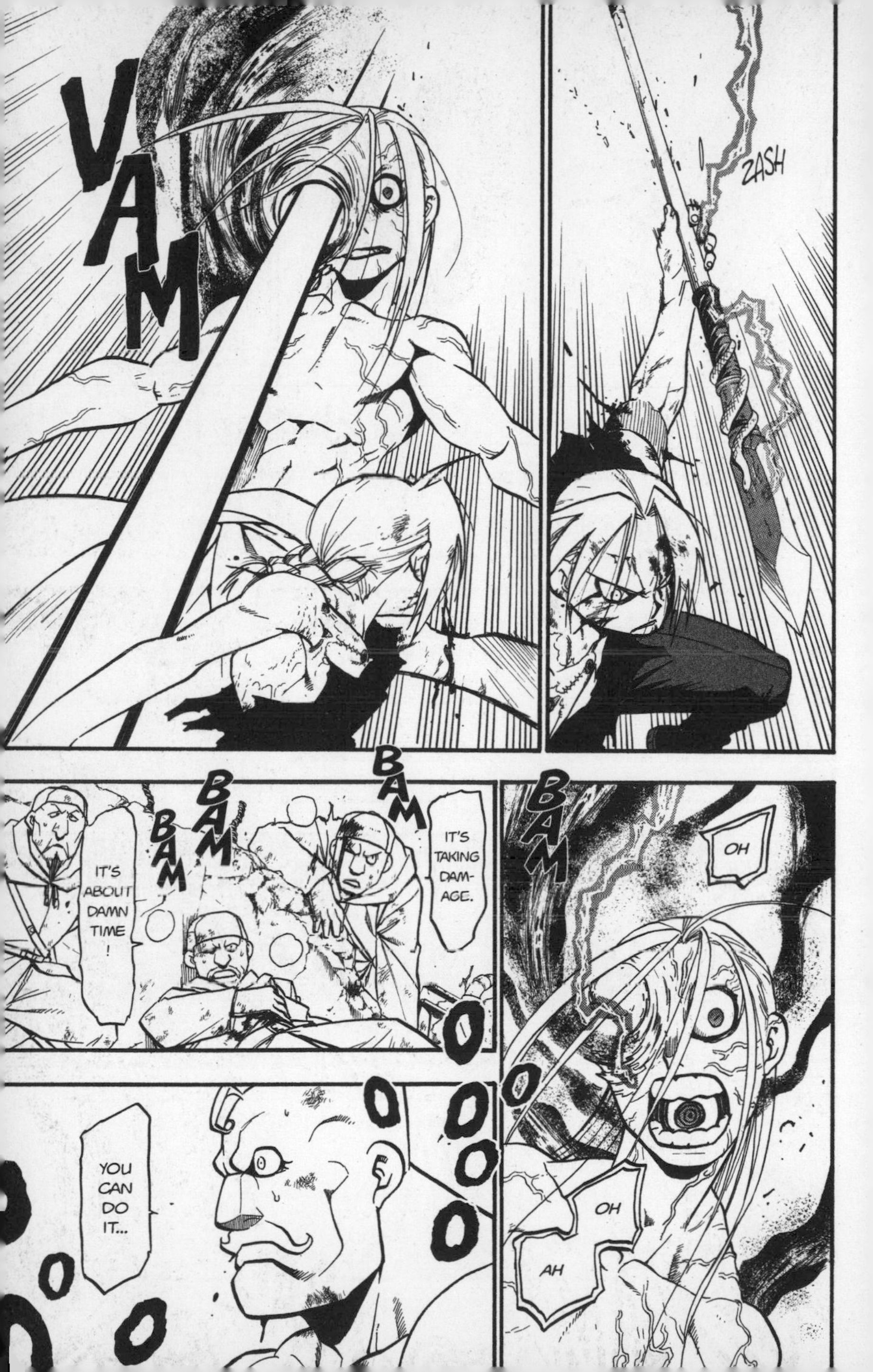
ZASH
VAM
BAM
OH
OH
AH
BAM
IT'S TAKING DAMAGE.
BAM
BAM
IT'S ABOUT DAMN TIME!
OOOOOOO
YOU CAN DO IT...

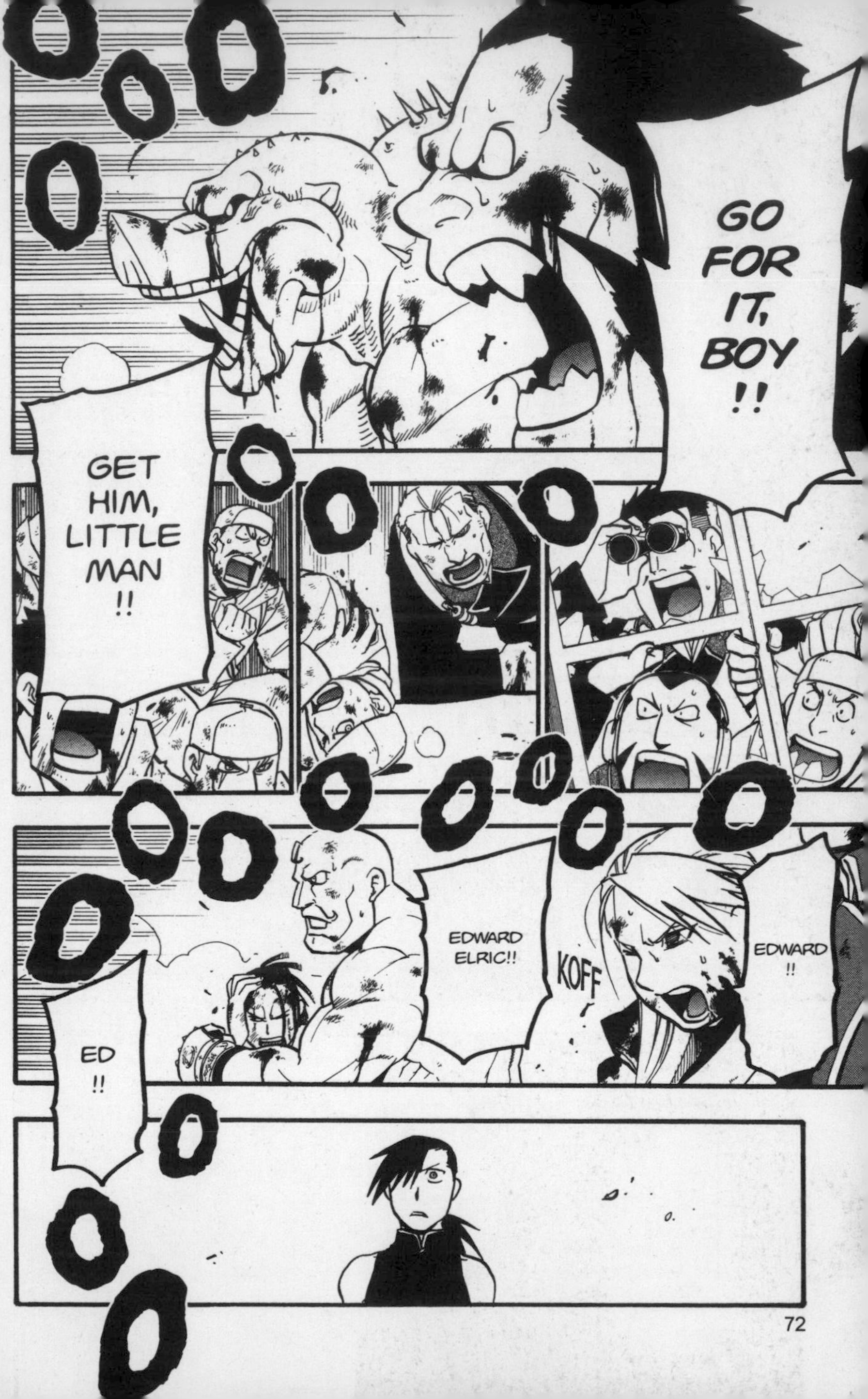
GO FOR IT, BOY!!
GET HIM, LITTLE MAN!!
EDWARD!!
KOFF
EDWARD ELRIC!!
ED!!

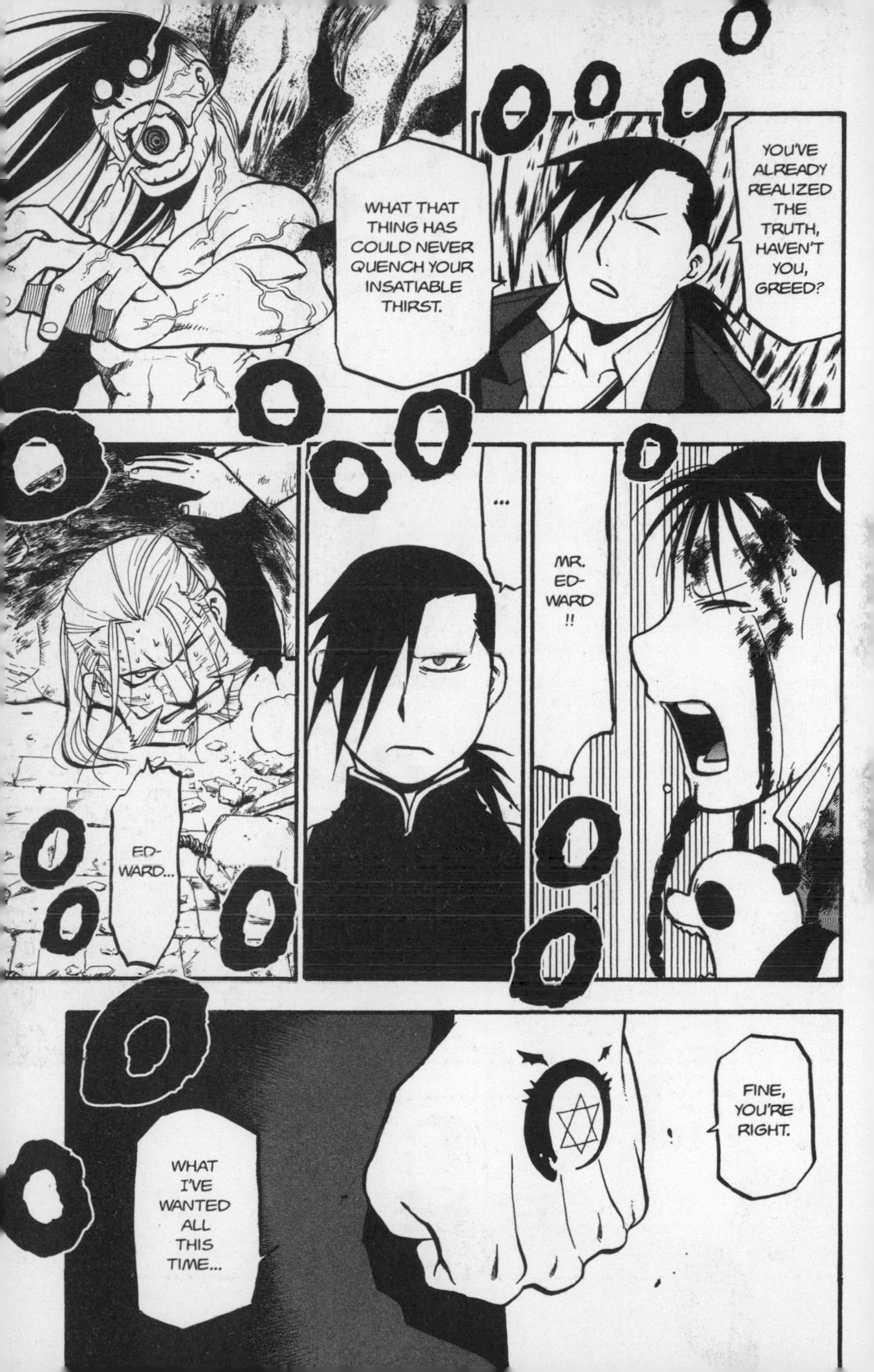
YOU'VE ALREADY REALIZED THE TRUTH, HAVEN'T YOU, GREED?
WHAT THAT THING HAS COULD NEVER QUENCH YOUR INSATIABLE THIRST.
MR. ED-WARD!!
...
ED-WARD...
FINE, YOU'RE RIGHT.
WHAT I'VE WANTED ALL THIS TIME...

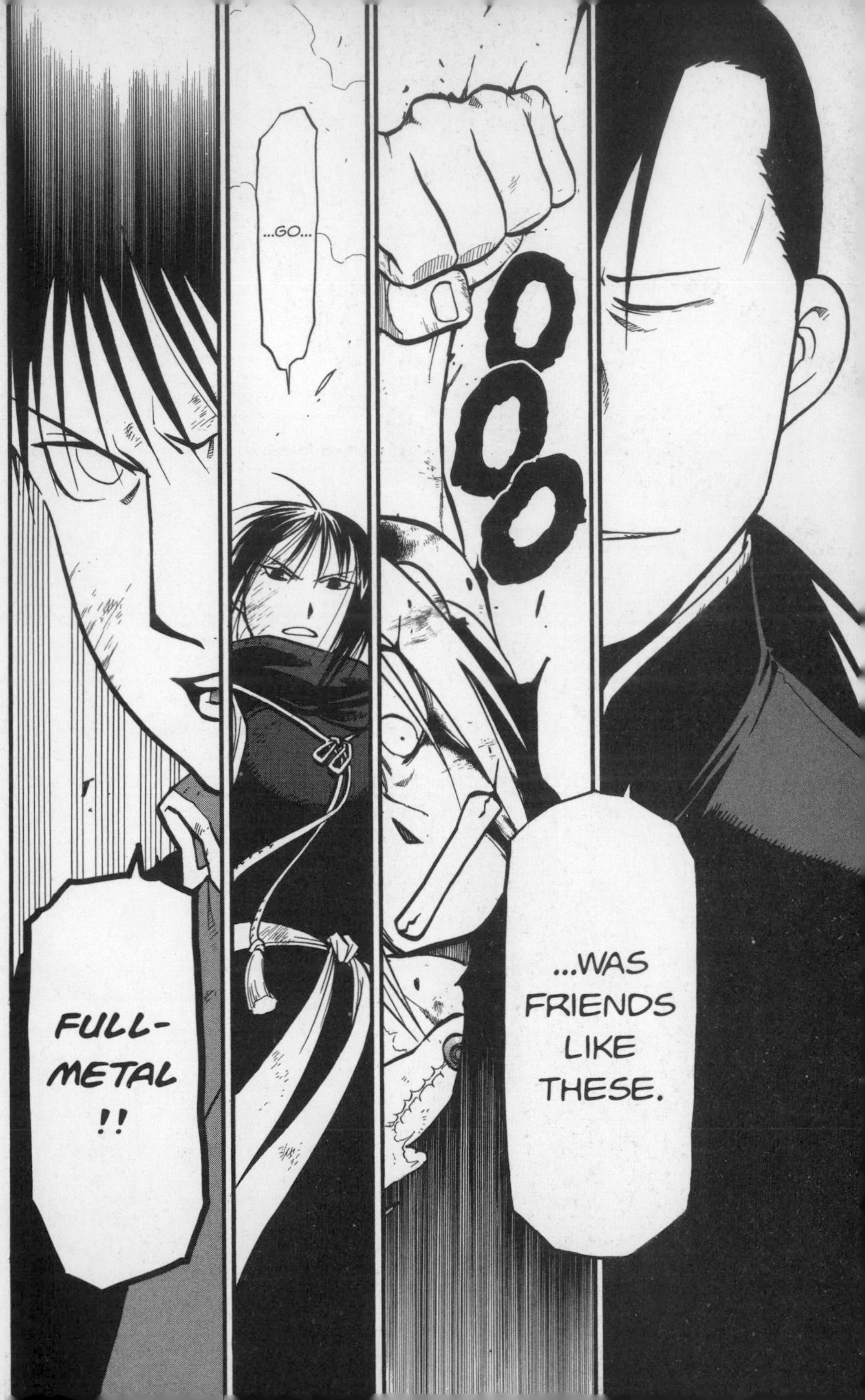
...WAS FRIENDS LIKE THESE.
...GO...
FULL-METAL !!

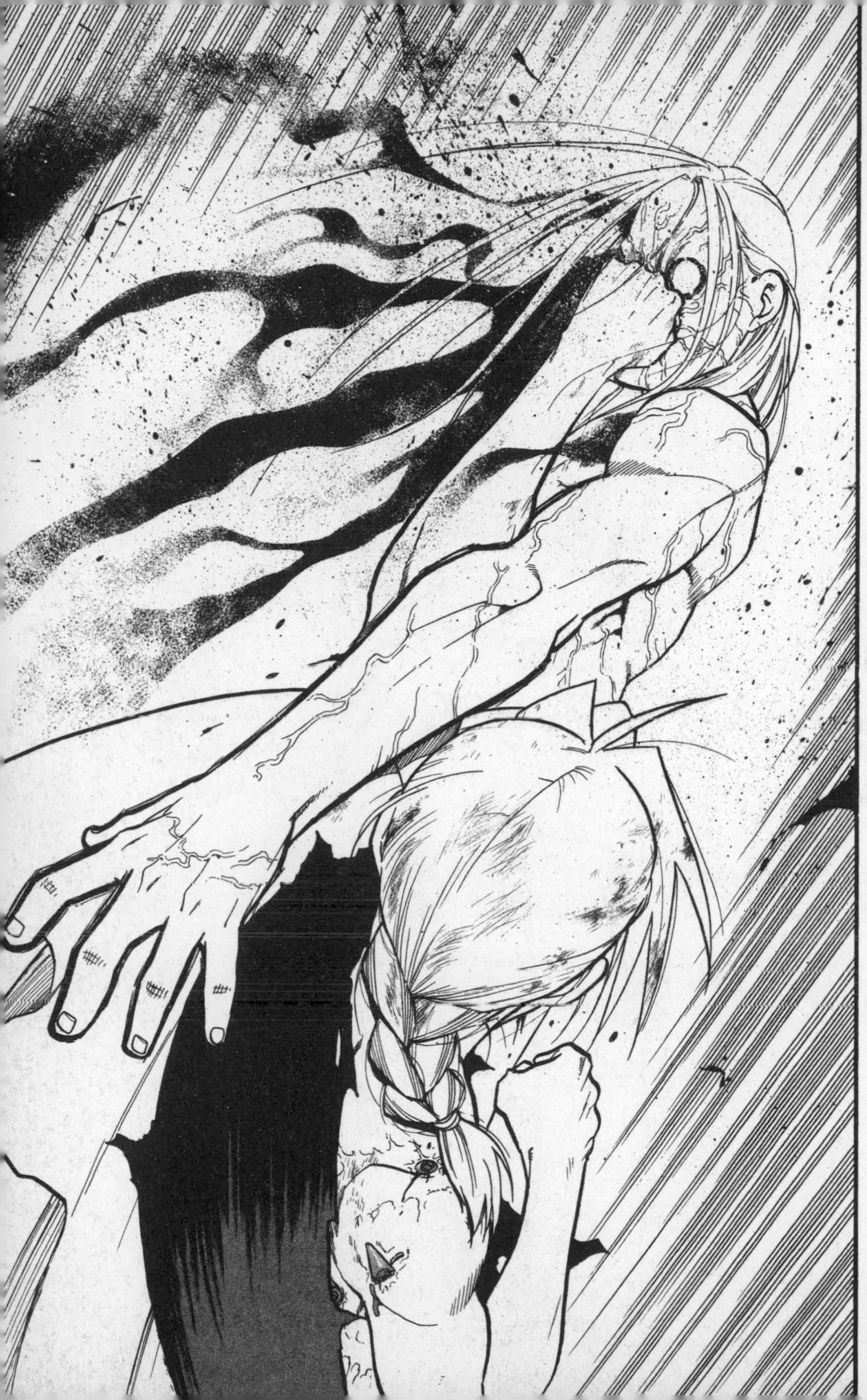

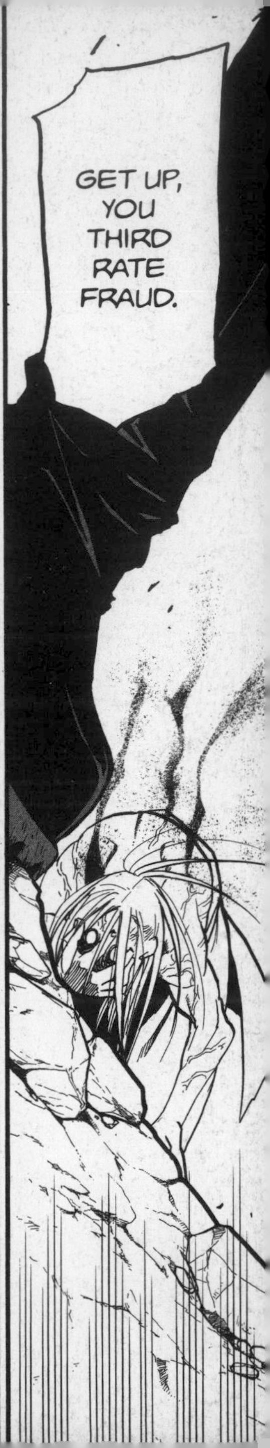
GET UP, YOU THIRD RATE FRAUD.

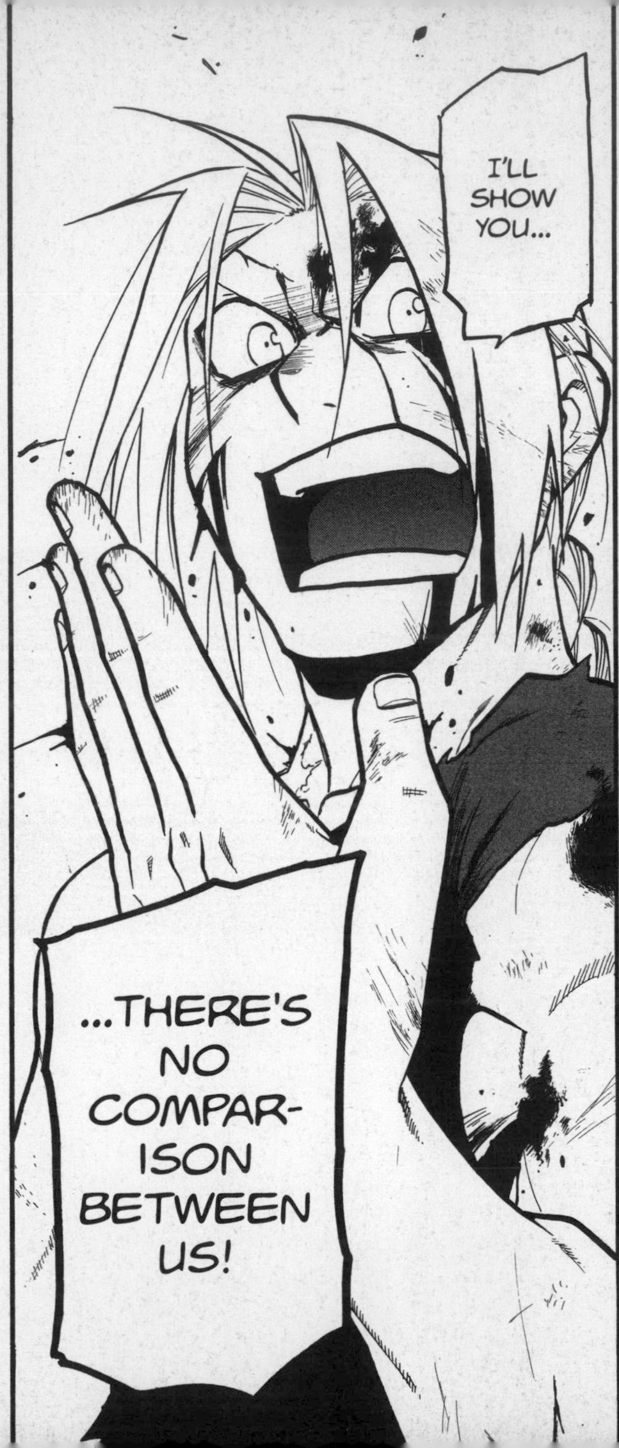
I'LL SHOW YOU...
...THERE'S NO COMPARISON BETWEEN US!

FULLMETAL
ALCHEMIST

WHY?

WHY IS THIS HAPPENING TO ME, THE BEARER OF GODHOOD?

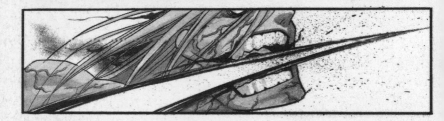

WHY AM I BEING FORCED TO ENDURE THESE ATTACKS...

...FROM A MERE HUMAN ALCHEMIST'S...

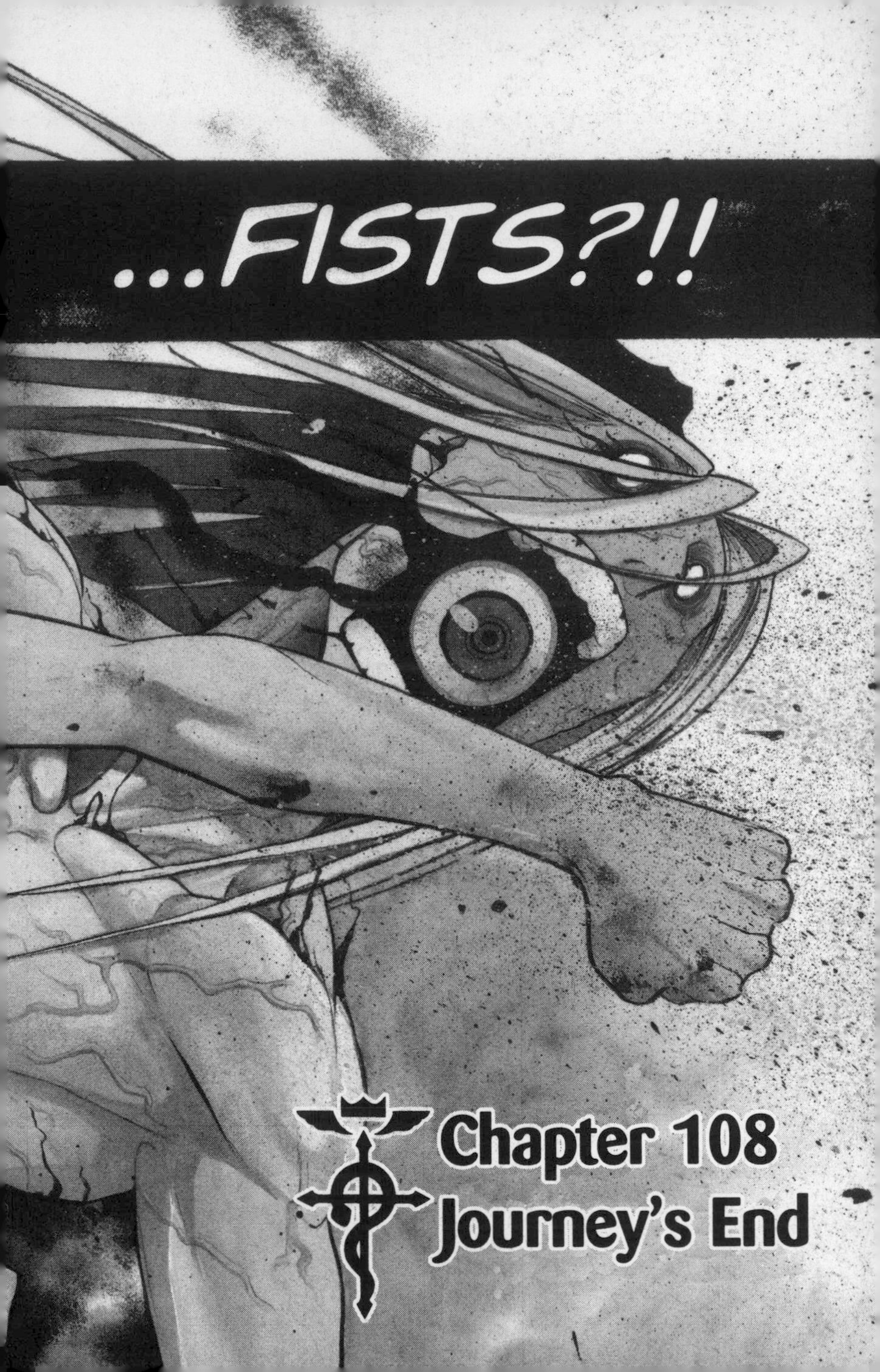
...FISTS?!!
Chapter 108
Journey's End

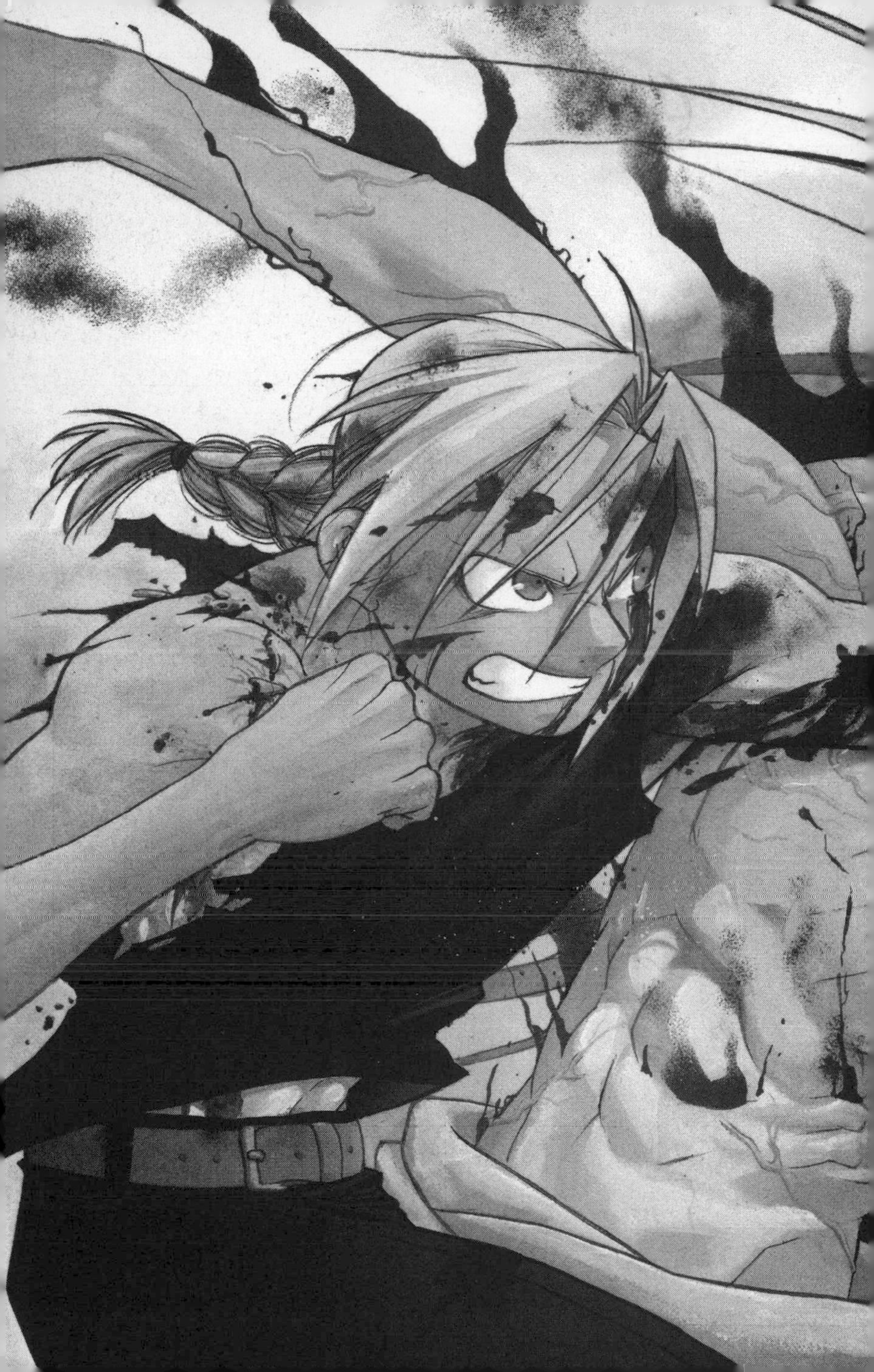

FULLMETAL
ALCHEMIST

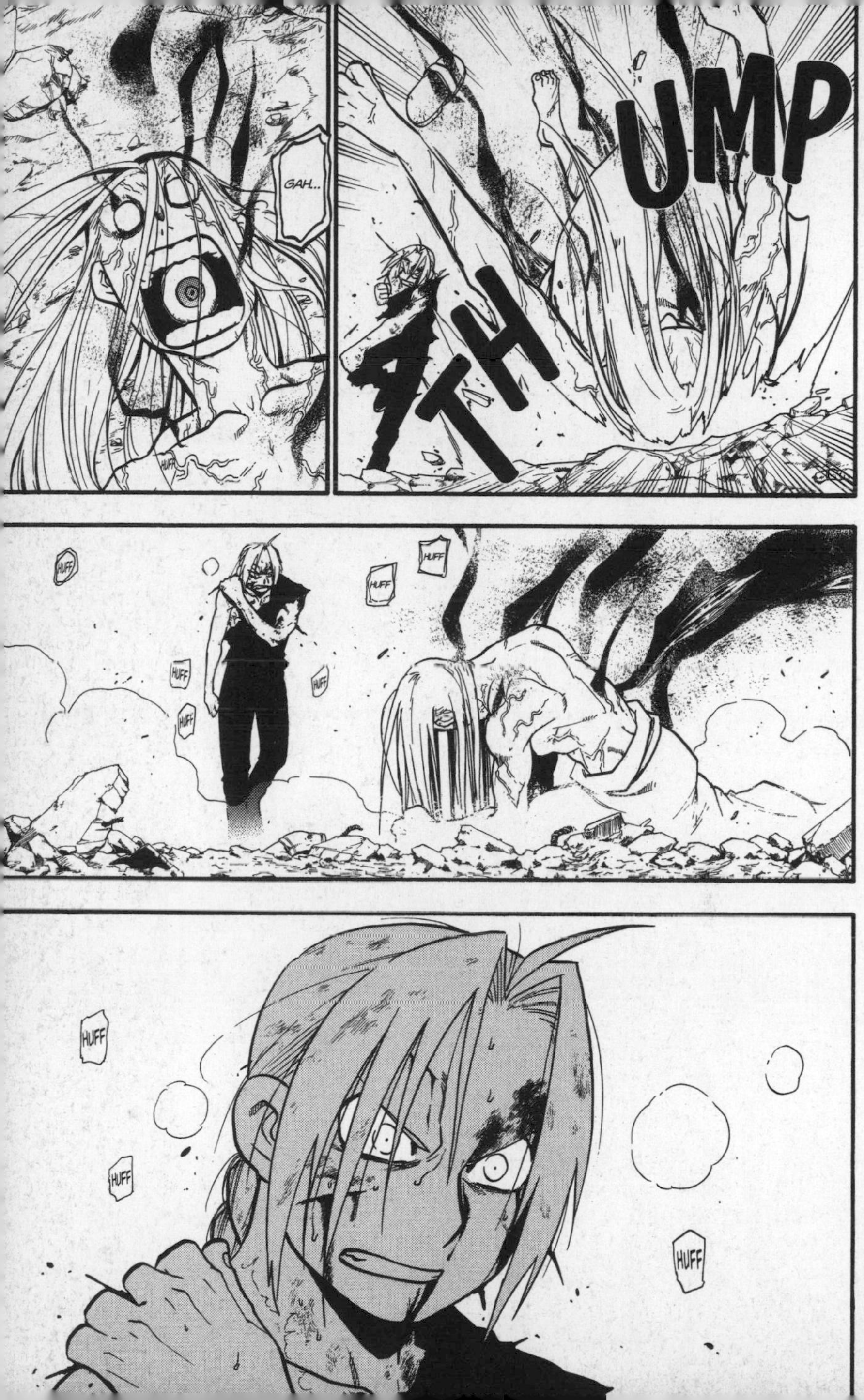
UMP
TH
GAH...
HUFF
HUFF
HUFF
HUFF
HUFF
HUFF
HUFF
HUFF
HUFF
HUFF

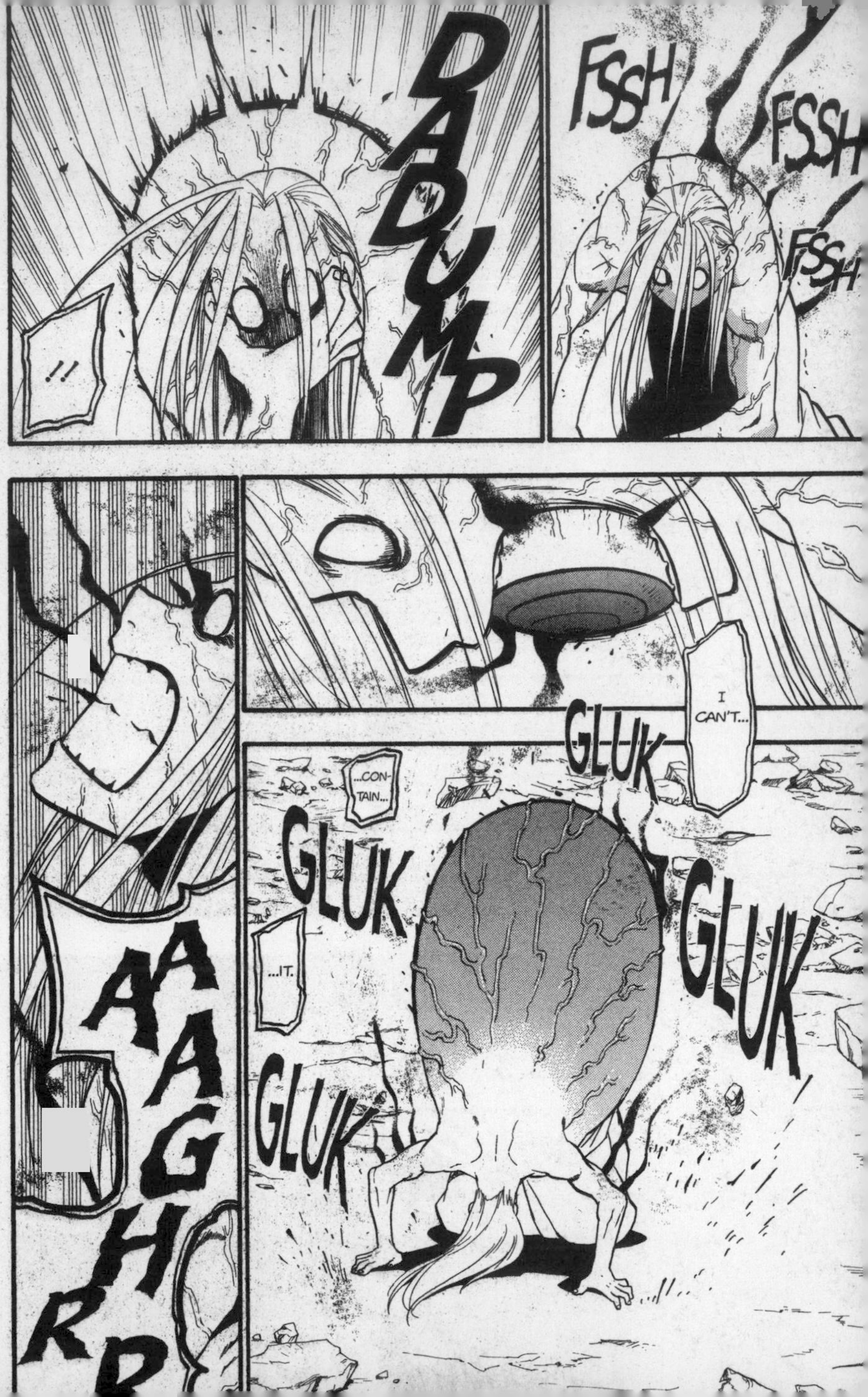
FSSH
FSSH
FSSH
DADUMP
!!
I CAN'T...
GLUK
...CON-TAIN...
GLUK
GLUK
...IT.
GLUK
AAAGHRR

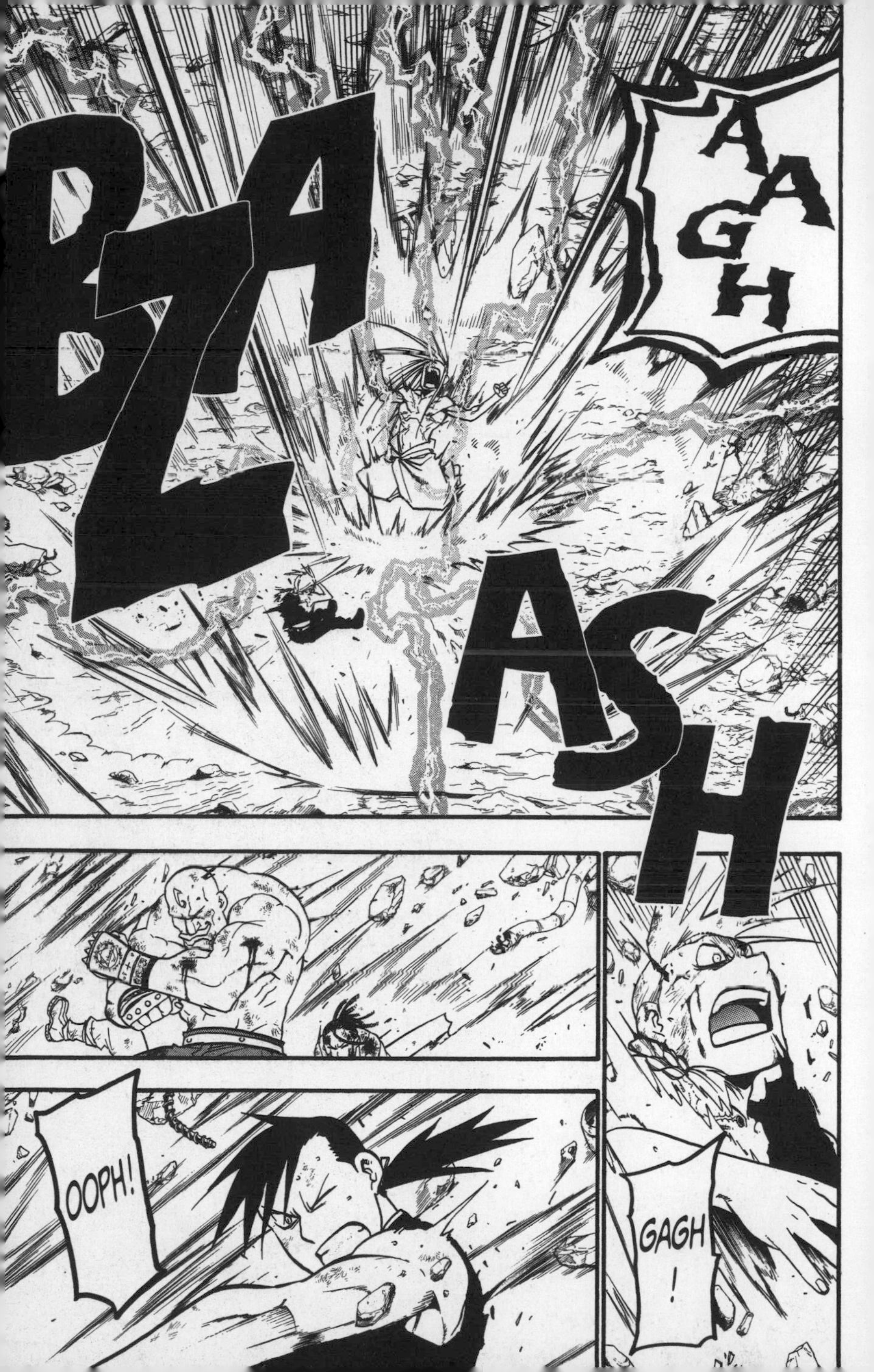
AAGH
BZAASH
GAGH!
OOPH!

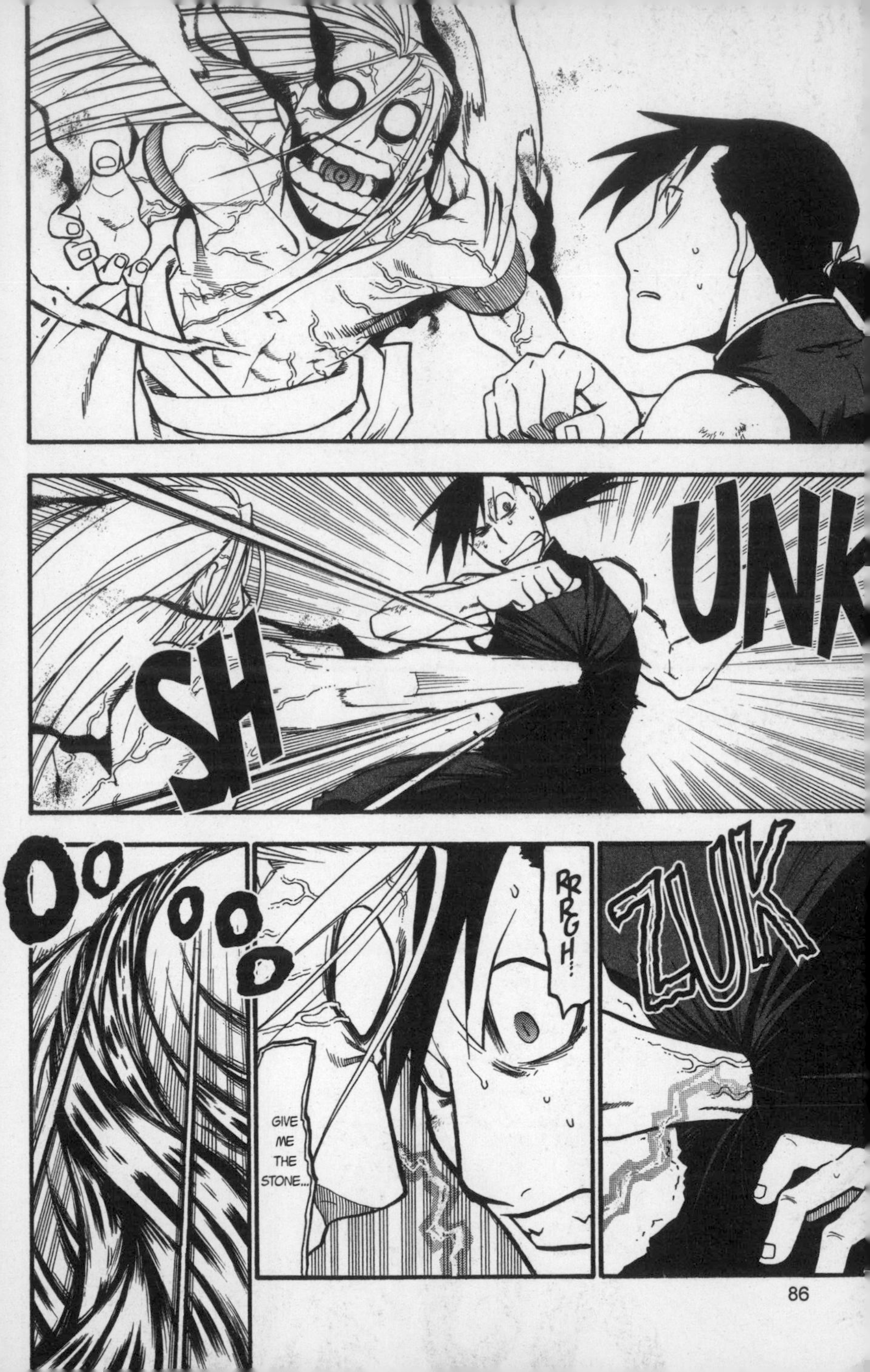
UNK
SH
ZUK
RRRGH!!
GIVE ME THE STONE...
OOOOO

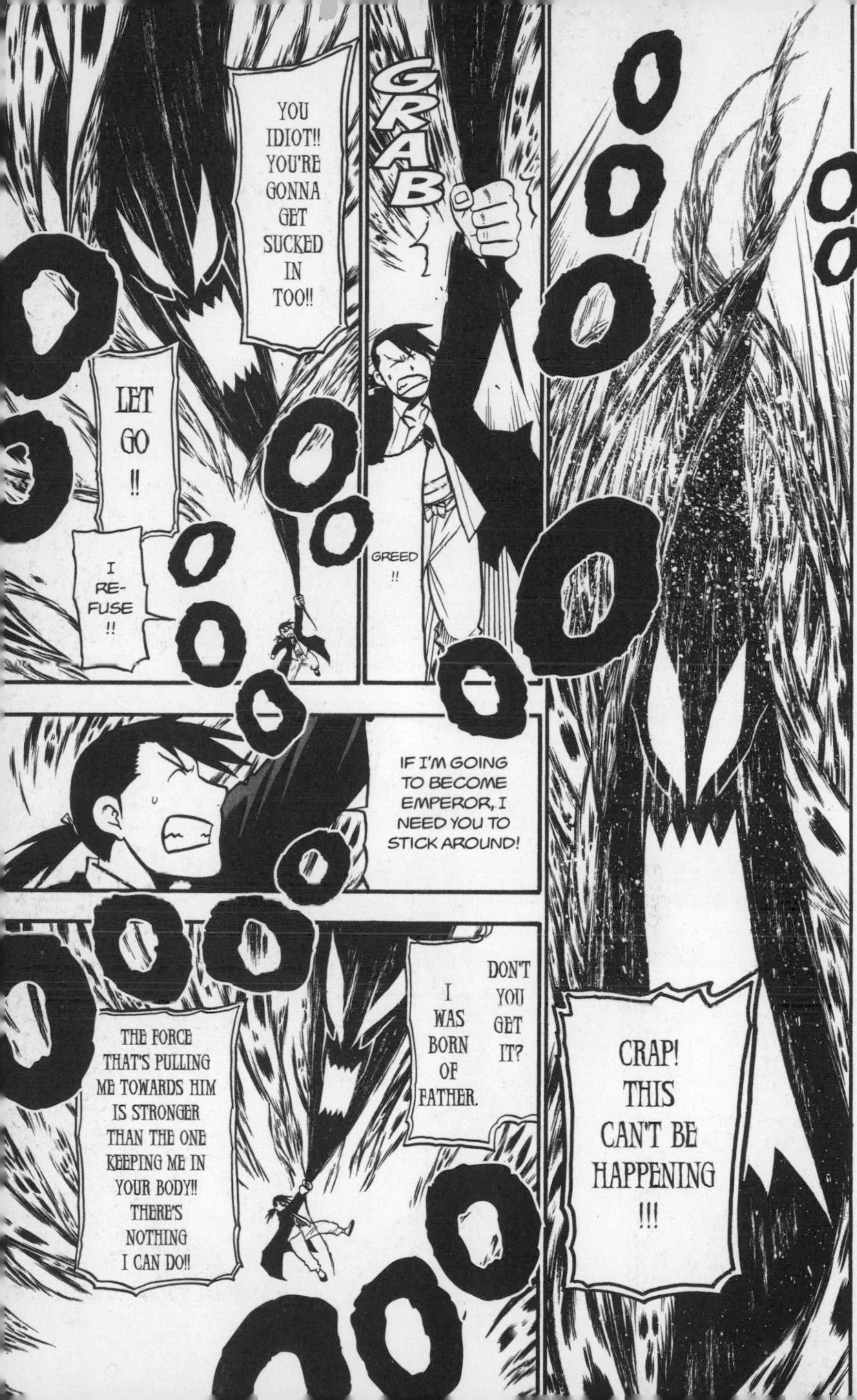
CRAP! THIS CAN'T BE HAPPENING!!!
GRAB
GREED!!
YOU IDIOT!! YOU'RE GONNA GET SUCKED IN TOO!!
LET GO!!
I REFUSE!!
IF I'M GOING TO BECOME EMPEROR, I NEED YOU TO STICK AROUND!
DON'T YOU GET IT?
I WAS BORN OF FATHER.
THE FORCE THAT'S PULLING ME TOWARDS HIM IS STRONGER THAN THE ONE KEEPING ME IN YOUR BODY!! THERE'S NOTHING I CAN DO!!

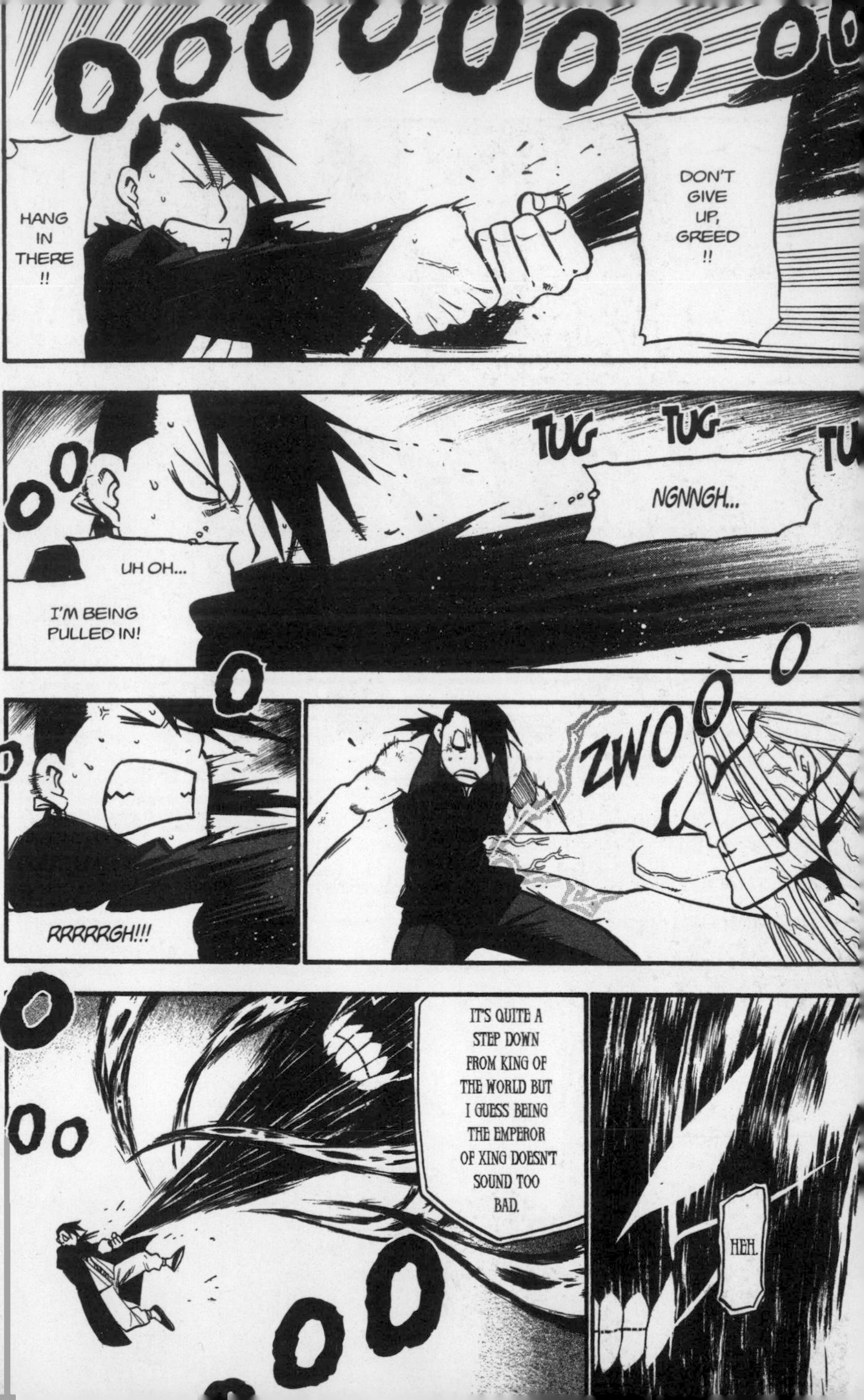
OOOOOOOOOO
DON'T GIVE UP, GREED!!
HANG IN THERE!!
TUG TUG
NGNNGH...
OOO
UH OH...
I'M BEING PULLED IN!
ZWOOOO
O
RRRRRGH!!!
HEH.
IT'S QUITE A STEP DOWN FROM KING OF THE WORLD BUT I GUESS BEING THE EMPEROR OF XING DOESN'T SOUND TOO BAD.
OOOOO

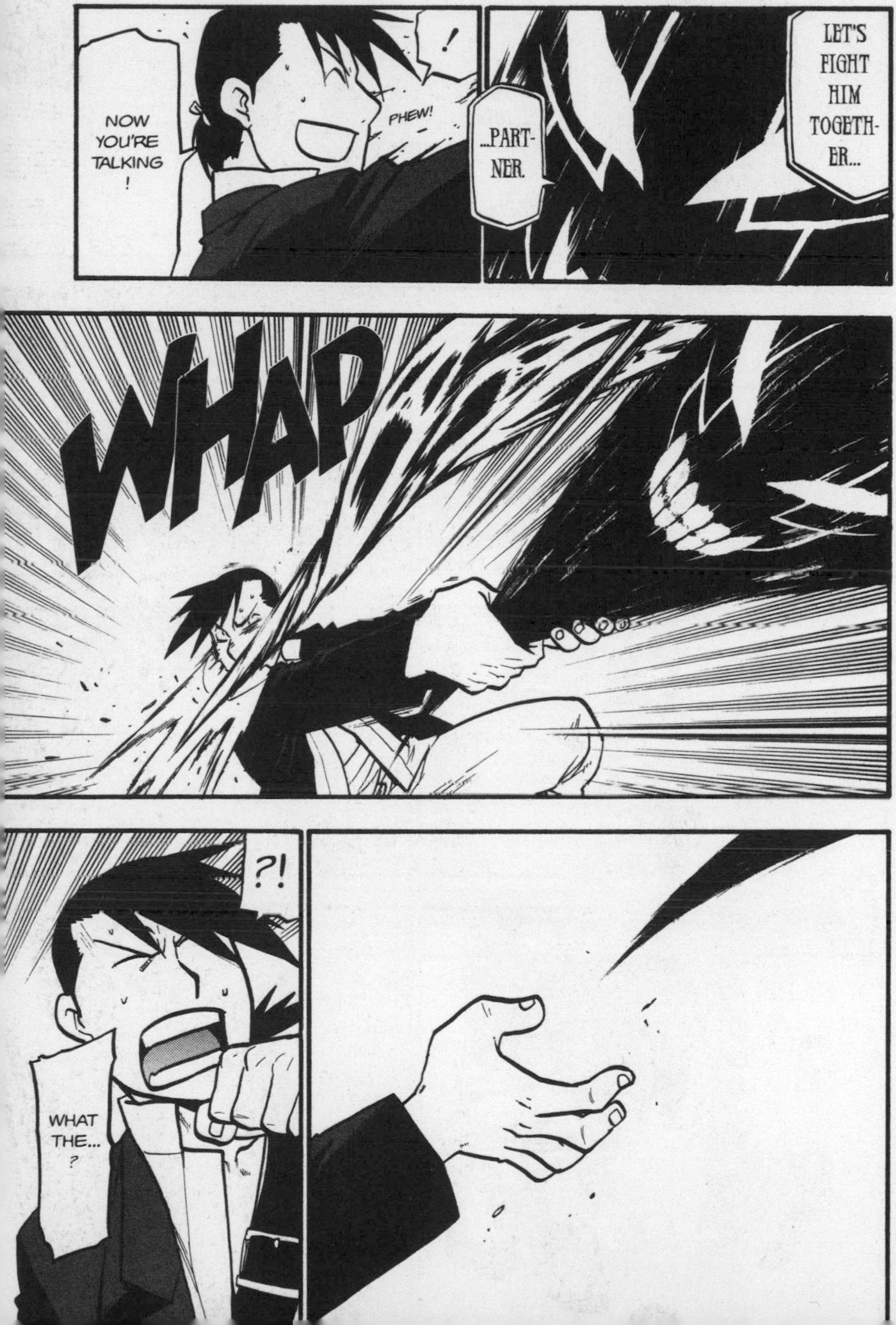
LET'S FIGHT HIM TOGETH-ER...
...PART-NER.
!
PHEW!
NOW YOU'RE TALKING!
WHAP
?!
WHAT THE...?

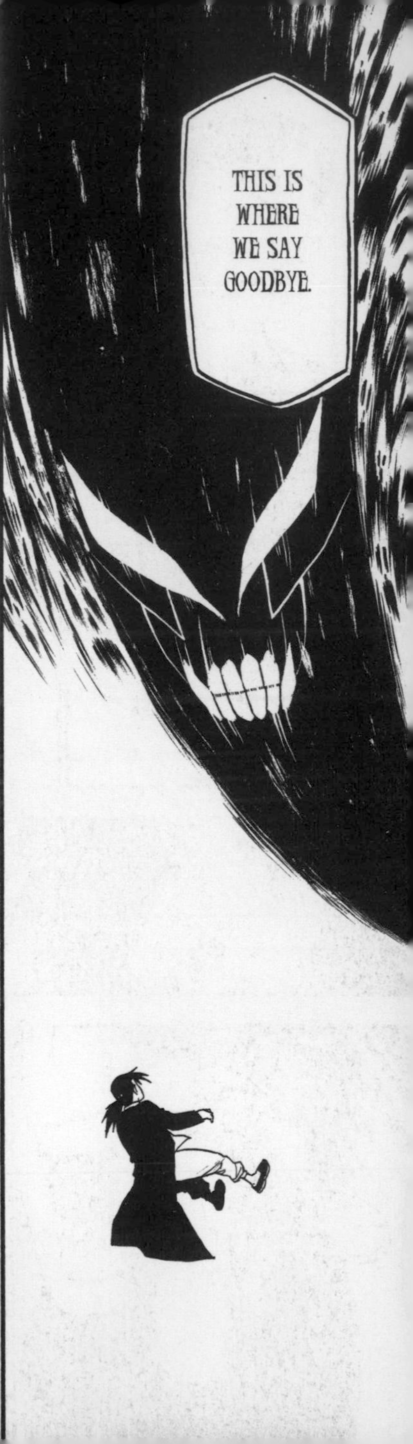
THIS IS WHERE WE SAY GOODBYE.

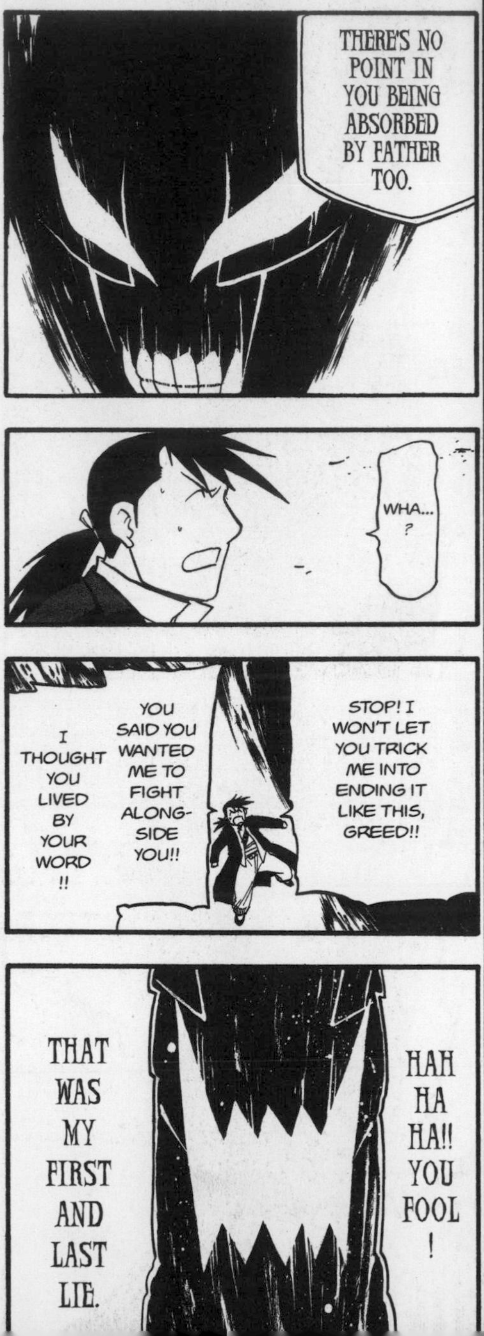
THERE'S NO POINT IN YOU BEING ABSORBED BY FATHER TOO.
WHA...?
STOP! I WON'T LET YOU TRICK ME INTO ENDING IT LIKE THIS, GREED!!
YOU SAID YOU WANTED ME TO FIGHT ALONG-SIDE YOU!!
I THOUGHT YOU LIVED BY YOUR WORD!!
HAH HA HA!! YOU FOOL!
THAT WAS MY FIRST AND LAST LIE.

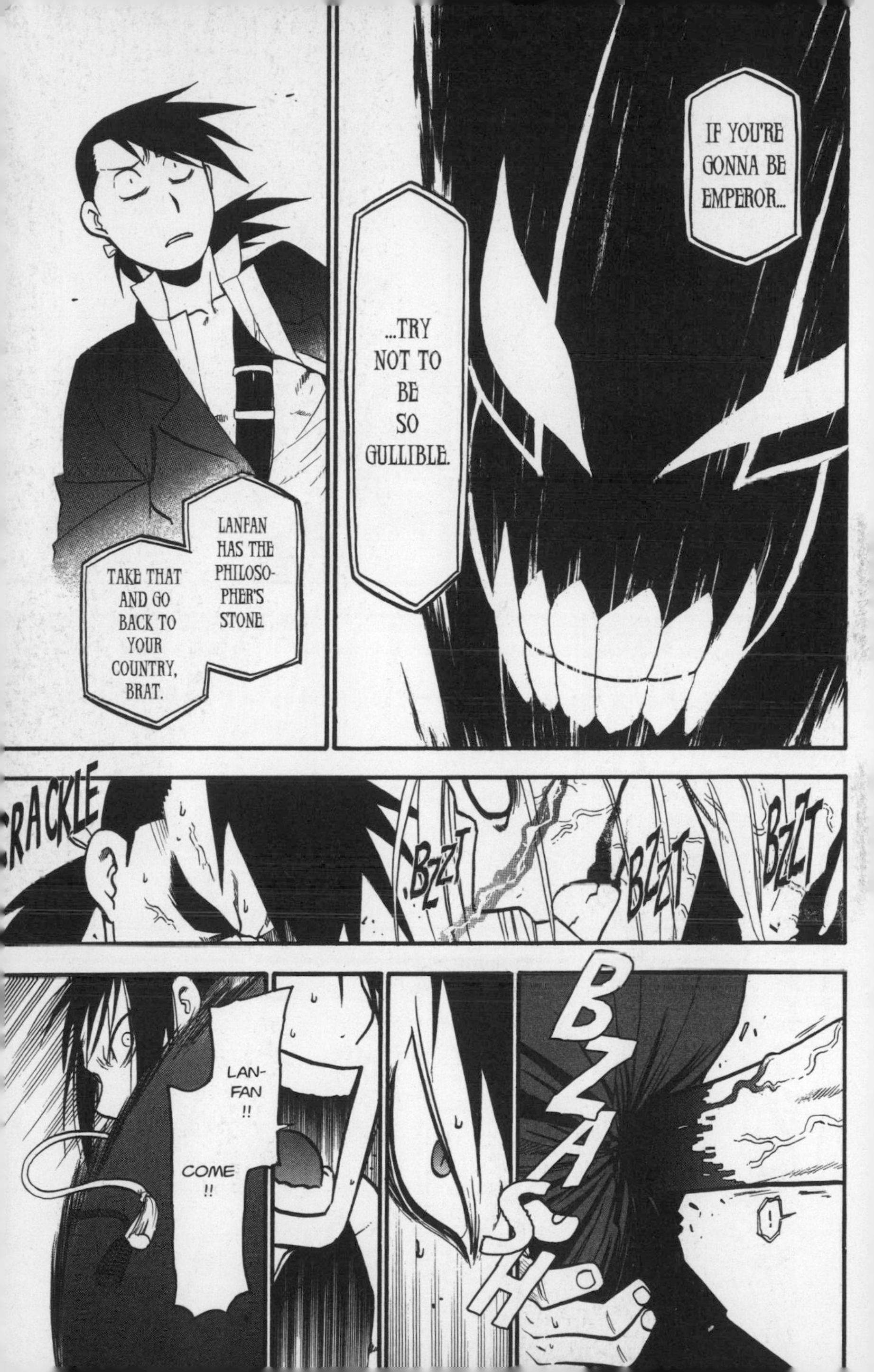
IF YOU'RE GONNA BE EMPEROR...
...TRY NOT TO BE SO GULLIBLE.
LANFAN HAS THE PHILOSO-PHER'S STONE.
TAKE THAT AND GO BACK TO YOUR COUNTRY, BRAT.
BZZT
BZZT
BZZT
RACKLE
BZASH
!
LAN-FAN !!
COME !!

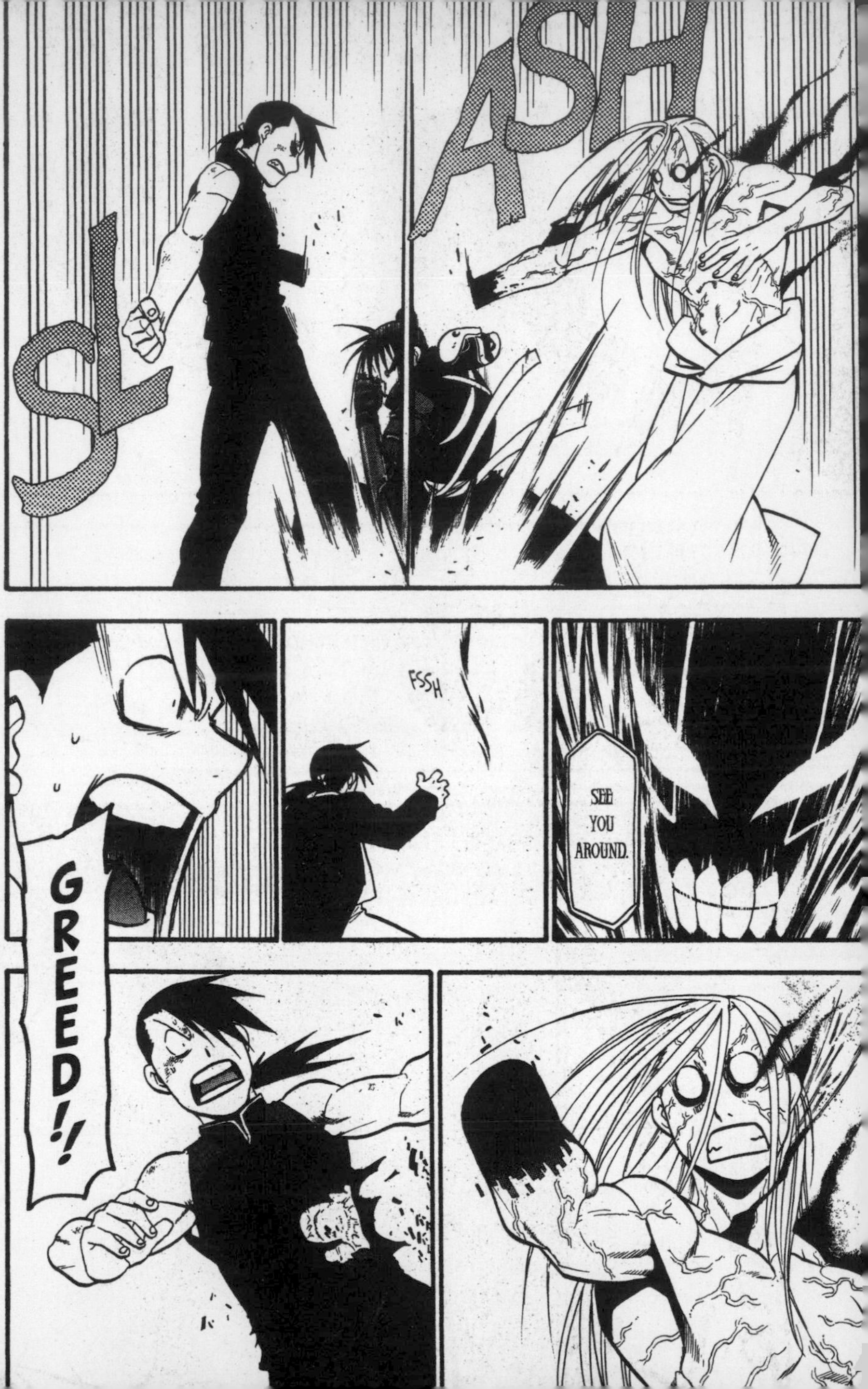
SLASH
SEE YOU AROUND.
FSSH
GREED!!

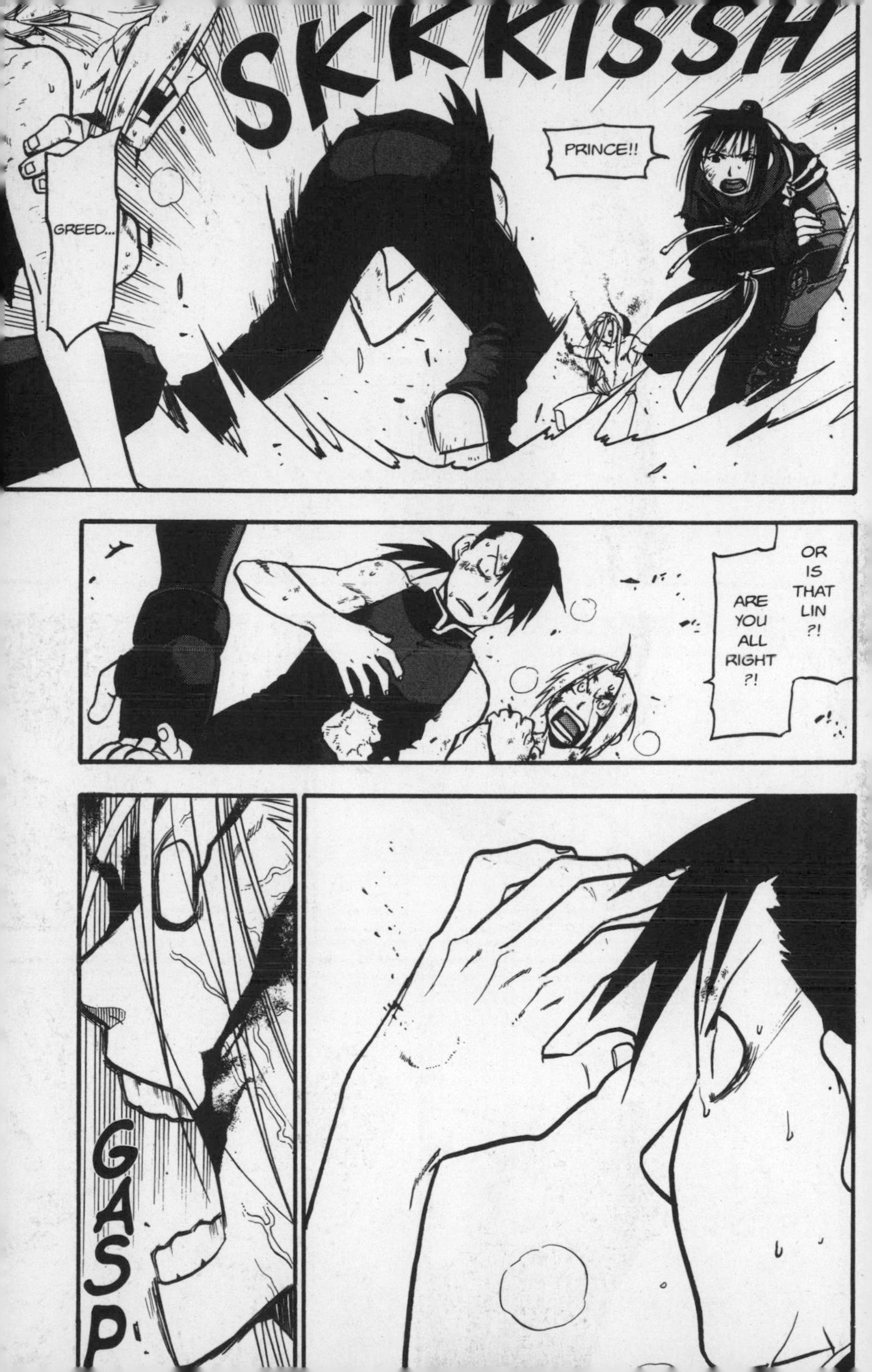
SKKKISSH
PRINCE!!
GREED...
ARE YOU ALL RIGHT ?!
OR IS THAT LIN ?!
GASP

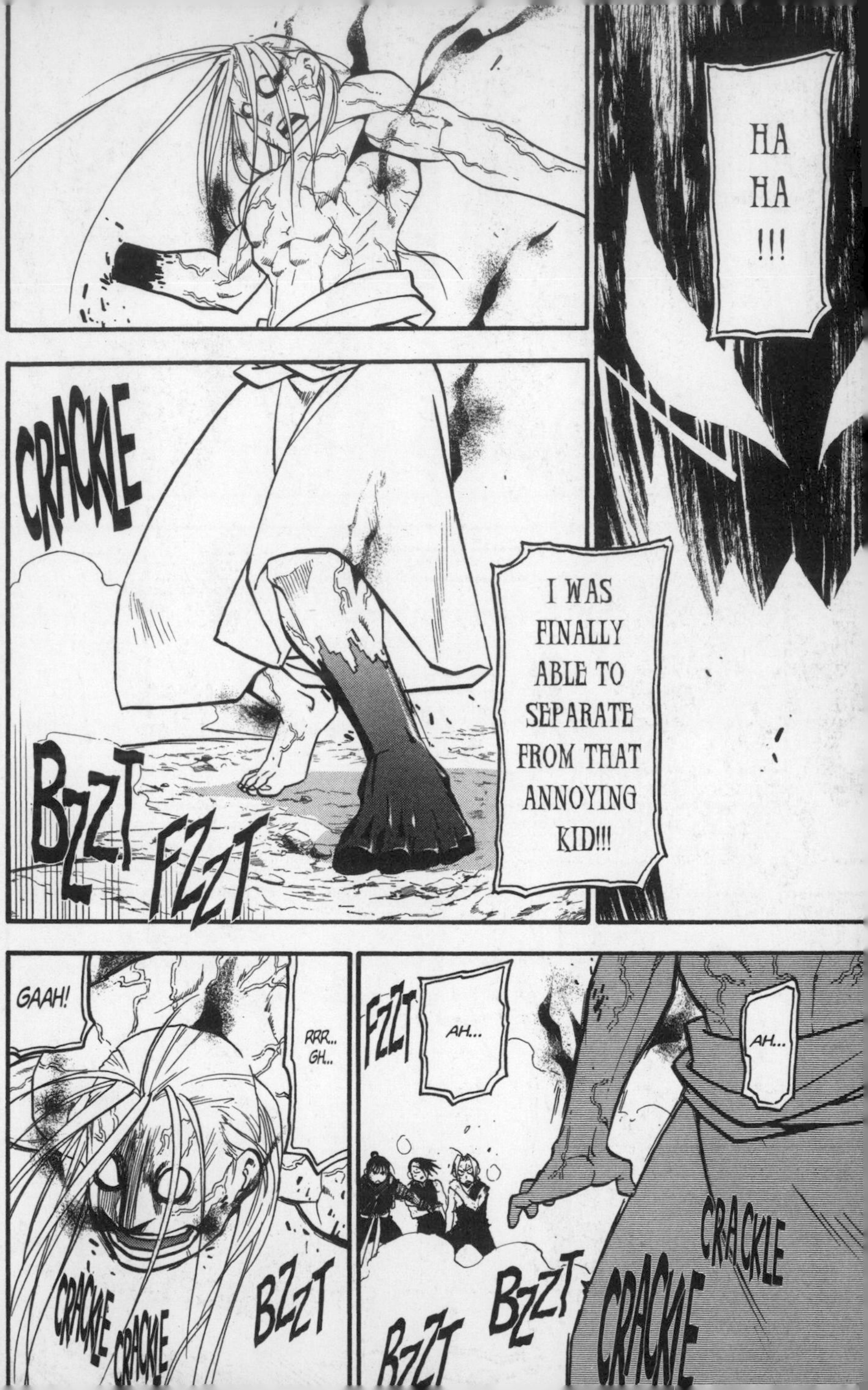
HA
HA
!!!
I WAS FINALLY ABLE TO SEPARATE FROM THAT ANNOYING KID!!!
CRACKLE
BZZT
FZZT
AH...
AH...
FZZT
CRACKLE
CRACKLE
BZZT
BZZT
RRR... GH..
GAAH!
BZZT
CRACKLE
CRACKLE

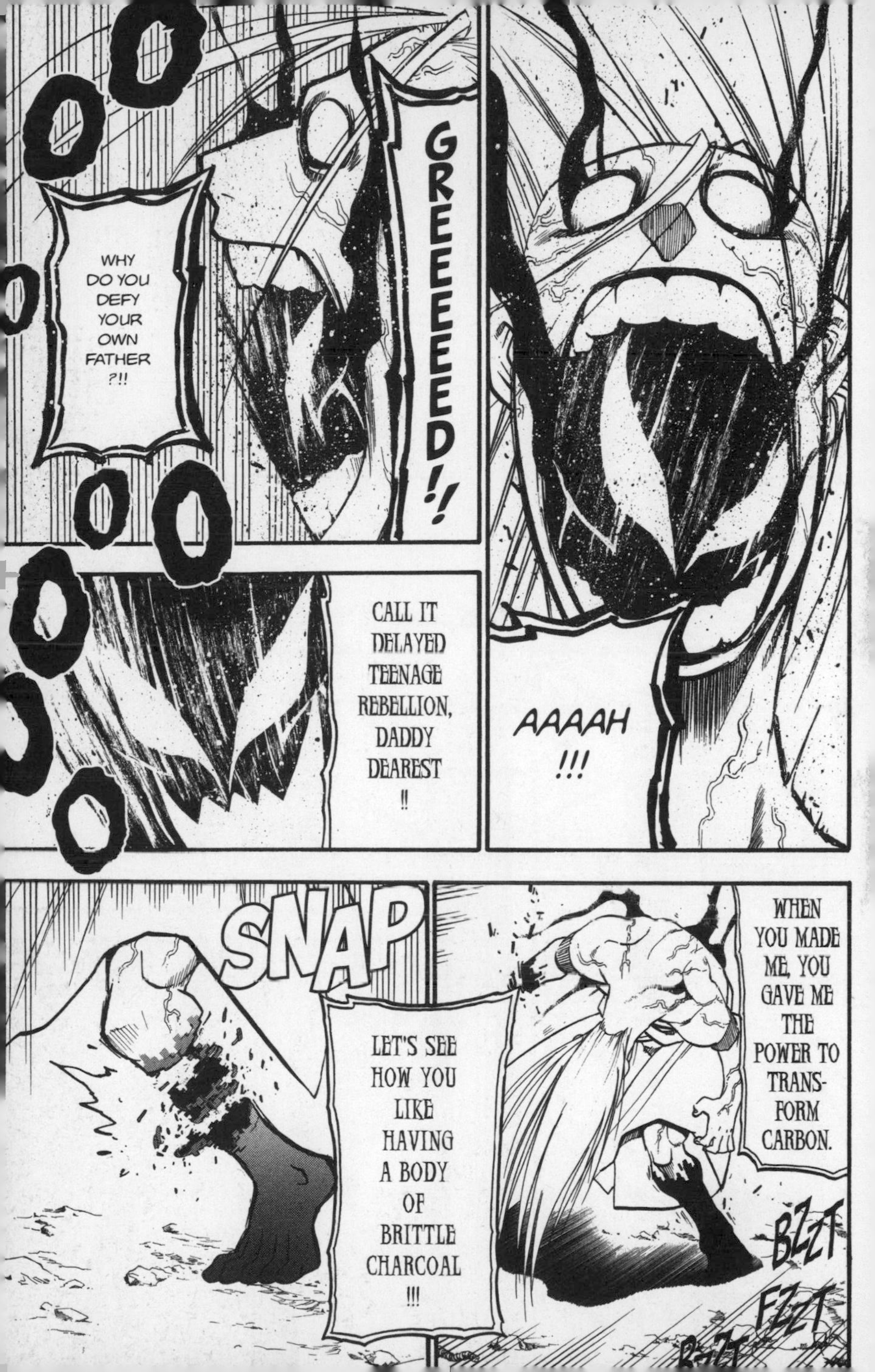
AAAAH !!!
WHY DO YOU DEFY YOUR OWN FATHER ?!!
GREEEEEED!!
CALL IT DELAYED TEENAGE REBELLION, DADDY DEAREST !!
WHEN YOU MADE ME, YOU GAVE ME THE POWER TO TRANS-FORM CARBON.
BZZT
FZZT
SNAP
LET'S SEE HOW YOU LIKE HAVING A BODY OF BRITTLE CHARCOAL !!!

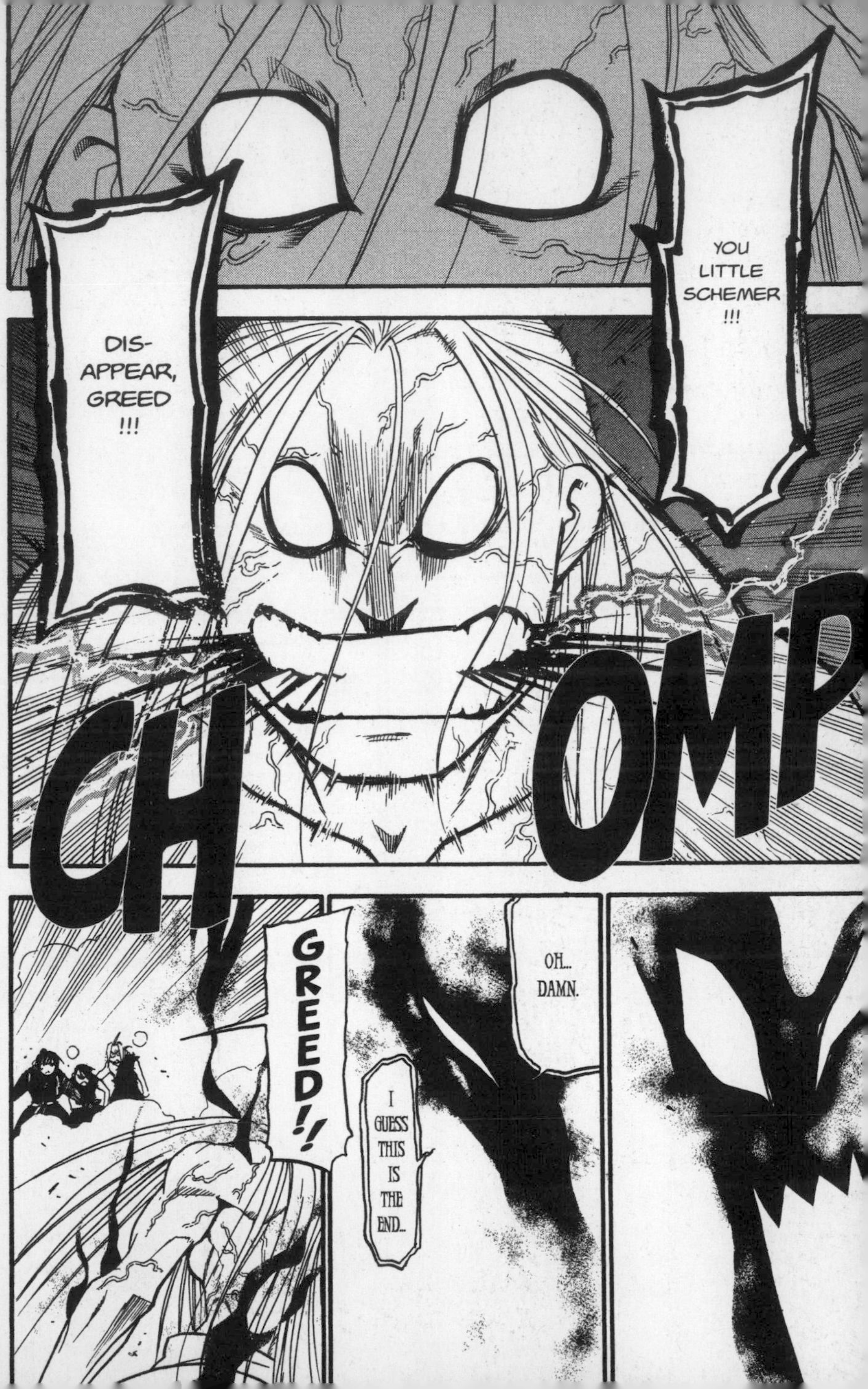
YOU LITTLE SCHEMER!!!
DIS-APPEAR, GREED!!!
CHOMP
OH.. DAMN.
I GUESS THIS IS THE END..
GREED!!

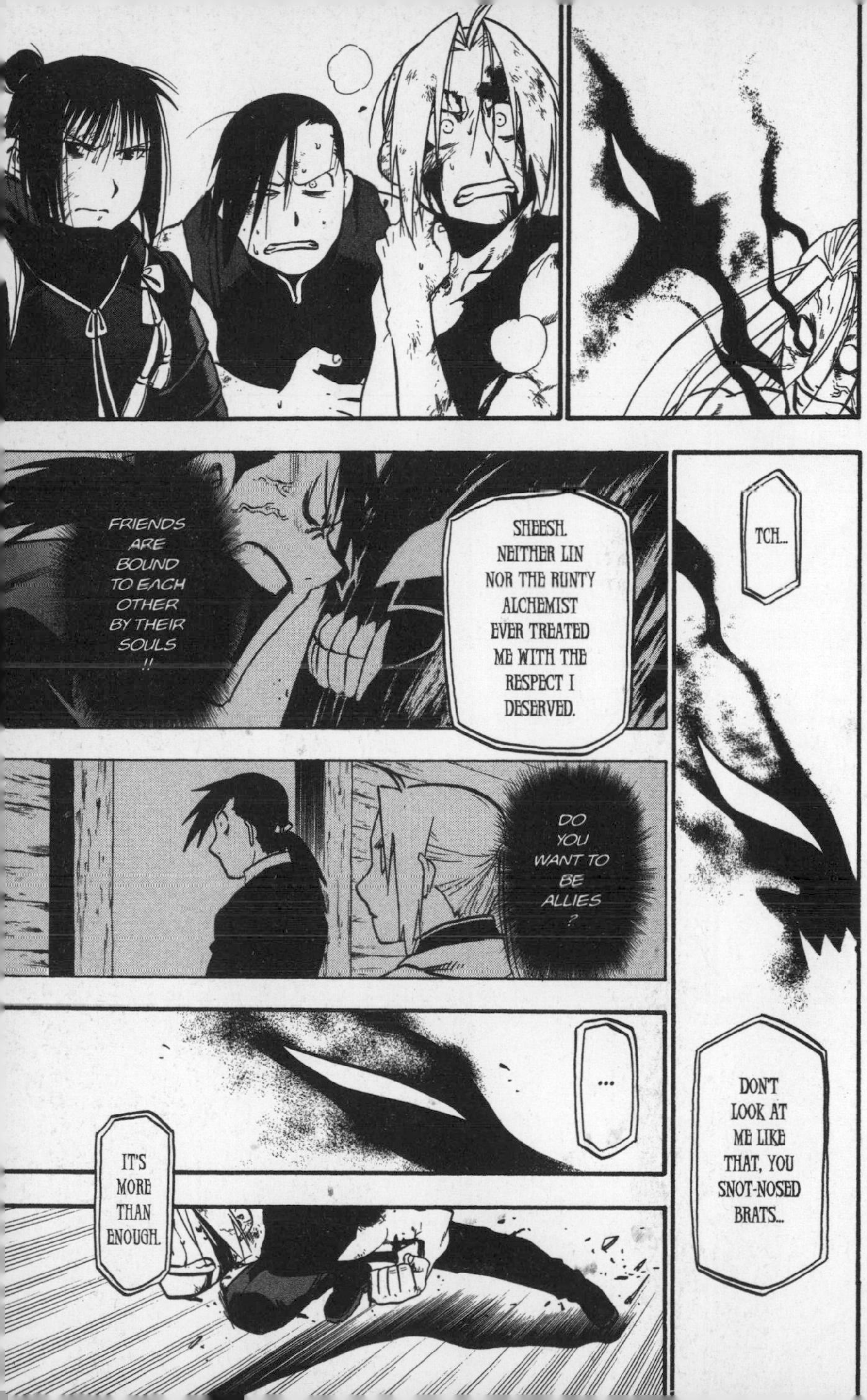
TCH...
DON'T LOOK AT ME LIKE THAT, YOU SNOT-NOSED BRATS...
SHEESH. NEITHER LIN NOR THE RUNTY ALCHEMIST EVER TREATED ME WITH THE RESPECT I DESERVED.
FRIENDS ARE BOUND TO EACH OTHER BY THEIR SOULS !!
DO YOU WANT TO BE ALLIES ?
...
IT'S MORE THAN ENOUGH.

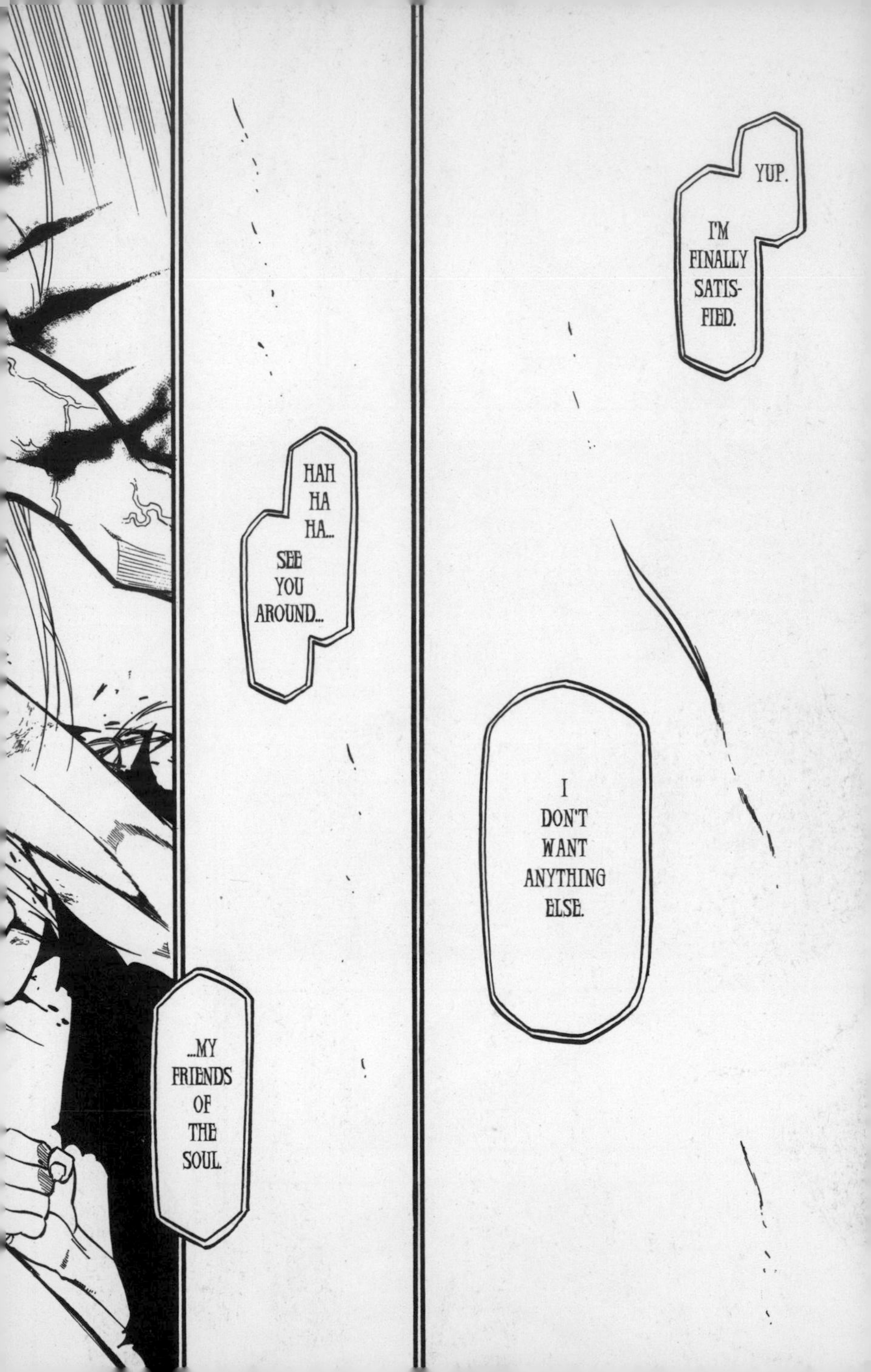
YUP. I'M FINALLY SATIS-FIED.
I DON'T WANT ANYTHING ELSE.
HAH HA HA... SEE YOU AROUND...
...MY FRIENDS OF THE SOUL.

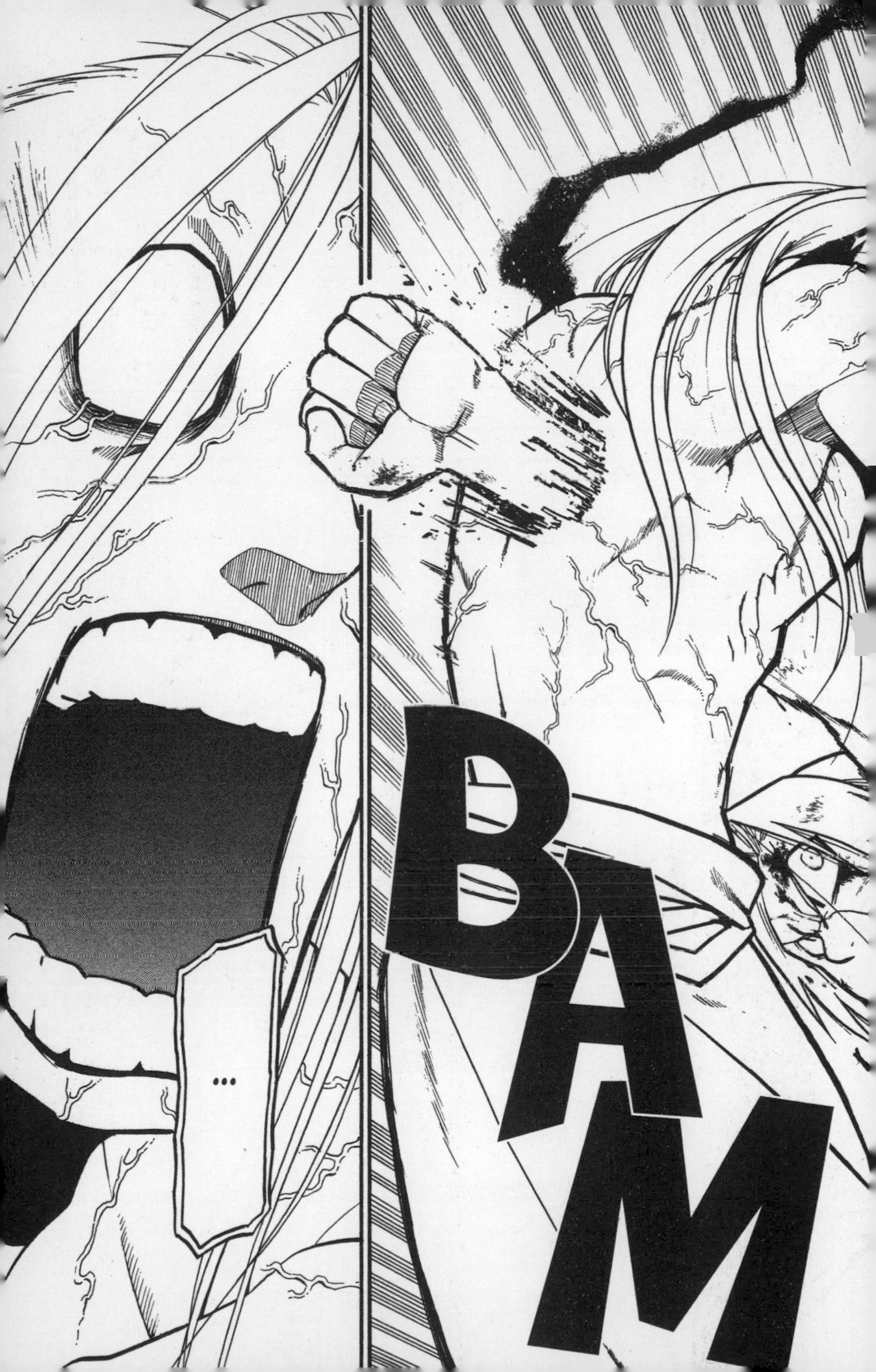
BAM
...

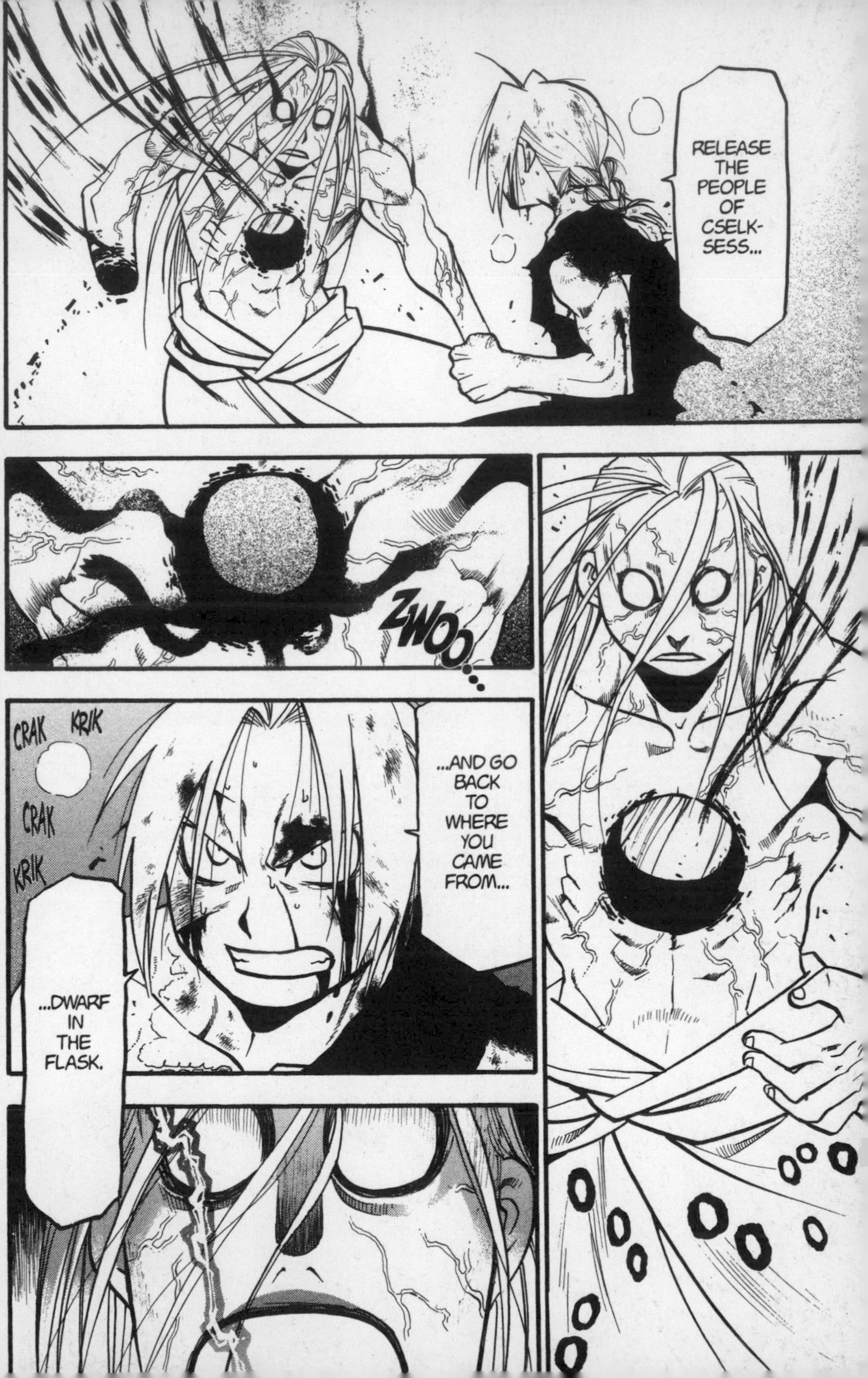
RELEASE THE PEOPLE OF CSELK-SESS...
ZWOO...
CRAK KRIK
CRAK
KRIK
...AND GO BACK TO WHERE YOU CAME FROM...
...DWARF IN THE FLASK.

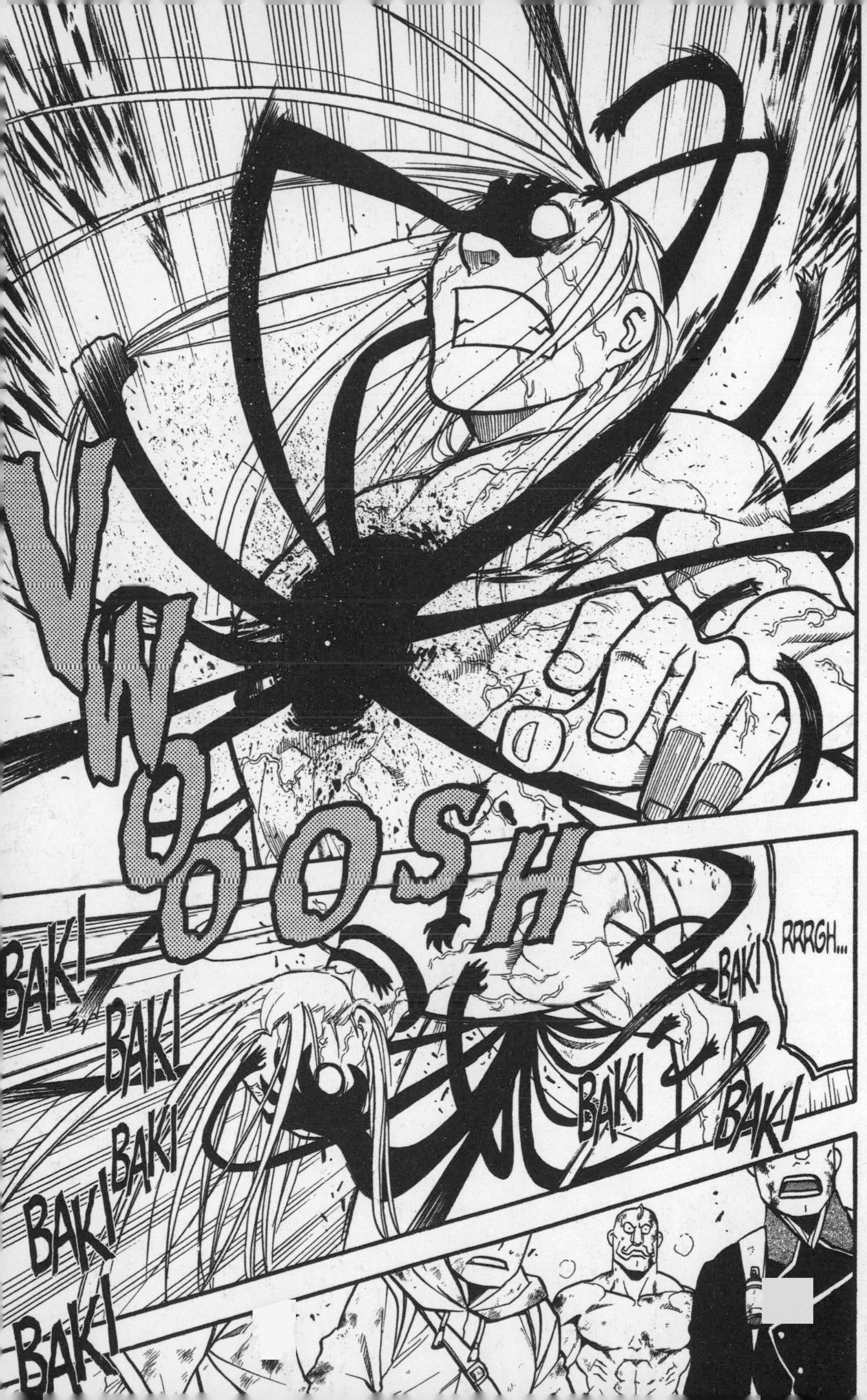
VWOOOSH
RRRGH...
BAKI
BAKI
BAKI
BAKI
BAKI
BAKI
BAKI
BAKI

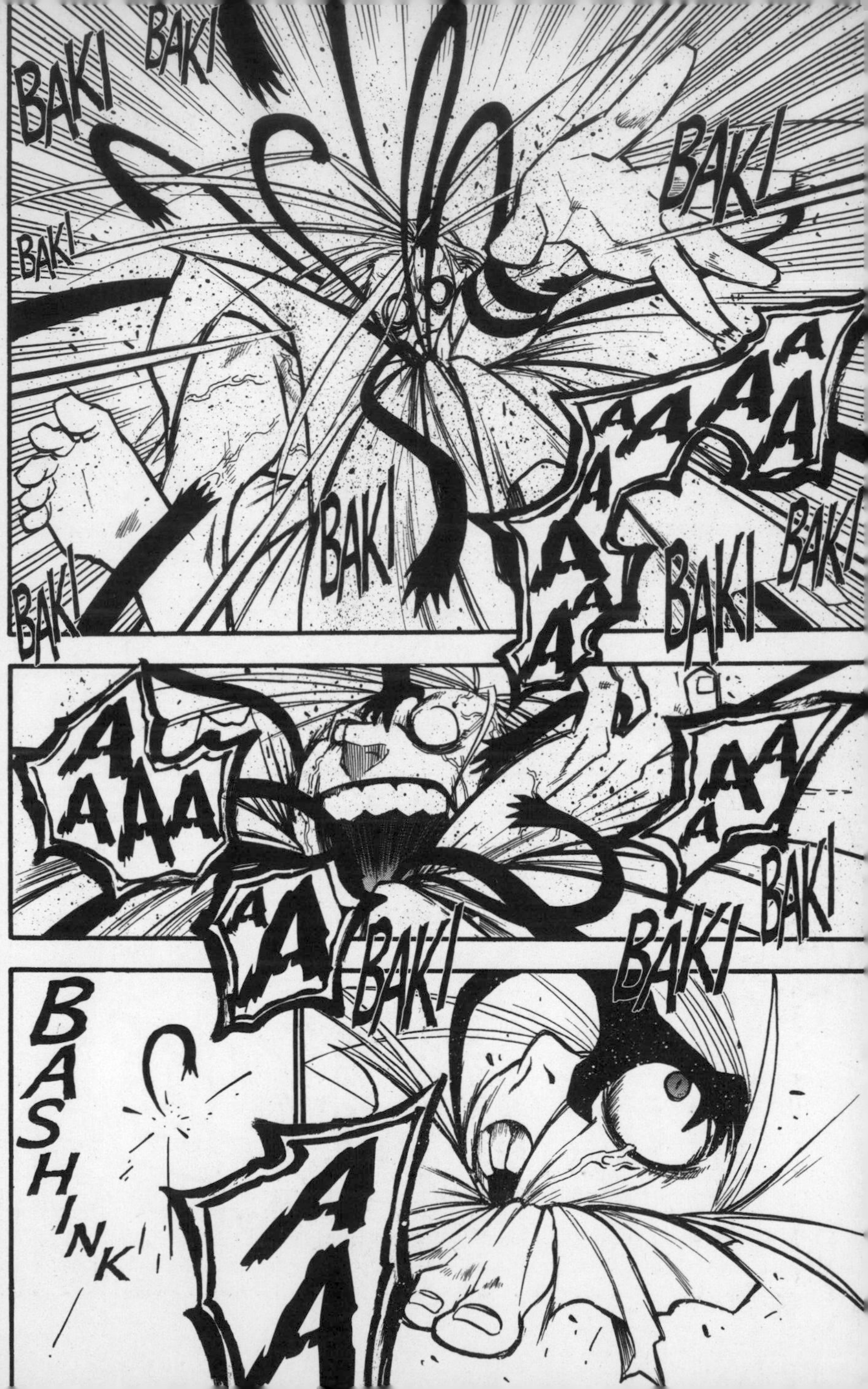
BAKI
BAKI
BAKI
BAKI
AAAAAAAAAAAAA
BAKI
BAKI
BAKI
BAKI
BAKI
AAAAA
BAKI
BAKI
AAAAAA
BAKI
AA
BASHINK
AA

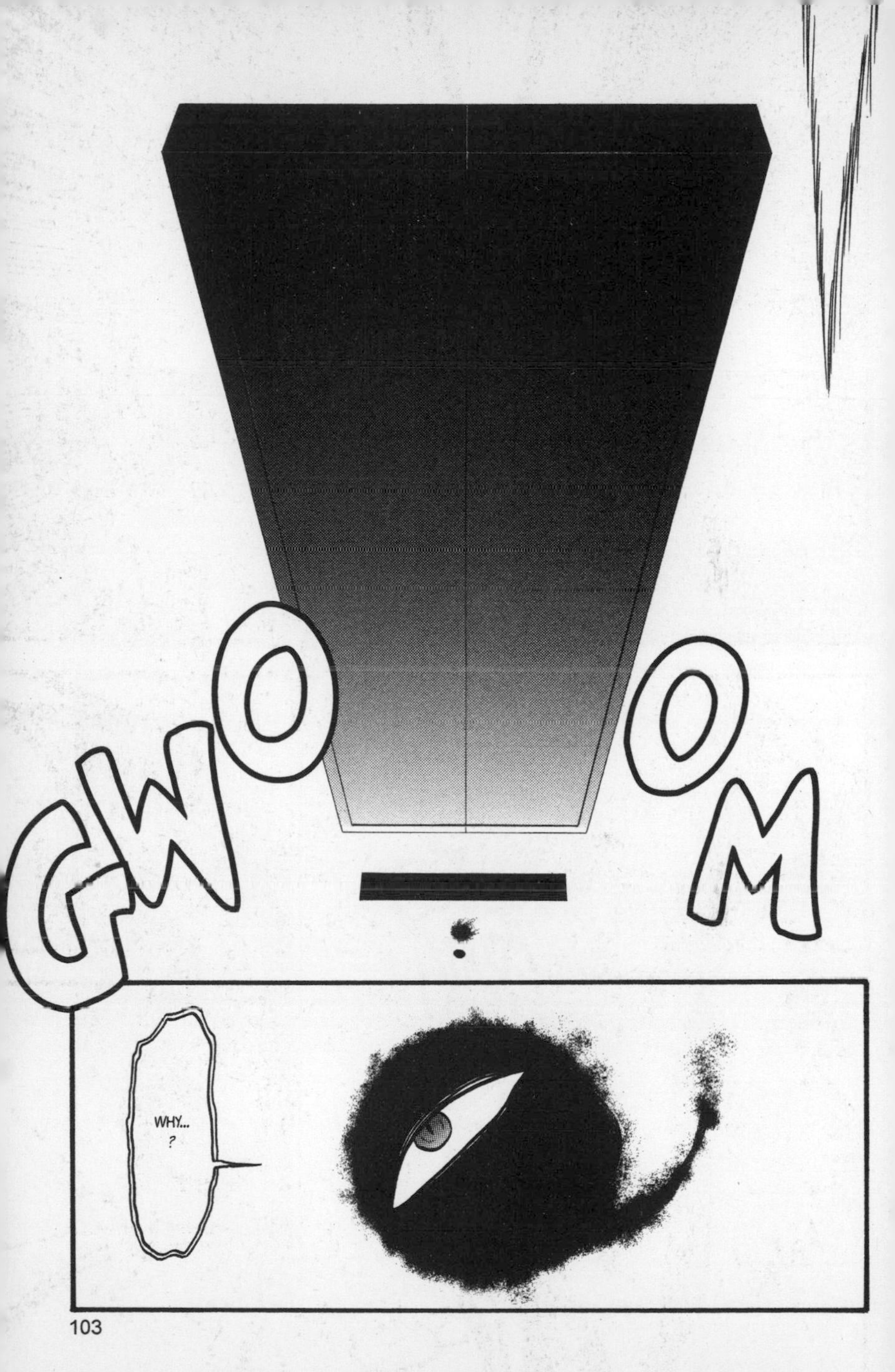
GWOOM
WHY...
?

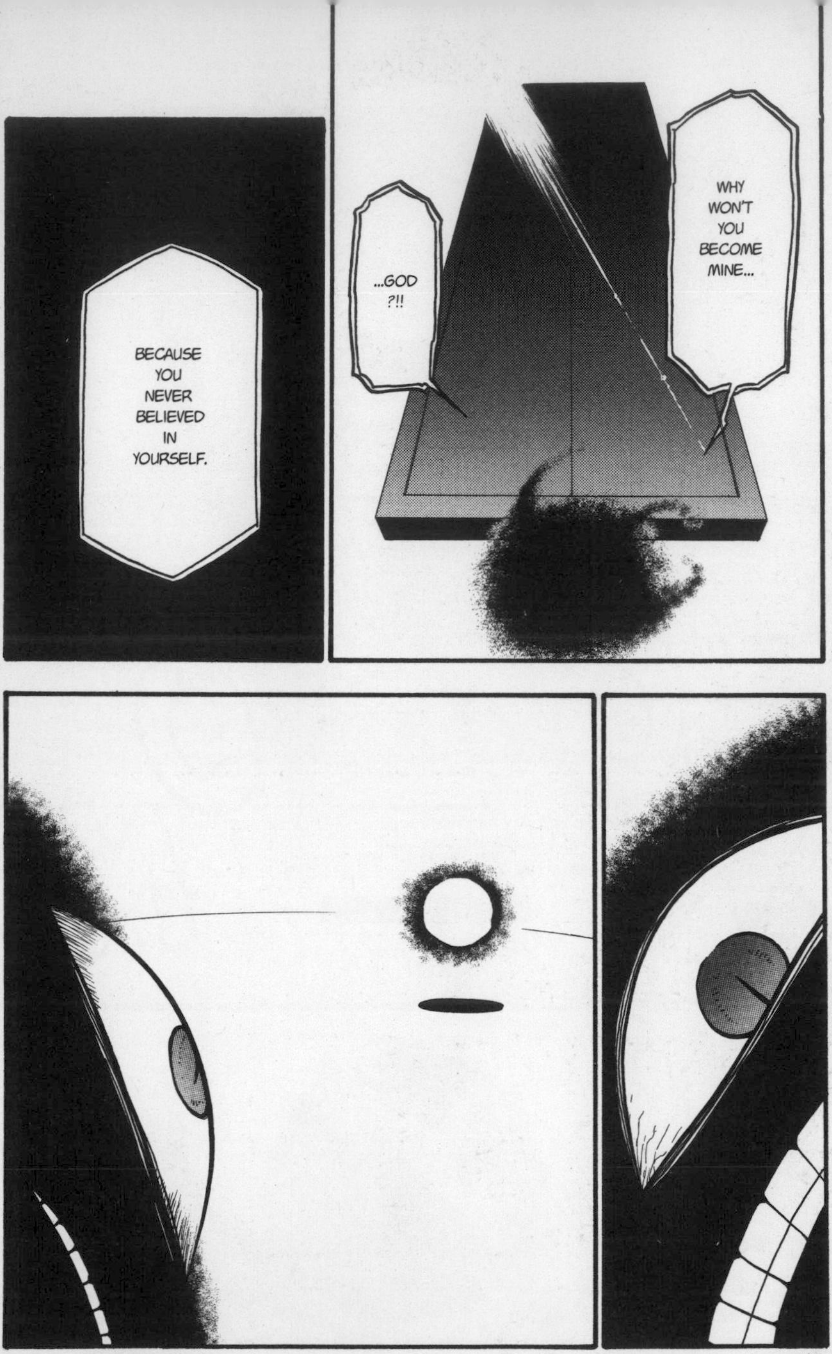
WHY WON'T YOU BECOME MINE...
...GOD ?!!
BECAUSE YOU NEVER BELIEVED IN YOURSELF.

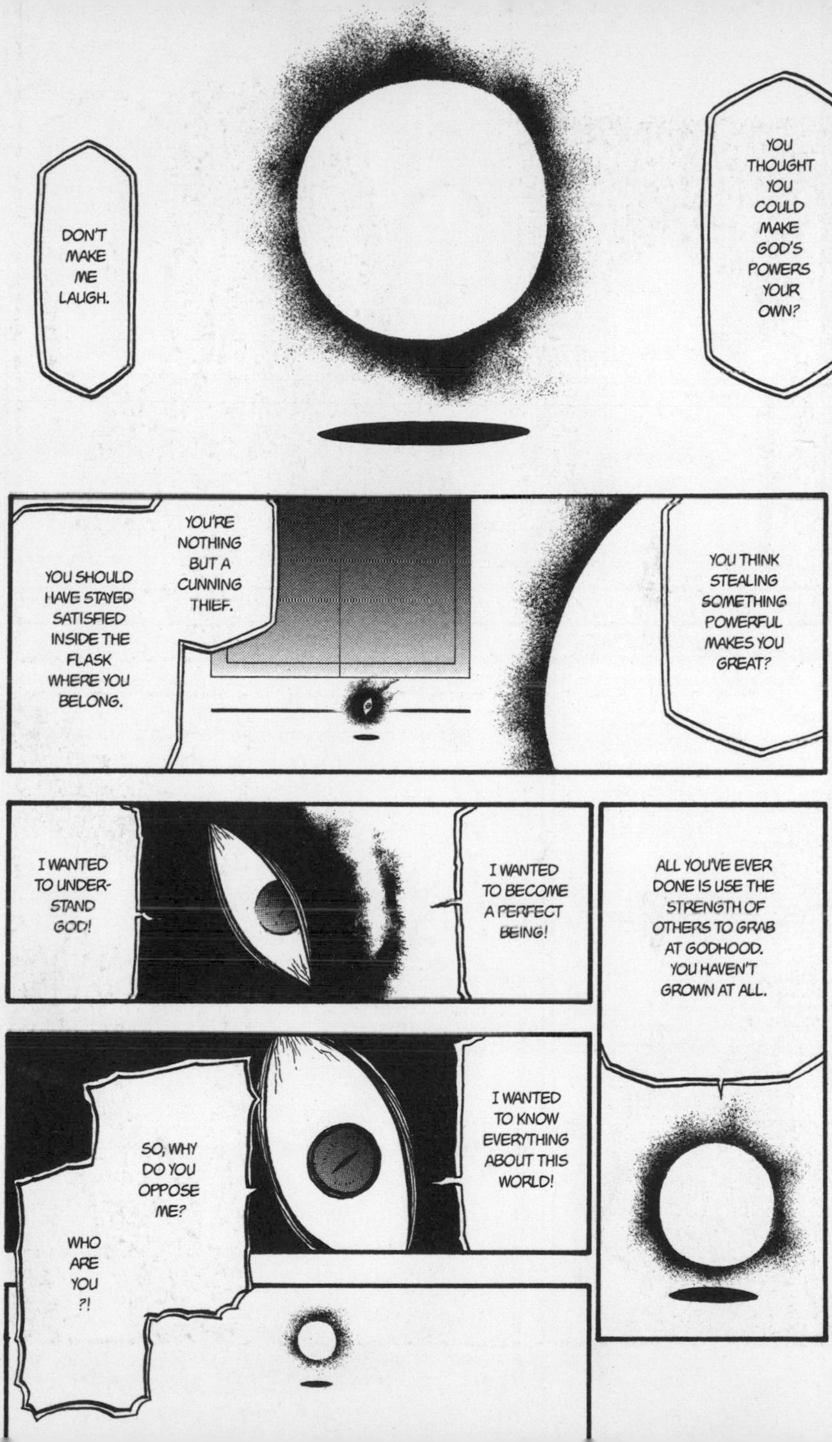
YOU THOUGHT YOU COULD MAKE GOD'S POWERS YOUR OWN?
DON'T MAKE ME LAUGH.
YOU THINK STEALING SOMETHING POWERFUL MAKES YOU GREAT?
YOU'RE NOTHING BUT A CUNNING THIEF.
YOU SHOULD HAVE STAYED SATISFIED INSIDE THE FLASK WHERE YOU BELONG.
ALL YOU'VE EVER DONE IS USE THE STRENGTH OF OTHERS TO GRAB AT GODHOOD. YOU HAVEN'T GROWN AT ALL.
I WANTED TO BECOME A PERFECT BEING!
I WANTED TO UNDER-STAND GOD!
I WANTED TO KNOW EVERYTHING ABOUT THIS WORLD!
SO, WHY DO YOU OPPOSE ME?
WHO ARE YOU ?!

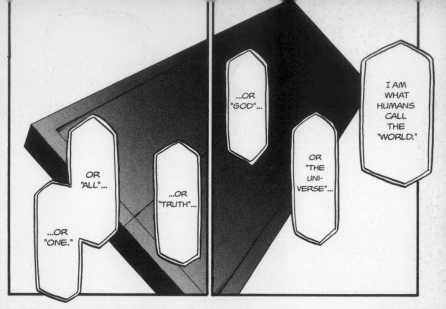

...OR
"GOD"...

I AM
WHAT
HUMANS
CALL
THE
"WORLD."

OR
"ALL"...

...OR
"TRUTH"...

OR
"THE
UNI-
VERSE"...

...OR
"ONE."

YOU CALLED
TRUTH "THE
ARBITER OF
ORDER" THAT
"KEEPS MEN
IN THEIR
PLACE."

THAT'S
WHAT
YOU
SAID,
WASN'T
IT?

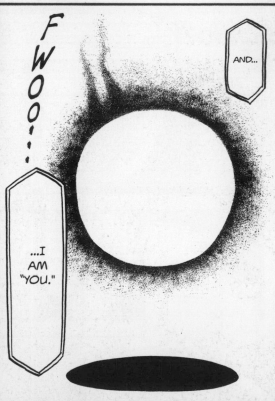

F
WOO...!!

AND...

...I
AM
"YOU."

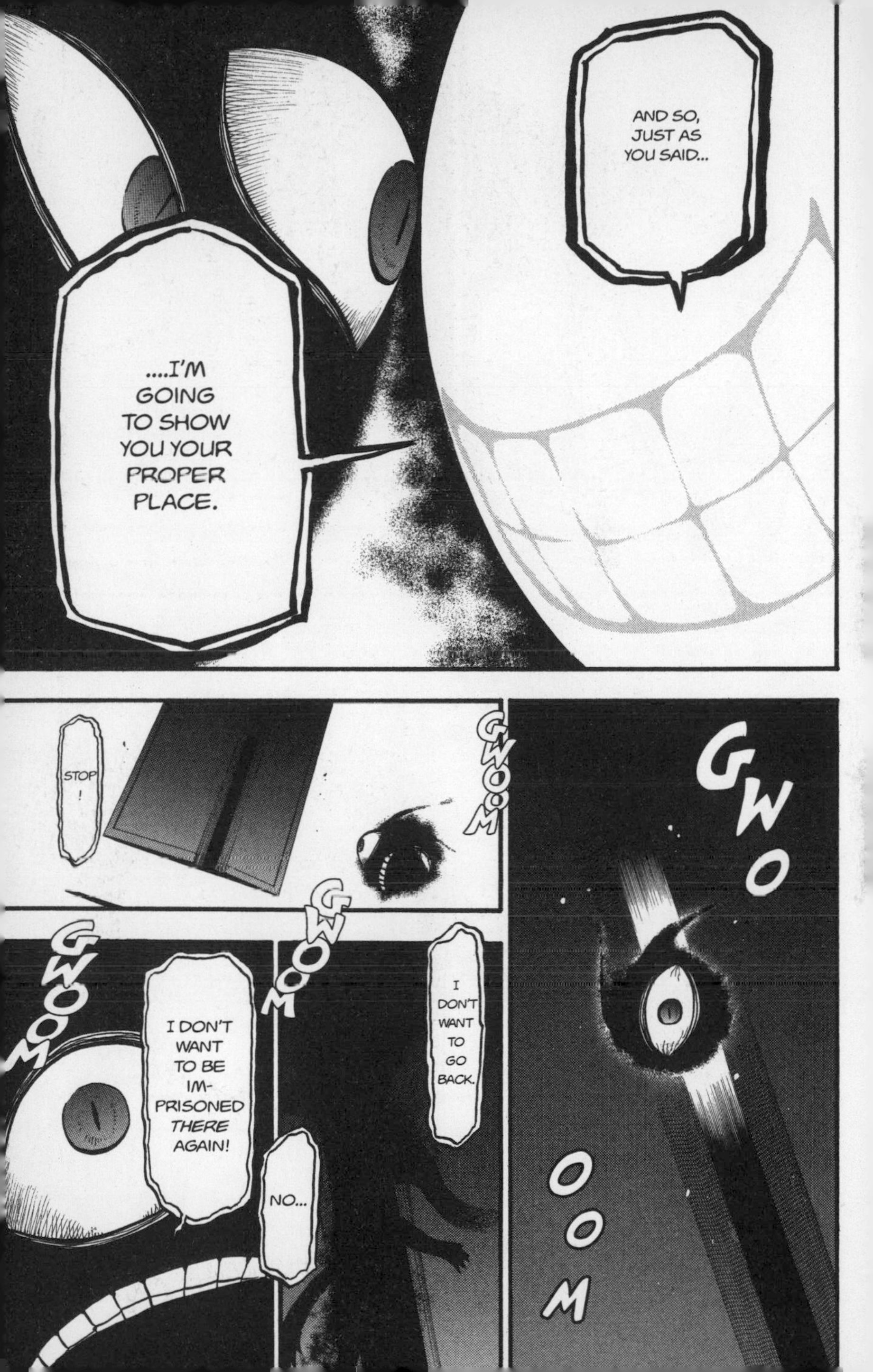
AND SO, JUST AS YOU SAID...
....I'M GOING TO SHOW YOU YOUR PROPER PLACE.
GWOOOOM
GWOOM
STOP!
GWOOM
I DON'T WANT TO GO BACK.
NO...
GWOOM
I DON'T WANT TO BE IM-PRISONED THERE AGAIN!

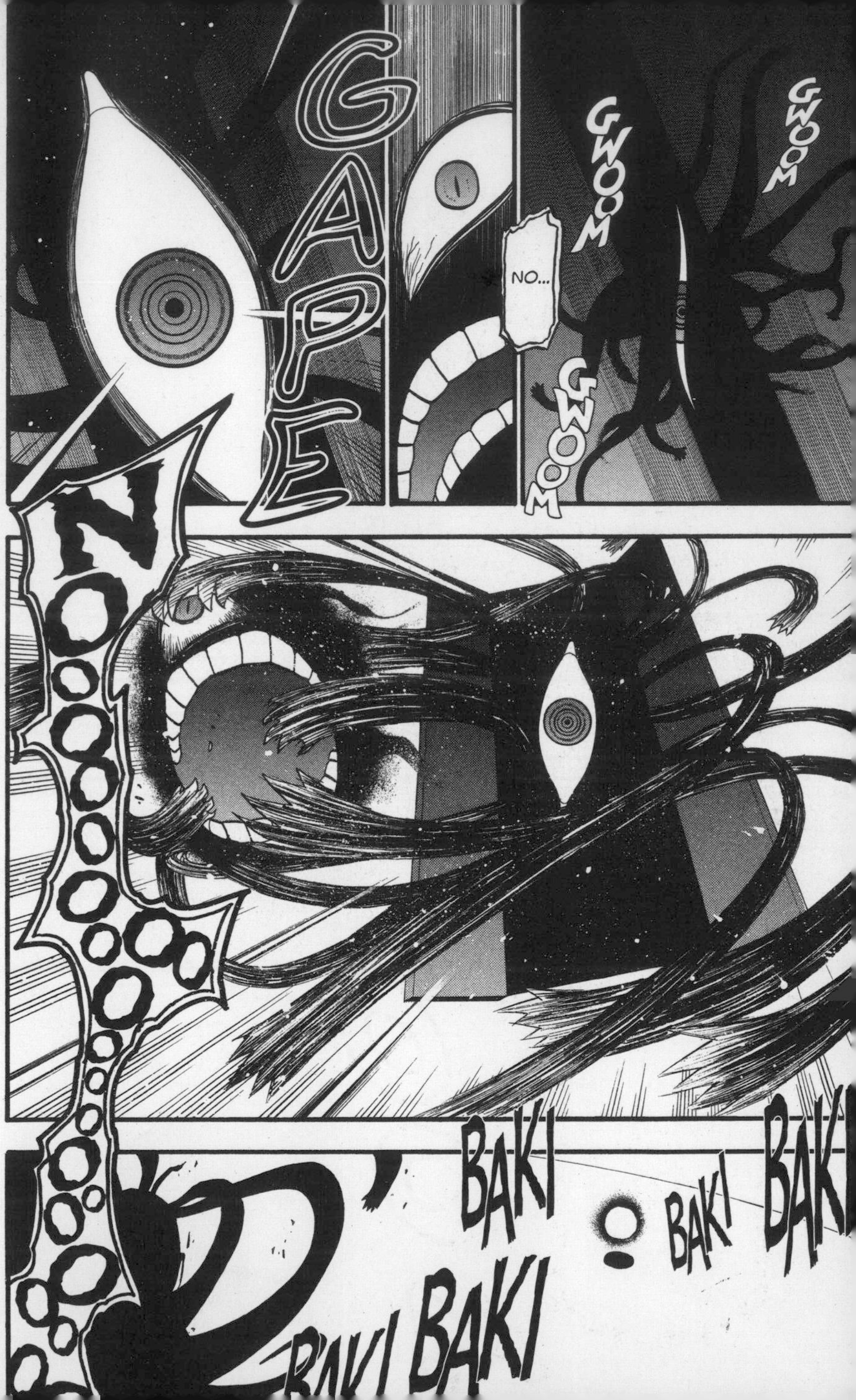
GWOOM
GWOOM
NO...
GWOOM
GAPE
NOOOOOOOOOOOOOOOOOOOOOO
BAKI
BAKI
BAKI
BAKI
BAKI

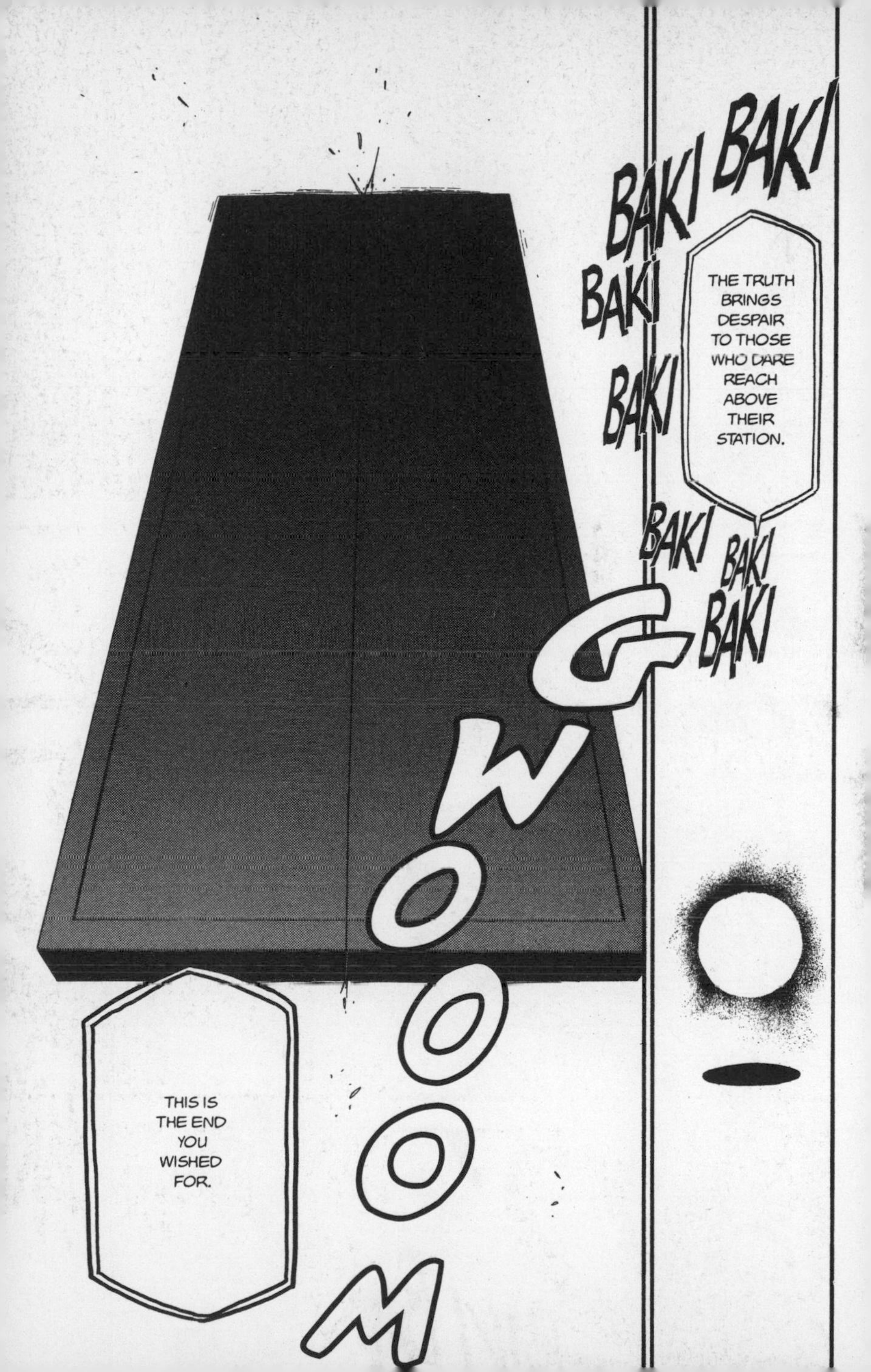
BAKI BAKI
BAKI
BAKI
THE TRUTH BRINGS DESPAIR TO THOSE WHO DARE REACH ABOVE THEIR STATION.
BAKI BAKI
BAKI
GWOOOM
THIS IS THE END YOU WISHED FOR.

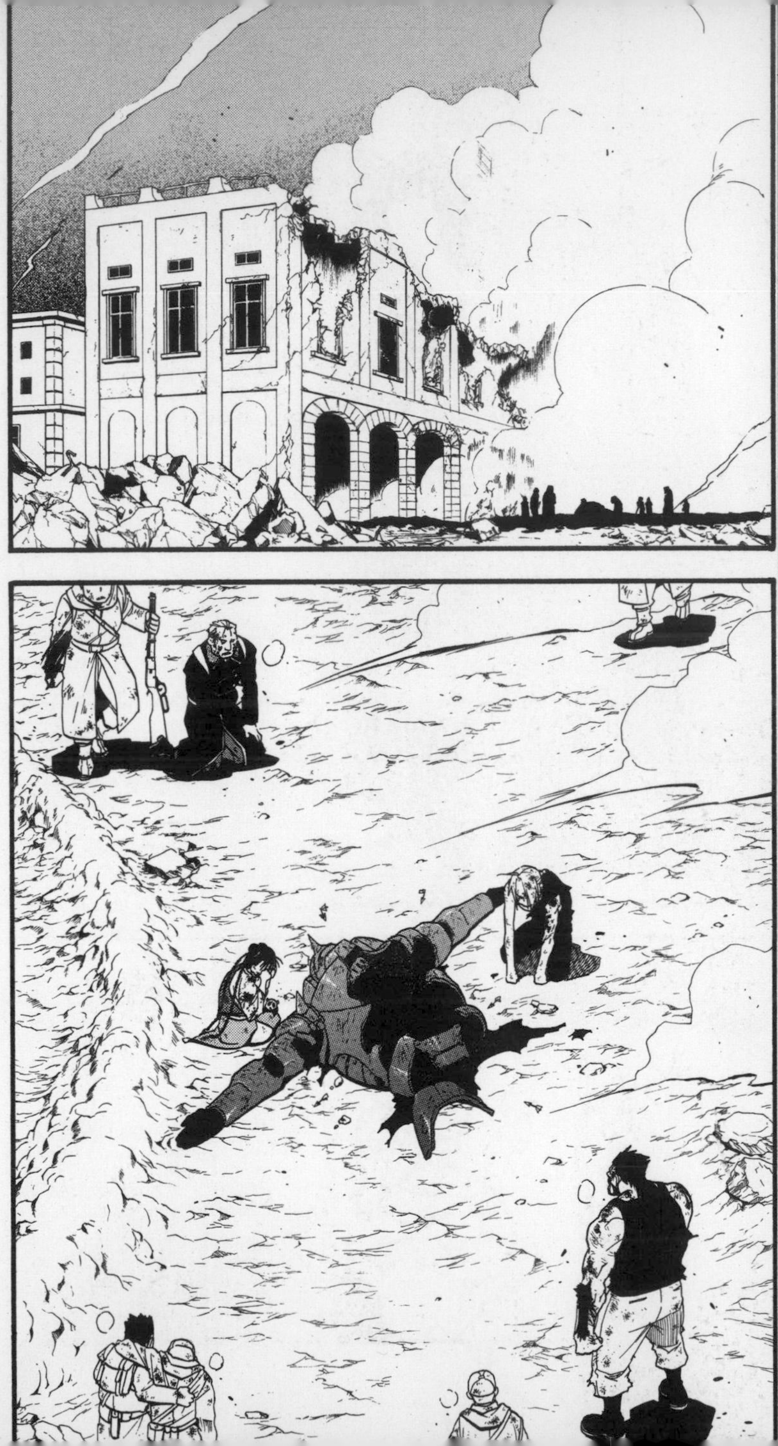

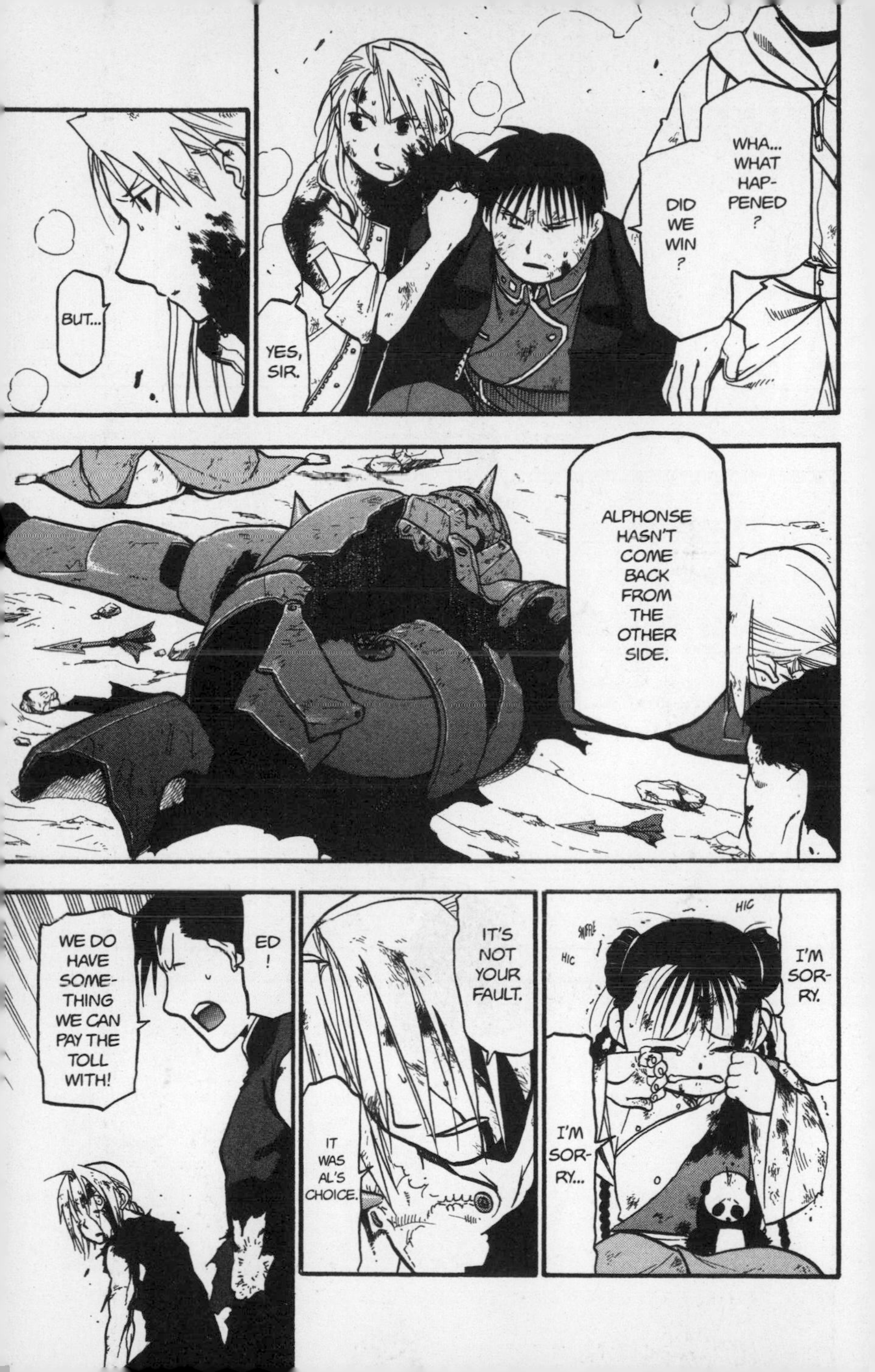
WHA... WHAT HAP-PENED?
DID WE WIN?
YES, SIR.
BUT...
ALPHONSE HASN'T COME BACK FROM THE OTHER SIDE.
HIC
I'M SOR-RY.
SNIFFLE
HIC
I'M SOR-RY...
IT'S NOT YOUR FAULT.
IT WAS AL'S CHOICE.
ED!
WE DO HAVE SOME-THING WE CAN PAY THE TOLL WITH!

A PHILOSOPHER'S STONE!

USE THIS TO BRING ED BACK.

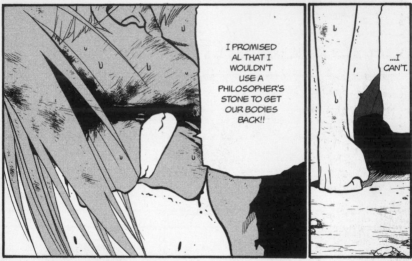

I PROMISED AL THAT I WOULDN'T USE A PHILOSOPHER'S STONE TO GET OUR BODIES BACK!!

...I CAN'T.

AL-PHONSE ELRIC...

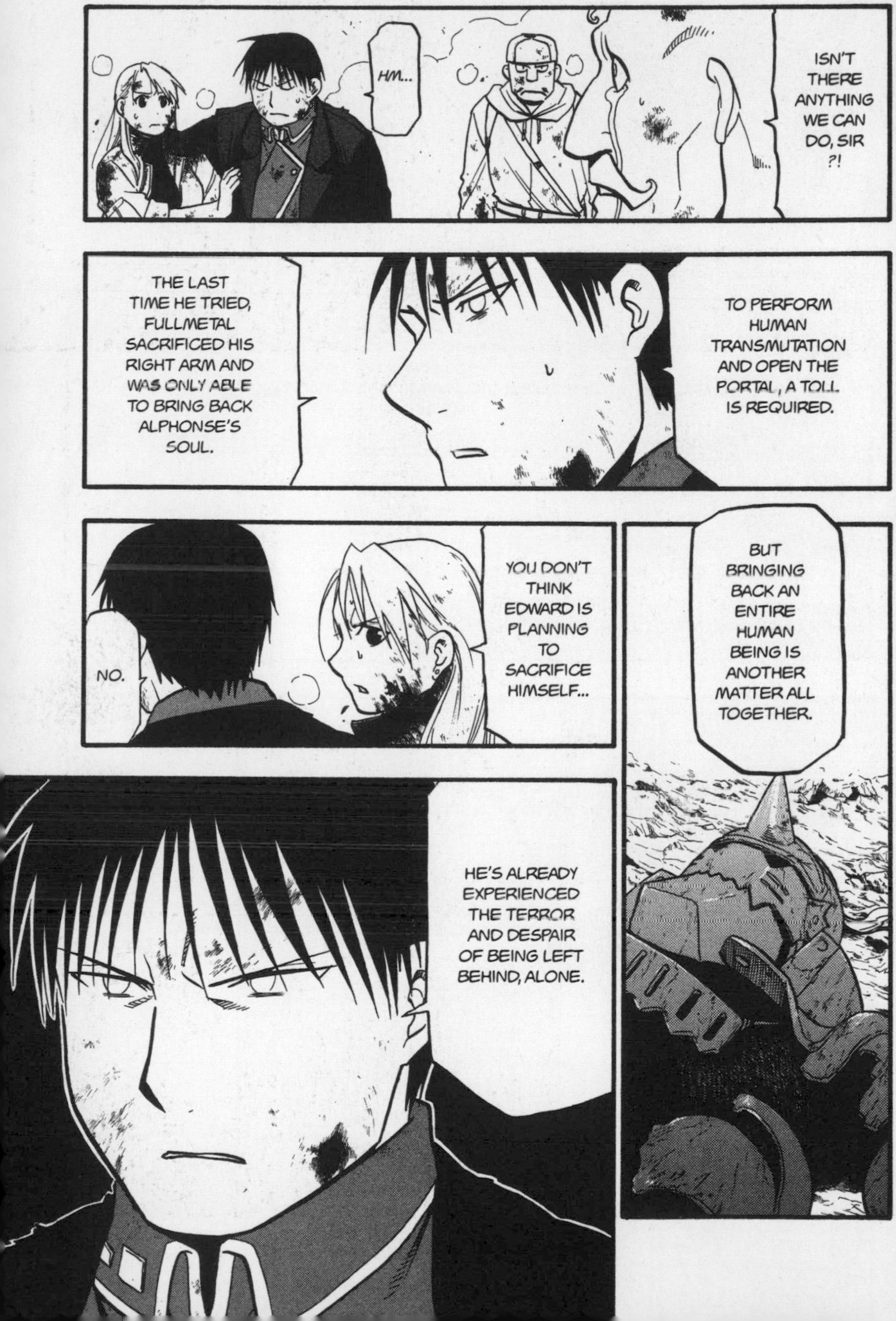
ISN'T THERE ANYTHING WE CAN DO, SIR ?!
HM...
TO PERFORM HUMAN TRANSMUTATION AND OPEN THE PORTAL, A TOLL IS REQUIRED.
THE LAST TIME HE TRIED, FULLMETAL SACRIFICED HIS RIGHT ARM AND WAS ONLY ABLE TO BRING BACK ALPHONSE'S SOUL.
BUT BRINGING BACK AN ENTIRE HUMAN BEING IS ANOTHER MATTER ALL TOGETHER.
YOU DON'T THINK EDWARD IS PLANNING TO SACRIFICE HIMSELF...
NO.
HE'S ALREADY EXPERIENCED THE TERROR AND DESPAIR OF BEING LEFT BEHIND, ALONE.

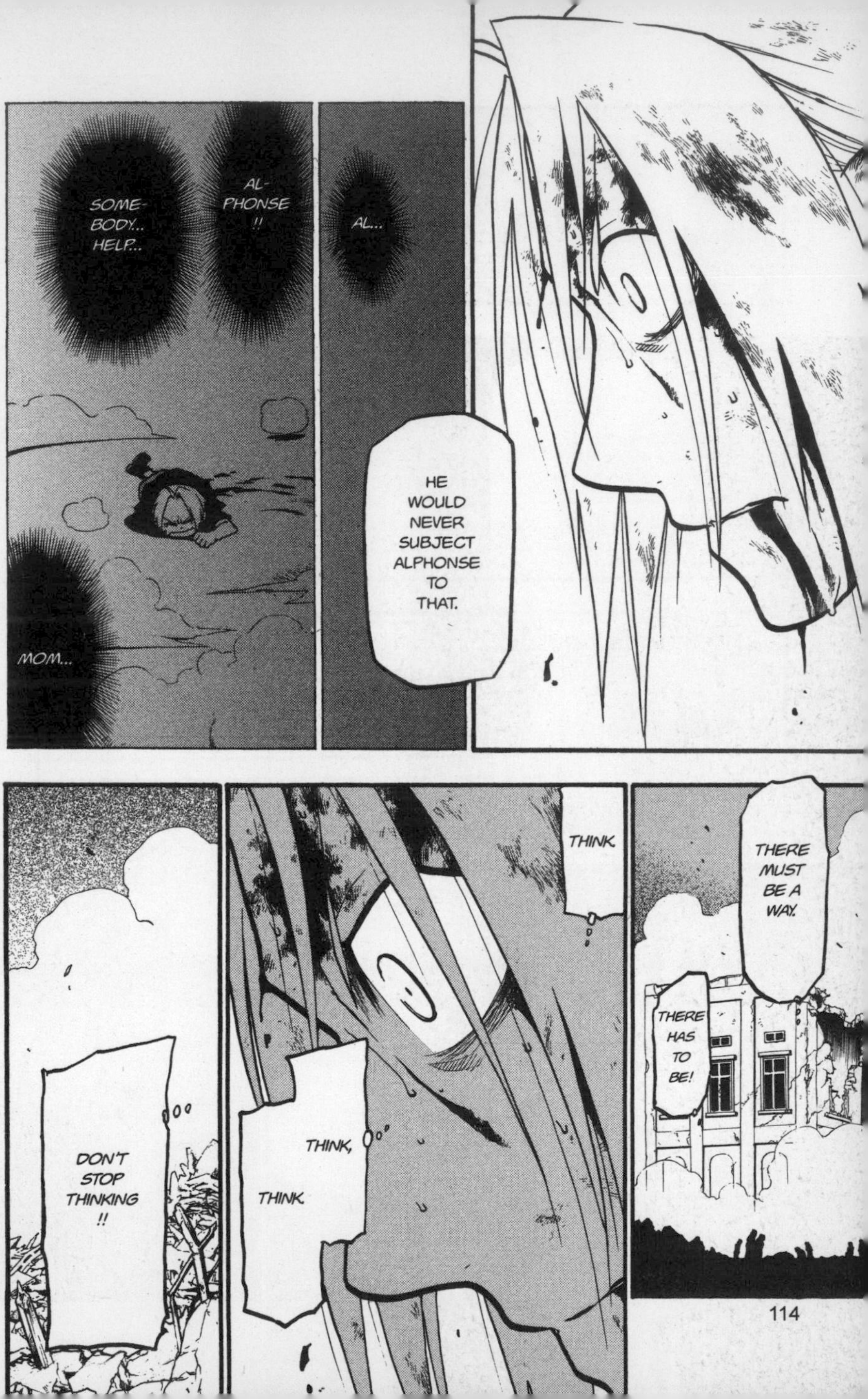
HE WOULD NEVER SUBJECT ALPHONSE TO THAT.
AL...
AL-PHONSE !!
SOME-BODY... HELP...
MOM...
THERE MUST BE A WAY.
THERE HAS TO BE!
THINK.
THINK,
THINK.
DON'T STOP THINKING !!

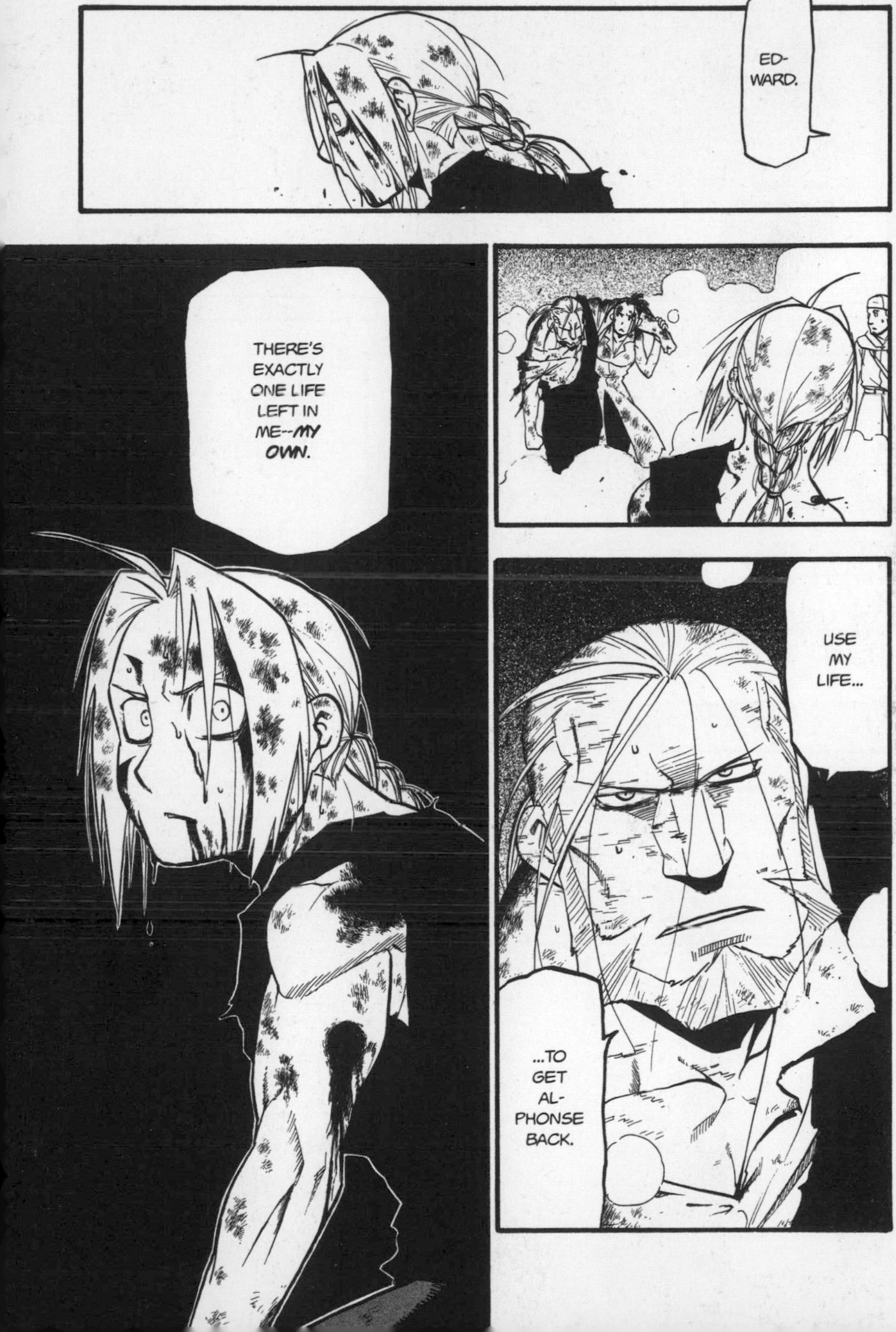
ED-WARD.
USE MY LIFE...
...TO GET AL-PHONSE BACK.
THERE'S EXACTLY ONE LIFE LEFT IN ME--MY OWN.

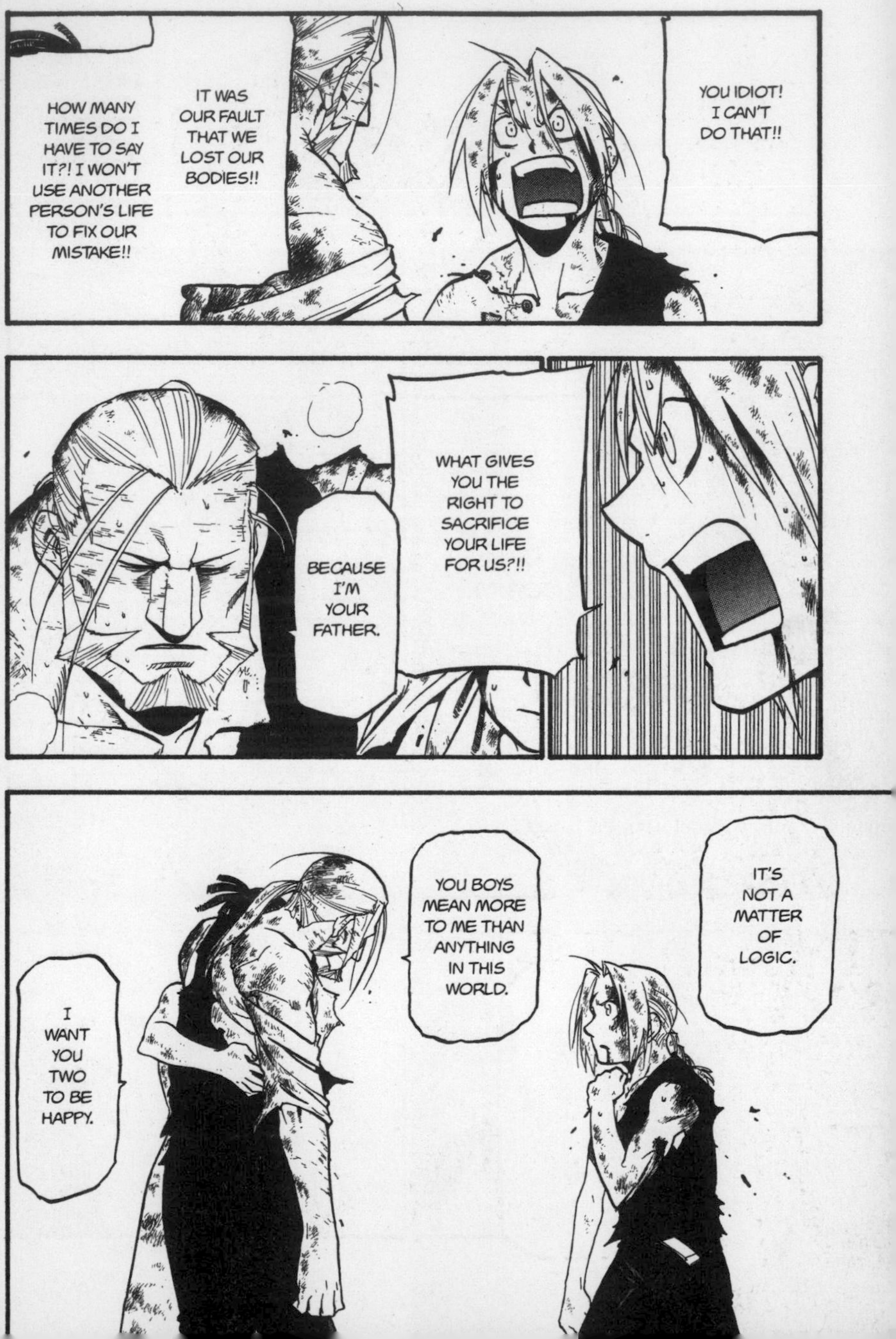
YOU IDIOT! I CAN'T DO THAT!!
IT WAS OUR FAULT THAT WE LOST OUR BODIES!!
HOW MANY TIMES DO I HAVE TO SAY IT?! I WON'T USE ANOTHER PERSON'S LIFE TO FIX OUR MISTAKE!!
WHAT GIVES YOU THE RIGHT TO SACRIFICE YOUR LIFE FOR US?!!
BECAUSE I'M YOUR FATHER.
IT'S NOT A MATTER OF LOGIC.
YOU BOYS MEAN MORE TO ME THAN ANYTHING IN THIS WORLD.
I WANT YOU TWO TO BE HAPPY.

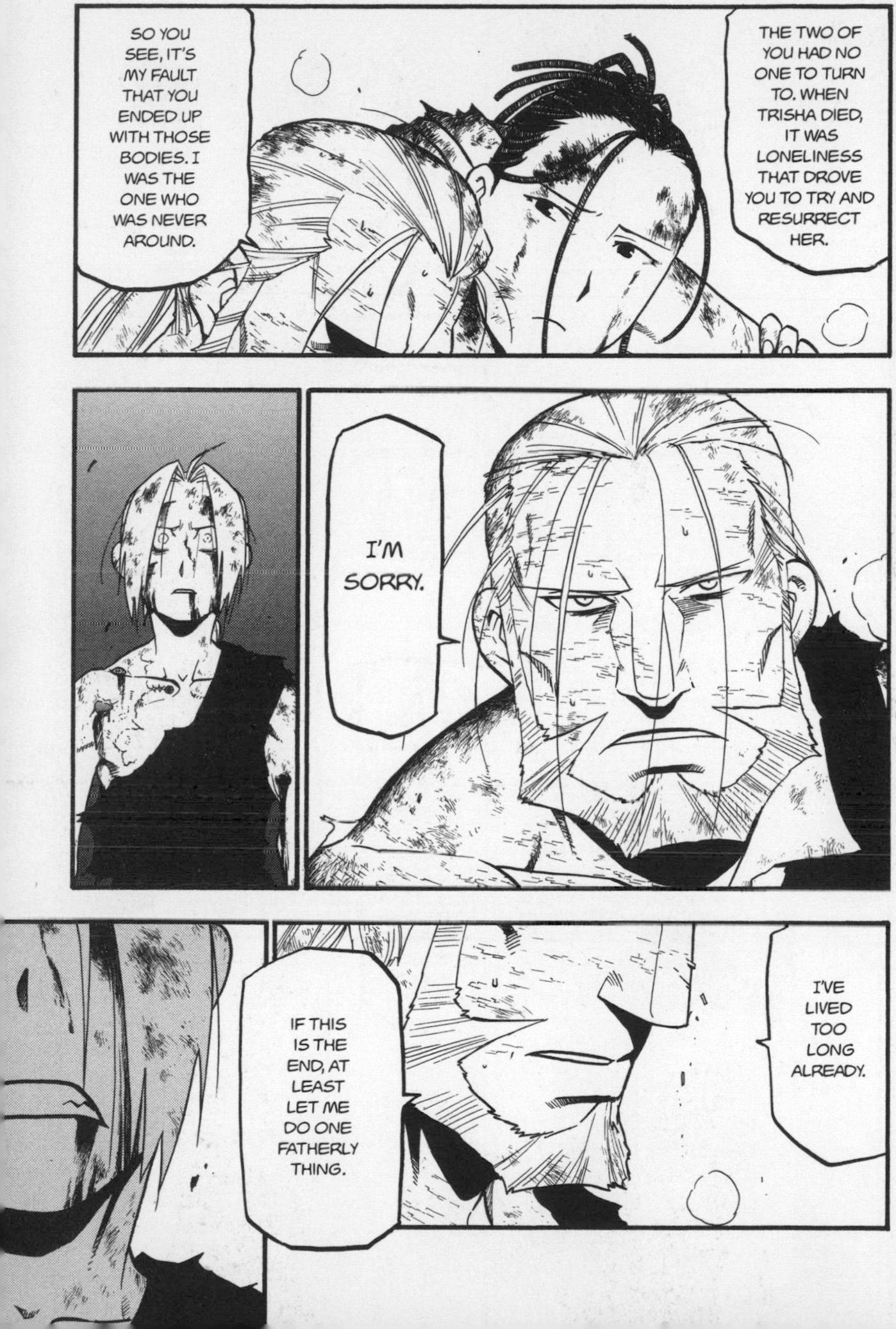
THE TWO OF YOU HAD NO ONE TO TURN TO. WHEN TRISHA DIED, IT WAS LONELINESS THAT DROVE YOU TO TRY AND RESURRECT HER.
SO YOU SEE, IT'S MY FAULT THAT YOU ENDED UP WITH THOSE BODIES. I WAS THE ONE WHO WAS NEVER AROUND.
I'M SORRY.
I'VE LIVED TOO LONG ALREADY.
IF THIS IS THE END, AT LEAST LET ME DO ONE FATHERLY THING.

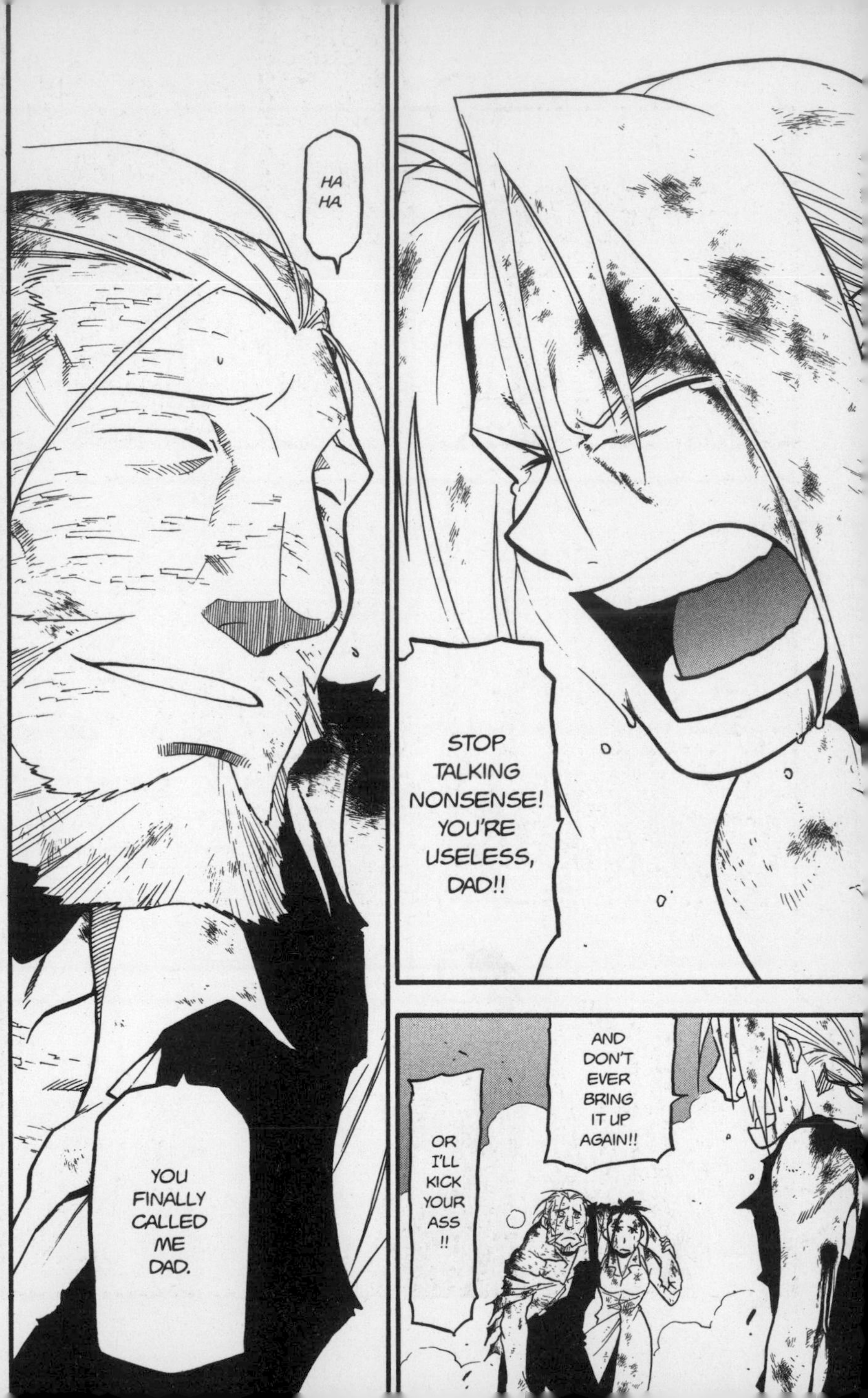
STOP TALKING NONSENSE! YOU'RE USELESS, DAD!!
AND DON'T EVER BRING IT UP AGAIN!!
OR I'LL KICK YOUR ASS!!
HA HA.
YOU FINALLY CALLED ME DAD.

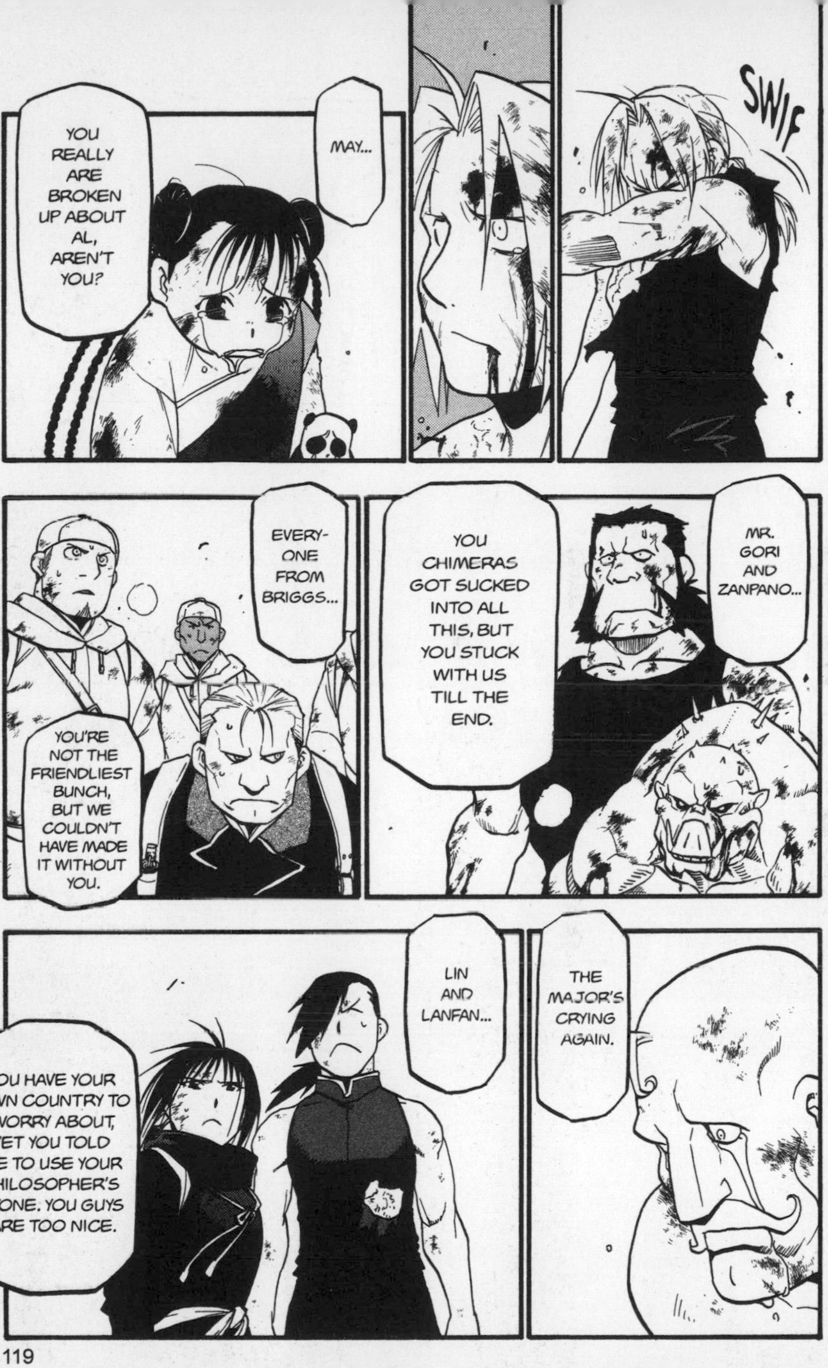
SWIF
MAY...
YOU REALLY ARE BROKEN UP ABOUT AL, AREN'T YOU?
MR. GORI AND ZANPANO...
YOU CHIMERAS GOT SUCKED INTO ALL THIS, BUT YOU STUCK WITH US TILL THE END.
EVERY-ONE FROM BRIGGS...
YOU'RE NOT THE FRIENDLIEST BUNCH, BUT WE COULDN'T HAVE MADE IT WITHOUT YOU.
THE MAJOR'S CRYING AGAIN.
LIN AND LANFAN...
YOU HAVE YOUR OWN COUNTRY TO WORRY ABOUT, YET YOU TOLD ME TO USE YOUR PHILOSOPHER'S STONE. YOU GUYS ARE TOO NICE.

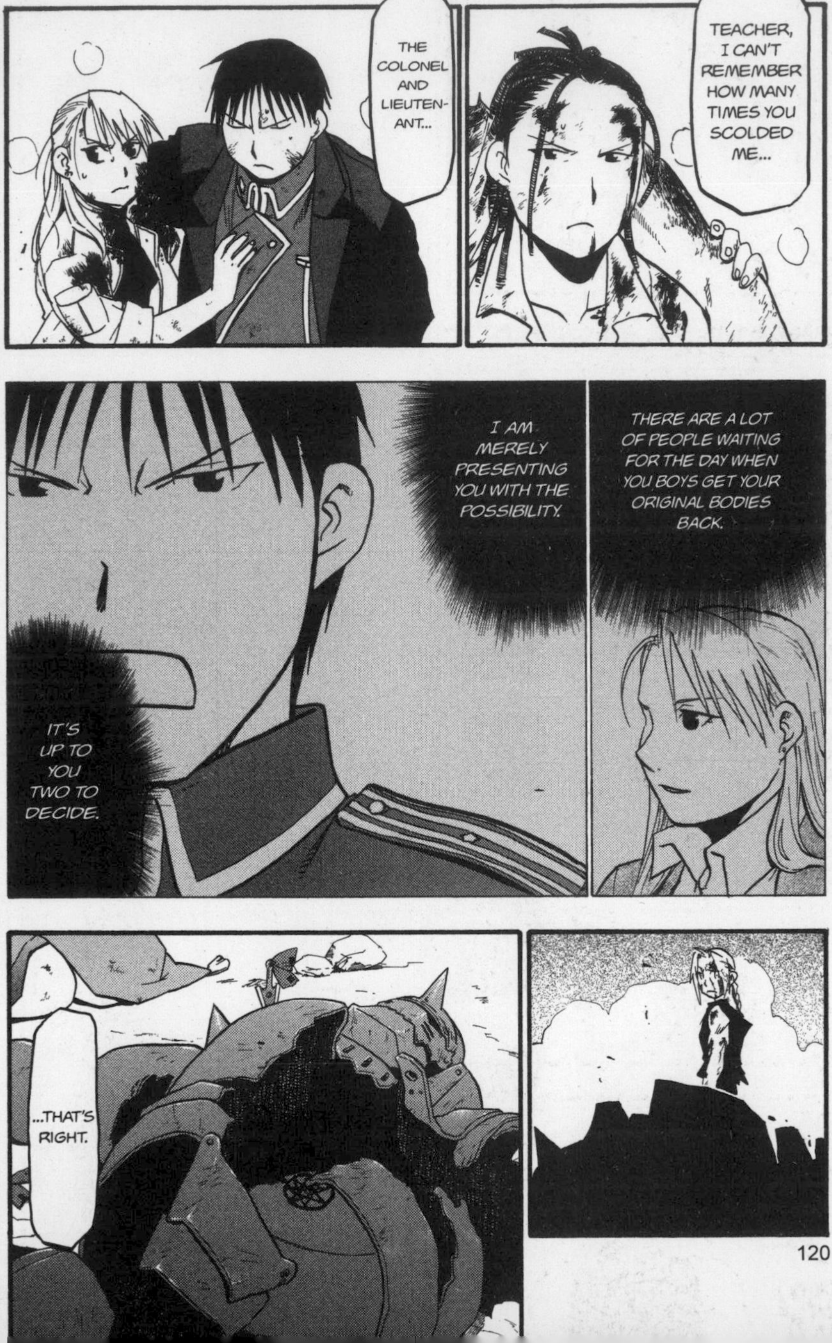
TEACHER, I CAN'T REMEMBER HOW MANY TIMES YOU SCOLDED ME...
THE COLONEL AND LIEUTEN-ANT...
THERE ARE A LOT OF PEOPLE WAITING FOR THE DAY WHEN YOU BOYS GET YOUR ORIGINAL BODIES BACK.
I AM MERELY PRESENTING YOU WITH THE POSSIBILITY.
IT'S UP TO YOU TWO TO DECIDE.
...THAT'S RIGHT.

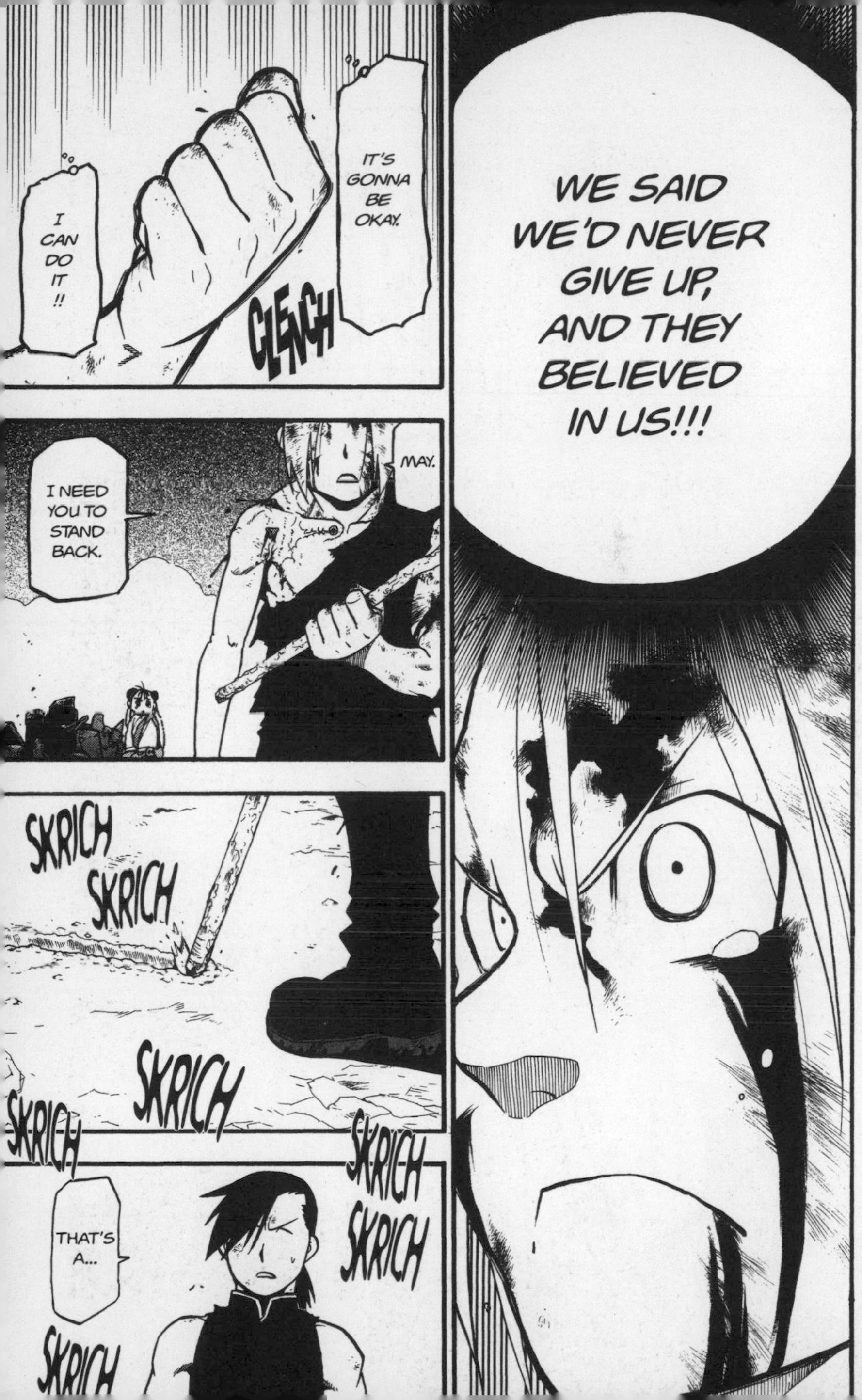
WE SAID WE'D NEVER GIVE UP, AND THEY BELIEVED IN US!!!
IT'S GONNA BE OKAY.
I CAN DO IT!!
CLENCH
MAY.
I NEED YOU TO STAND BACK.
SKRICH
SKRICH
SKRICH
SKRICH
SKRICH
SKRICH
THAT'S A...
SKRICH

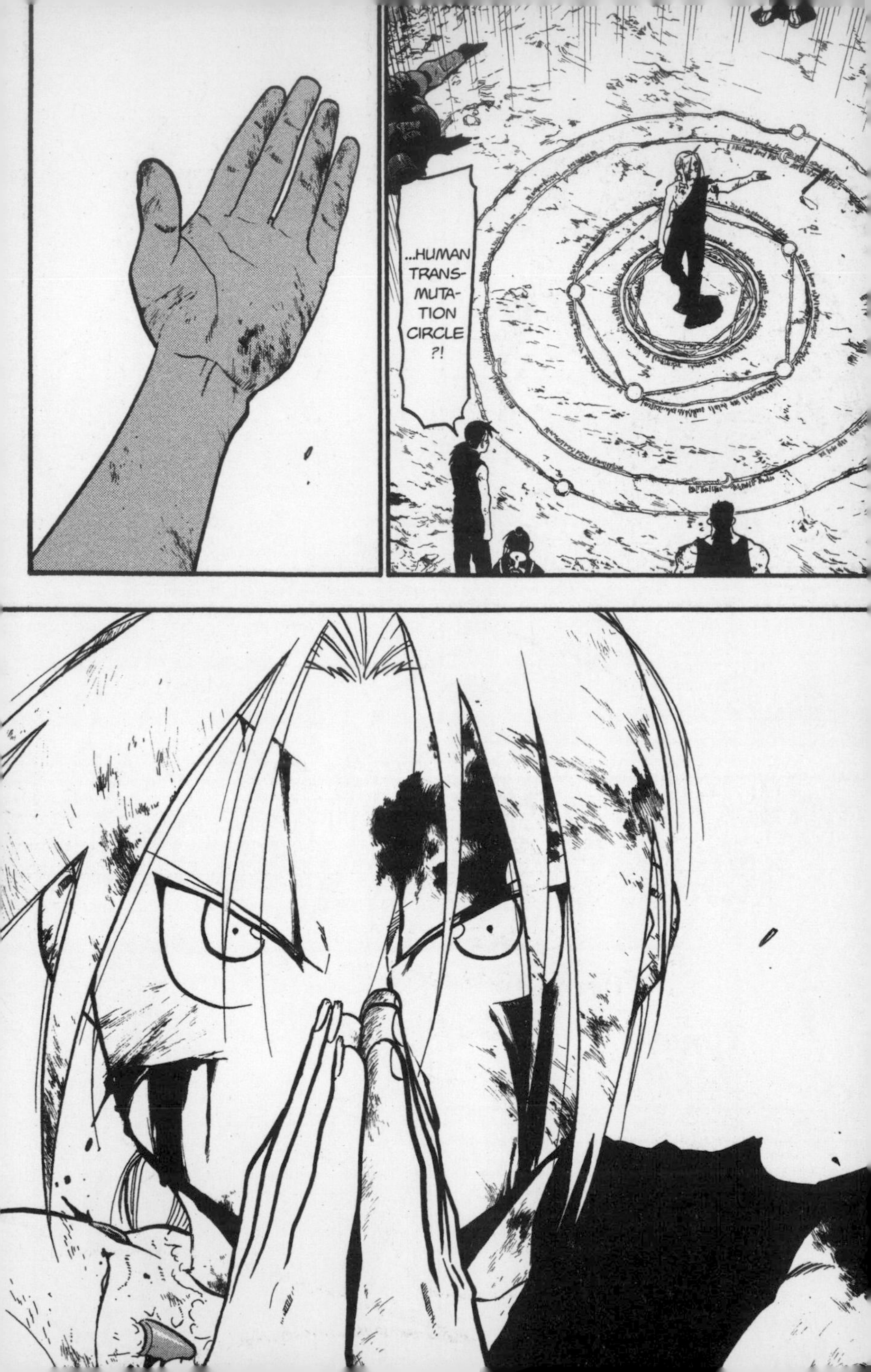
...HUMAN TRANS-MUTATION CIRCLE ?!

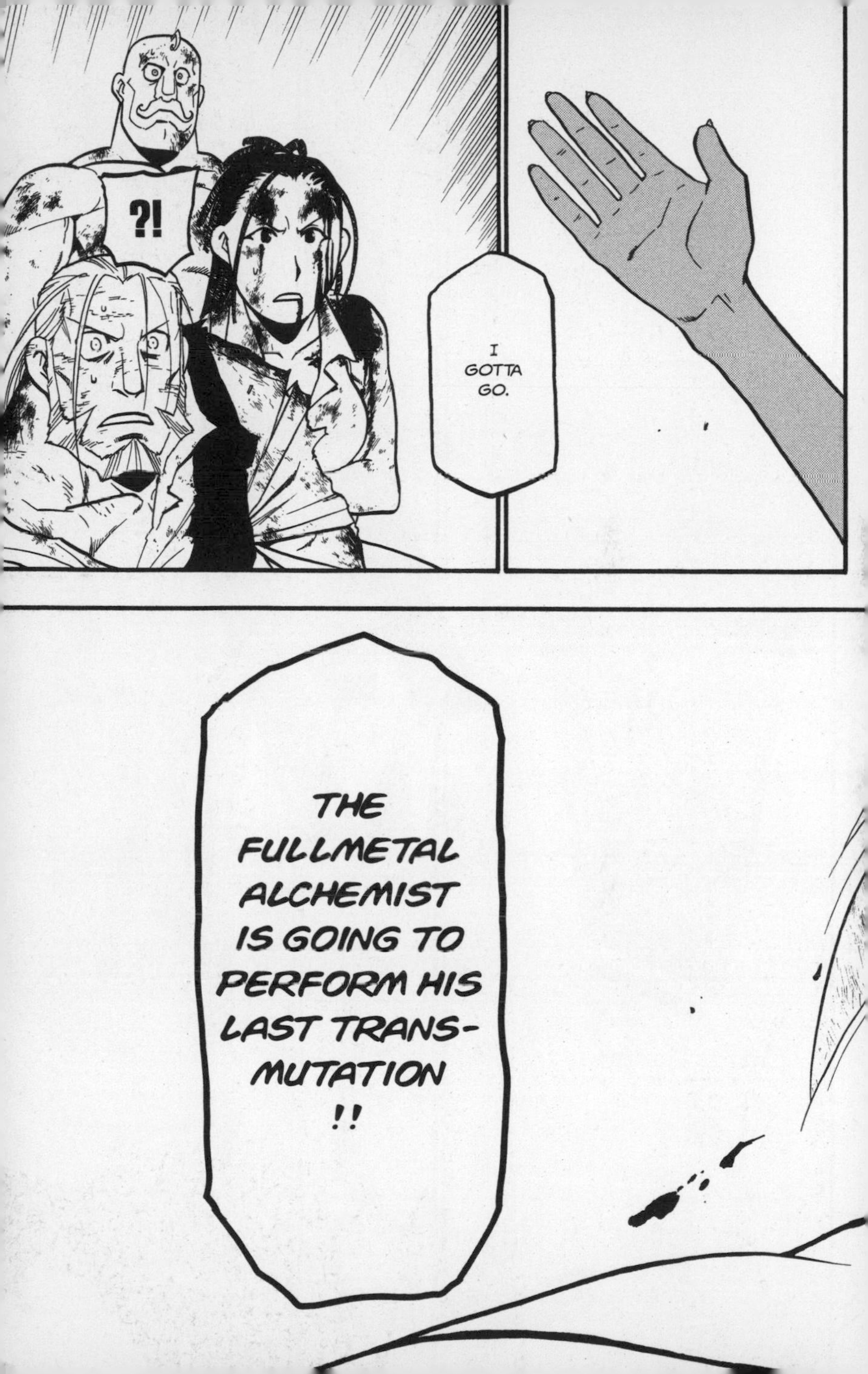
I GOTTA GO.
?!
THE FULLMETAL ALCHEMIST IS GOING TO PERFORM HIS LAST TRANS-MUTATION!!

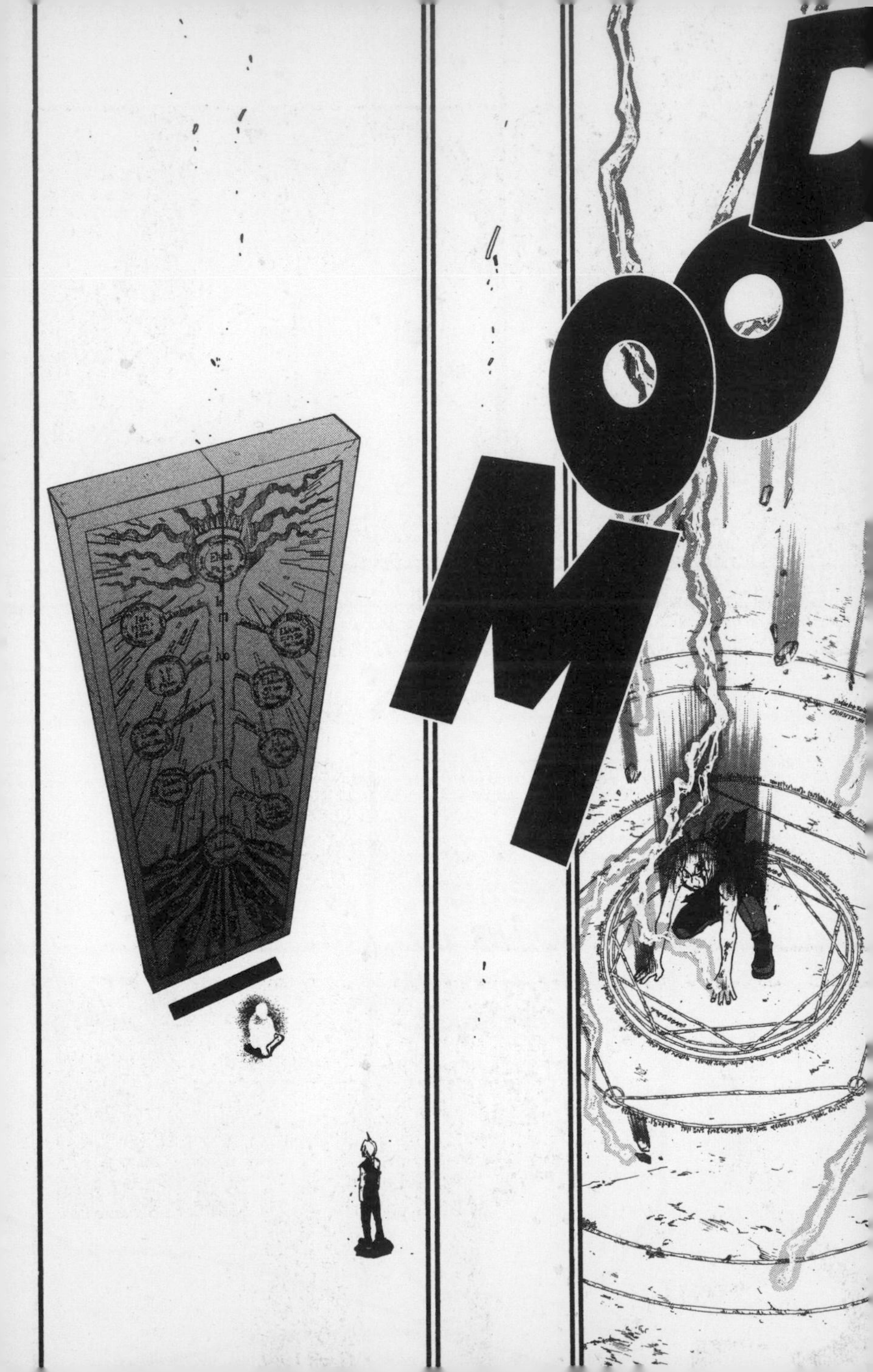
DOOM

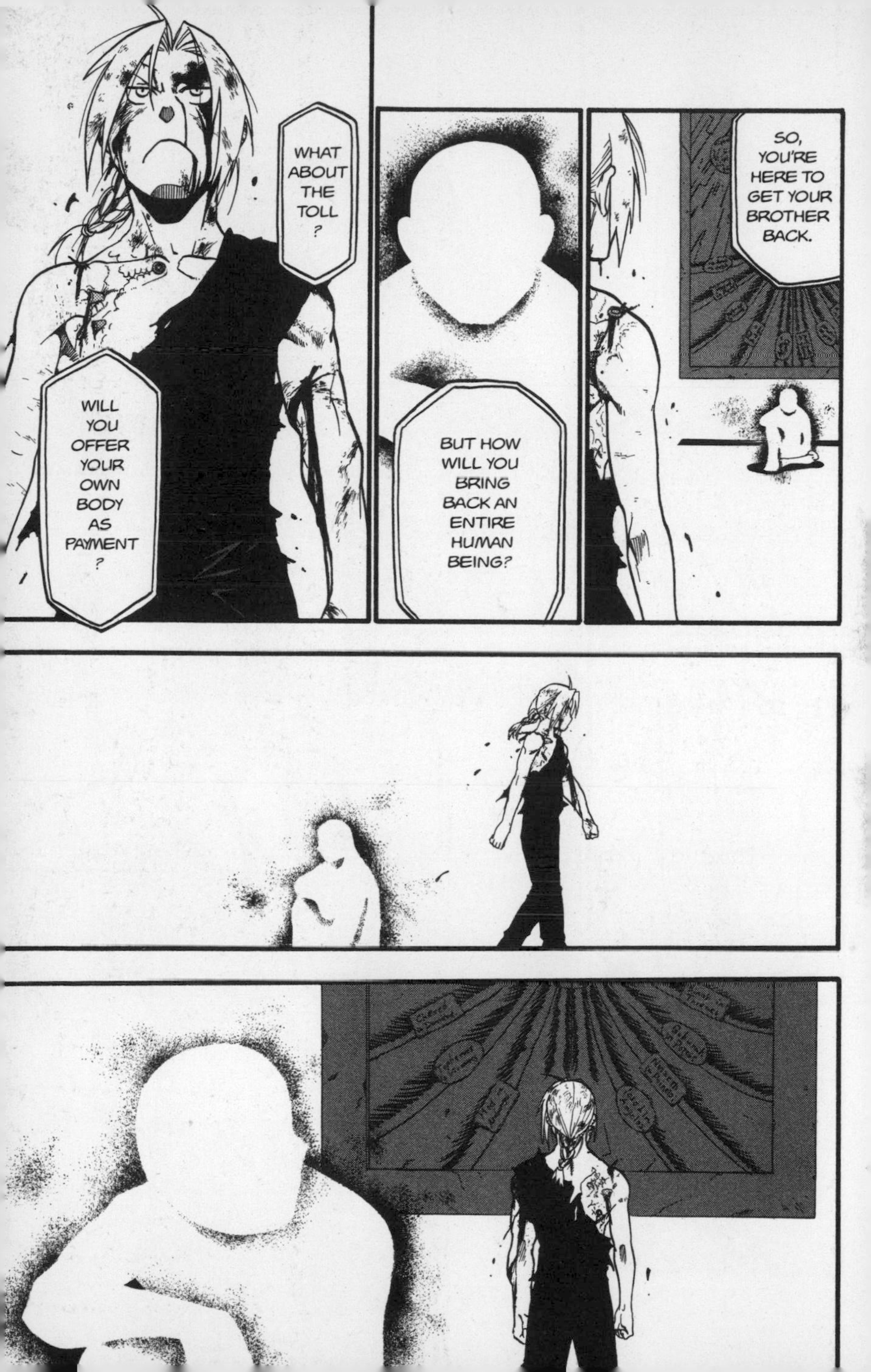
SO, YOU'RE HERE TO GET YOUR BROTHER BACK.
BUT HOW WILL YOU BRING BACK AN ENTIRE HUMAN BEING?
WHAT ABOUT THE TOLL?
WILL YOU OFFER YOUR OWN BODY AS PAYMENT?

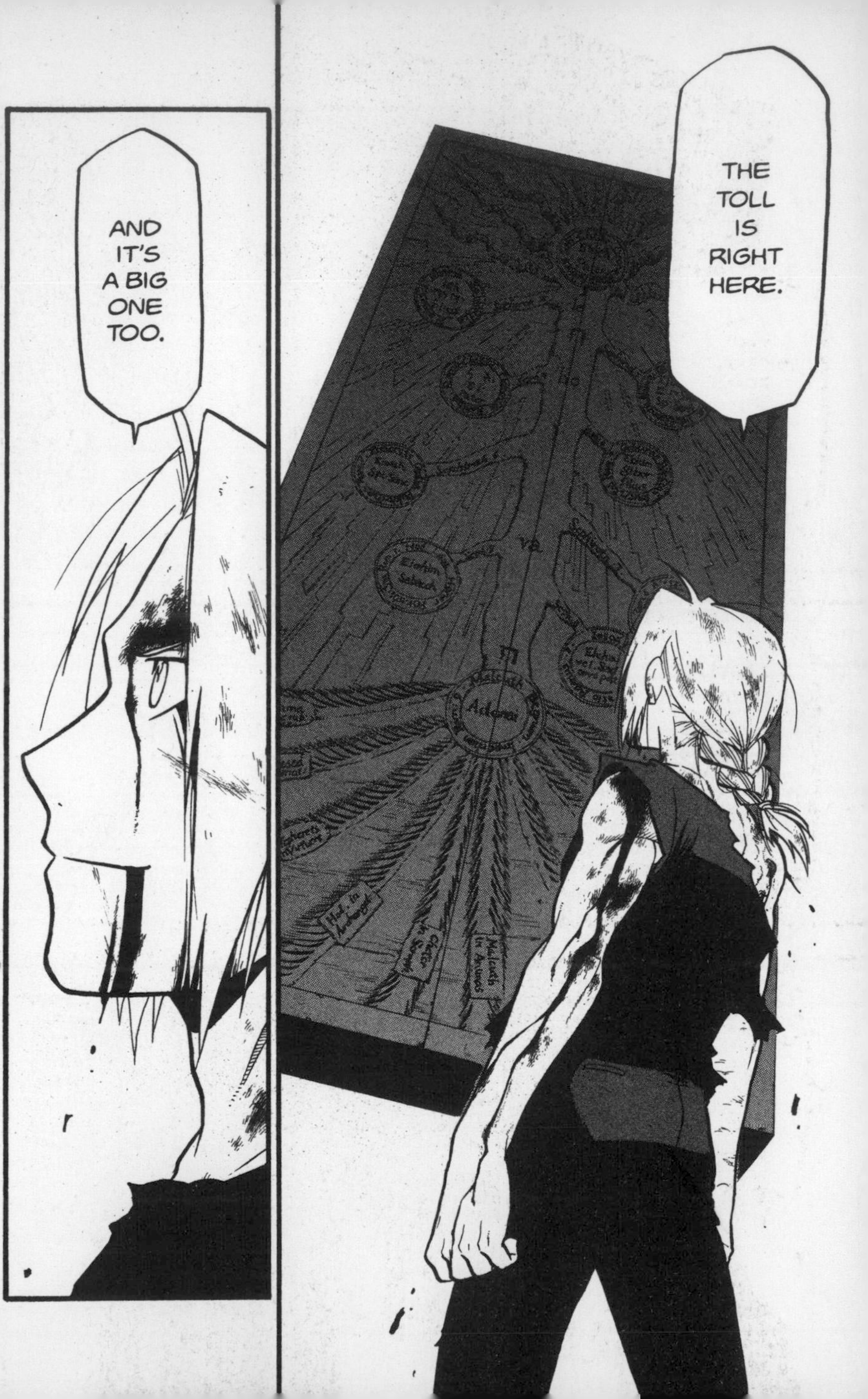
THE TOLL IS RIGHT HERE.
AND IT'S A BIG ONE TOO.

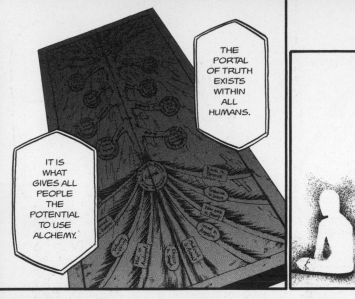

THE PORTAL OF TRUTH EXISTS WITHIN ALL HUMANS.
IT IS WHAT GIVES ALL PEOPLE THE POTENTIAL TO USE ALCHEMY.
WILL YOU REALLY FALL TO THE LEVEL OF AN ***ORDINARY HUMAN***, UNABLE TO USE ALCHEMY?
FALL TO THEIR LEVEL? I'VE NEVER BEEN ANYTHING BUT AN ORDINARY HUMAN.
I'M NOTHING BUT A HOPELESS HUMAN BEING WHO COULDN'T EVEN SAVE ONE LITTLE GIRL WHO WAS TURNED INTO A CHIMERA.
EVER SINCE I SAW THIS THING CALLED TRUTH, I GOT SUCKERED IN BY ITS POWER. I BECAME OVER-CONFIDENT, MAKING MISTAKE AFTER MISTAKE.
IT WAS A WILD RIDE, ALL RIGHT.

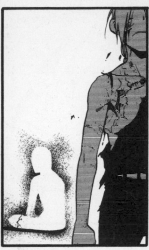

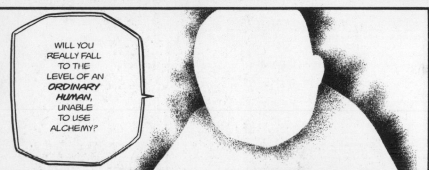

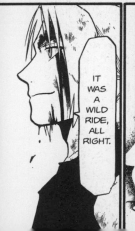

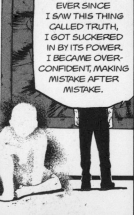

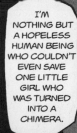

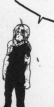

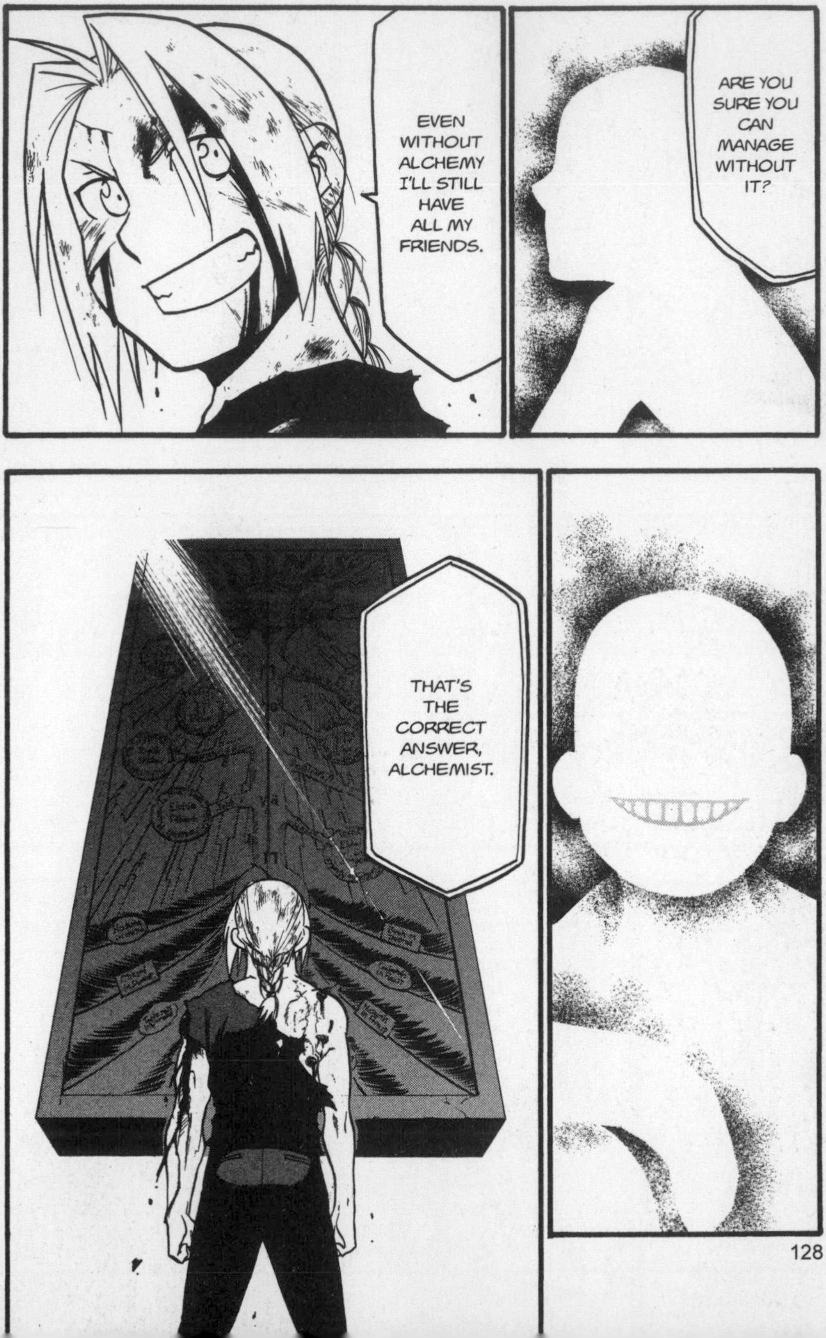
ARE YOU SURE YOU CAN MANAGE WITHOUT IT?
EVEN WITHOUT ALCHEMY I'LL STILL HAVE ALL MY FRIENDS.
THAT'S THE CORRECT ANSWER, ALCHEMIST.

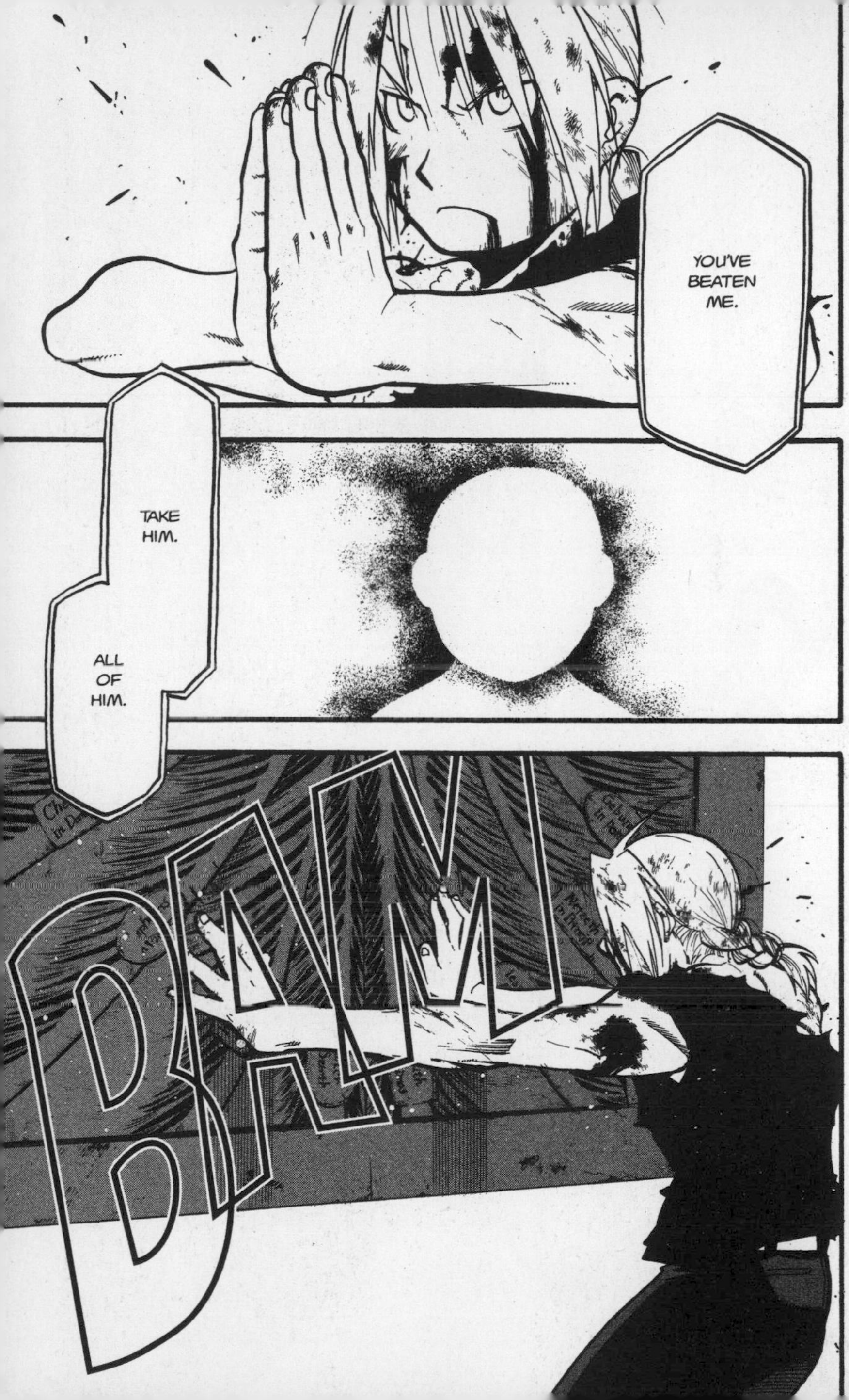
YOU'VE BEATEN ME.
TAKE HIM.
ALL OF HIM.
BAM

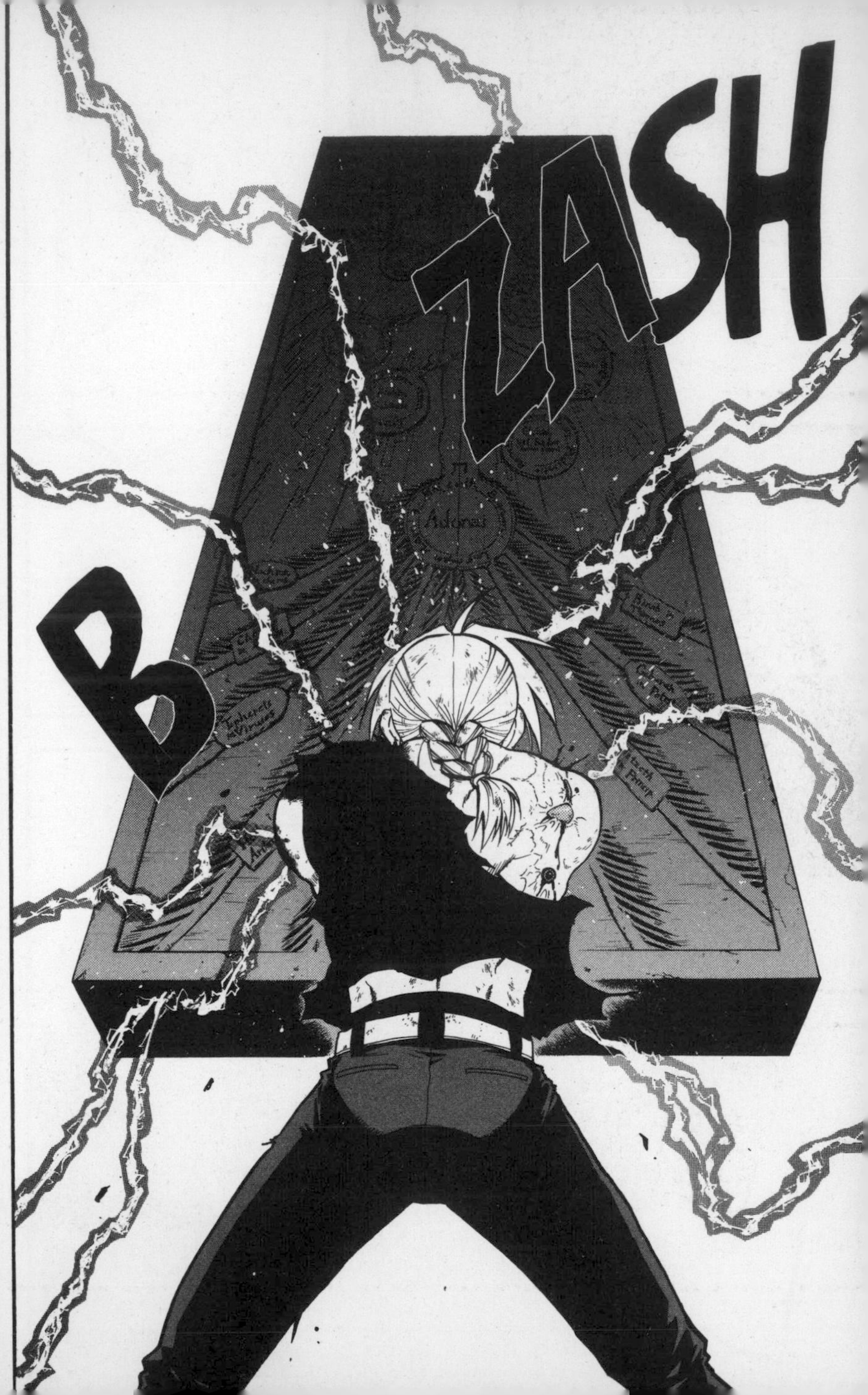
BZASH
Adonai

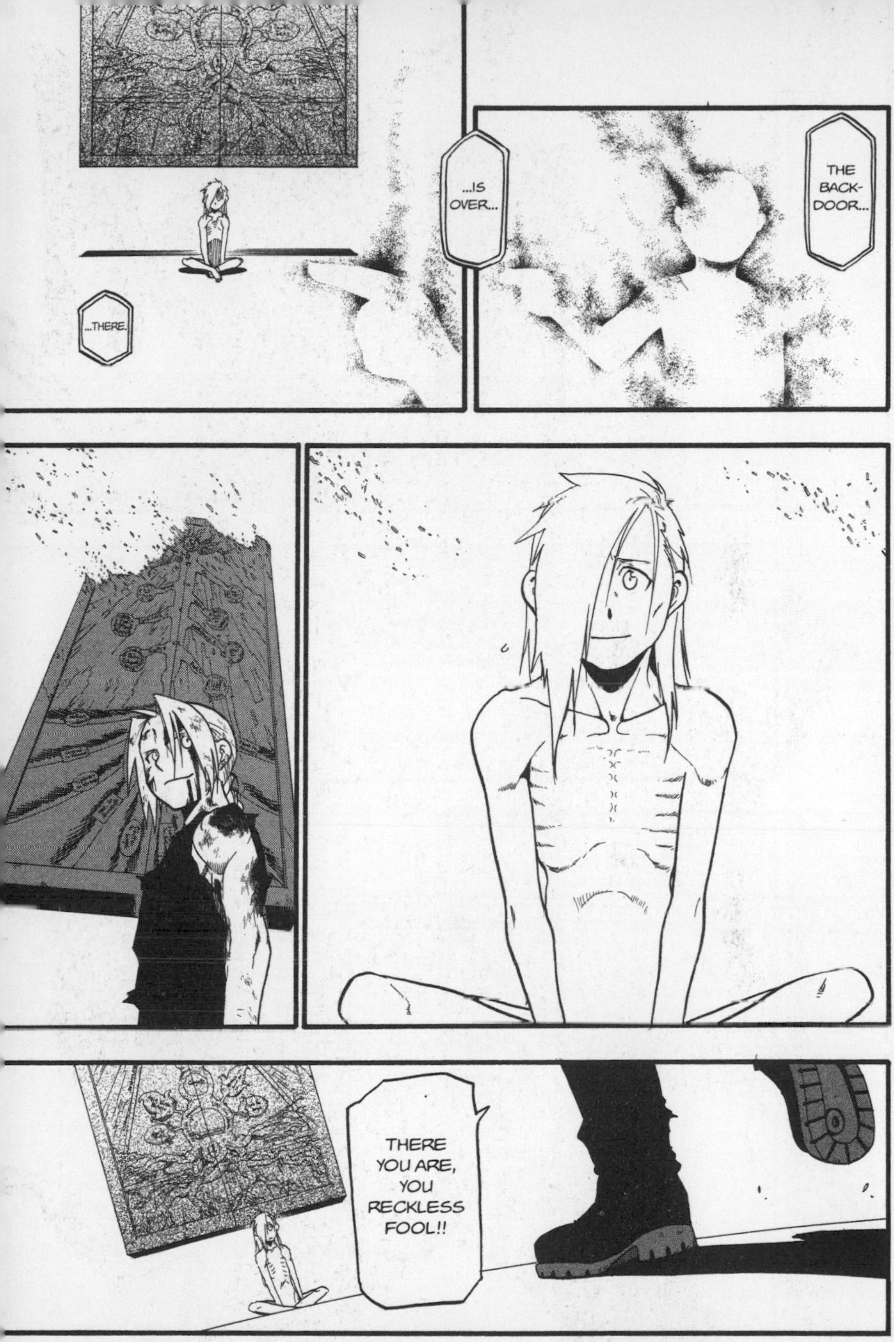
THE BACK-DOOR...
...IS OVER...
...THERE.
THERE YOU ARE, YOU RECKLESS FOOL!!

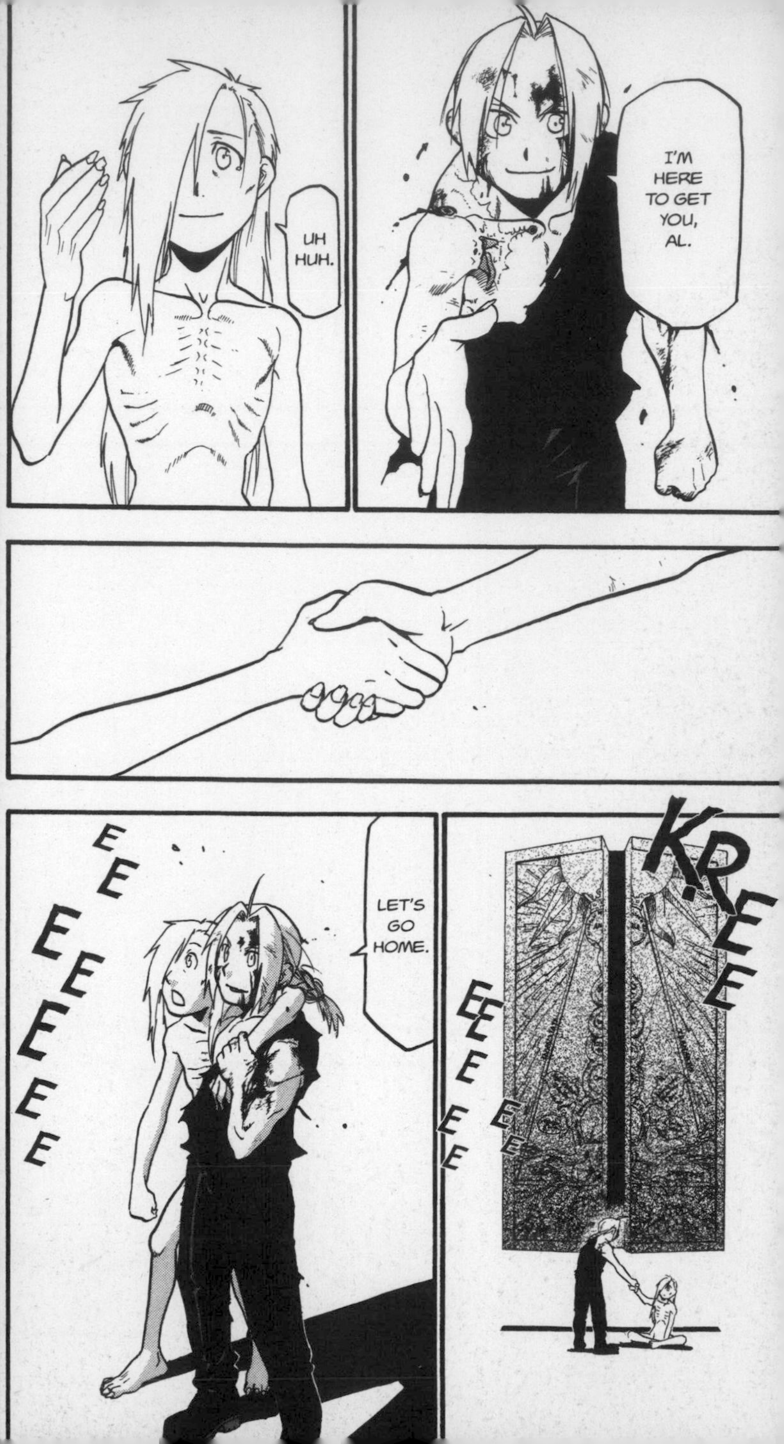

I'M HERE TO GET YOU, AL.
UH HUH.
KREEE
EEEEEEEE
LET'S GO HOME.
EEEEEEEE

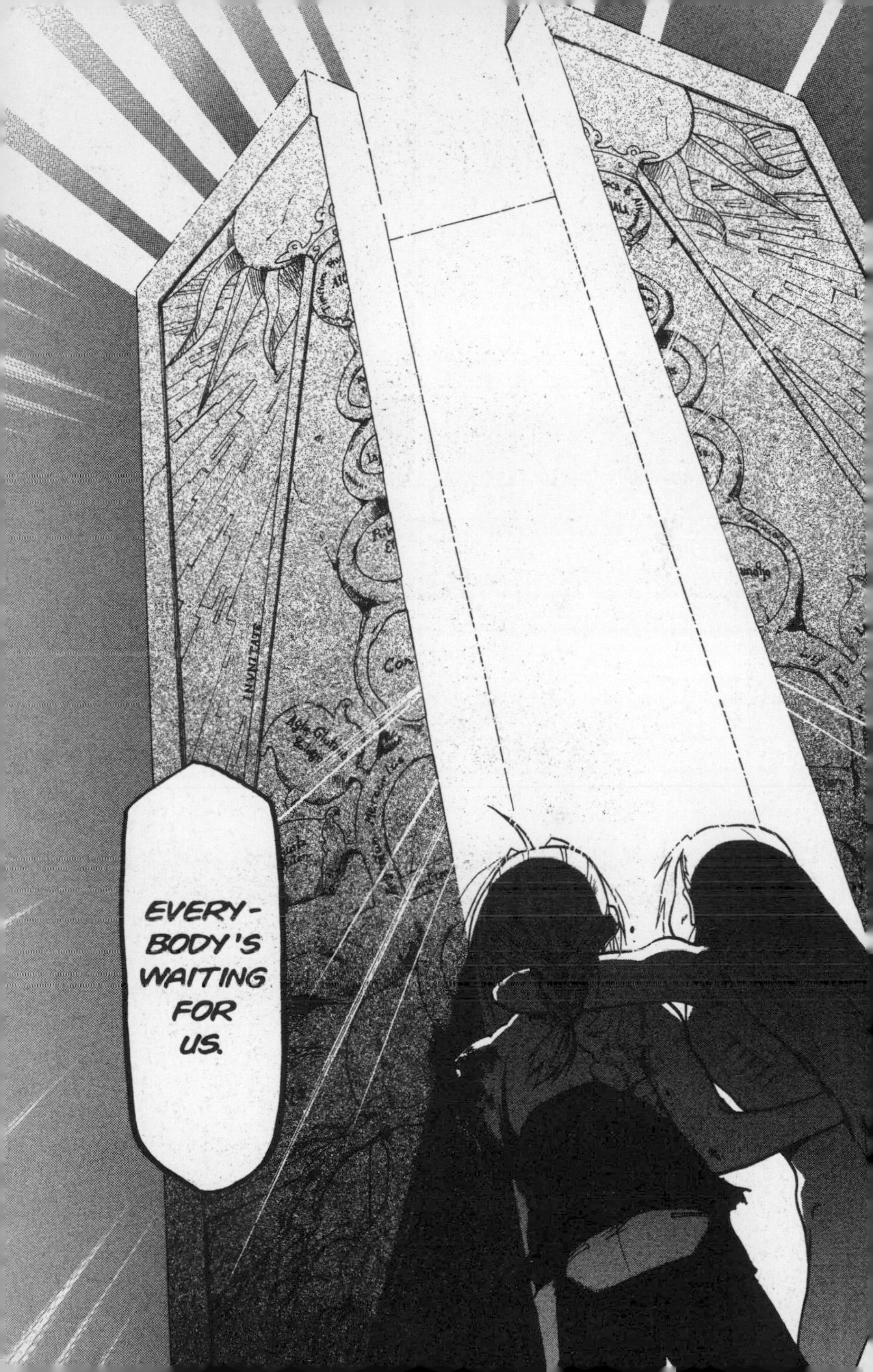
EVERY-BODY'S WAITING FOR US.

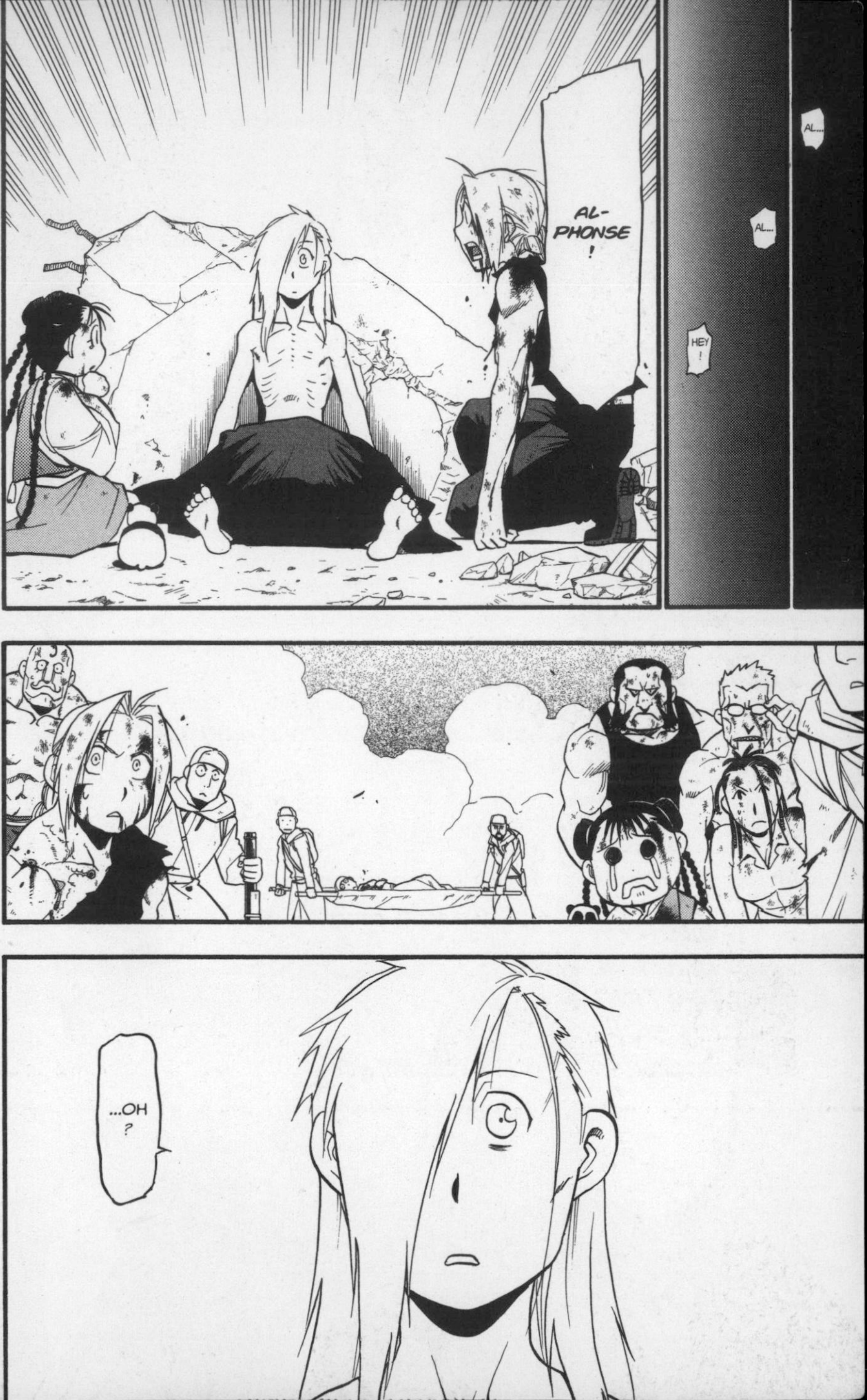
AL...
AL...
HEY!
AL-PHONSE!
...OH?

WHOA!!

GLOM

MR. ALPHONSE!!!

MR...

SNIFFLE

SNIFFLE

I'M SORRY.

I KNOW I PUT YOU THROUGH A LOT.

...

WAAAAAAA

WAAAAA

HEY.

DAD...

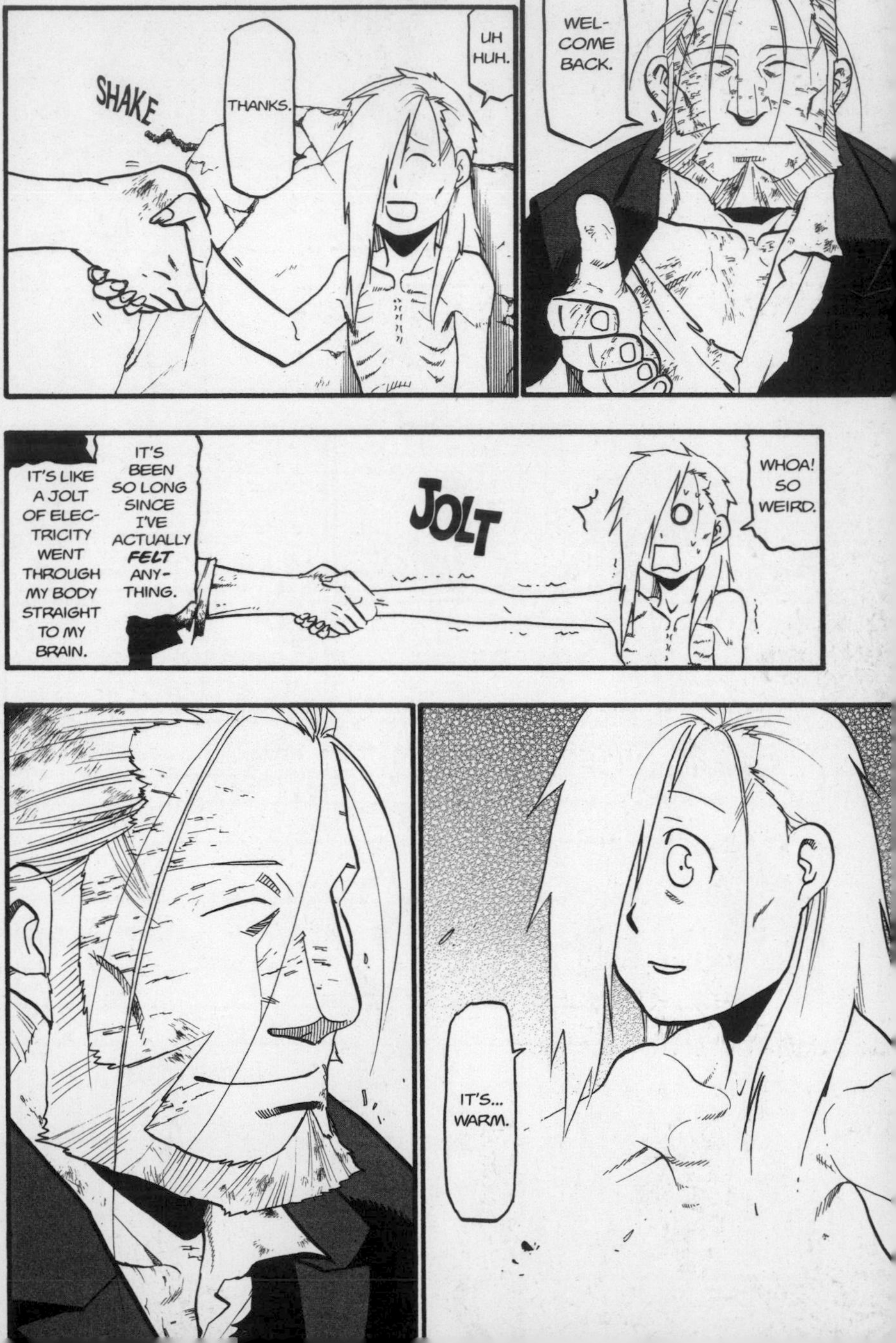
WELCOME BACK.
UH HUH.
THANKS.
SHAKE
WHOA! SO WEIRD.
JOLT
IT'S BEEN SO LONG SINCE I'VE ACTUALLY *FELT* ANYTHING.
IT'S LIKE A JOLT OF ELECTRICITY WENT THROUGH MY BODY STRAIGHT TO MY BRAIN.
IT'S... WARM.

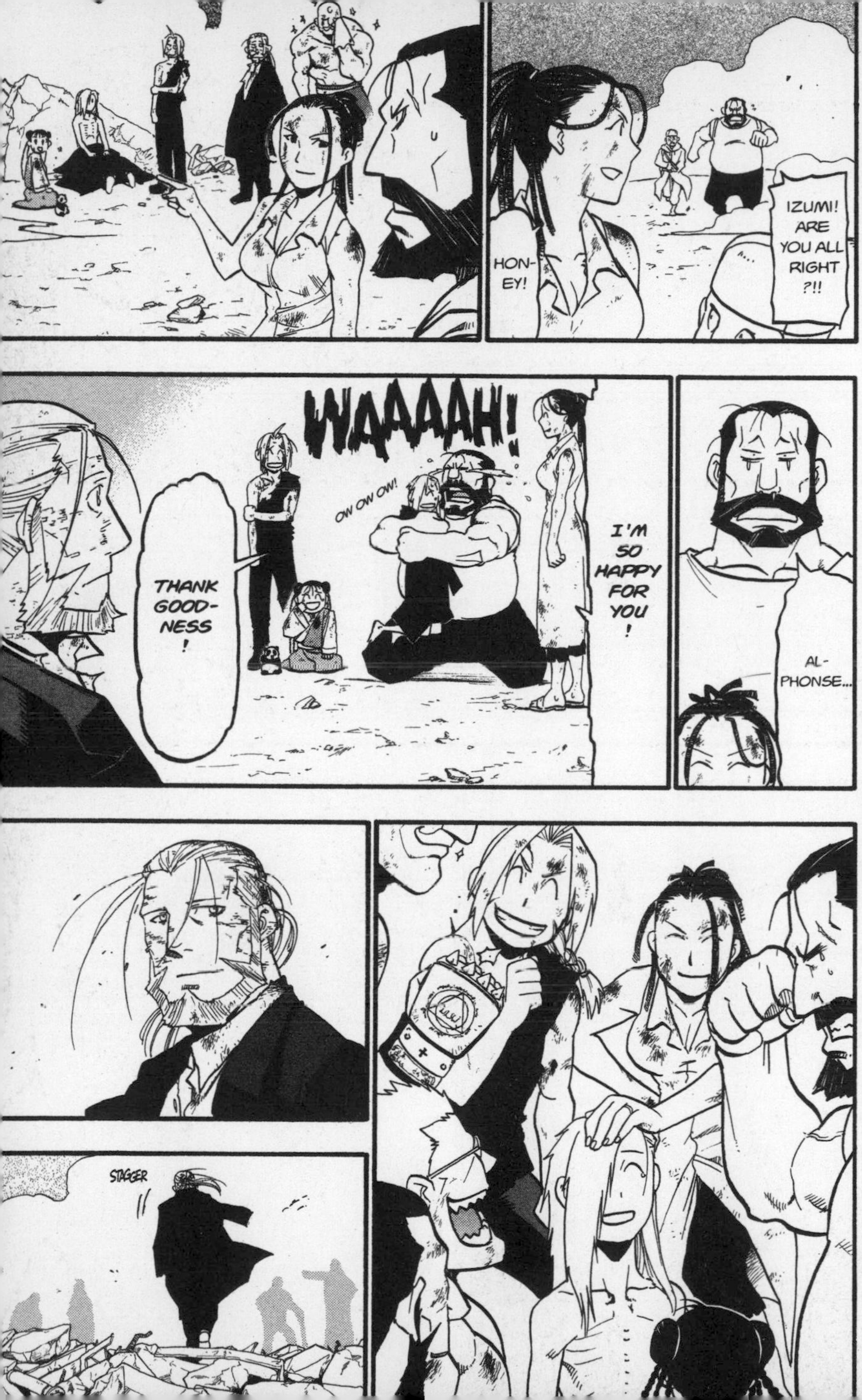
IZUMI! ARE YOU ALL RIGHT?!!
HON-EY!
AL-PHONSE...
WAAAAH!
I'M SO HAPPY FOR YOU!
OW OW OW!
THANK GOOD-NESS!
STAGGER

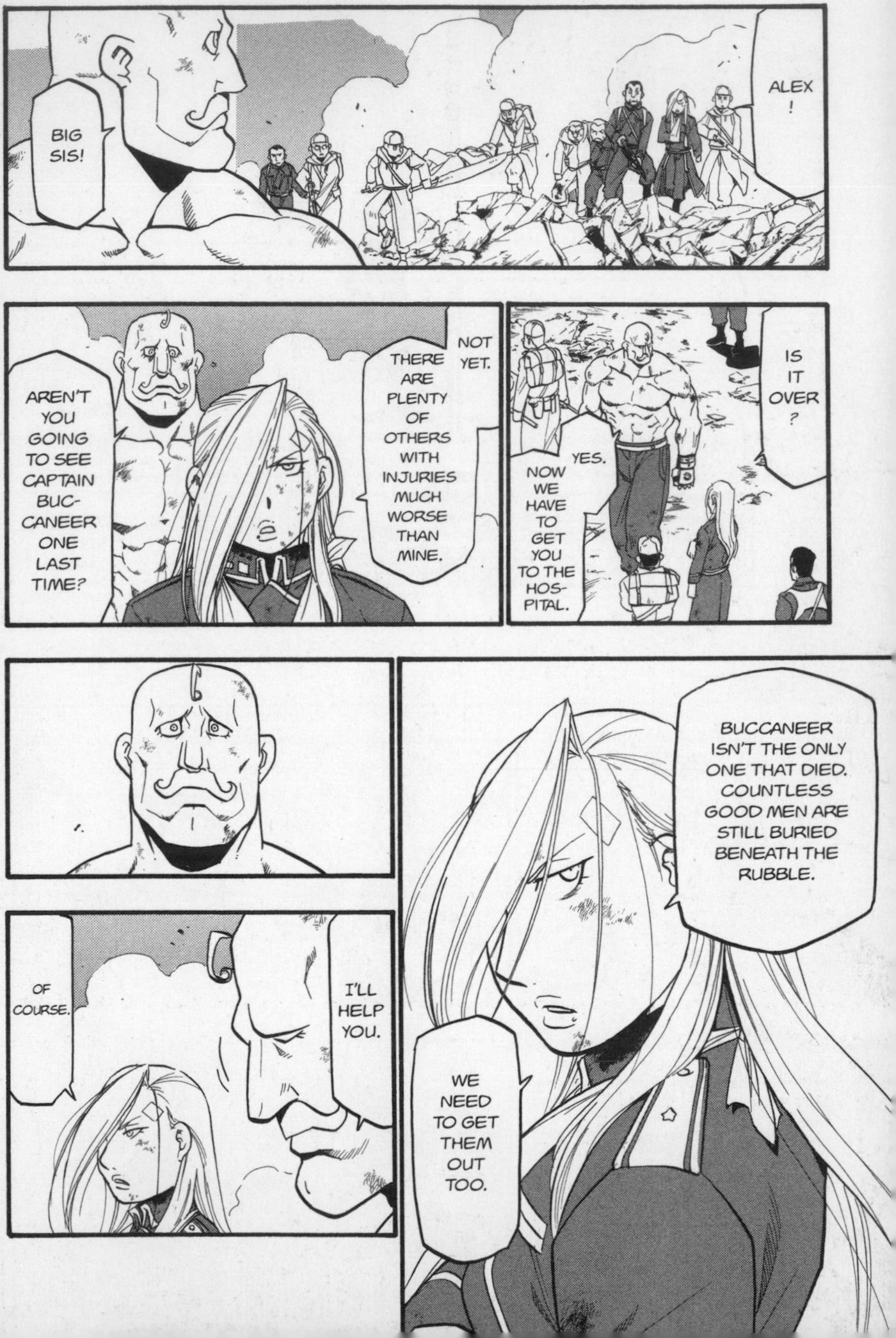
ALEX!
BIG SIS!
IS IT OVER?
YES. NOW WE HAVE TO GET YOU TO THE HOSPITAL.
NOT YET. THERE ARE PLENTY OF OTHERS WITH INJURIES MUCH WORSE THAN MINE.
AREN'T YOU GOING TO SEE CAPTAIN BUCCANEER ONE LAST TIME?
BUCCANEER ISN'T THE ONLY ONE THAT DIED. COUNTLESS GOOD MEN ARE STILL BURIED BENEATH THE RUBBLE.
WE NEED TO GET THEM OUT TOO.
I'LL HELP YOU.
OF COURSE.

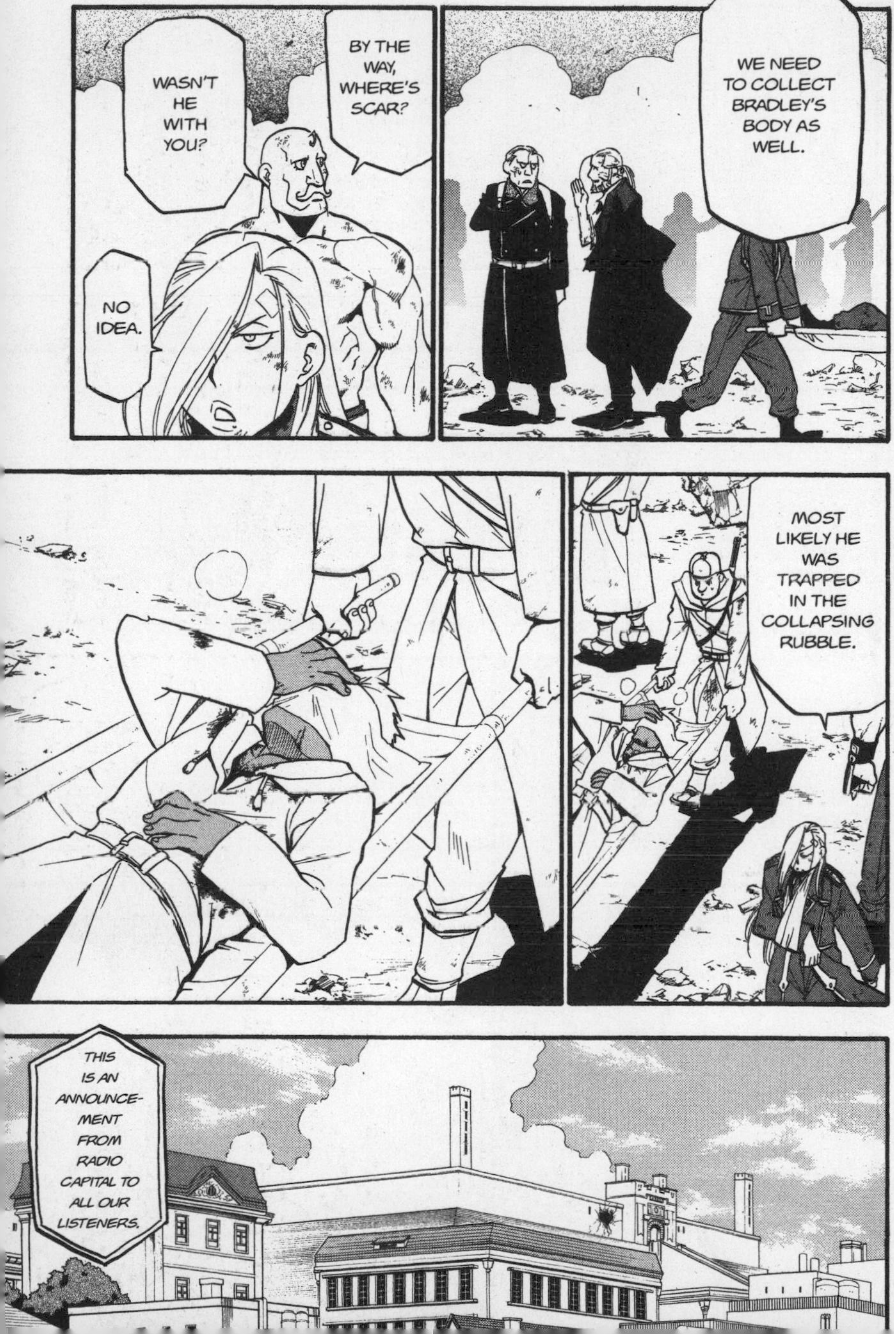
WE NEED TO COLLECT BRADLEY'S BODY AS WELL.
BY THE WAY, WHERE'S SCAR?
WASN'T HE WITH YOU?
NO IDEA.
MOST LIKELY HE WAS TRAPPED IN THE COLLAPSING RUBBLE.
THIS IS AN ANNOUNCE-MENT FROM RADIO CAPITAL TO ALL OUR LISTENERS.

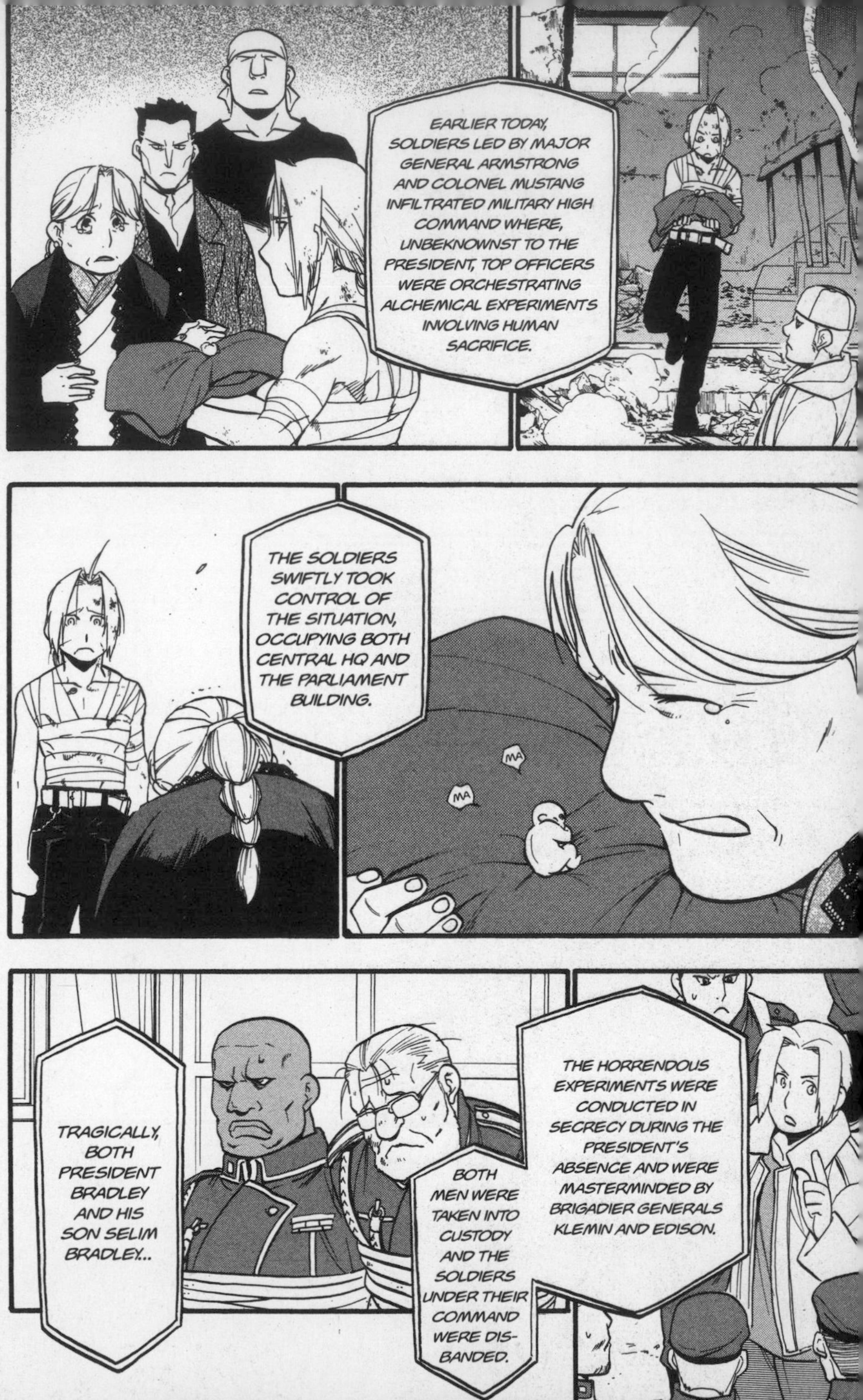
EARLIER TODAY, SOLDIERS LED BY MAJOR GENERAL ARMSTRONG AND COLONEL MUSTANG INFILTRATED MILITARY HIGH COMMAND WHERE, UNBEKNOWNST TO THE PRESIDENT, TOP OFFICERS WERE ORCHESTRATING ALCHEMICAL EXPERIMENTS INVOLVING HUMAN SACRIFICE.
MA
MA
THE SOLDIERS SWIFTLY TOOK CONTROL OF THE SITUATION, OCCUPYING BOTH CENTRAL HQ AND THE PARLIAMENT BUILDING.
THE HORRENDOUS EXPERIMENTS WERE CONDUCTED IN SECRECY DURING THE PRESIDENT'S ABSENCE AND WERE MASTERMINDED BY BRIGADIER GENERALS KLEMIN AND EDISON.
BOTH MEN WERE TAKEN INTO CUSTODY AND THE SOLDIERS UNDER THEIR COMMAND WERE DIS-BANDED.
TRAGICALLY, BOTH PRESIDENT BRADLEY AND HIS SON SELIM BRADLEY...

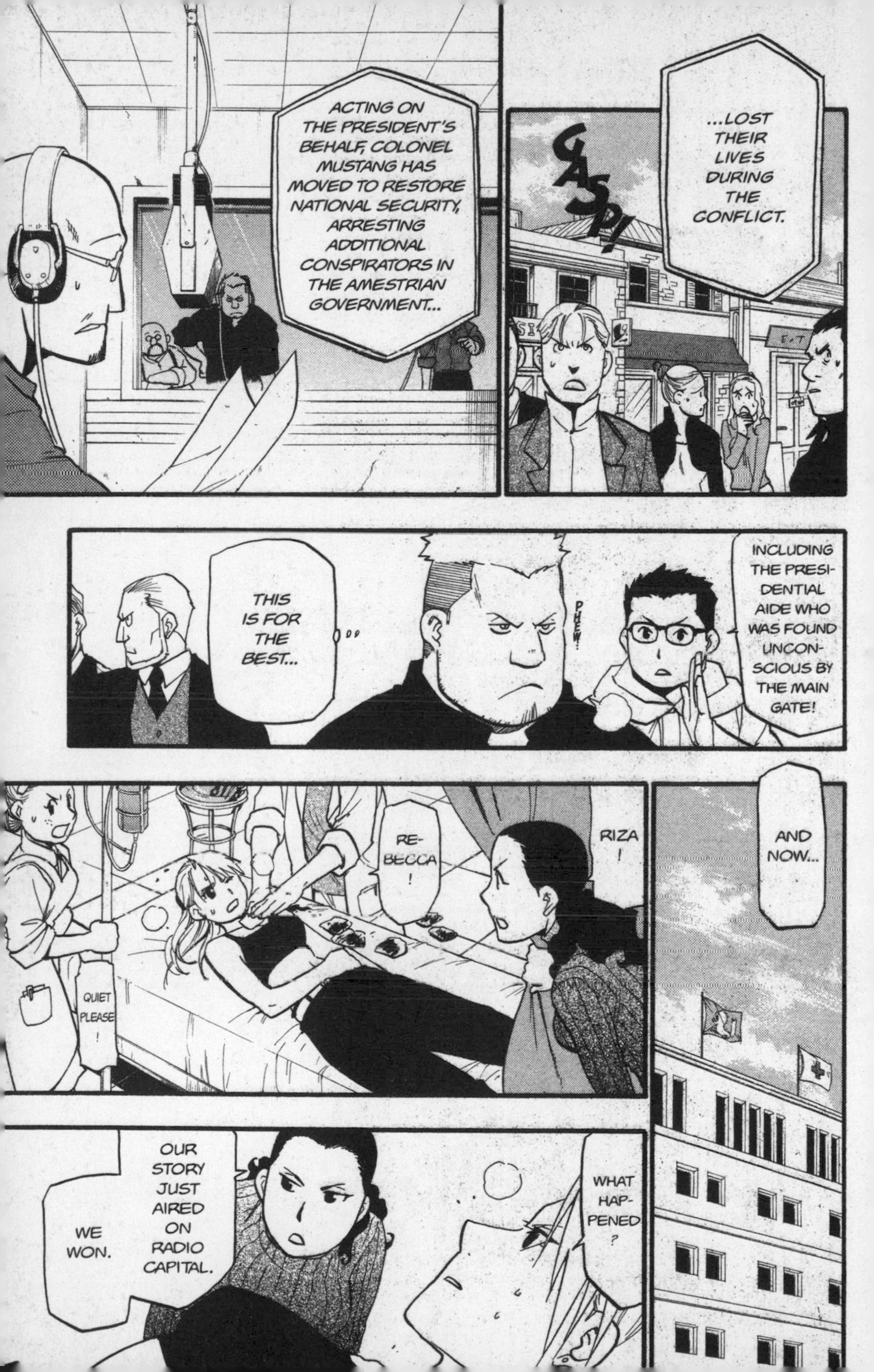
...LOST THEIR LIVES DURING THE CONFLICT.
GASP!
ACTING ON THE PRESIDENT'S BEHALF, COLONEL MUSTANG HAS MOVED TO RESTORE NATIONAL SECURITY, ARRESTING ADDITIONAL CONSPIRATORS IN THE AMESTRIAN GOVERNMENT...
INCLUDING THE PRESIDENTIAL AIDE WHO WAS FOUND UNCONSCIOUS BY THE MAIN GATE!
PHEW!
THIS IS FOR THE BEST...
AND NOW...
RIZA!
REBECCA!
QUIET PLEASE!
WHAT HAPPENED?
OUR STORY JUST AIRED ON RADIO CAPITAL.
WE WON.

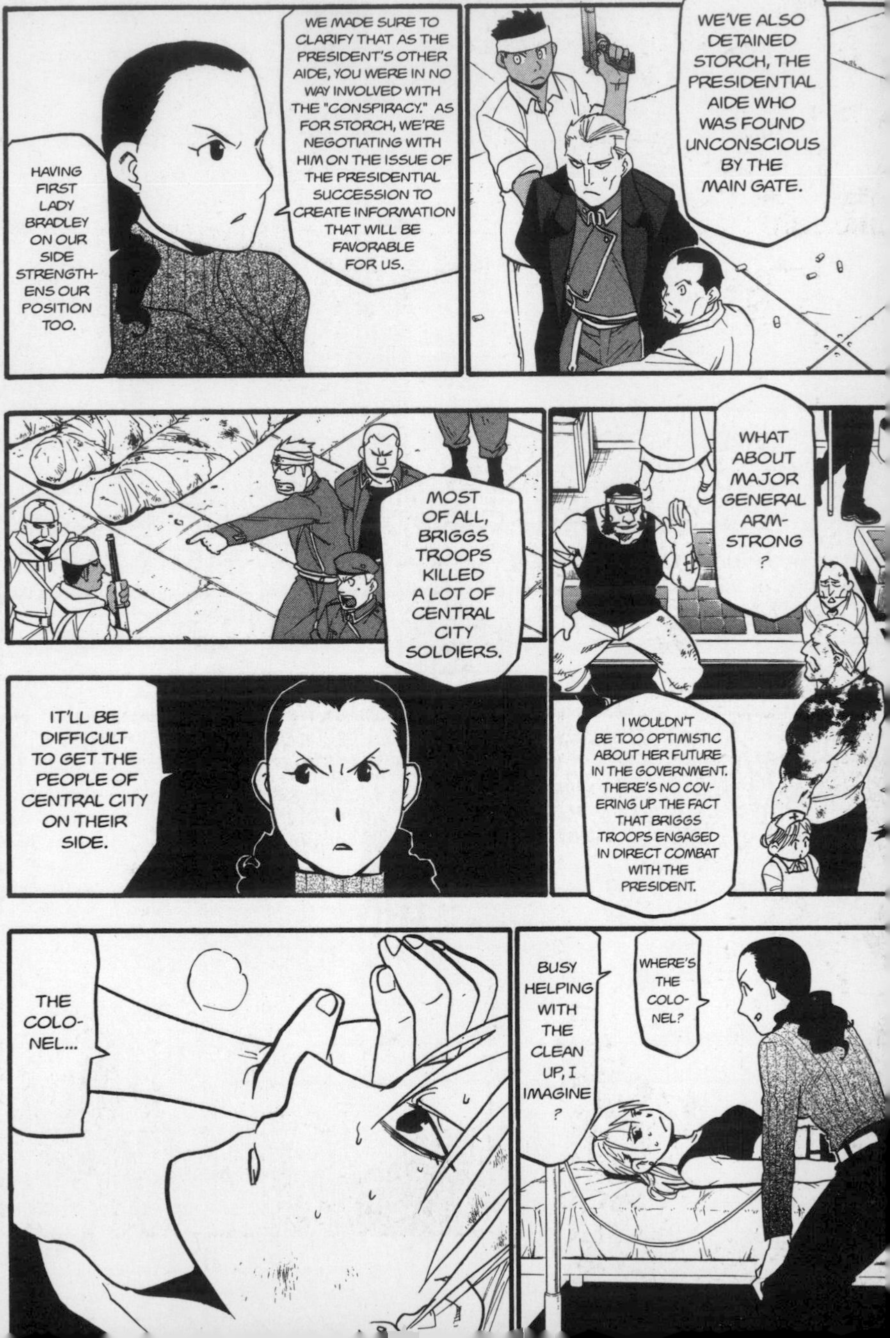
WE'VE ALSO DETAINED STORCH, THE PRESIDENTIAL AIDE WHO WAS FOUND UNCONSCIOUS BY THE MAIN GATE.
WE MADE SURE TO CLARIFY THAT AS THE PRESIDENT'S OTHER AIDE, YOU WERE IN NO WAY INVOLVED WITH THE "CONSPIRACY." AS FOR STORCH, WE'RE NEGOTIATING WITH HIM ON THE ISSUE OF THE PRESIDENTIAL SUCCESSION TO CREATE INFORMATION THAT WILL BE FAVORABLE FOR US.
HAVING FIRST LADY BRADLEY ON OUR SIDE STRENGTHENS OUR POSITION TOO.
WHAT ABOUT MAJOR GENERAL ARMSTRONG?
I WOULDN'T BE TOO OPTIMISTIC ABOUT HER FUTURE IN THE GOVERNMENT. THERE'S NO COVERING UP THE FACT THAT BRIGGS TROOPS ENGAGED IN DIRECT COMBAT WITH THE PRESIDENT.
MOST OF ALL, BRIGGS TROOPS KILLED A LOT OF CENTRAL CITY SOLDIERS.
IT'LL BE DIFFICULT TO GET THE PEOPLE OF CENTRAL CITY ON THEIR SIDE.
WHERE'S THE COLONEL?
BUSY HELPING WITH THE CLEAN UP, I IMAGINE?
THE COLONEL...

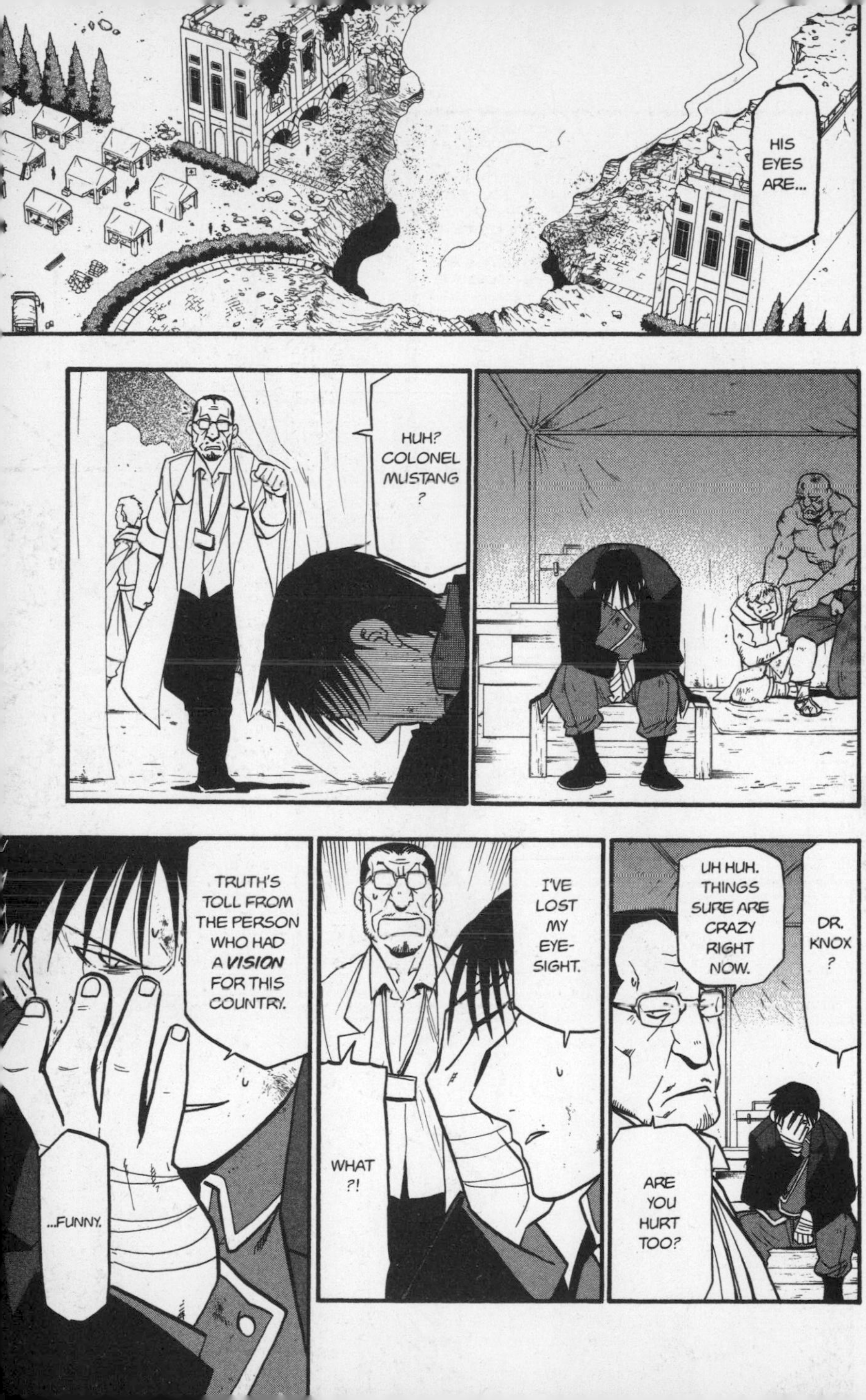
HIS EYES ARE...
HUH? COLONEL MUSTANG ?
DR. KNOX ?
UH HUH. THINGS SURE ARE CRAZY RIGHT NOW.
ARE YOU HURT TOO?
I'VE LOST MY EYE-SIGHT.
WHAT ?!
TRUTH'S TOLL FROM THE PERSON WHO HAD A VISION FOR THIS COUNTRY.
...FUNNY.

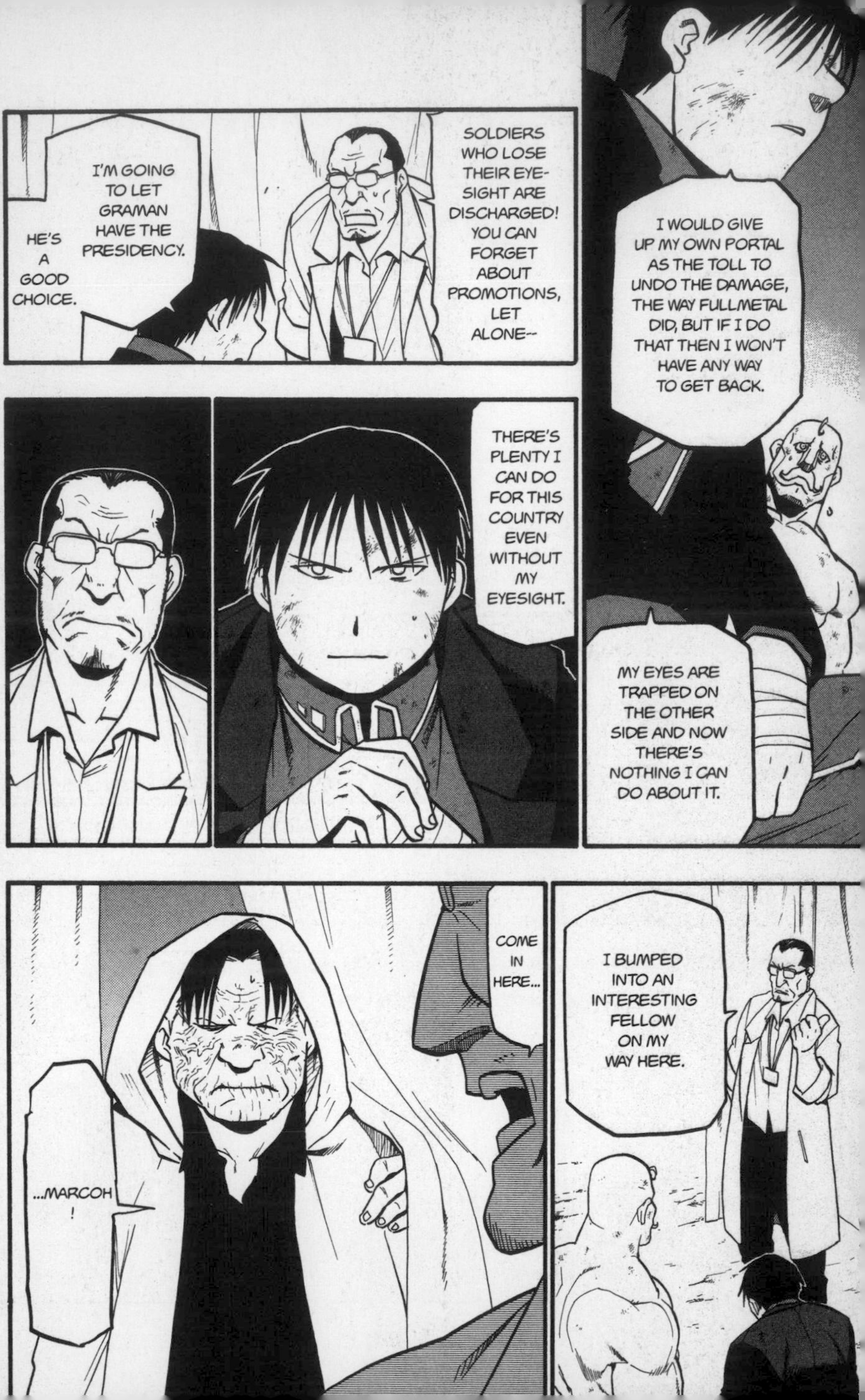
I WOULD GIVE UP MY OWN PORTAL AS THE TOLL TO UNDO THE DAMAGE, THE WAY FULLMETAL DID, BUT IF I DO THAT THEN I WON'T HAVE ANY WAY TO GET BACK.
MY EYES ARE TRAPPED ON THE OTHER SIDE AND NOW THERE'S NOTHING I CAN DO ABOUT IT.
SOLDIERS WHO LOSE THEIR EYE-SIGHT ARE DISCHARGED! YOU CAN FORGET ABOUT PROMOTIONS, LET ALONE--
I'M GOING TO LET GRAMAN HAVE THE PRESIDENCY.
HE'S A GOOD CHOICE.
THERE'S PLENTY I CAN DO FOR THIS COUNTRY EVEN WITHOUT MY EYESIGHT.
I BUMPED INTO AN INTERESTING FELLOW ON MY WAY HERE.
COME IN HERE...
...MARCOH!

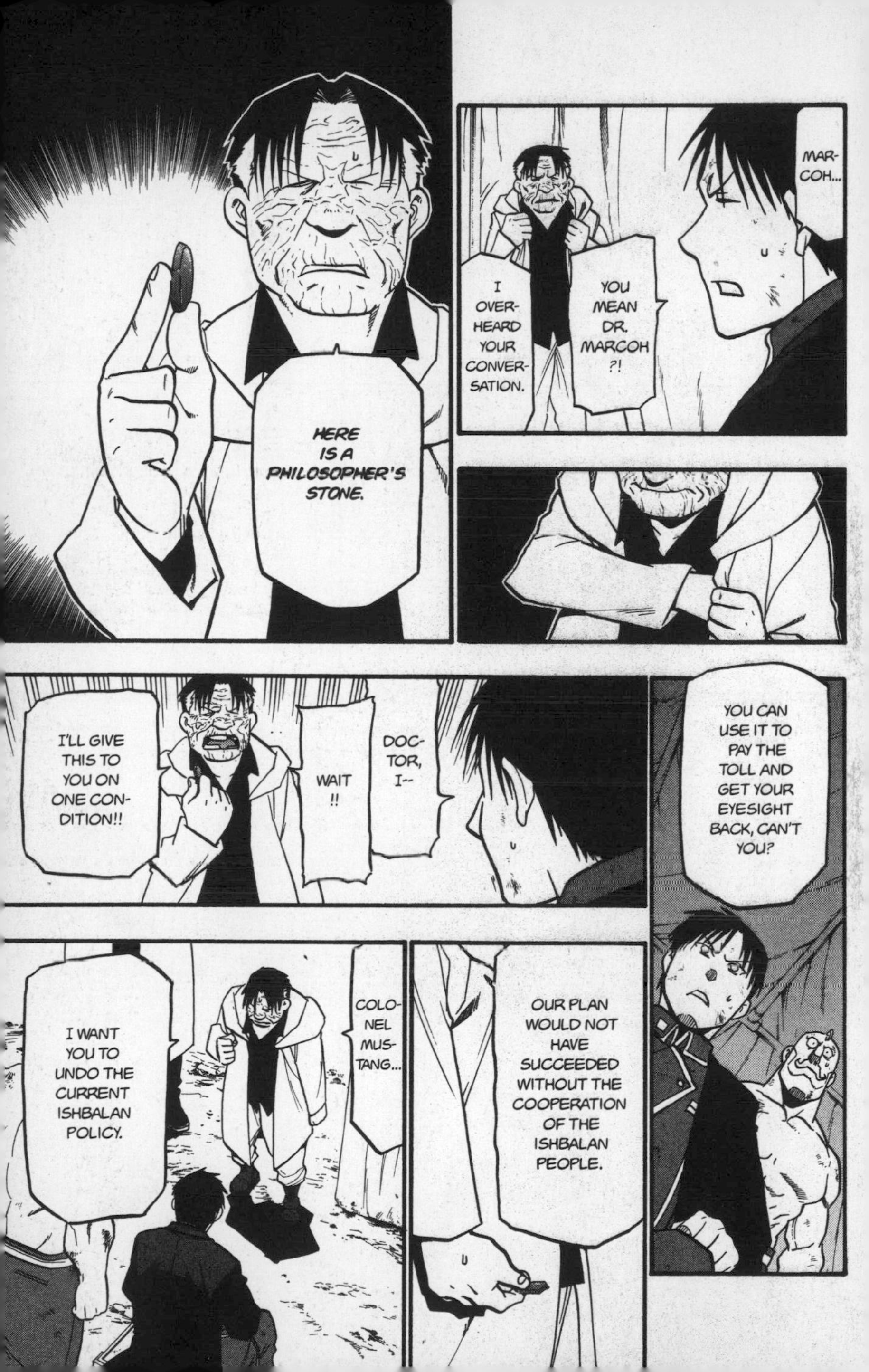

MAR-COH...
YOU MEAN DR. MARCOH?!
I OVERHEARD YOUR CONVERSATION.
HERE IS A PHILOSOPHER'S STONE.
YOU CAN USE IT TO PAY THE TOLL AND GET YOUR EYESIGHT BACK, CAN'T YOU?
DOCTOR, I--
WAIT!!
I'LL GIVE THIS TO YOU ON ONE CONDITION!!
OUR PLAN WOULD NOT HAVE SUCCEEDED WITHOUT THE COOPERATION OF THE ISHBALAN PEOPLE.
COLONEL MUSTANG...
I WANT YOU TO UNDO THE CURRENT ISHBALAN POLICY.

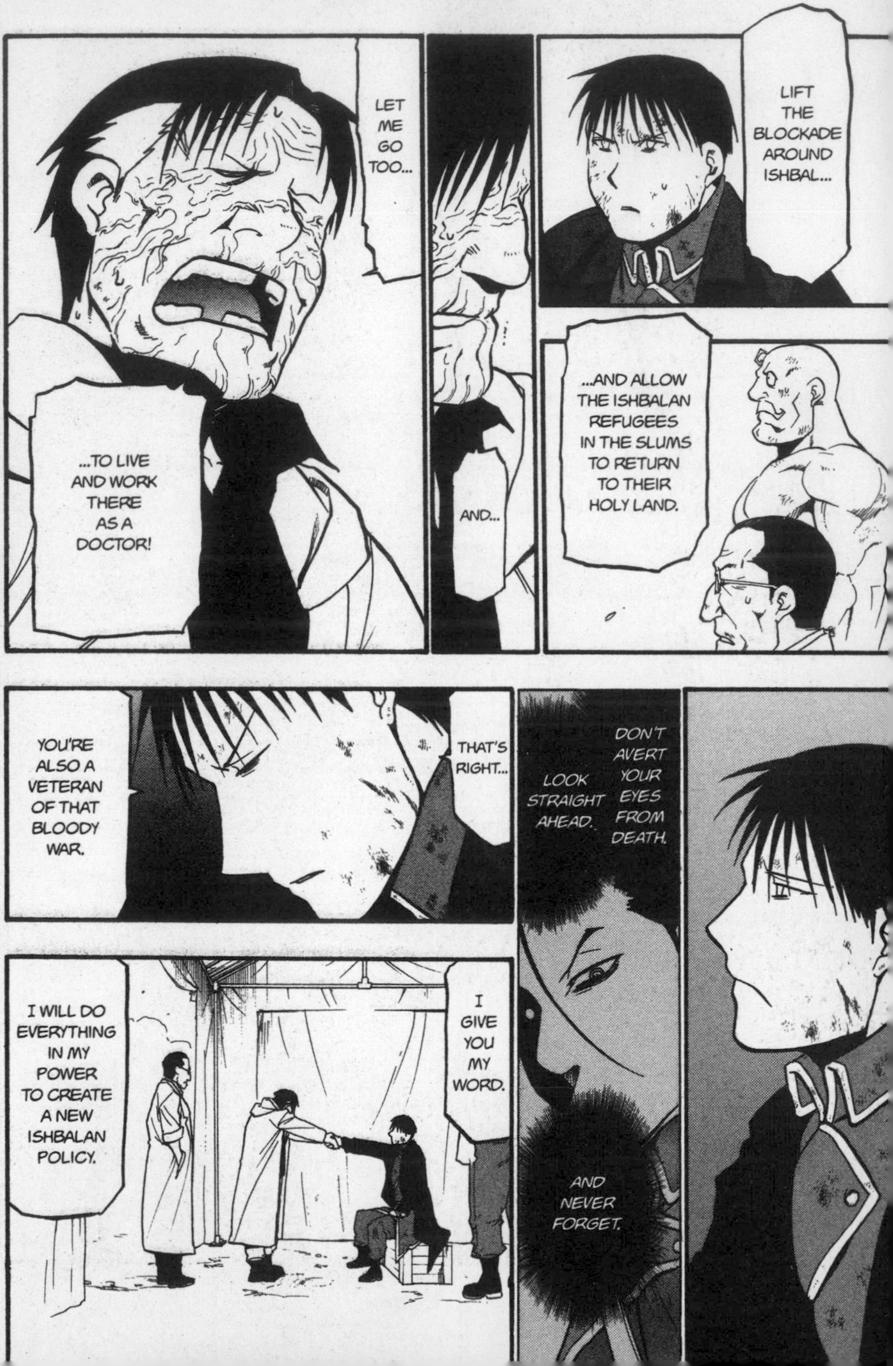
LIFT THE BLOCKADE AROUND ISHBAL...
...AND ALLOW THE ISHBALAN REFUGEES IN THE SLUMS TO RETURN TO THEIR HOLY LAND.
AND...
LET ME GO TOO...
...TO LIVE AND WORK THERE AS A DOCTOR!
DON'T AVERT YOUR EYES FROM DEATH.
LOOK STRAIGHT AHEAD.
AND NEVER FORGET.
THAT'S RIGHT...
YOU'RE ALSO A VETERAN OF THAT BLOODY WAR.
I GIVE YOU MY WORD.
I WILL DO EVERYTHING IN MY POWER TO CREATE A NEW ISHBALAN POLICY.

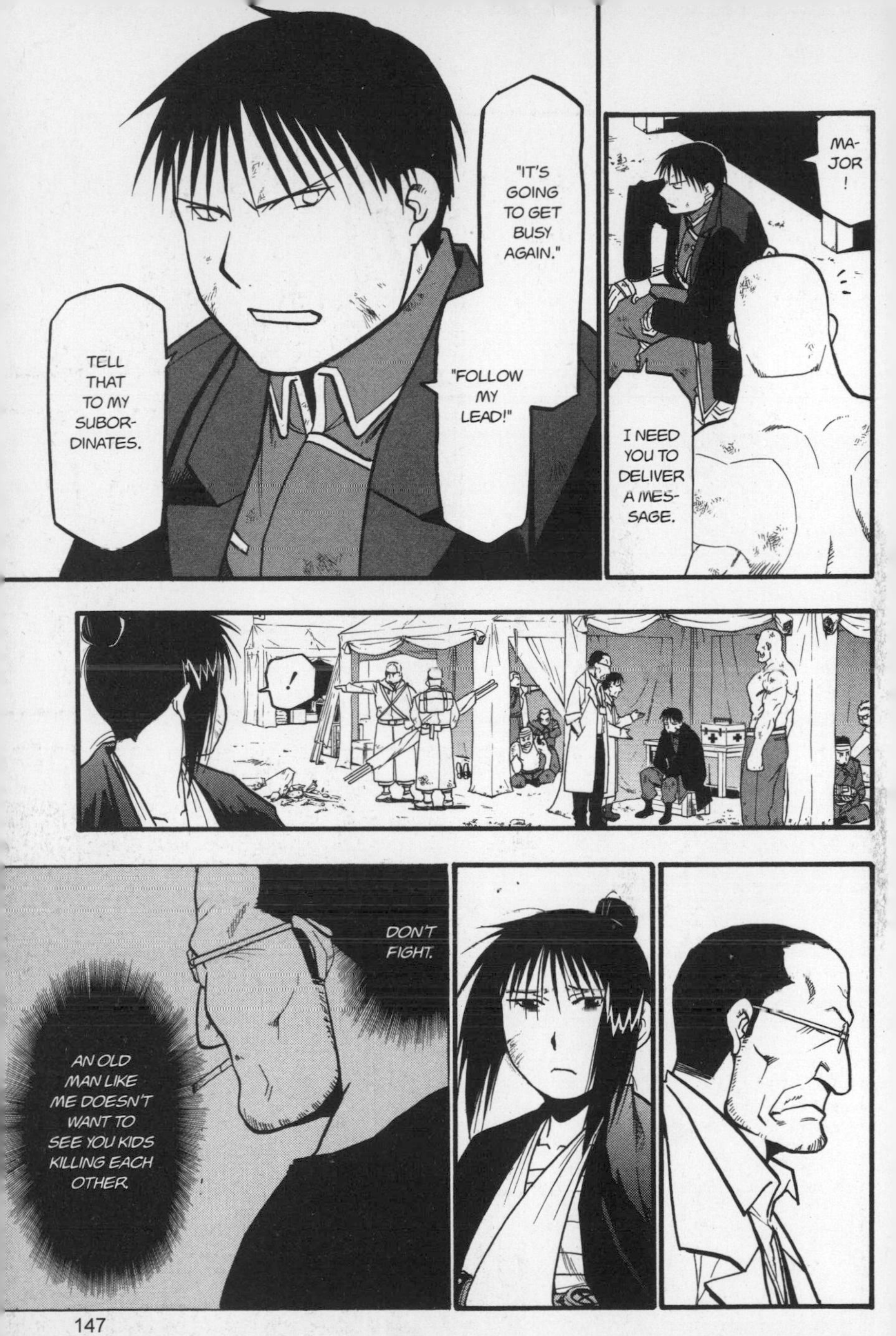
MAJOR!
I NEED YOU TO DELIVER A MESSAGE.
"IT'S GOING TO GET BUSY AGAIN."
"FOLLOW MY LEAD!"
TELL THAT TO MY SUBORDINATES.
!
DON'T FIGHT.
AN OLD MAN LIKE ME DOESN'T WANT TO SEE YOU KIDS KILLING EACH OTHER.

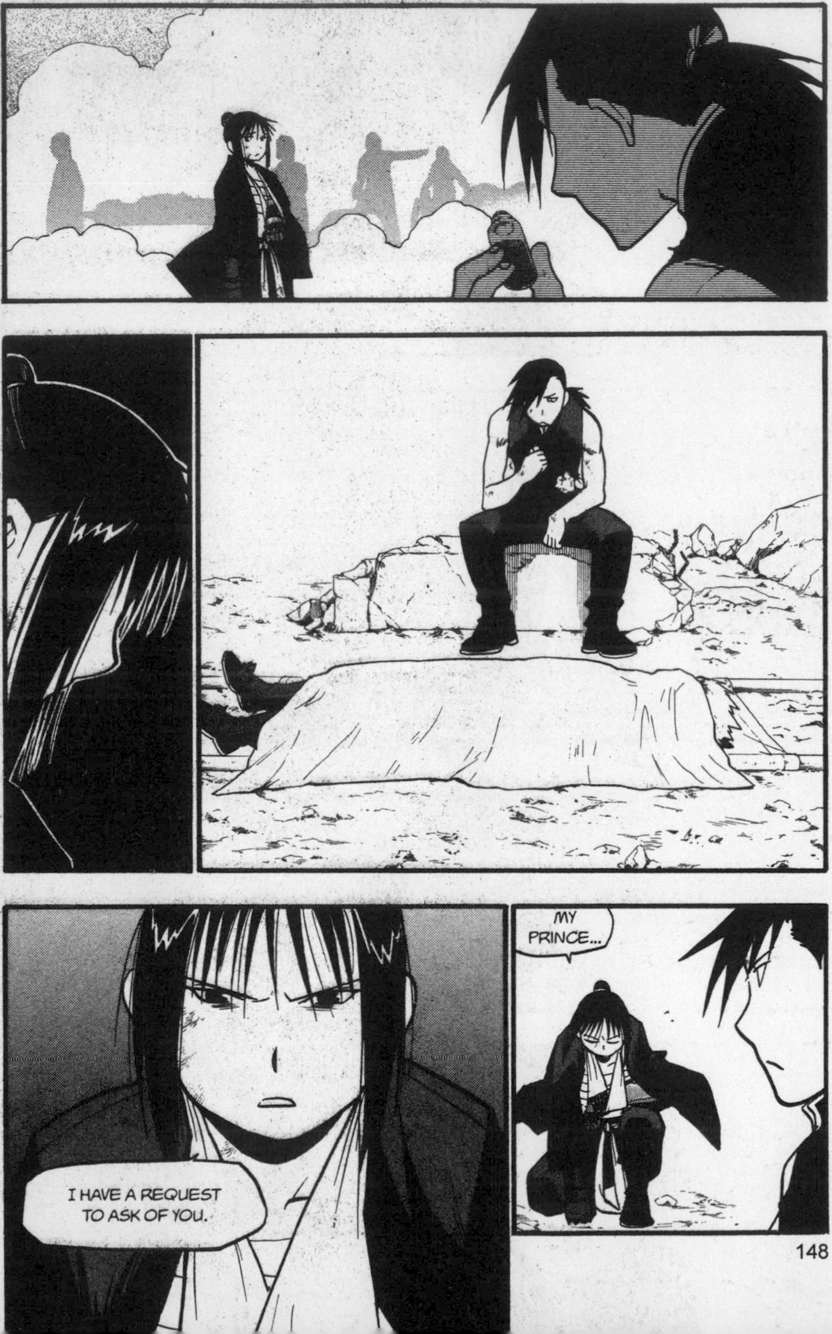
MY PRINCE...
I HAVE A REQUEST TO ASK OF YOU.

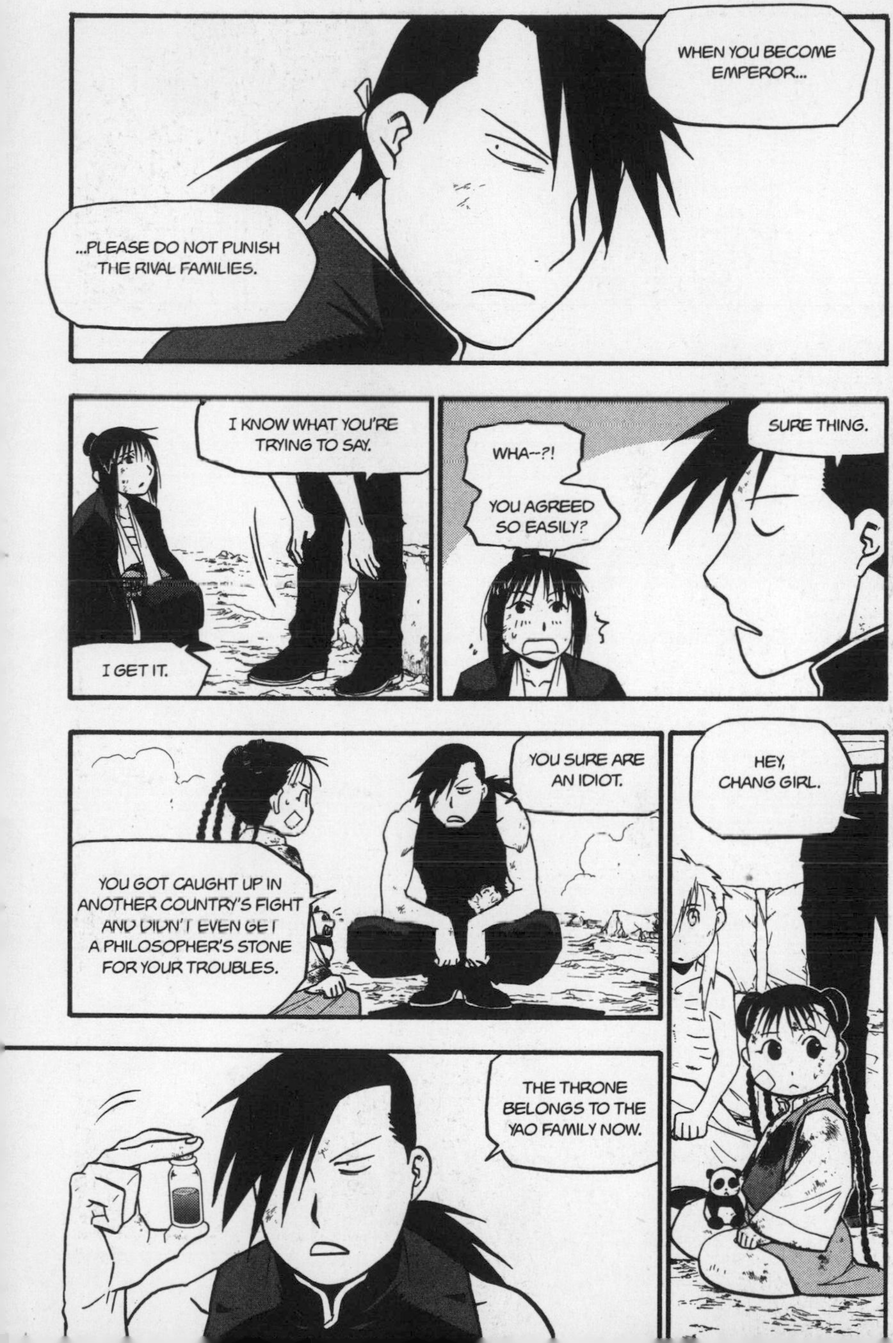
WHEN YOU BECOME EMPEROR...
...PLEASE DO NOT PUNISH THE RIVAL FAMILIES.
SURE THING.
WHA--?!
YOU AGREED SO EASILY?
I KNOW WHAT YOU'RE TRYING TO SAY.
I GET IT.
HEY, CHANG GIRL.
YOU SURE ARE AN IDIOT.
YOU GOT CAUGHT UP IN ANOTHER COUNTRY'S FIGHT AND DIDN'T EVEN GET A PHILOSOPHER'S STONE FOR YOUR TROUBLES.
THE THRONE BELONGS TO THE YAO FAMILY NOW.

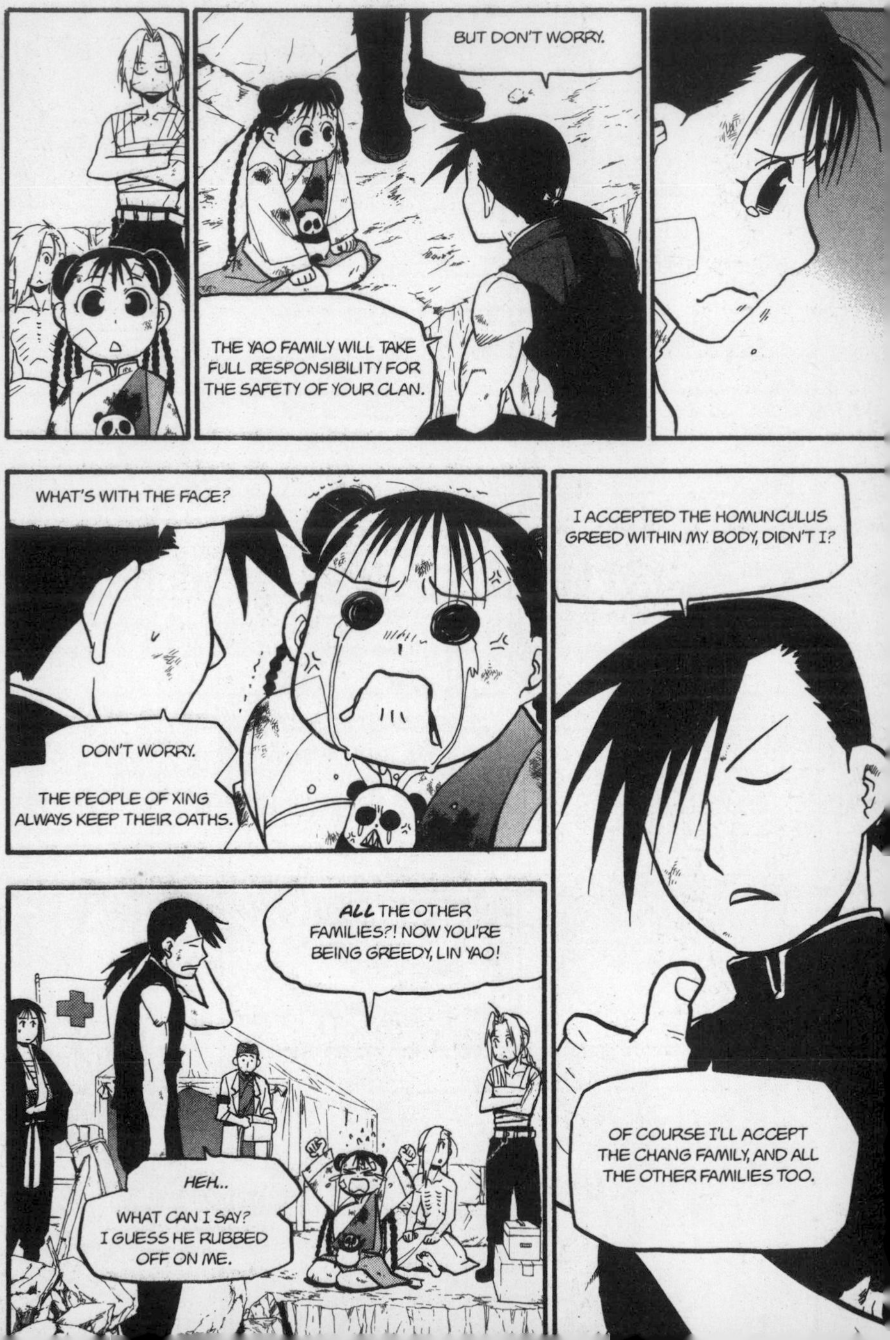
BUT DON'T WORRY.
THE YAO FAMILY WILL TAKE FULL RESPONSIBILITY FOR THE SAFETY OF YOUR CLAN.
I ACCEPTED THE HOMUNCULUS GREED WITHIN MY BODY, DIDN'T I?
OF COURSE I'LL ACCEPT THE CHANG FAMILY, AND ALL THE OTHER FAMILIES TOO.
WHAT'S WITH THE FACE?
DON'T WORRY.
THE PEOPLE OF XING ALWAYS KEEP THEIR OATHS.
ALL THE OTHER FAMILIES?! NOW YOU'RE BEING GREEDY, LIN YAO!
HEH..
WHAT CAN I SAY? I GUESS HE RUBBED OFF ON ME.

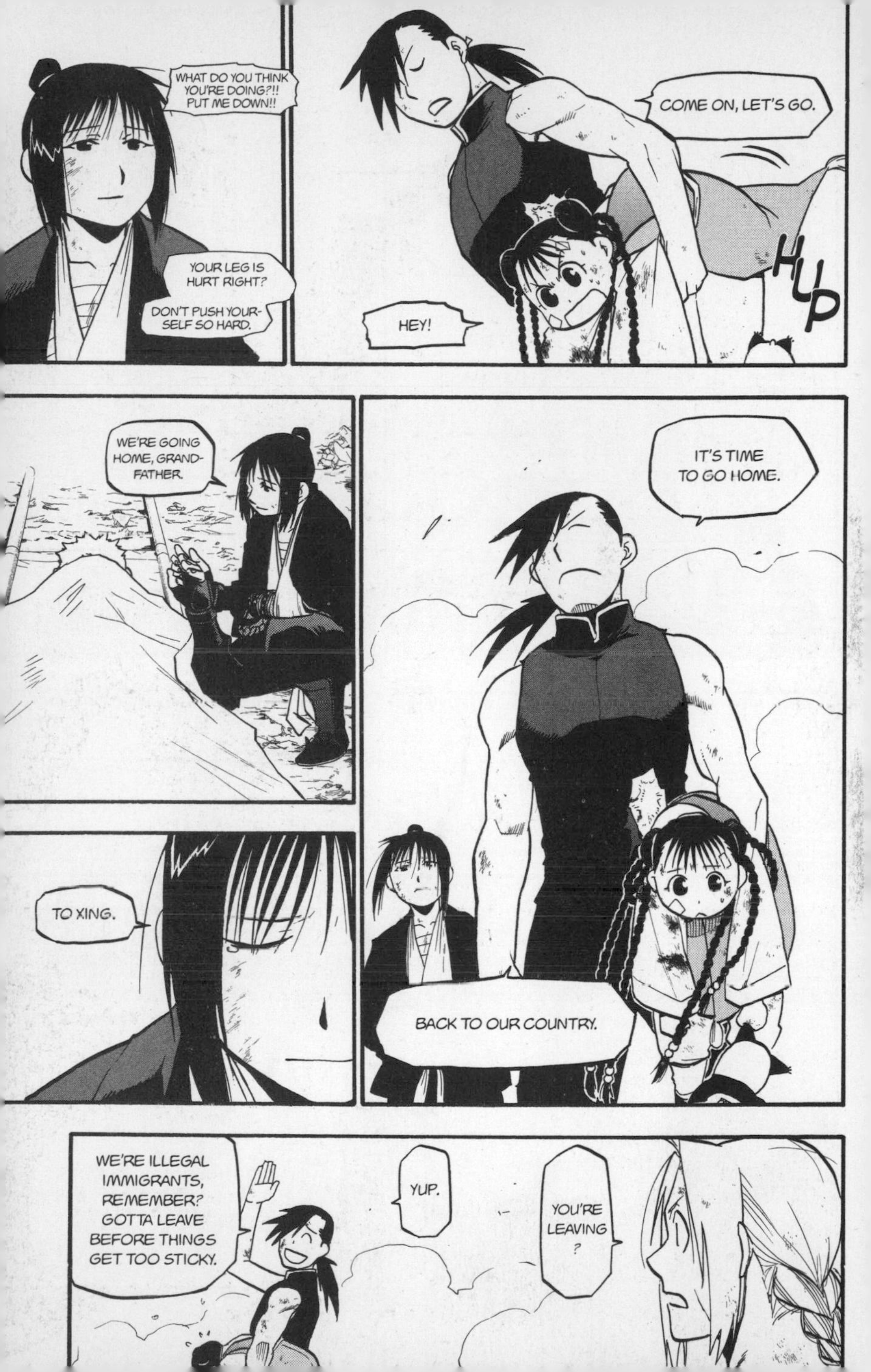
COME ON, LET'S GO.
HUP
HEY!
WHAT DO YOU THINK YOU'RE DOING?!! PUT ME DOWN!!
YOUR LEG IS HURT RIGHT?
DON'T PUSH YOURSELF SO HARD.
IT'S TIME TO GO HOME.
BACK TO OUR COUNTRY.
WE'RE GOING HOME, GRANDFATHER.
TO XING.
YOU'RE LEAVING?
YUP.
WE'RE ILLEGAL IMMIGRANTS, REMEMBER? GOTTA LEAVE BEFORE THINGS GET TOO STICKY.

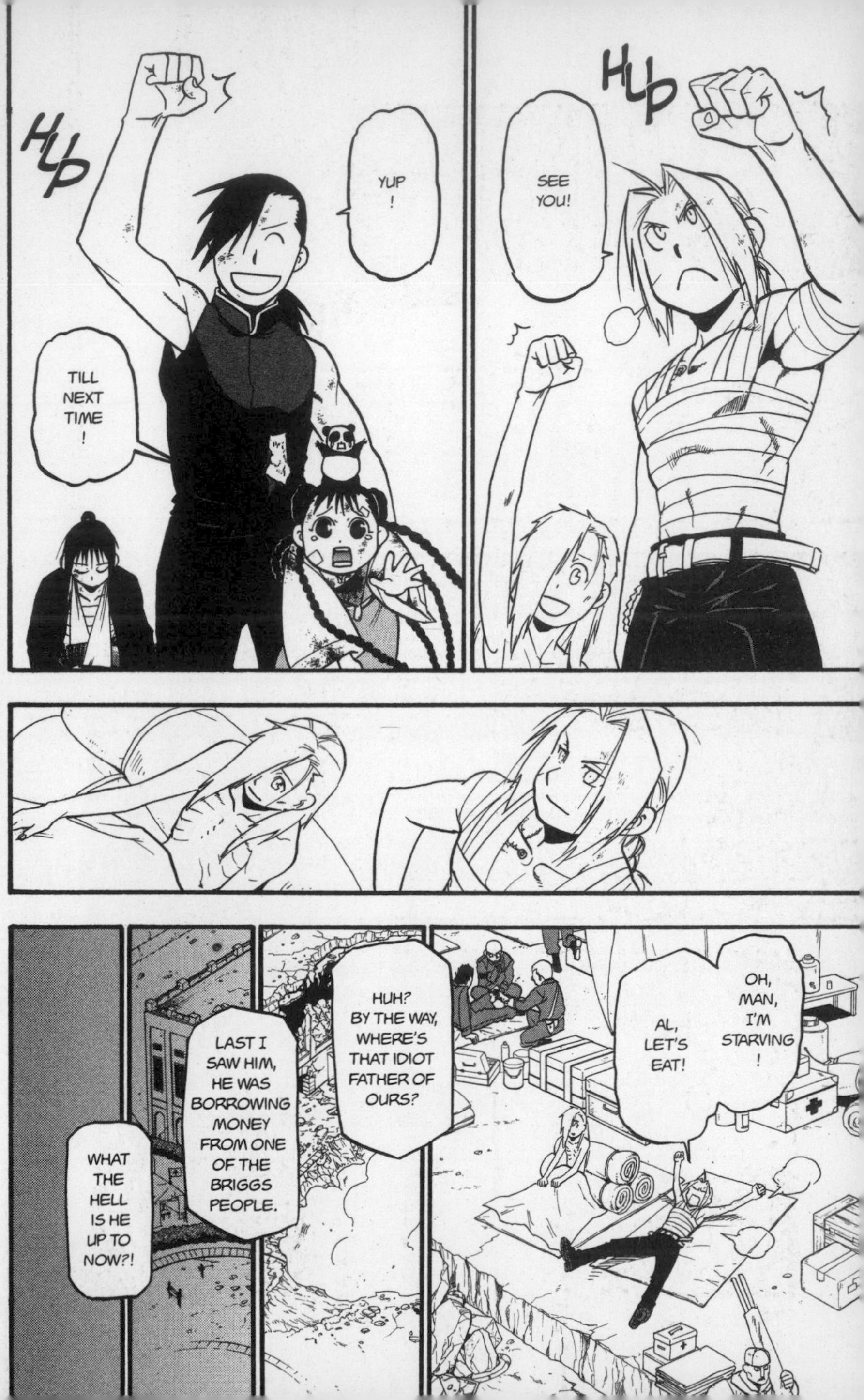
HUP
SEE YOU!
YUP!
HUP
TILL NEXT TIME!
OH, MAN, I'M STARVING!
AL, LET'S EAT!
HUH? BY THE WAY, WHERE'S THAT IDIOT FATHER OF OURS?
LAST I SAW HIM, HE WAS BORROWING MONEY FROM ONE OF THE BRIGGS PEOPLE.
WHAT THE HELL IS HE UP TO NOW?!

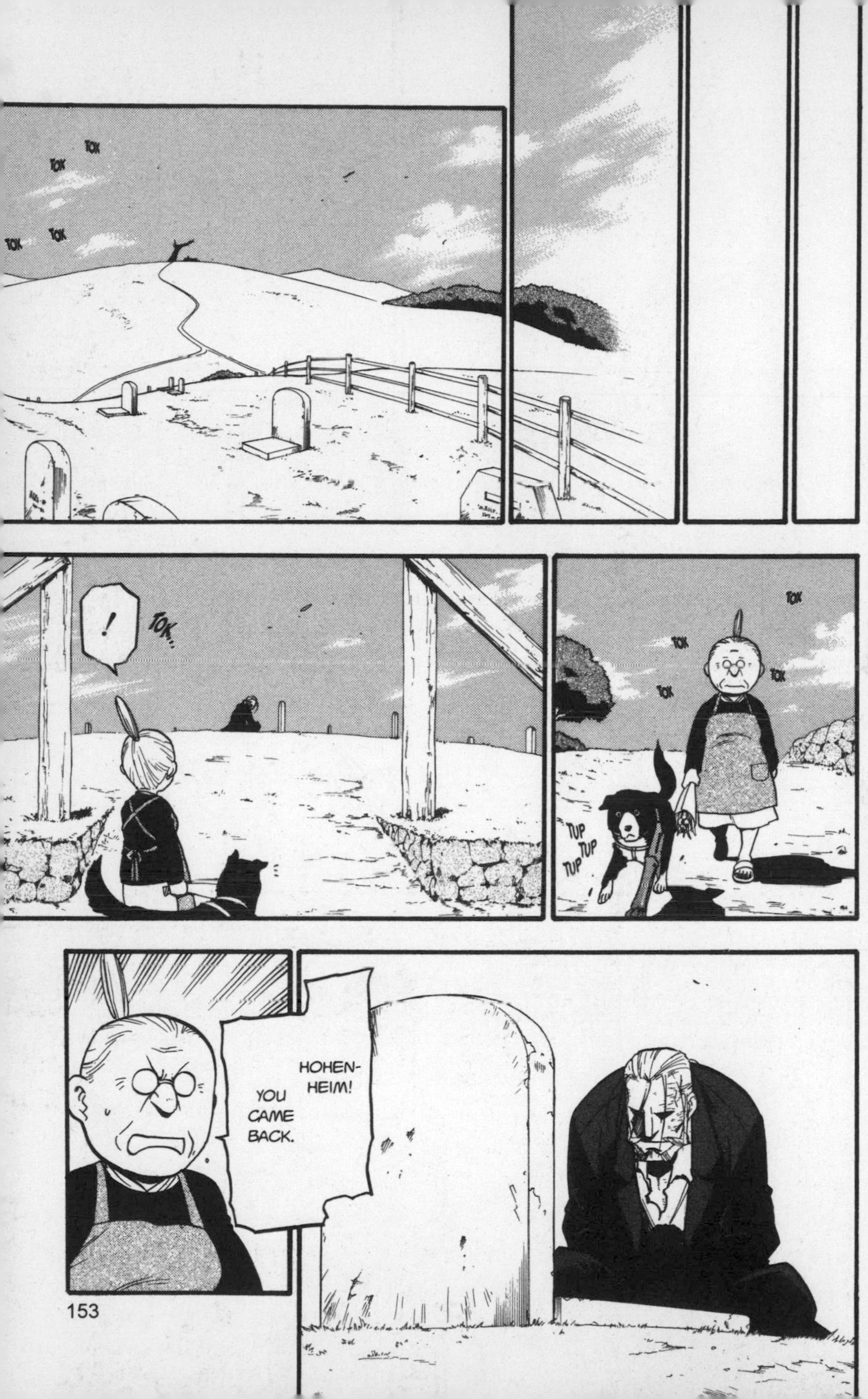
TOK
TOK
TOK
TOK
TOK
TOK
TOK
TUP TUP TUP TUP
!
TOK
HOHEN-HEIM! YOU CAME BACK.

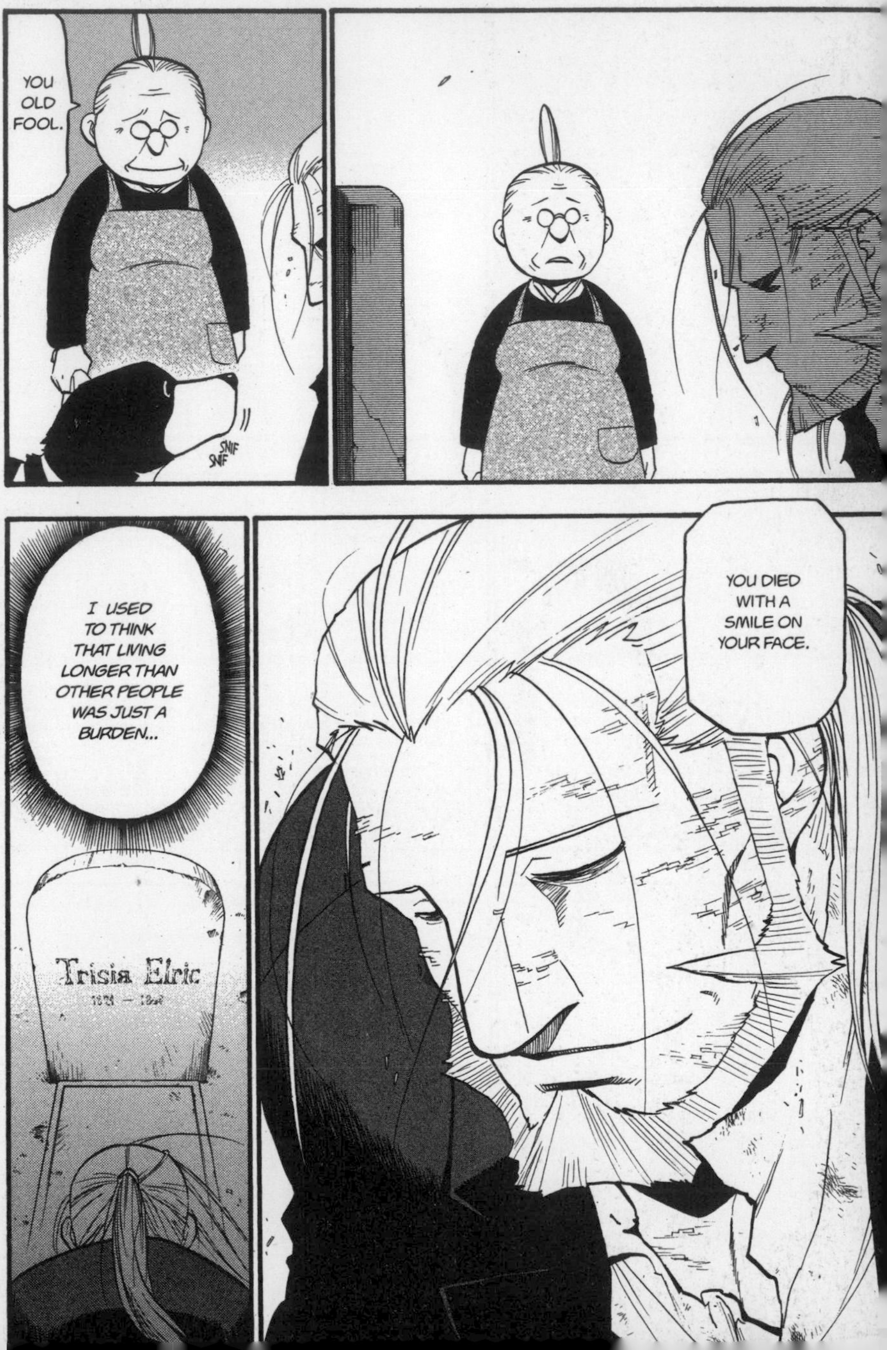
YOU OLD FOOL.
SNIF SNIF
YOU DIED WITH A SMILE ON YOUR FACE.
I USED TO THINK THAT LIVING LONGER THAN OTHER PEOPLE WAS JUST A BURDEN...
Trisia Elric

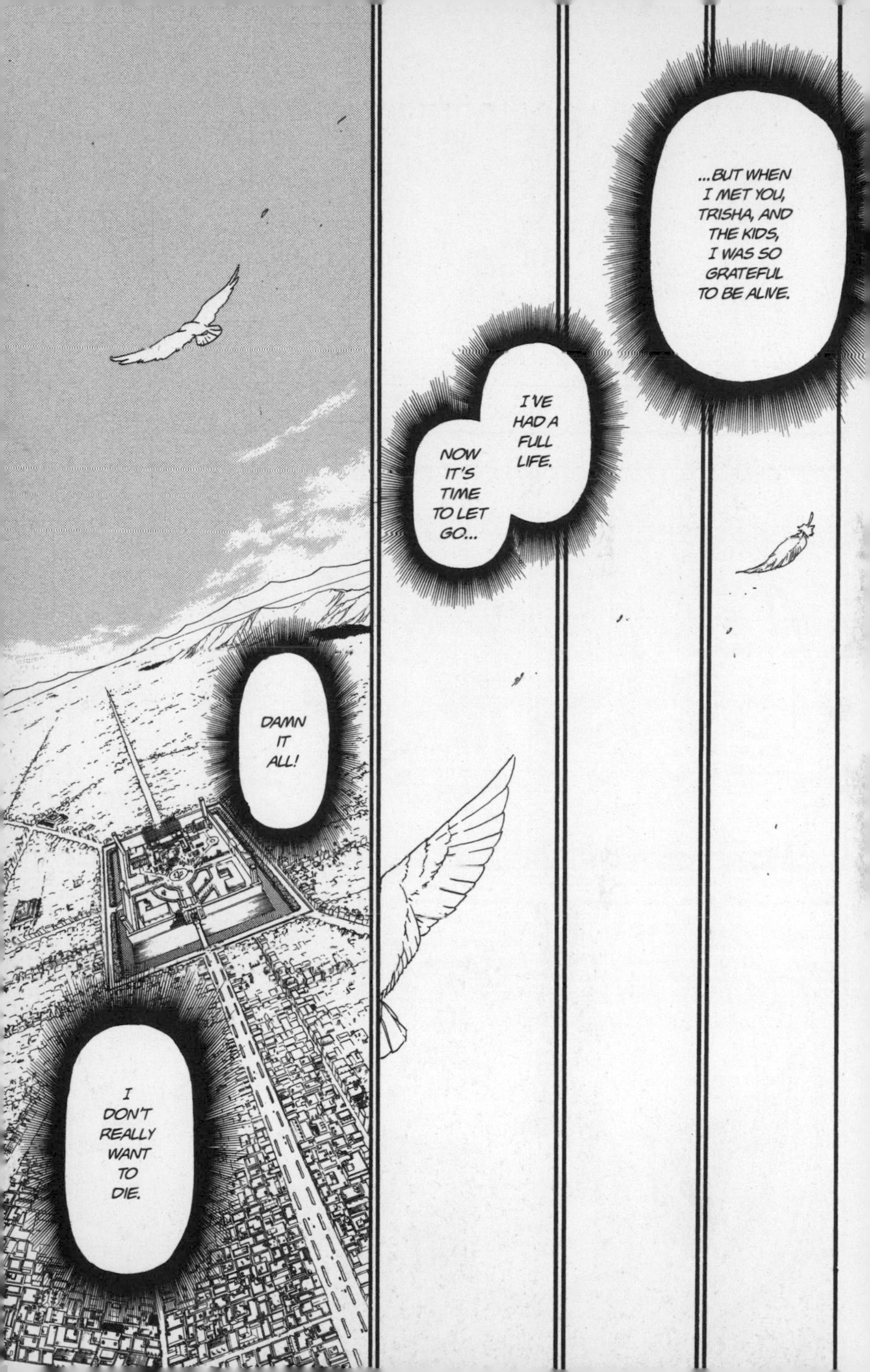
...BUT WHEN I MET YOU, TRISHA, AND THE KIDS, I WAS SO GRATEFUL TO BE ALIVE.
I'VE HAD A FULL LIFE.
NOW IT'S TIME TO LET GO...
DAMN IT ALL!
I DON'T REALLY WANT TO DIE.

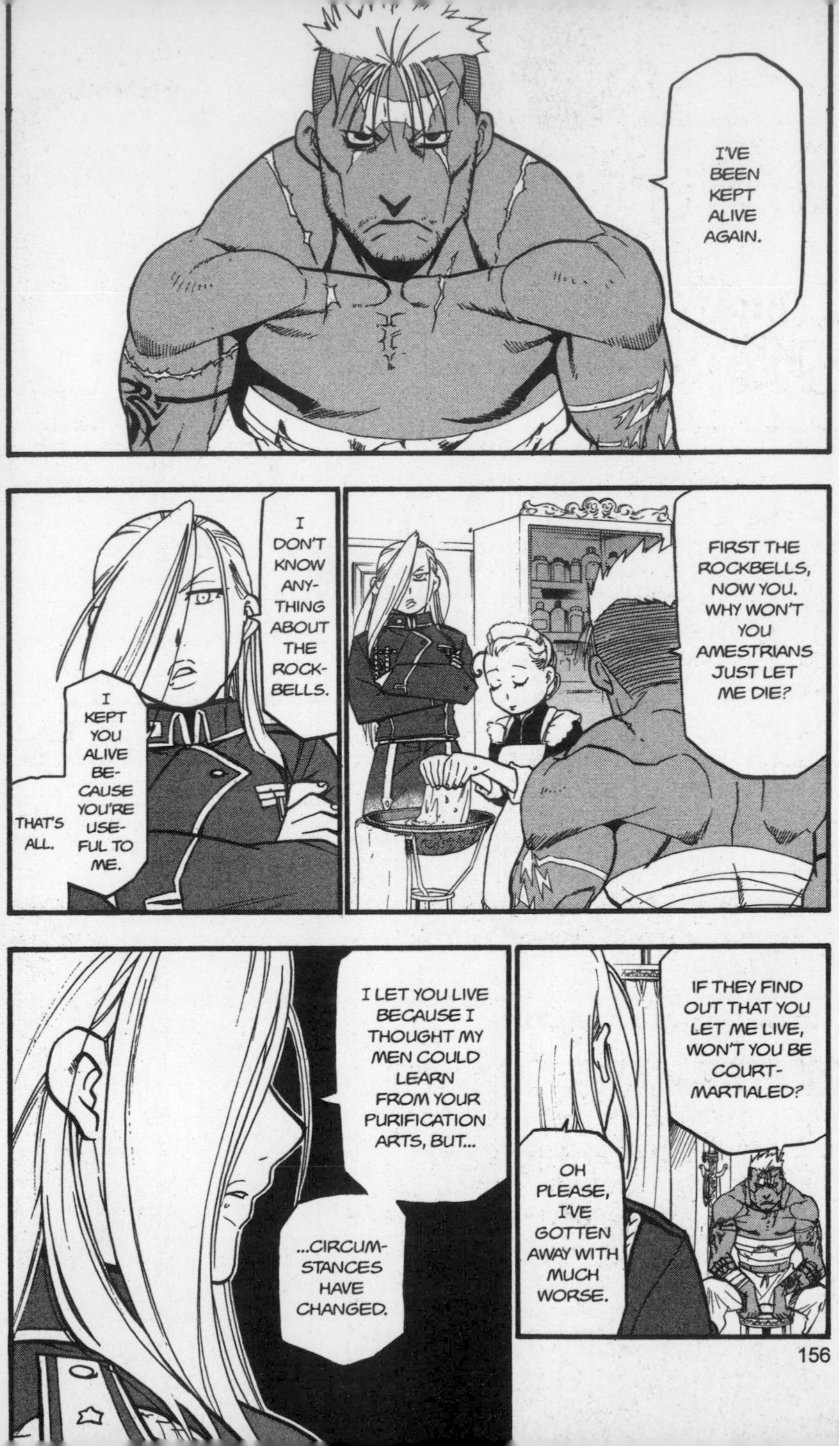

I'VE BEEN KEPT ALIVE AGAIN.
FIRST THE ROCKBELLS, NOW YOU. WHY WON'T YOU AMESTRIANS JUST LET ME DIE?
I DON'T KNOW ANYTHING ABOUT THE ROCKBELLS.
I KEPT YOU ALIVE BECAUSE YOU'RE USEFUL TO ME.
THAT'S ALL.
IF THEY FIND OUT THAT YOU LET ME LIVE, WON'T YOU BE COURT-MARTIALED?
OH PLEASE, I'VE GOTTEN AWAY WITH MUCH WORSE.
I LET YOU LIVE BECAUSE I THOUGHT MY MEN COULD LEARN FROM YOUR PURIFICATION ARTS, BUT...
...CIRCUMSTANCES HAVE CHANGED.

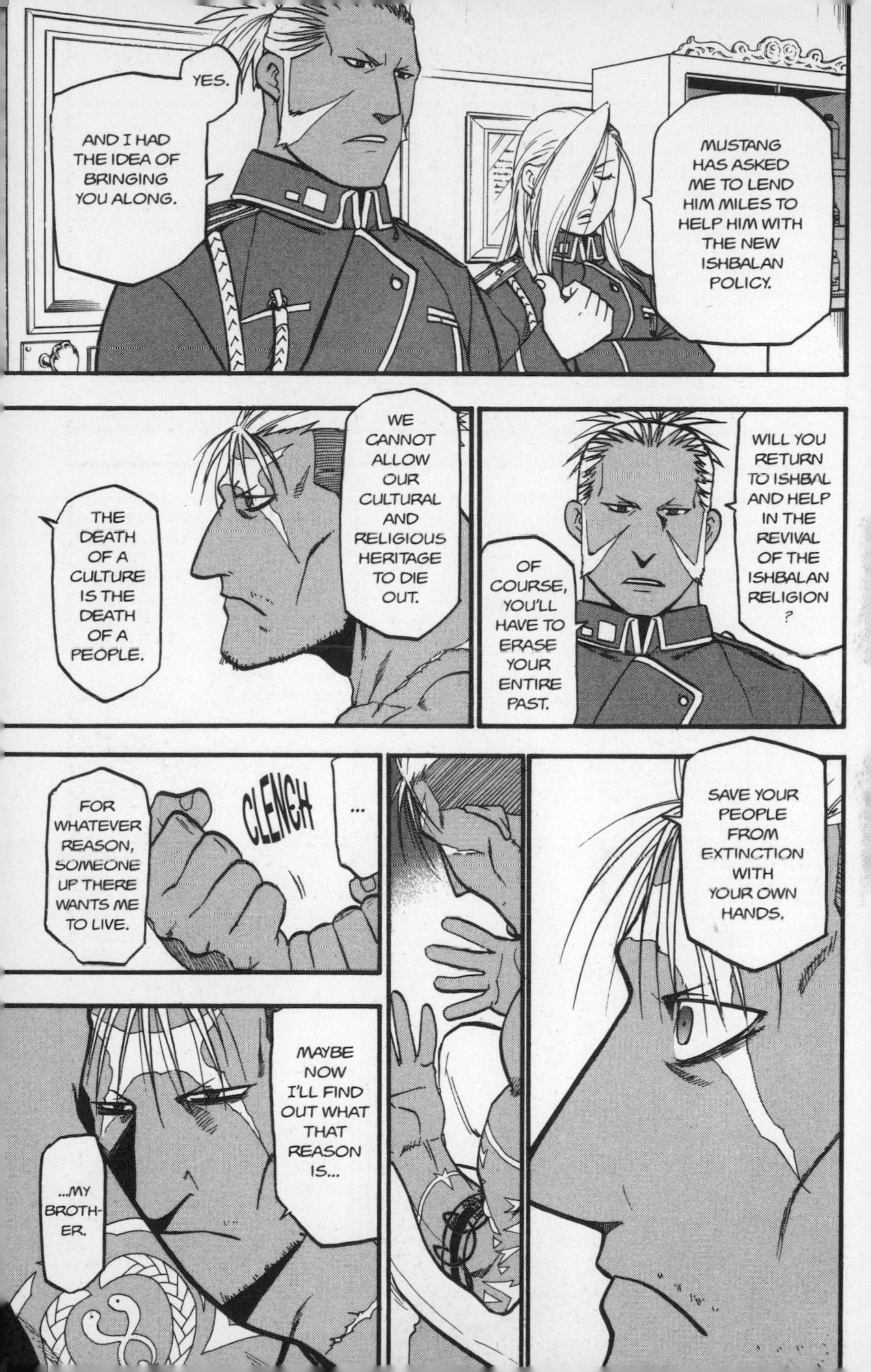
MUSTANG HAS ASKED ME TO LEND HIM MILES TO HELP HIM WITH THE NEW ISHBALAN POLICY.
YES.
AND I HAD THE IDEA OF BRINGING YOU ALONG.
WILL YOU RETURN TO ISHBAL AND HELP IN THE REVIVAL OF THE ISHBALAN RELIGION?
OF COURSE, YOU'LL HAVE TO ERASE YOUR ENTIRE PAST.
WE CANNOT ALLOW OUR CULTURAL AND RELIGIOUS HERITAGE TO DIE OUT.
THE DEATH OF A CULTURE IS THE DEATH OF A PEOPLE.
SAVE YOUR PEOPLE FROM EXTINCTION WITH YOUR OWN HANDS.
...
CLENCH
FOR WHATEVER REASON, SOMEONE UP THERE WANTS ME TO LIVE.
MAYBE NOW I'LL FIND OUT WHAT THAT REASON IS...
...MY BROTHER.

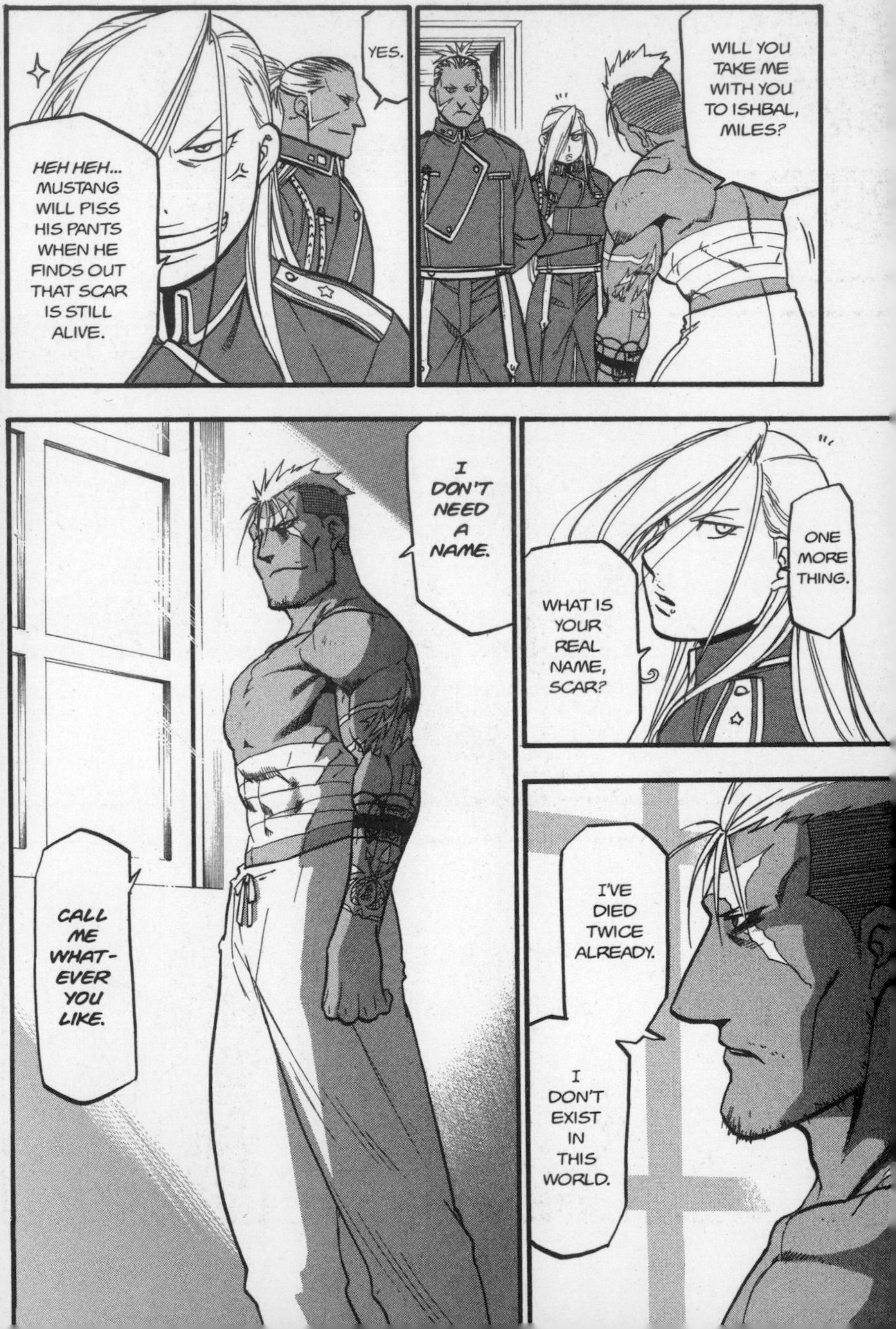
WILL YOU TAKE ME WITH YOU TO ISHBAL, MILES?
YES.
HEH HEH... MUSTANG WILL PISS HIS PANTS WHEN HE FINDS OUT THAT SCAR IS STILL ALIVE.
ONE MORE THING.
WHAT IS YOUR REAL NAME, SCAR?
I'VE DIED TWICE ALREADY.
I DON'T EXIST IN THIS WORLD.
I DON'T NEED A NAME.
CALL ME WHATEVER YOU LIKE.

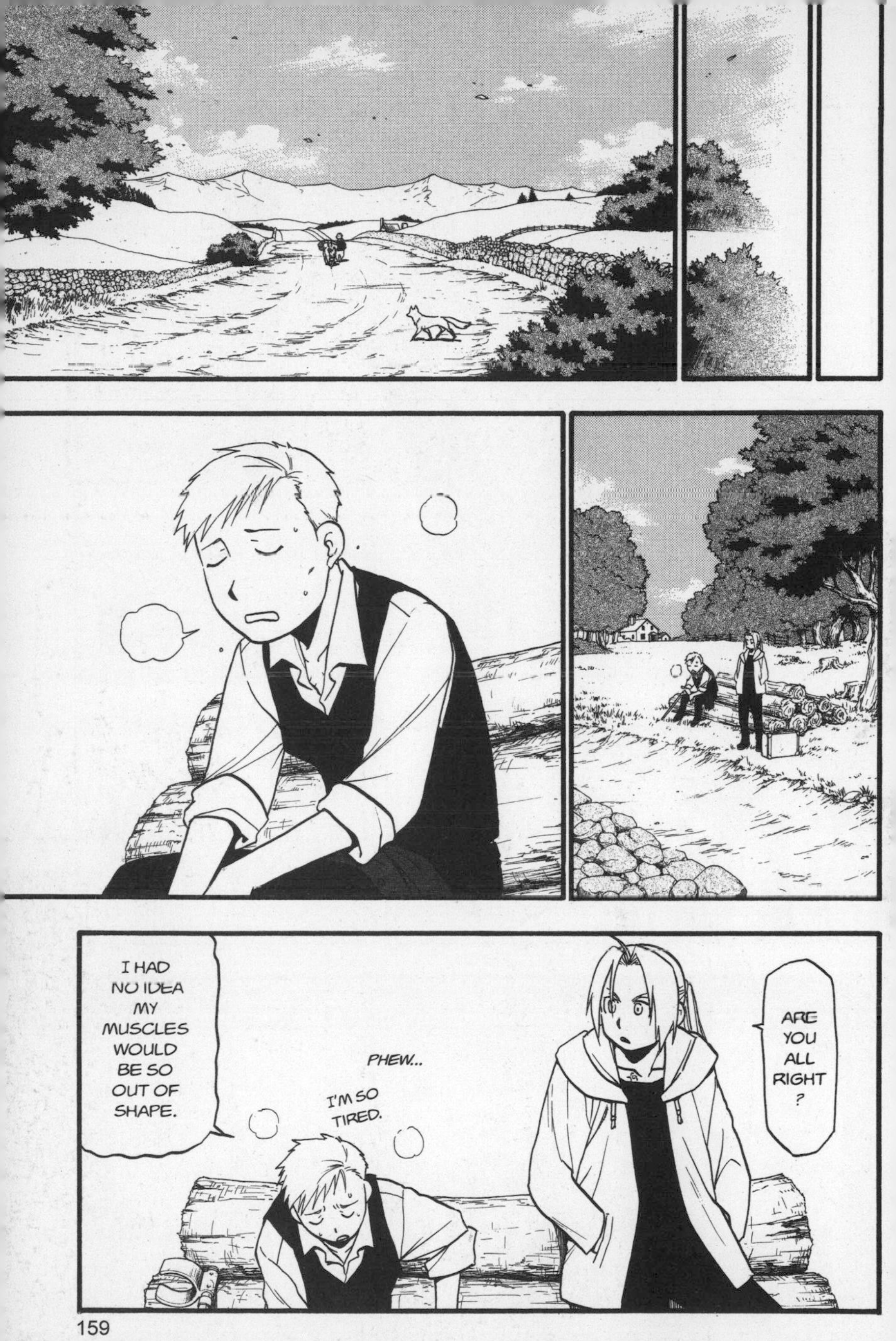
ARE YOU ALL RIGHT?
PHEW...
I'M SO TIRED.
I HAD NO IDEA MY MUSCLES WOULD BE SO OUT OF SHAPE.

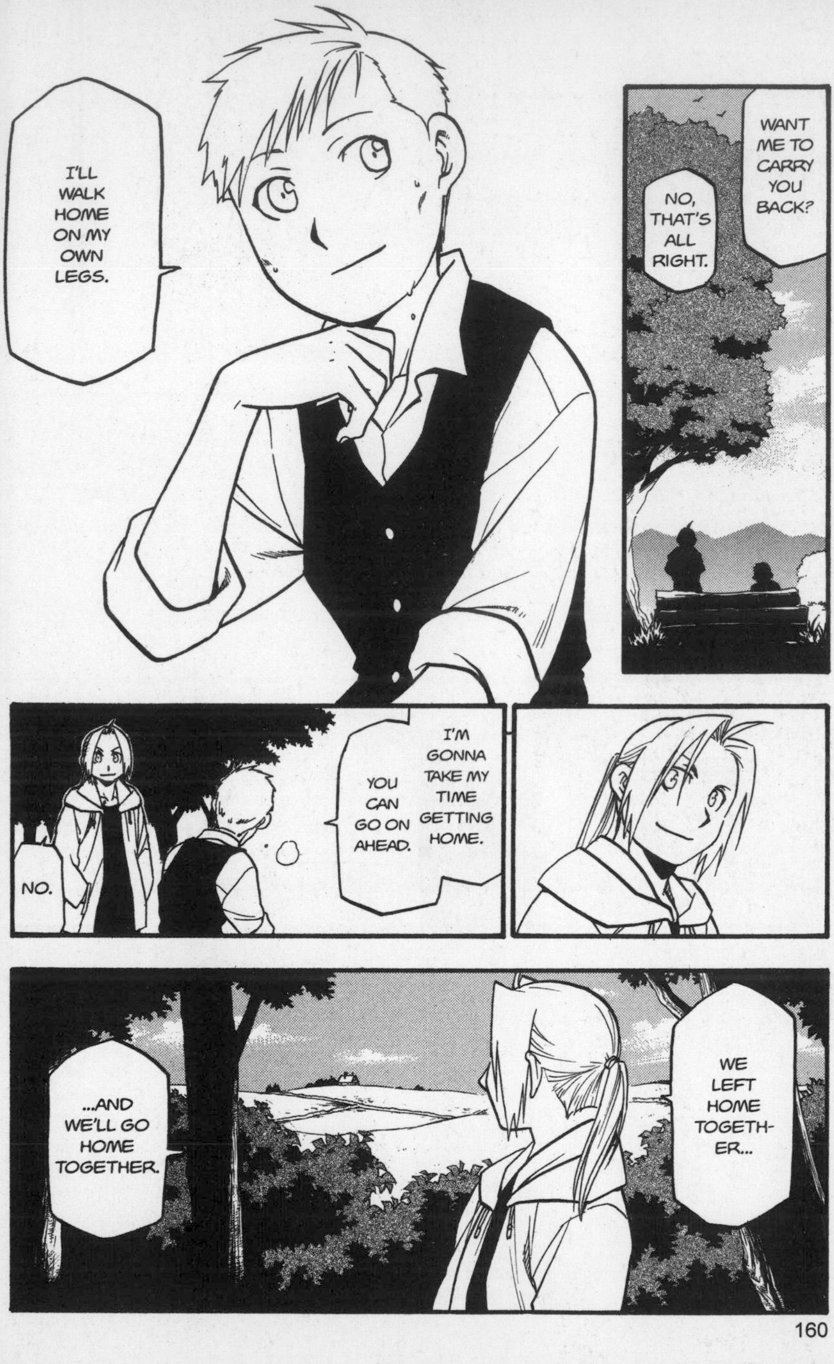
WANT ME TO CARRY YOU BACK?
NO, THAT'S ALL RIGHT.
I'LL WALK HOME ON MY OWN LEGS.
I'M GONNA TAKE MY TIME GETTING HOME.
YOU CAN GO ON AHEAD.
NO.
WE LEFT HOME TOGETHER...
...AND WE'LL GO HOME TOGETHER.

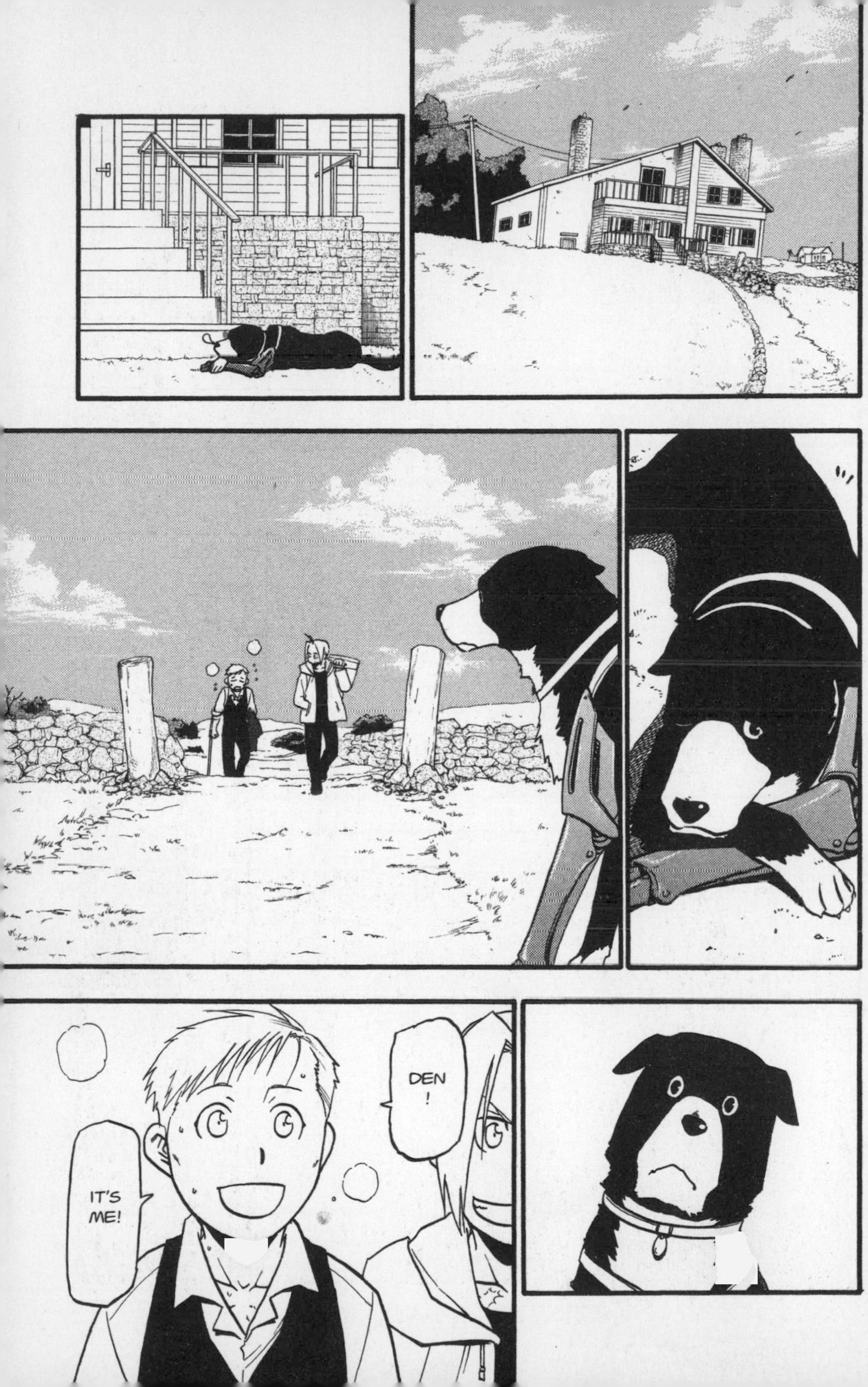
DEN!
IT'S ME!

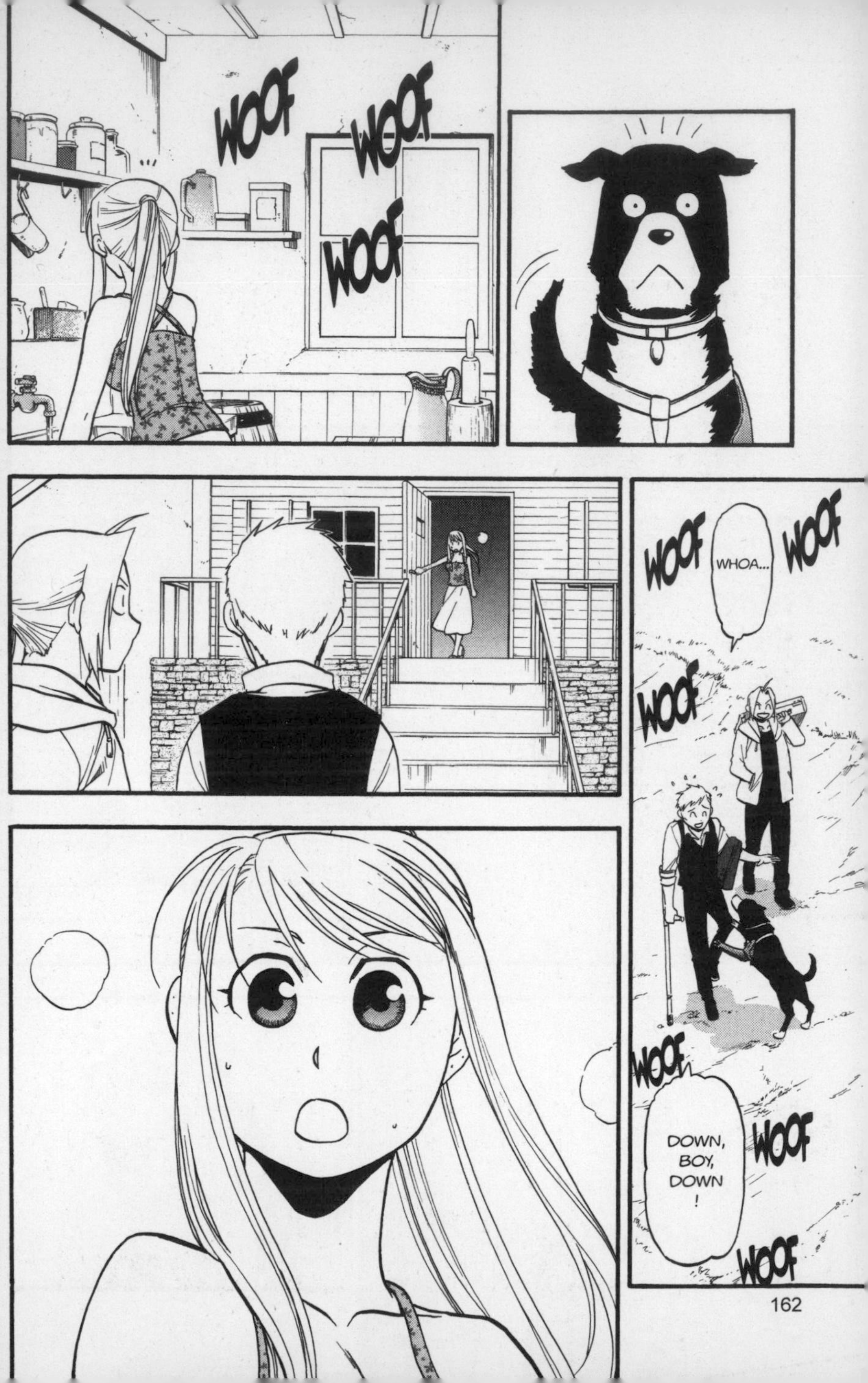
WOOF
WOOF
WOOF
WOOF
WHOA...
WOOF
WOOF
WOOF
DOWN, BOY, DOWN!
WOOF
WOOF

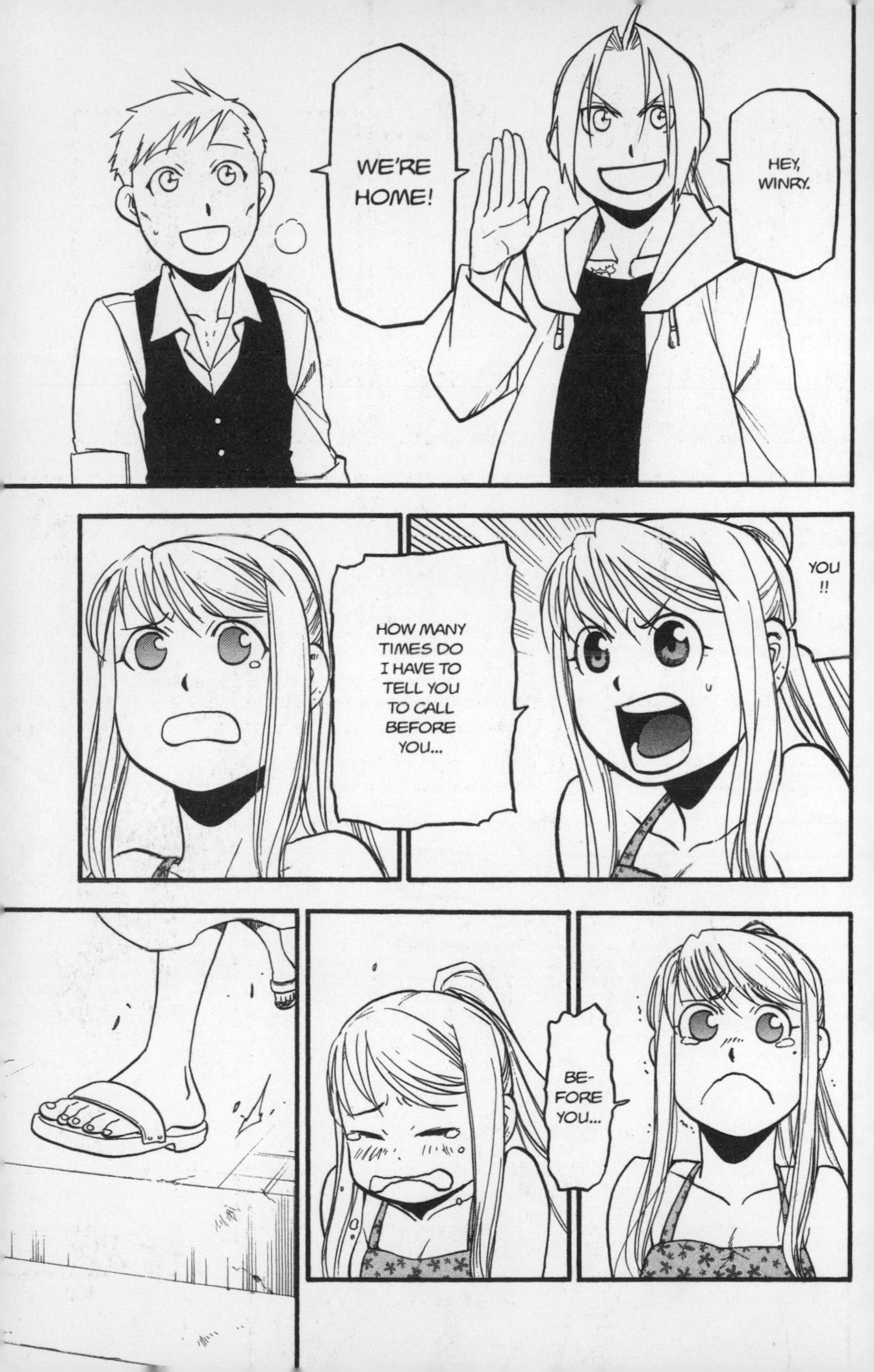
HEY, WINRY.
WE'RE HOME!
YOU !!
HOW MANY TIMES DO I HAVE TO TELL YOU TO CALL BEFORE YOU...
BE-FORE YOU...

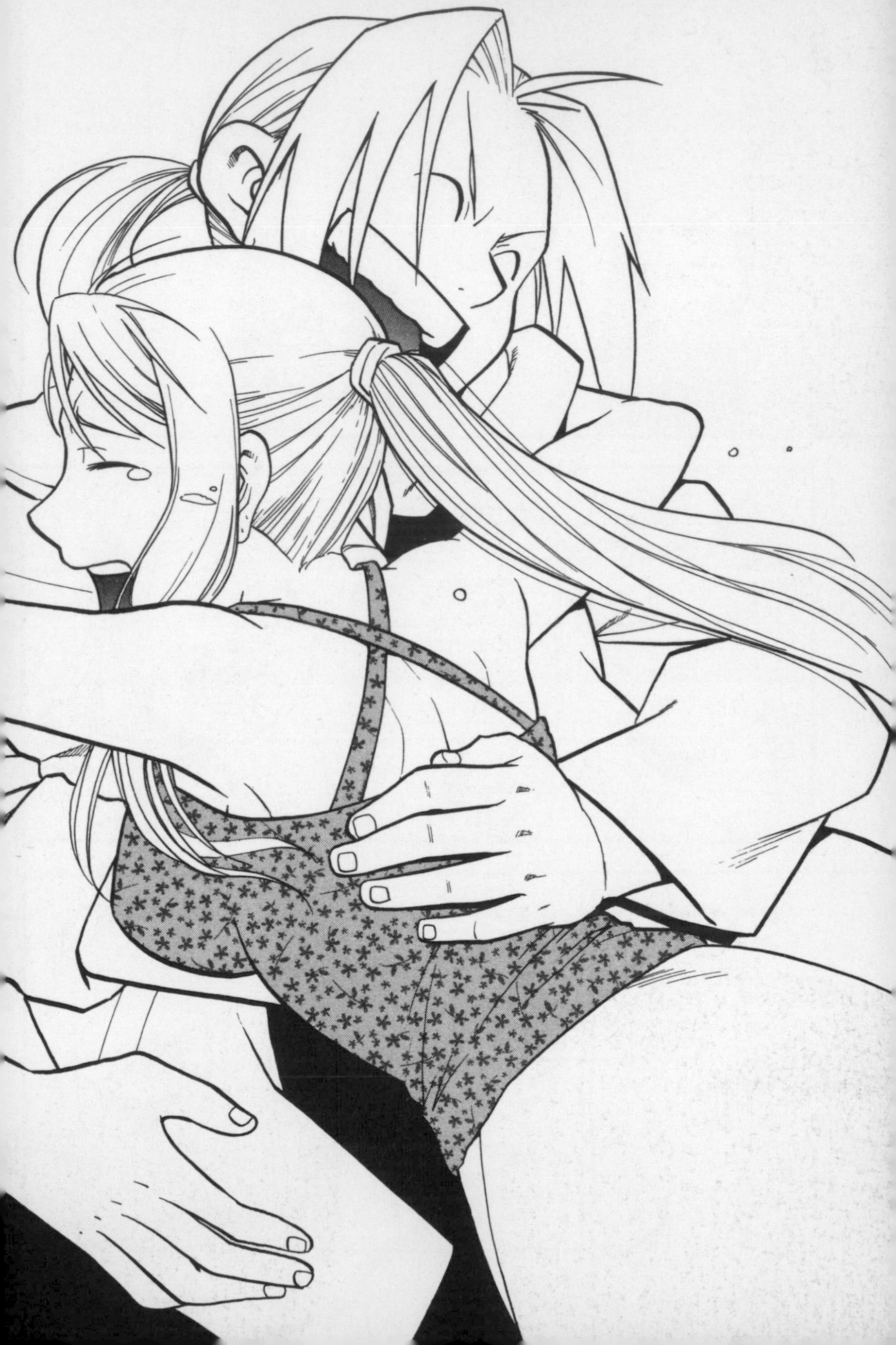

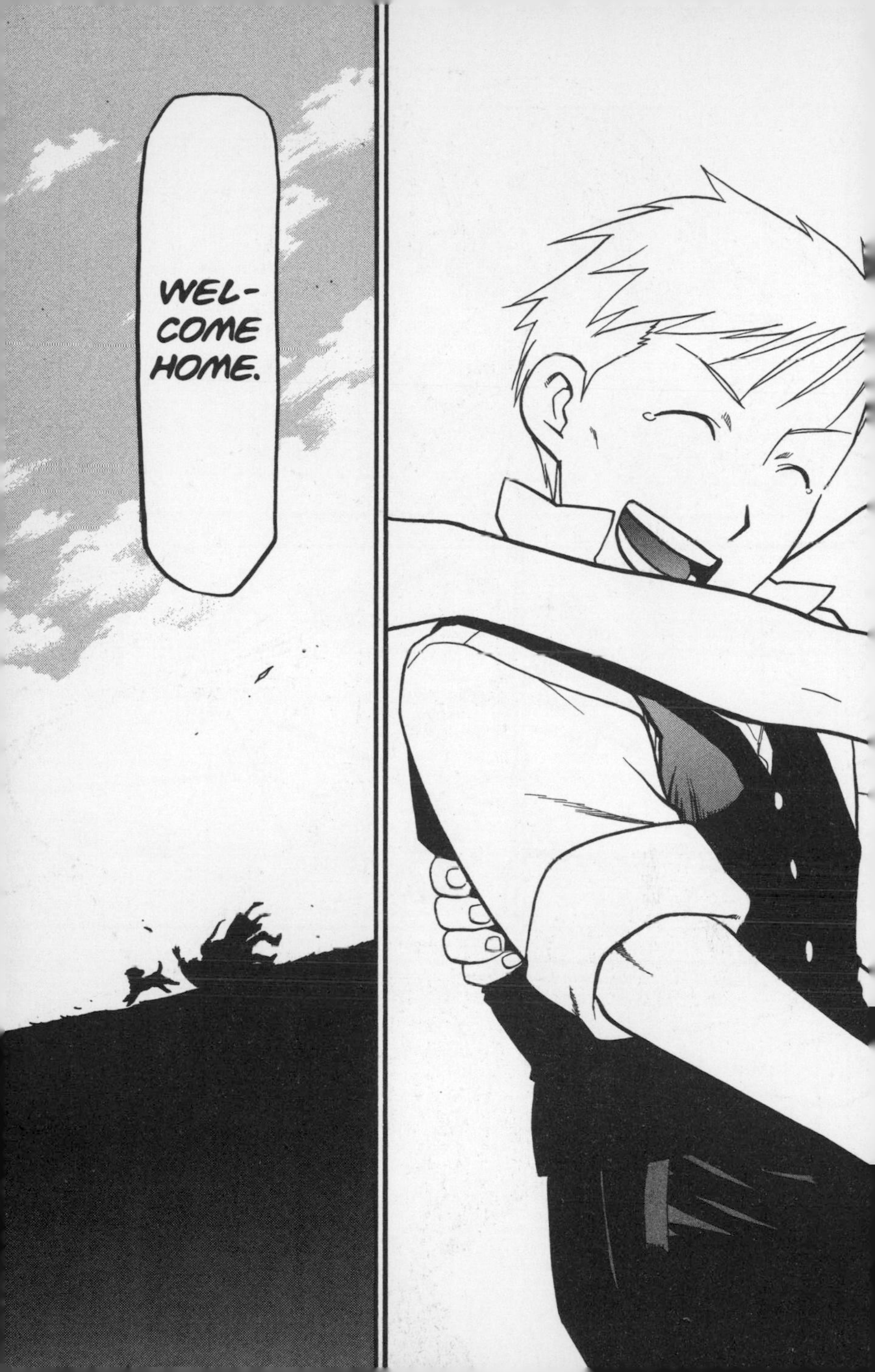
WEL-COME HOME.

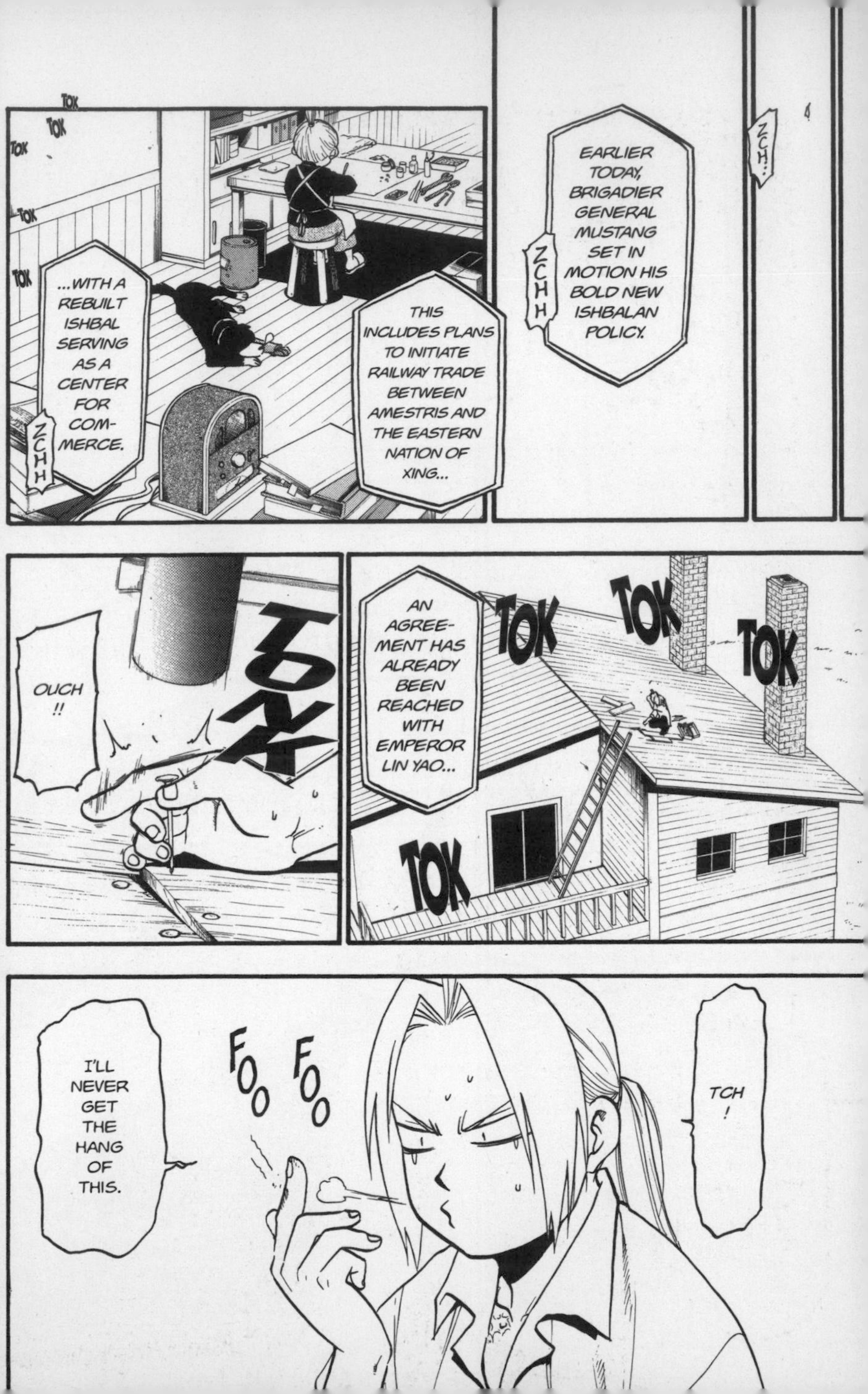
ZCH...
EARLIER TODAY, BRIGADIER GENERAL MUSTANG SET IN MOTION HIS BOLD NEW ISHBALAN POLICY.
ZCHH
TOK
TOK
TOK
TOK
TOK
THIS INCLUDES PLANS TO INITIATE RAILWAY TRADE BETWEEN AMESTRIS AND THE EASTERN NATION OF XING...
...WITH A REBUILT ISHBAL SERVING AS A CENTER FOR COM-MERCE.
ZCHH
AN AGREE-MENT HAS ALREADY BEEN REACHED WITH EMPEROR LIN YAO...
TOK
TOK
TOK
TOK
TONK
OUCH !!
TCH !
FOO
FOO
I'LL NEVER GET THE HANG OF THIS.

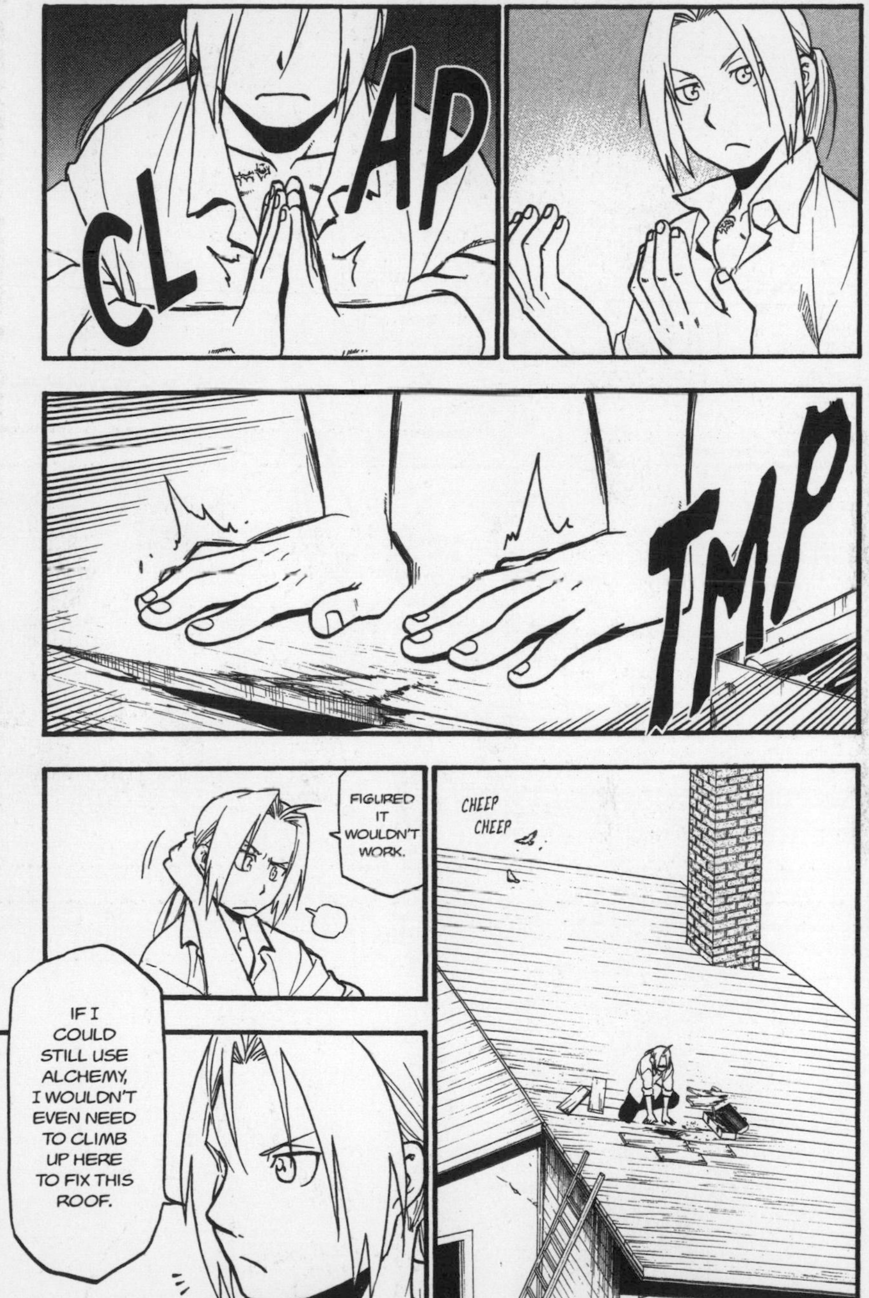

CLAP
TMP
CHEEP CHEEP
FIGURED IT WOULDN'T WORK.
IF I COULD STILL USE ALCHEMY, I WOULDN'T EVEN NEED TO CLIMB UP HERE TO FIX THIS ROOF.

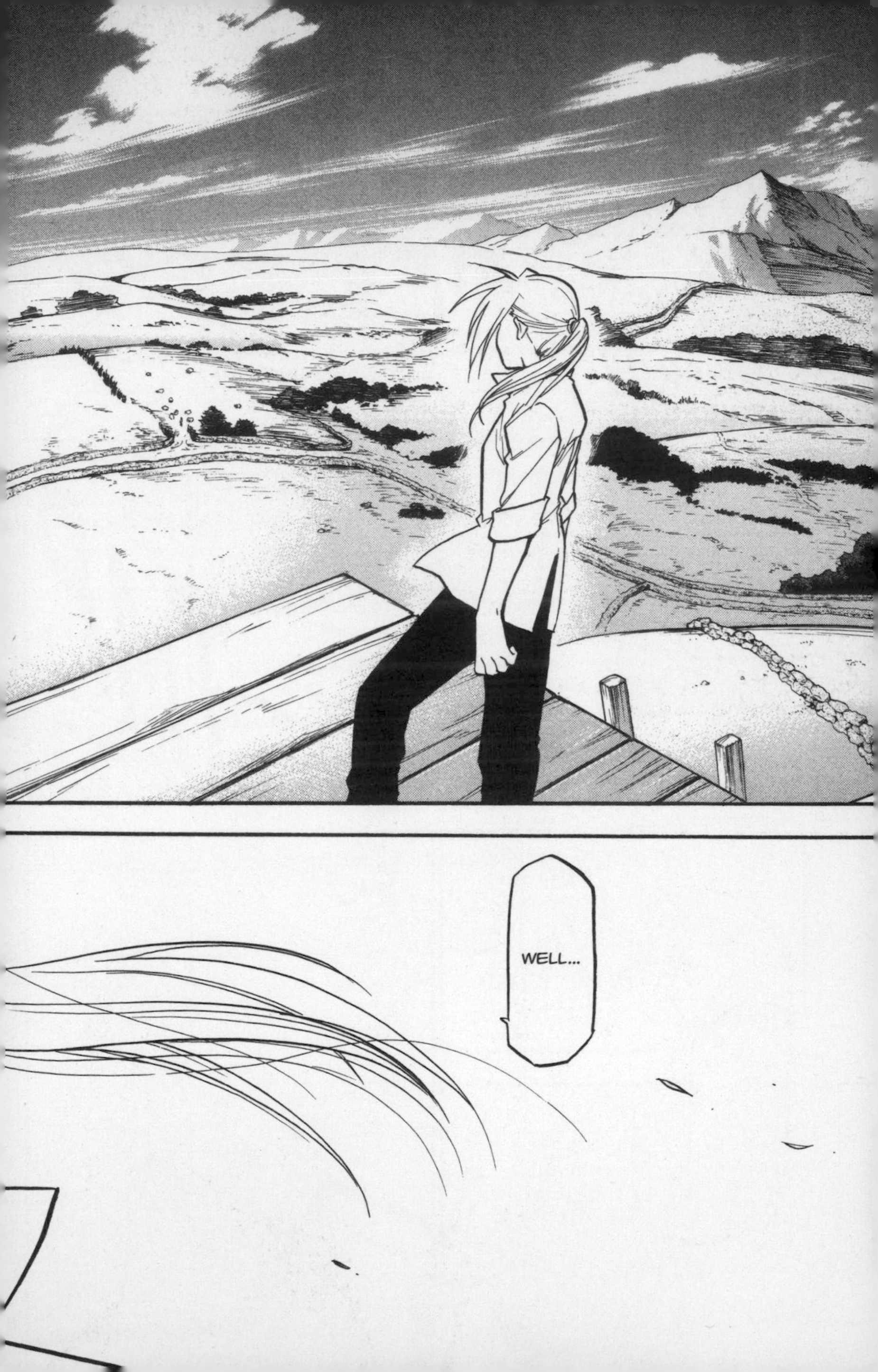
WELL...

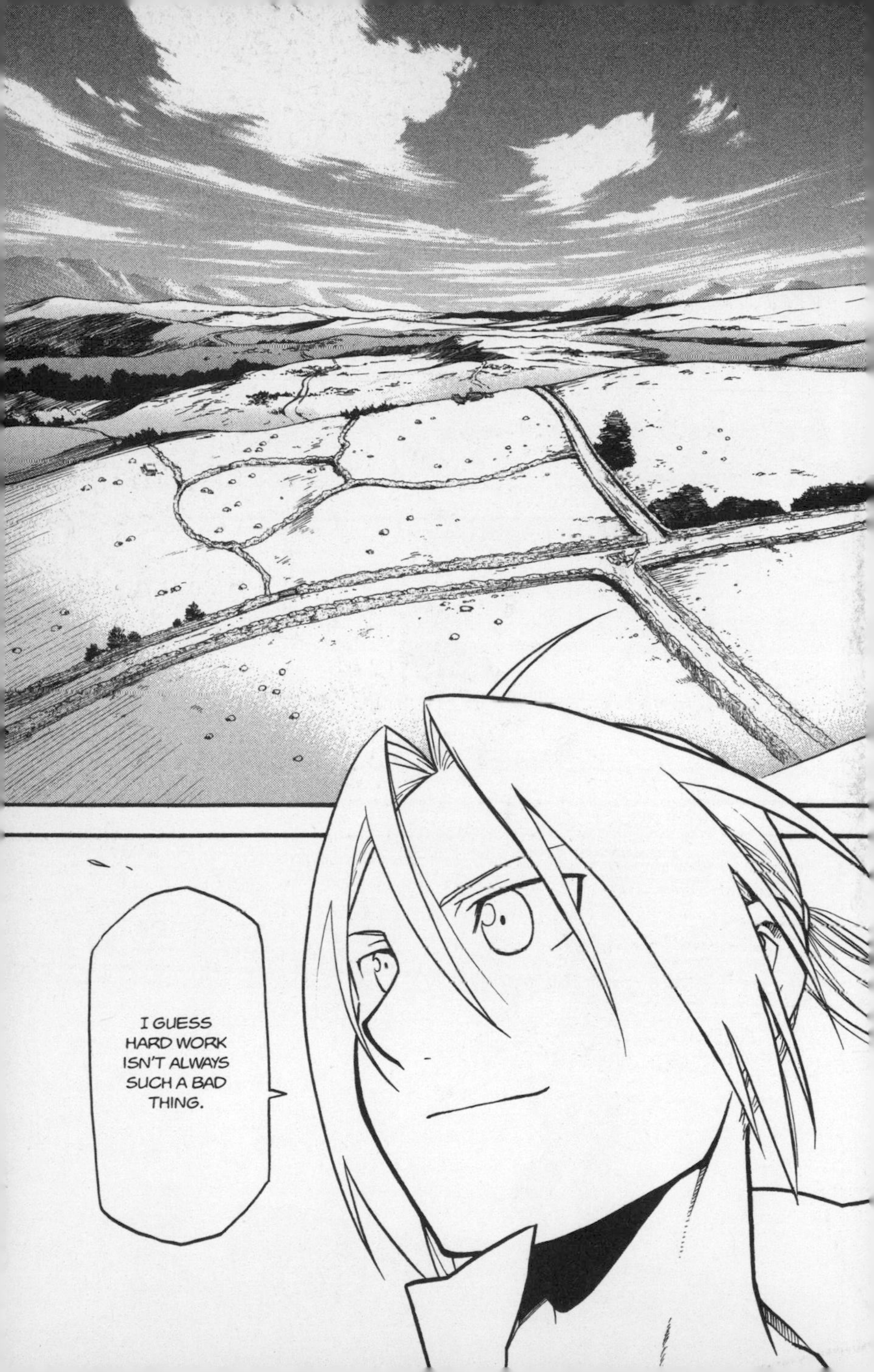
I GUESS HARD WORK ISN'T ALWAYS SUCH A BAD THING.

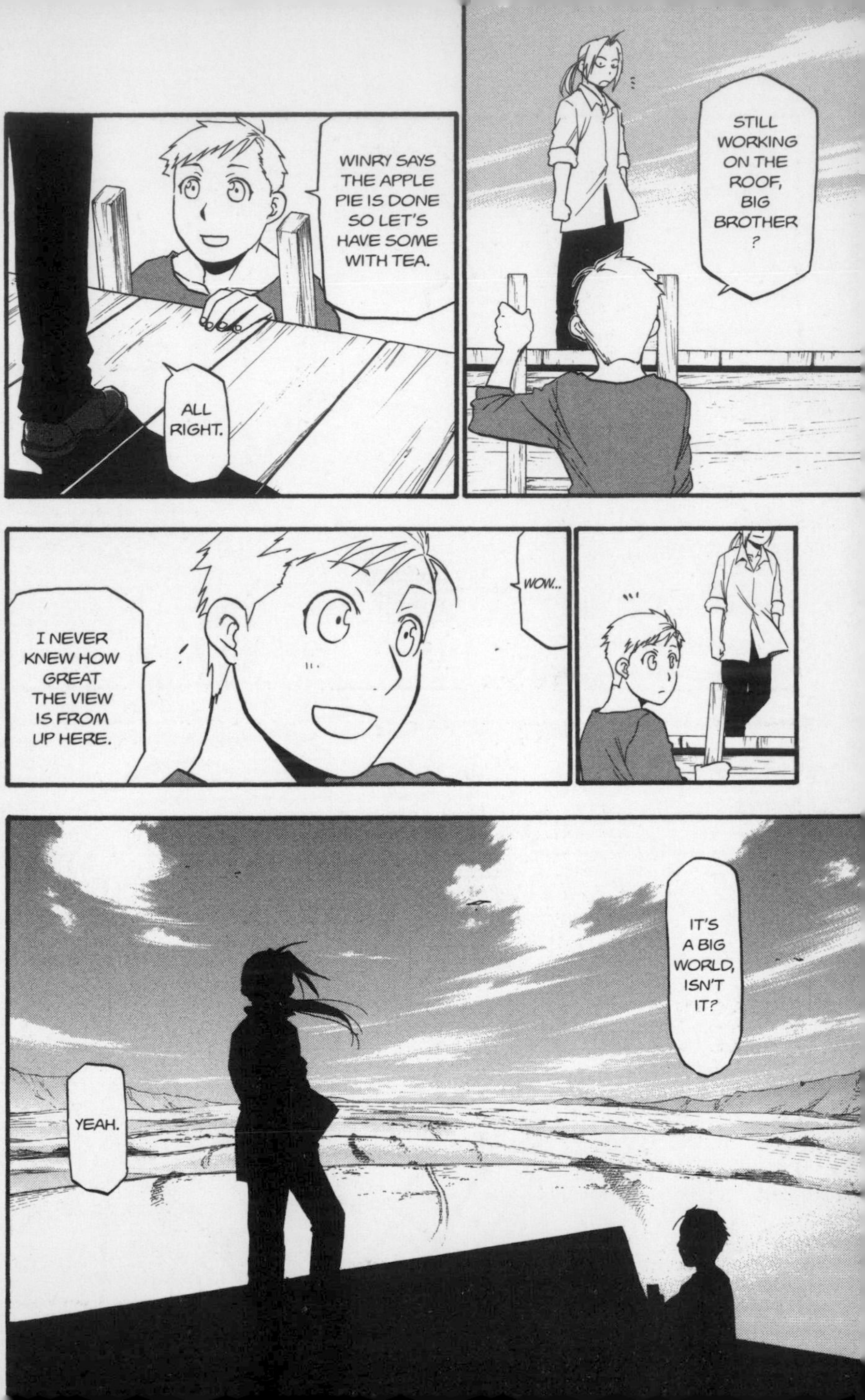
STILL WORKING ON THE ROOF, BIG BROTHER?
WINRY SAYS THE APPLE PIE IS DONE SO LET'S HAVE SOME WITH TEA.
ALL RIGHT.
WOW...
I NEVER KNEW HOW GREAT THE VIEW IS FROM UP HERE.
IT'S A BIG WORLD, ISN'T IT?
YEAH.

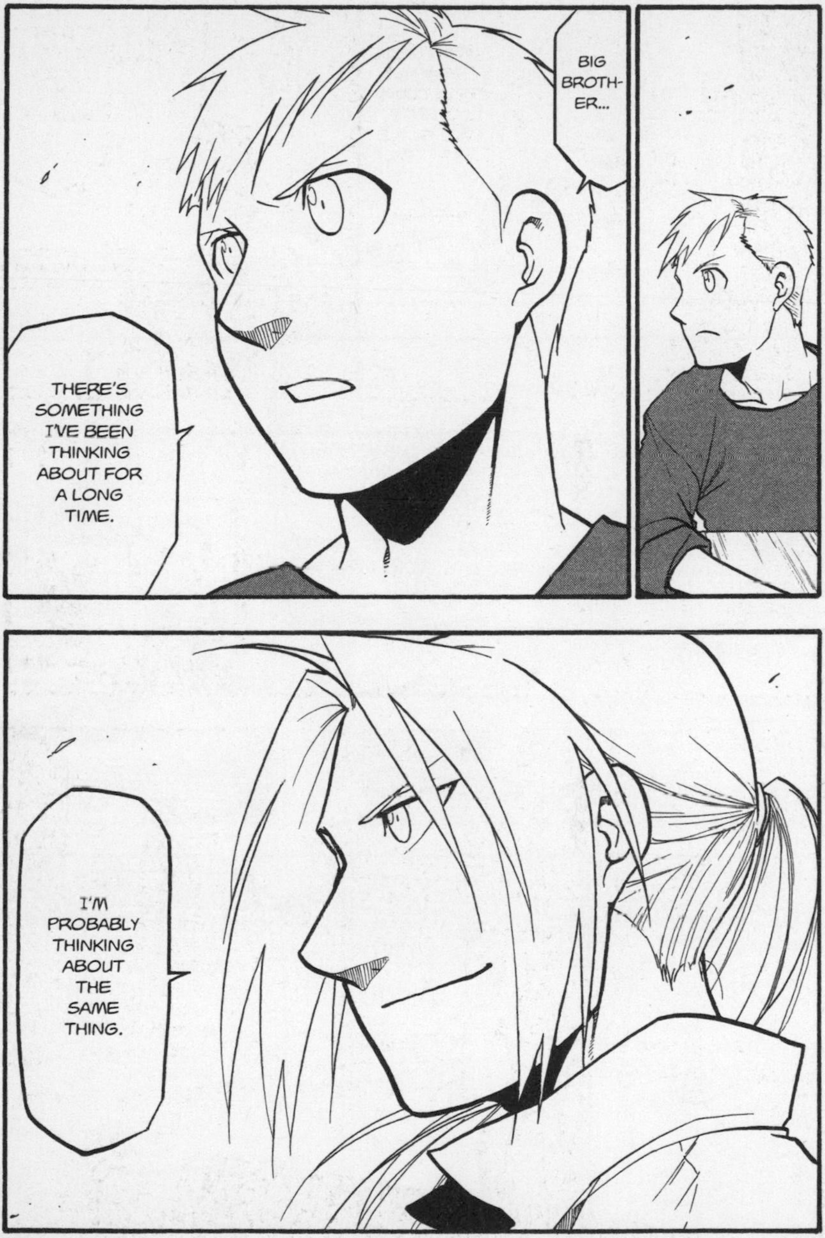
BIG BROTH-ER...
THERE'S SOMETHING I'VE BEEN THINKING ABOUT FOR A LONG TIME.
I'M PROBABLY THINKING ABOUT THE SAME THING.

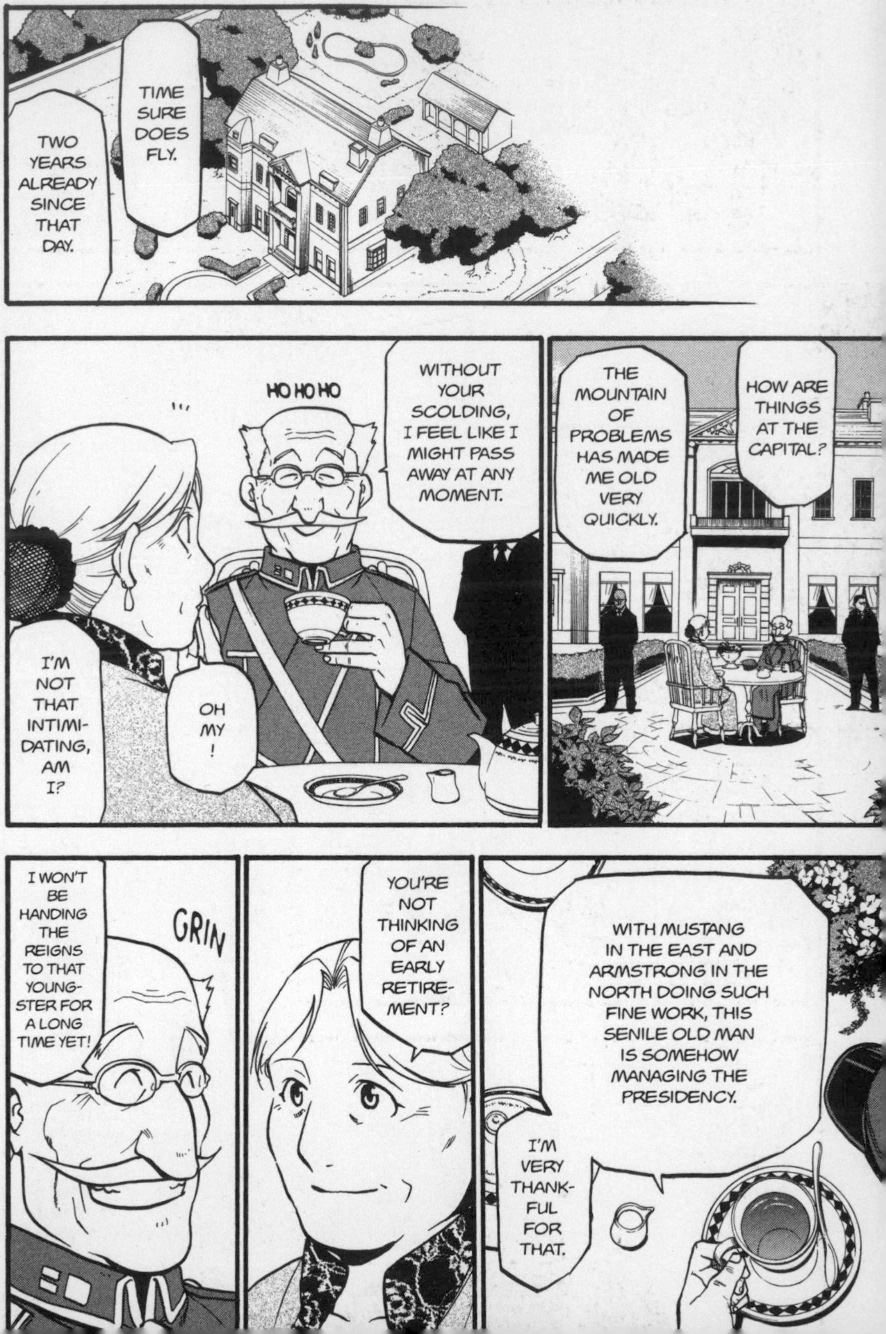
TIME SURE DOES FLY.
TWO YEARS ALREADY SINCE THAT DAY.
HOW ARE THINGS AT THE CAPITAL?
THE MOUNTAIN OF PROBLEMS HAS MADE ME OLD VERY QUICKLY.
HO HO HO
WITHOUT YOUR SCOLDING, I FEEL LIKE I MIGHT PASS AWAY AT ANY MOMENT.
OH MY!
I'M NOT THAT INTIMIDATING, AM I?
WITH MUSTANG IN THE EAST AND ARMSTRONG IN THE NORTH DOING SUCH FINE WORK, THIS SENILE OLD MAN IS SOMEHOW MANAGING THE PRESIDENCY.
I'M VERY THANKFUL FOR THAT.
YOU'RE NOT THINKING OF AN EARLY RETIREMENT?
GRIN
I WON'T BE HANDING THE REIGNS TO THAT YOUNGSTER FOR A LONG TIME YET!

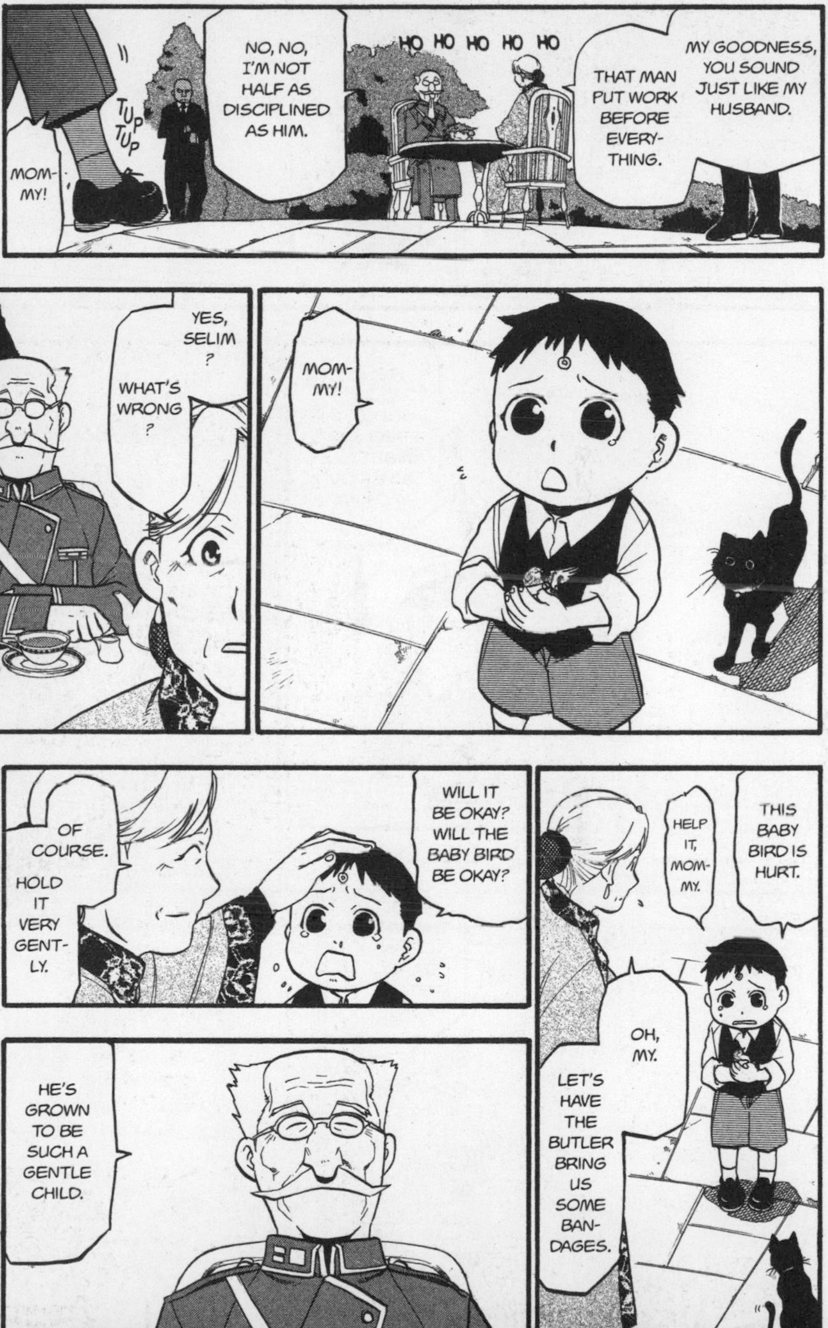
MY GOODNESS, YOU SOUND JUST LIKE MY HUSBAND.
THAT MAN PUT WORK BEFORE EVERY-THING.
HO HO HO HO HO
NO, NO, I'M NOT HALF AS DISCIPLINED AS HIM.
TUP TUP
MOM-MY!
MOM-MY!
YES, SELIM?
WHAT'S WRONG?
THIS BABY BIRD IS HURT.
HELP IT, MOM-MY.
OH, MY.
LET'S HAVE THE BUTLER BRING US SOME BAN-DAGES.
WILL IT BE OKAY? WILL THE BABY BIRD BE OKAY?
OF COURSE.
HOLD IT VERY GENT-LY.
HE'S GROWN TO BE SUCH A GENTLE CHILD.

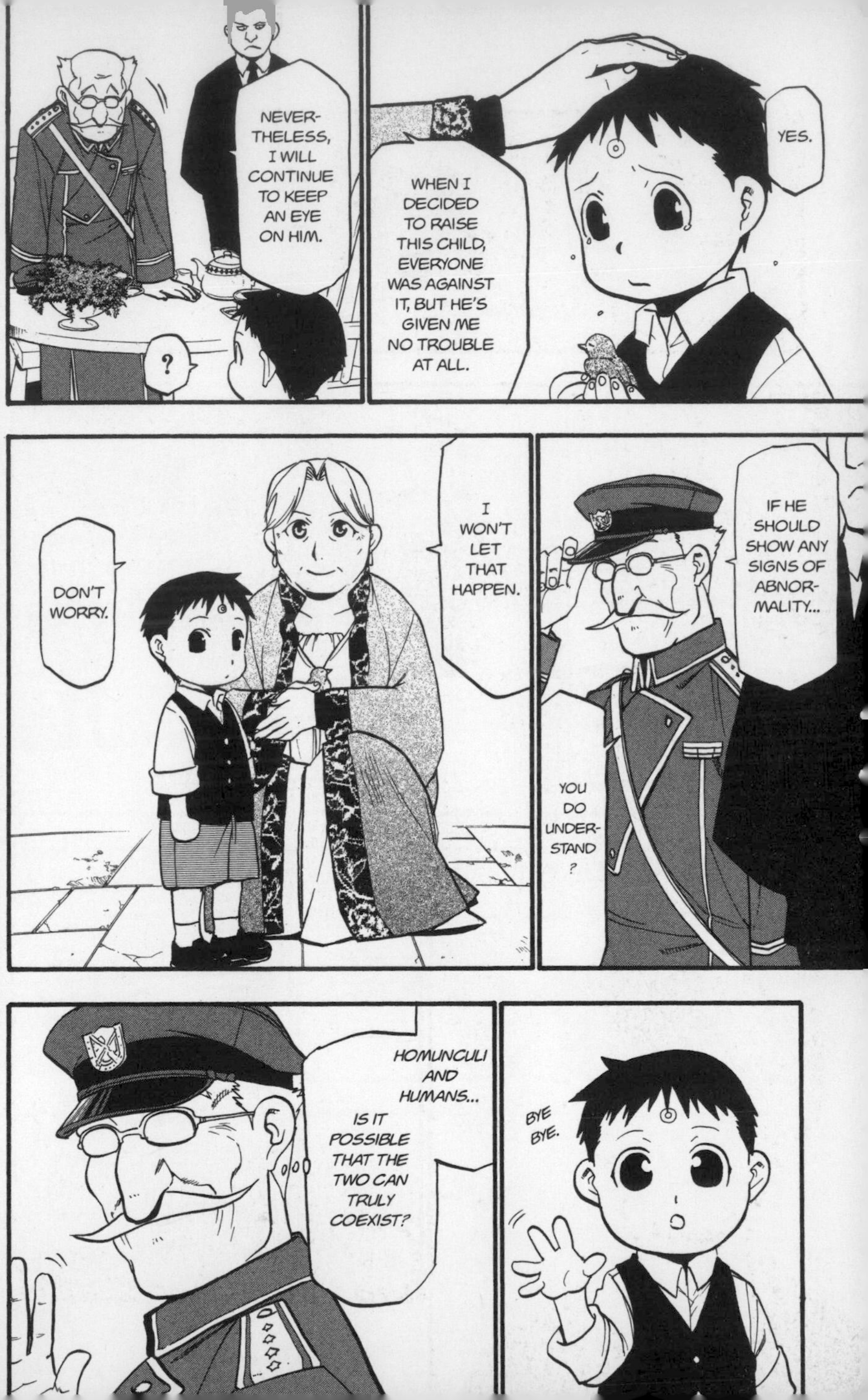
YES.
WHEN I DECIDED TO RAISE THIS CHILD, EVERYONE WAS AGAINST IT, BUT HE'S GIVEN ME NO TROUBLE AT ALL.
NEVER-THELESS, I WILL CONTINUE TO KEEP AN EYE ON HIM.
?
IF HE SHOULD SHOW ANY SIGNS OF ABNOR-MALITY...
YOU DO UNDER-STAND?
I WON'T LET THAT HAPPEN.
DON'T WORRY.
BYE BYE.
HOMUNCULI AND HUMANS...
IS IT POSSIBLE THAT THE TWO CAN TRULY COEXIST?

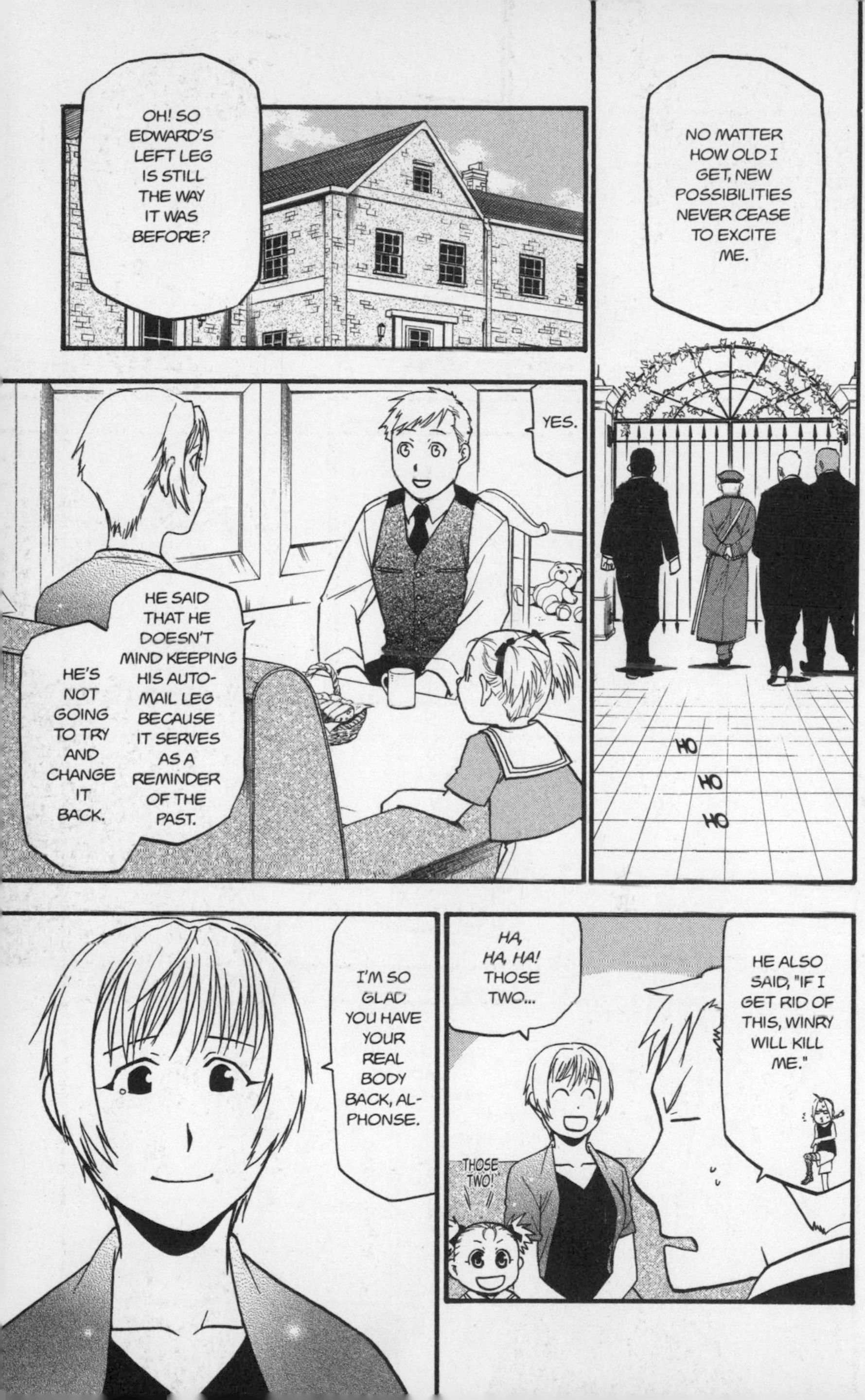
NO MATTER HOW OLD I GET, NEW POSSIBILITIES NEVER CEASE TO EXCITE ME.
HO
HO
HO
OH! SO EDWARD'S LEFT LEG IS STILL THE WAY IT WAS BEFORE?
YES.
HE SAID THAT HE DOESN'T MIND KEEPING HIS AUTO-MAIL LEG BECAUSE IT SERVES AS A REMINDER OF THE PAST.
HE'S NOT GOING TO TRY AND CHANGE IT BACK.
HE ALSO SAID, "IF I GET RID OF THIS, WINRY WILL KILL ME."
HA, HA, HA! THOSE TWO...
THOSE TWO!
I'M SO GLAD YOU HAVE YOUR REAL BODY BACK, AL-PHONSE.

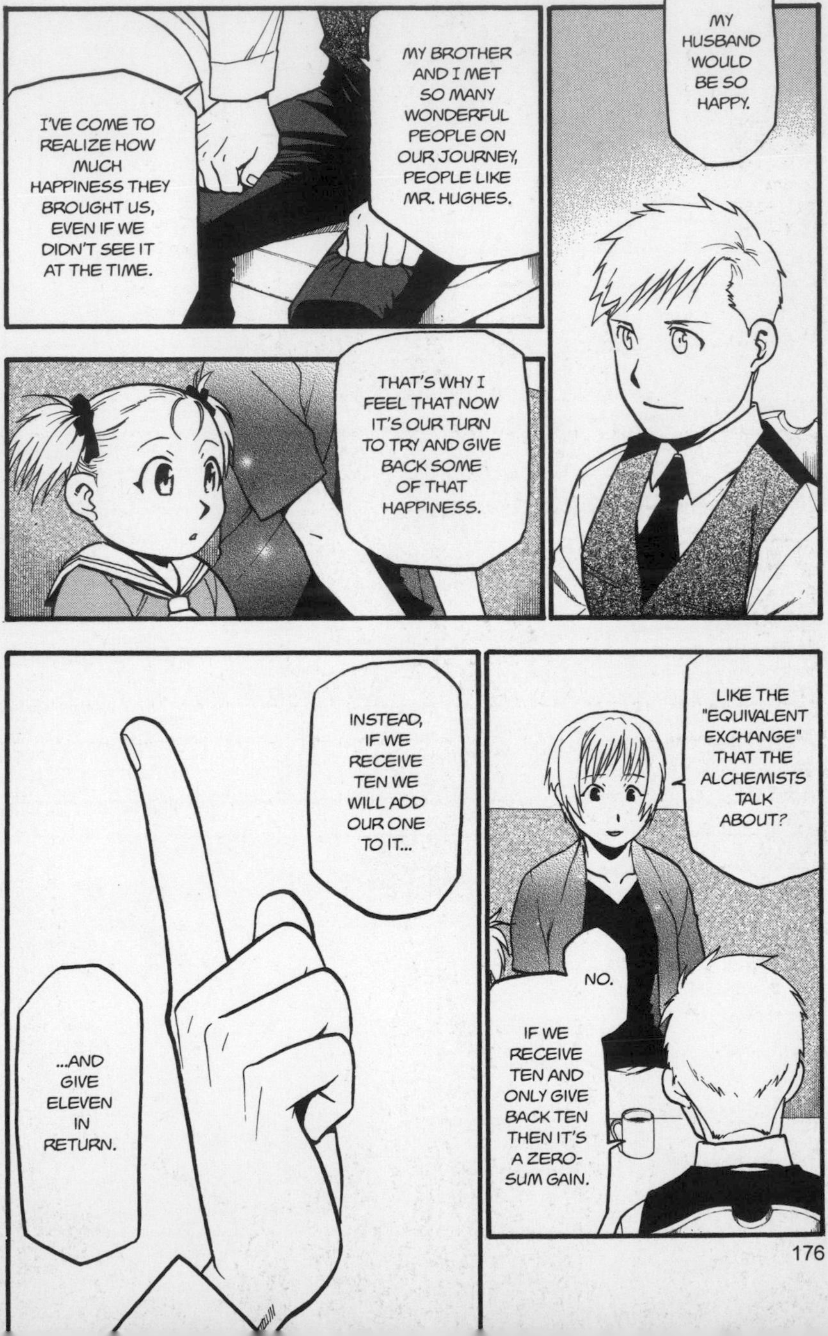
MY HUSBAND WOULD BE SO HAPPY.
MY BROTHER AND I MET SO MANY WONDERFUL PEOPLE ON OUR JOURNEY, PEOPLE LIKE MR. HUGHES.
I'VE COME TO REALIZE HOW MUCH HAPPINESS THEY BROUGHT US, EVEN IF WE DIDN'T SEE IT AT THE TIME.
THAT'S WHY I FEEL THAT NOW IT'S OUR TURN TO TRY AND GIVE BACK SOME OF THAT HAPPINESS.
LIKE THE "EQUIVALENT EXCHANGE" THAT THE ALCHEMISTS TALK ABOUT?
NO.
IF WE RECEIVE TEN AND ONLY GIVE BACK TEN THEN IT'S A ZERO-SUM GAIN.
INSTEAD, IF WE RECEIVE TEN WE WILL ADD OUR ONE TO IT...
...AND GIVE ELEVEN IN RETURN.

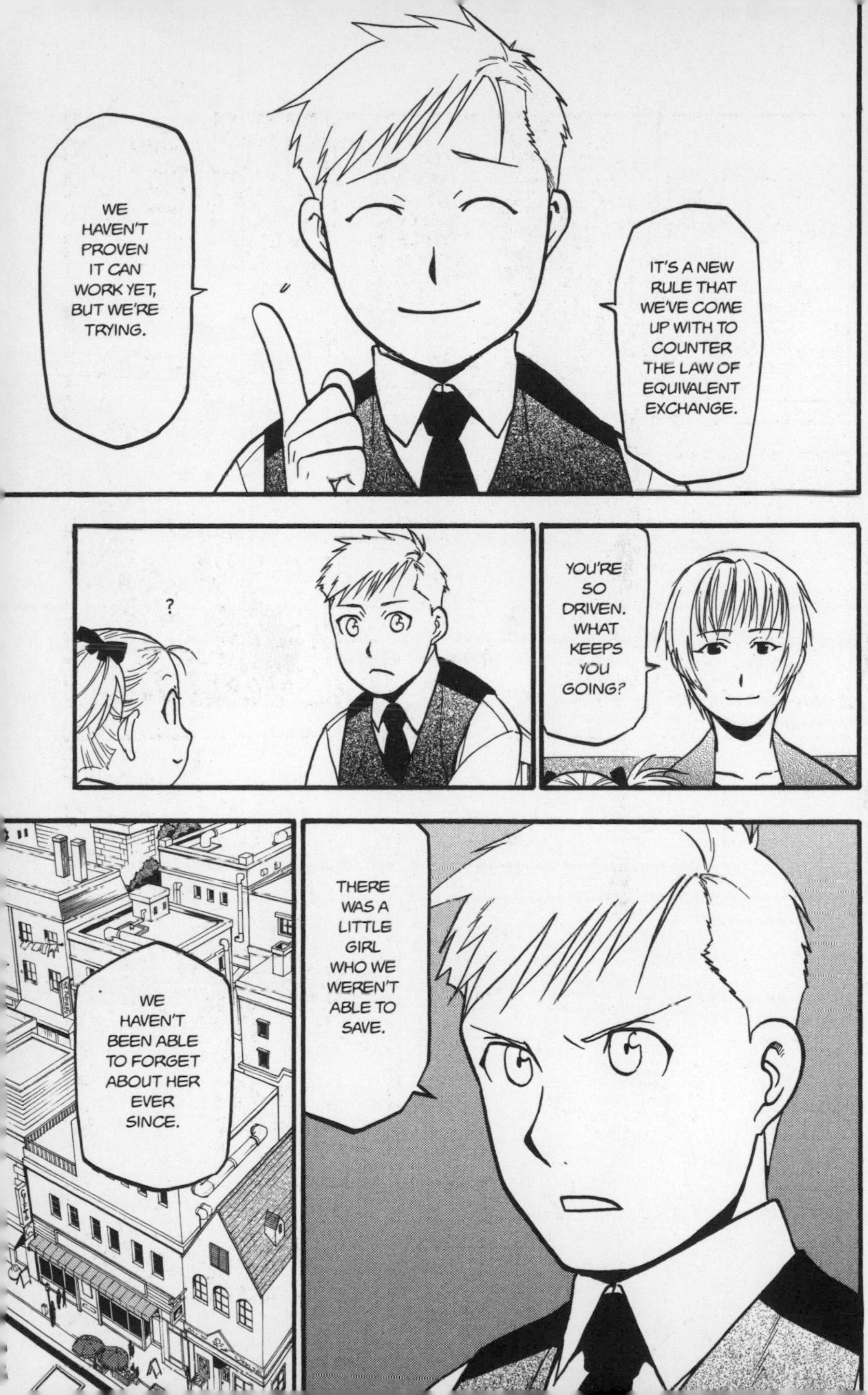
IT'S A NEW RULE THAT WE'VE COME UP WITH TO COUNTER THE LAW OF EQUIVALENT EXCHANGE.
WE HAVEN'T PROVEN IT CAN WORK YET, BUT WE'RE TRYING.
YOU'RE SO DRIVEN. WHAT KEEPS YOU GOING?
?
THERE WAS A LITTLE GIRL WHO WE WEREN'T ABLE TO SAVE.
WE HAVEN'T BEEN ABLE TO FORGET ABOUT HER EVER SINCE.

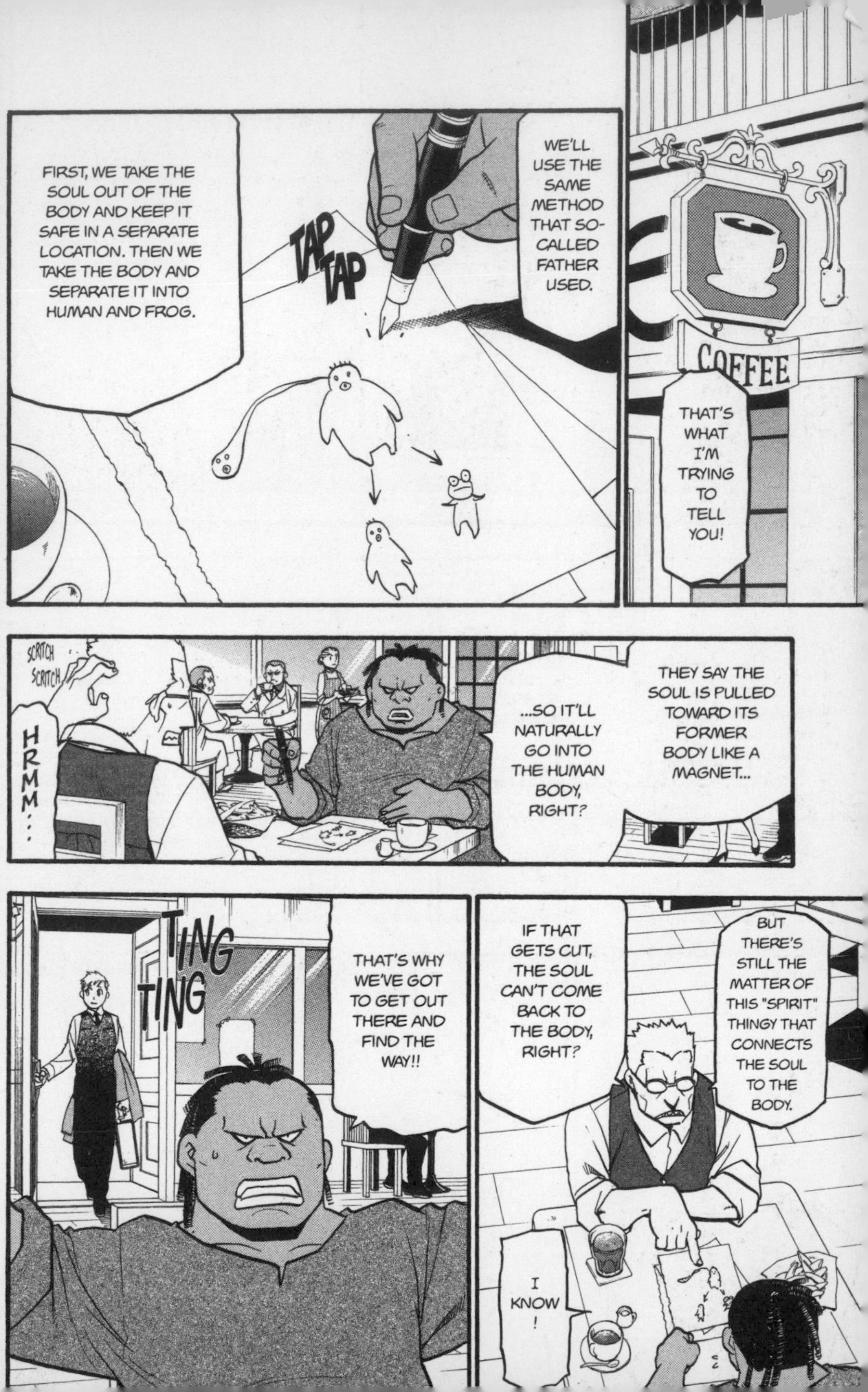
THAT'S WHAT I'M TRYING TO TELL YOU!
COFFEE
WE'LL USE THE SAME METHOD THAT SO-CALLED FATHER USED.
TAP TAP
FIRST, WE TAKE THE SOUL OUT OF THE BODY AND KEEP IT SAFE IN A SEPARATE LOCATION. THEN WE TAKE THE BODY AND SEPARATE IT INTO HUMAN AND FROG.
THEY SAY THE SOUL IS PULLED TOWARD ITS FORMER BODY LIKE A MAGNET...
...SO IT'LL NATURALLY GO INTO THE HUMAN BODY, RIGHT?
SCRATCH SCRATCH
HRMM...
BUT THERE'S STILL THE MATTER OF THIS "SPIRIT" THINGY THAT CONNECTS THE SOUL TO THE BODY.
IF THAT GETS CUT, THE SOUL CAN'T COME BACK TO THE BODY, RIGHT?
I KNOW!
THAT'S WHY WE'VE GOT TO GET OUT THERE AND FIND THE WAY!!
TING TING

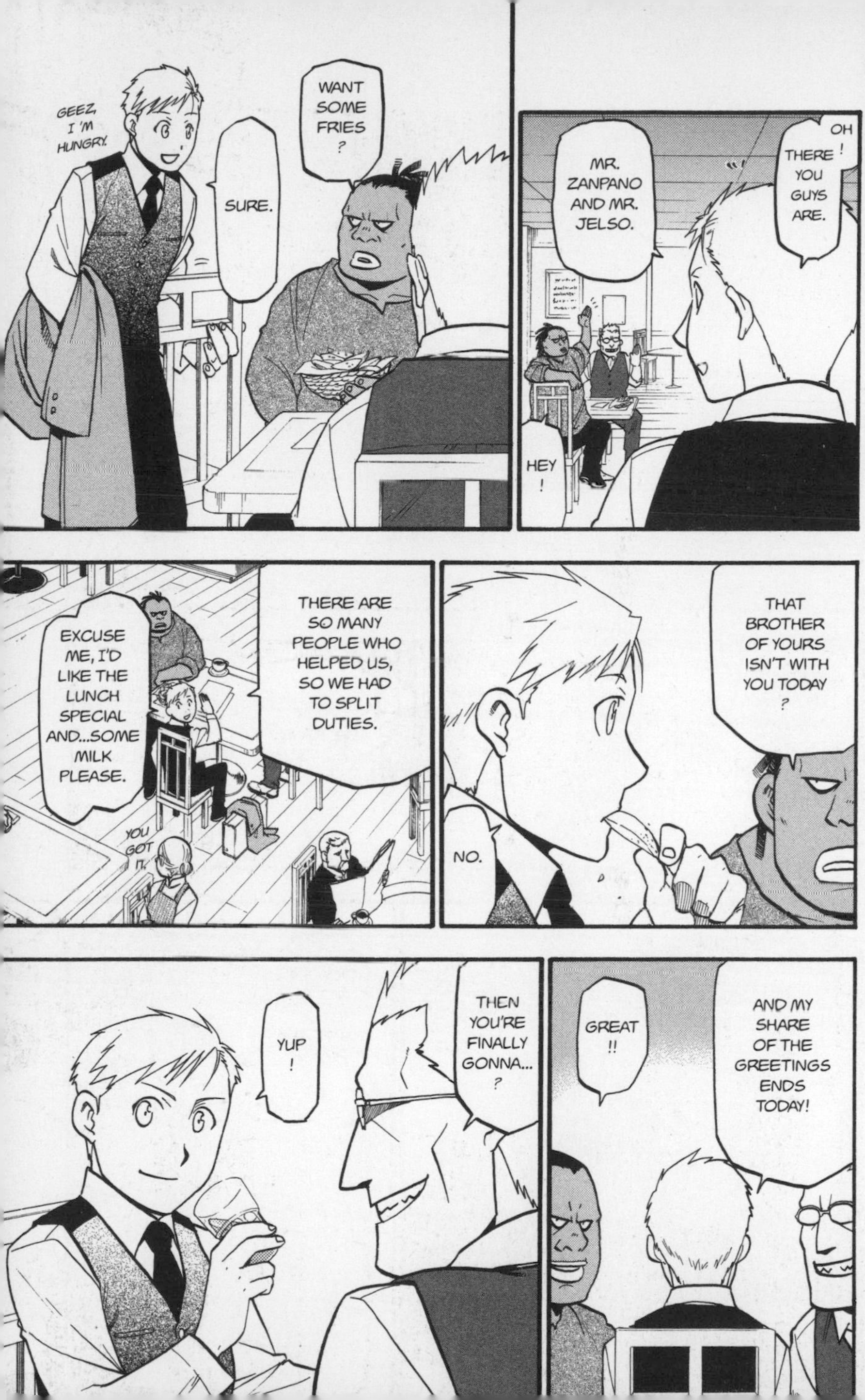
OH! THERE YOU GUYS ARE.
MR. ZANPANO AND MR. JELSO.
HEY!
WANT SOME FRIES?
GEEZ, I'M HUNGRY.
SURE.
THAT BROTHER OF YOURS ISN'T WITH YOU TODAY?
NO.
THERE ARE SO MANY PEOPLE WHO HELPED US, SO WE HAD TO SPLIT DUTIES.
EXCUSE ME, I'D LIKE THE LUNCH SPECIAL AND...SOME MILK PLEASE.
YOU GOT IT.
AND MY SHARE OF THE GREETINGS ENDS TODAY!
GREAT!!
THEN YOU'RE FINALLY GONNA...?
YUP!

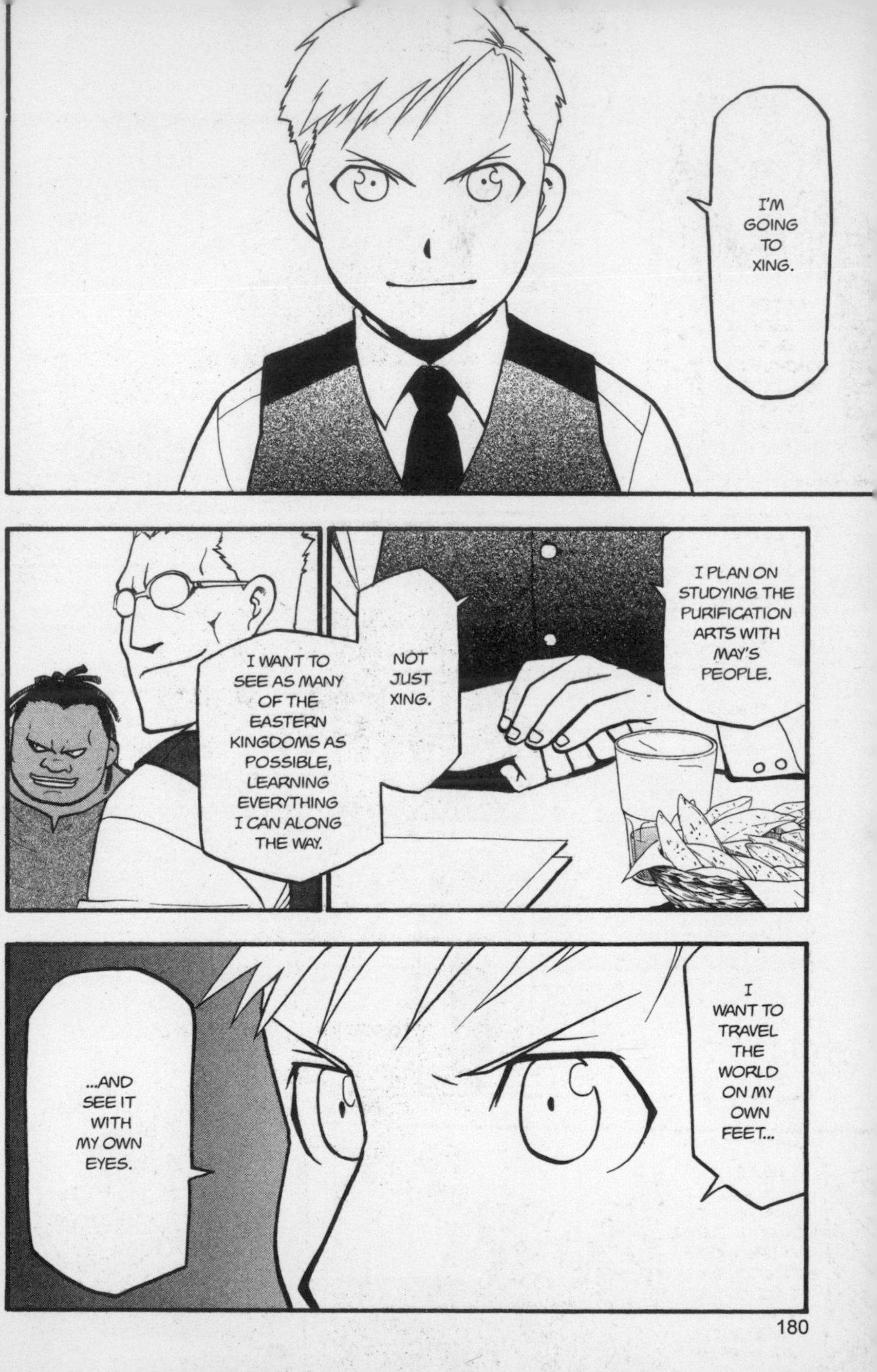
I'M GOING TO XING.
I PLAN ON STUDYING THE PURIFICATION ARTS WITH MAY'S PEOPLE.
NOT JUST XING.
I WANT TO SEE AS MANY OF THE EASTERN KINGDOMS AS POSSIBLE, LEARNING EVERYTHING I CAN ALONG THE WAY.
I WANT TO TRAVEL THE WORLD ON MY OWN FEET...
...AND SEE IT WITH MY OWN EYES.

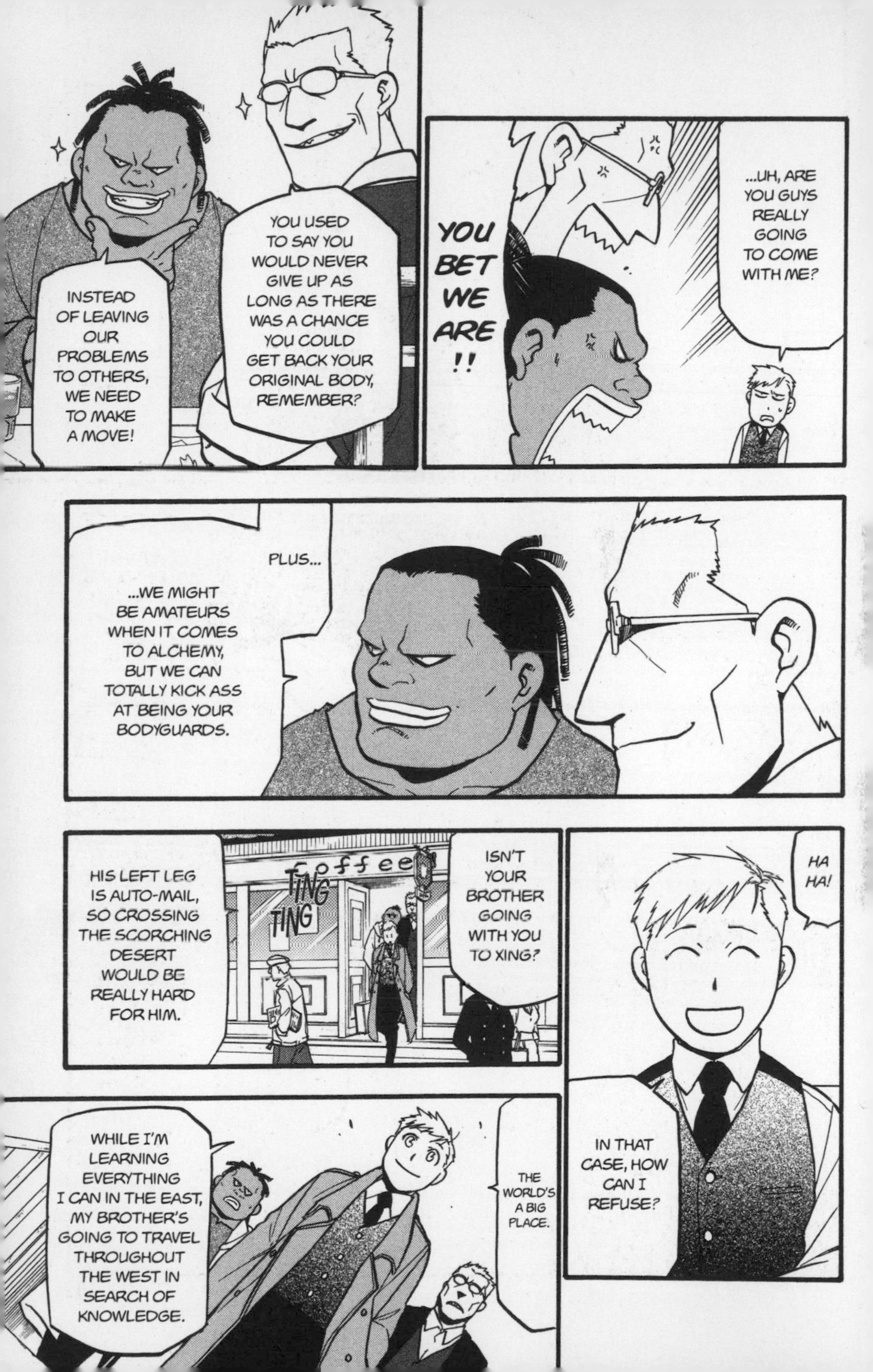
...UH, ARE YOU GUYS REALLY GOING TO COME WITH ME?
YOU BET WE ARE!!
YOU USED TO SAY YOU WOULD NEVER GIVE UP AS LONG AS THERE WAS A CHANCE YOU COULD GET BACK YOUR ORIGINAL BODY, REMEMBER?
INSTEAD OF LEAVING OUR PROBLEMS TO OTHERS, WE NEED TO MAKE A MOVE!
PLUS...
...WE MIGHT BE AMATEURS WHEN IT COMES TO ALCHEMY, BUT WE CAN TOTALLY KICK ASS AT BEING YOUR BODYGUARDS.
HA HA!
IN THAT CASE, HOW CAN I REFUSE?
ISN'T YOUR BROTHER GOING WITH YOU TO XING?
coffee
TING TING
HIS LEFT LEG IS AUTO-MAIL, SO CROSSING THE SCORCHING DESERT WOULD BE REALLY HARD FOR HIM.
THE WORLD'S A BIG PLACE.
WHILE I'M LEARNING EVERYTHING I CAN IN THE EAST, MY BROTHER'S GOING TO TRAVEL THROUGHOUT THE WEST IN SEARCH OF KNOWLEDGE.

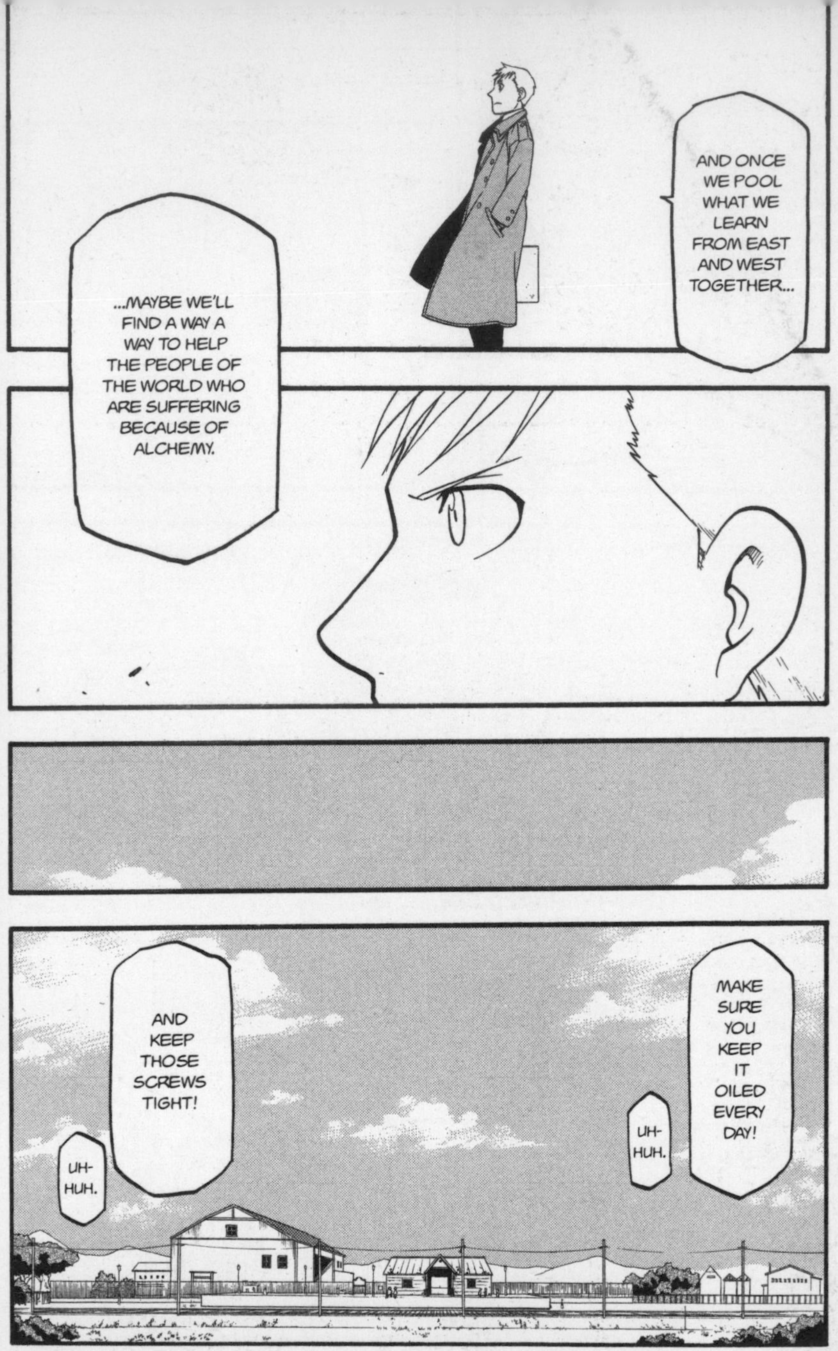
AND ONCE WE POOL WHAT WE LEARN FROM EAST AND WEST TOGETHER...
...MAYBE WE'LL FIND A WAY A WAY TO HELP THE PEOPLE OF THE WORLD WHO ARE SUFFERING BECAUSE OF ALCHEMY.
MAKE SURE YOU KEEP IT OILED EVERY DAY!
UH-HUH.
AND KEEP THOSE SCREWS TIGHT!
UH-HUH.

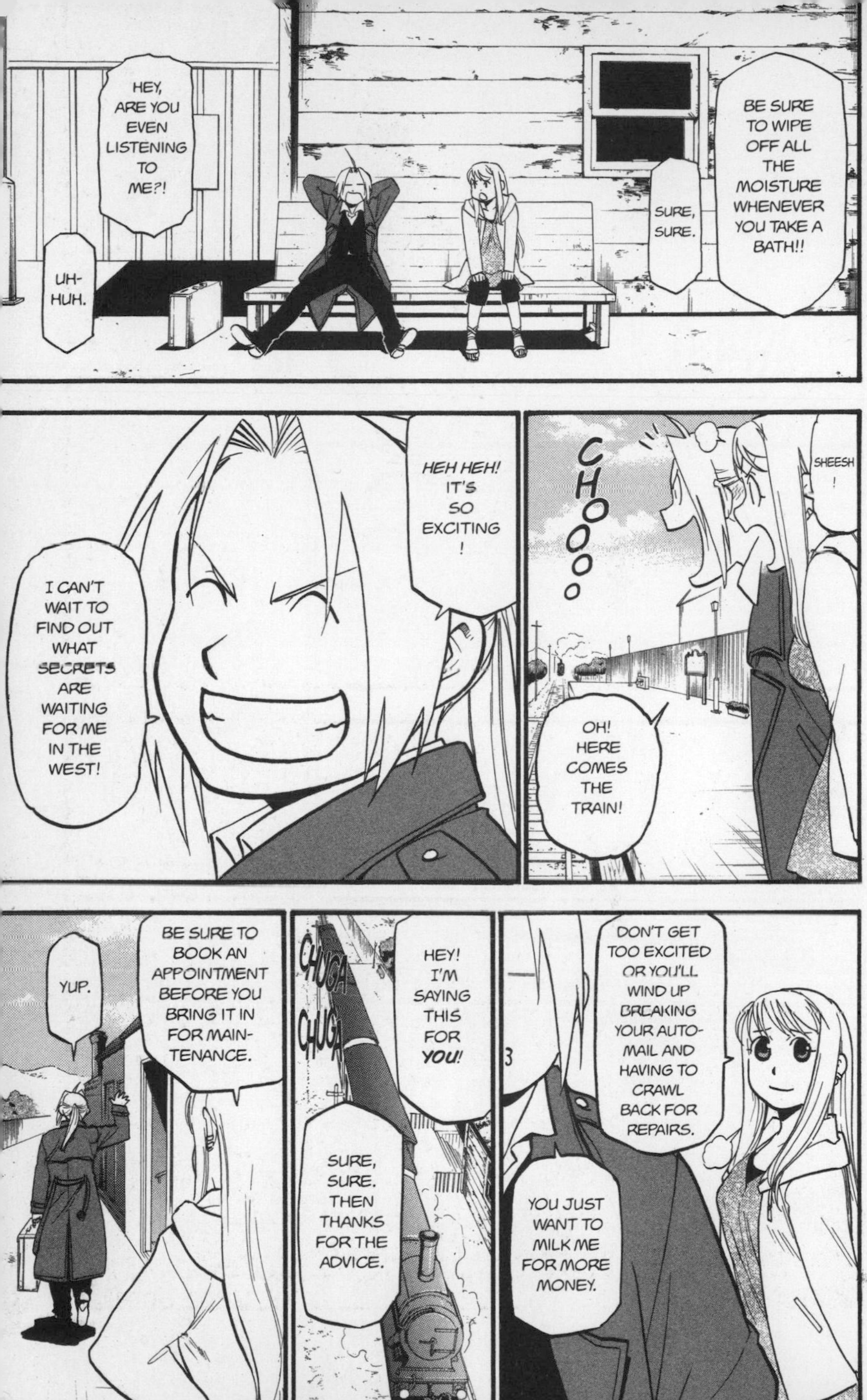
BE SURE TO WIPE OFF ALL THE MOISTURE WHENEVER YOU TAKE A BATH!!
SURE, SURE.
HEY, ARE YOU EVEN LISTENING TO ME?!
UH-HUH.
SHEESH!
CHOOOOO
OH! HERE COMES THE TRAIN!
HEH HEH! IT'S SO EXCITING!
I CAN'T WAIT TO FIND OUT WHAT SECRETS ARE WAITING FOR ME IN THE WEST!
DON'T GET TOO EXCITED OR YOU'LL WIND UP BREAKING YOUR AUTO-MAIL AND HAVING TO CRAWL BACK FOR REPAIRS.
YOU JUST WANT TO MILK ME FOR MORE MONEY.
HEY! I'M SAYING THIS FOR *YOU*!
CHUGA CHUGA
SURE, SURE. THEN THANKS FOR THE ADVICE.
BE SURE TO BOOK AN APPOINTMENT BEFORE YOU BRING IT IN FOR MAINTENANCE.
YUP.

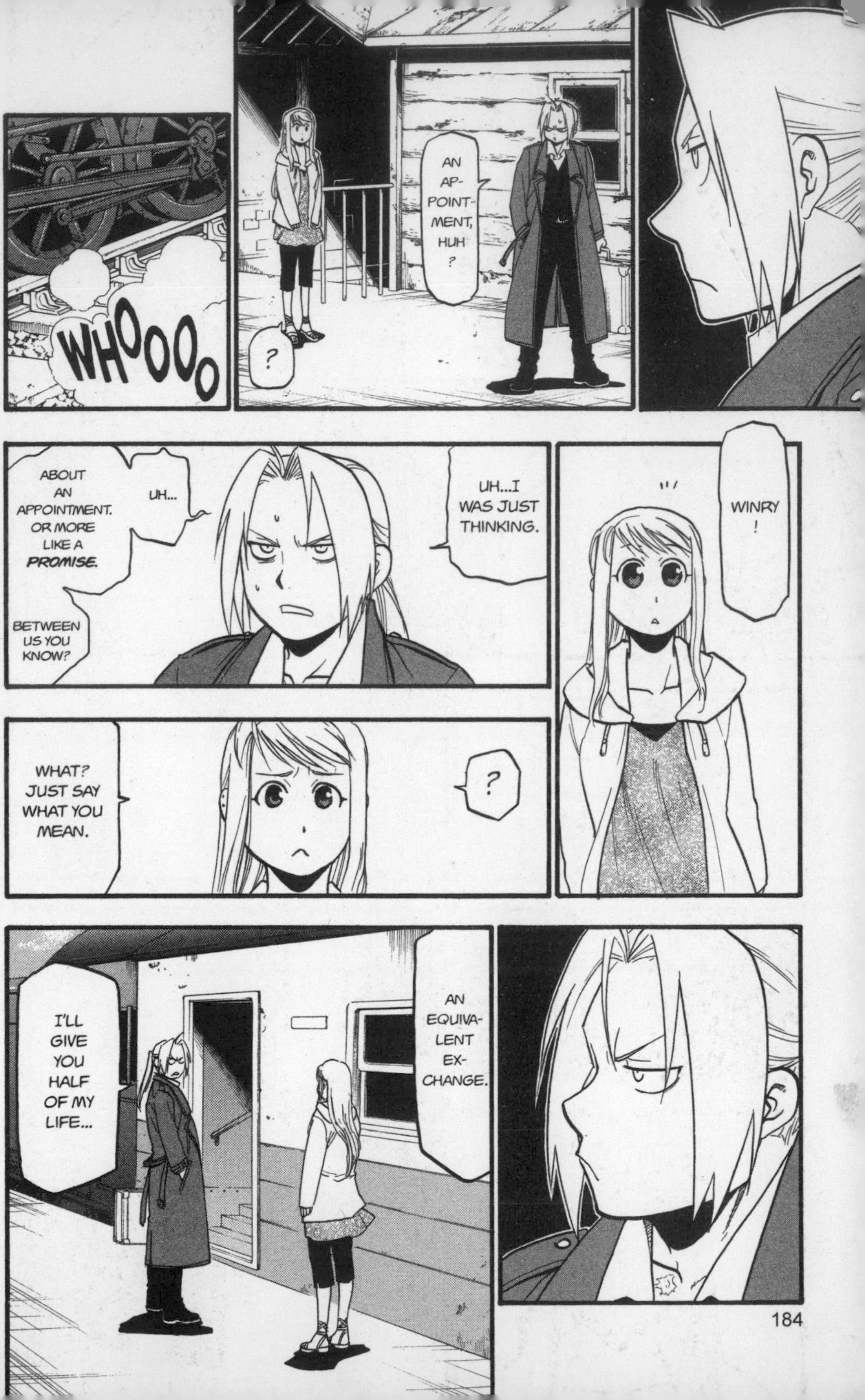
AN AP-POINT-MENT, HUH?
?
WHOOOO
WINRY!
UH...I WAS JUST THINKING.
UH...
ABOUT AN APPOINTMENT. OR MORE LIKE A **PROMISE.**
BETWEEN US YOU KNOW?
?
WHAT? JUST SAY WHAT YOU MEAN.
AN EQUIVA-LENT EX-CHANGE.
I'LL GIVE YOU HALF OF MY LIFE...

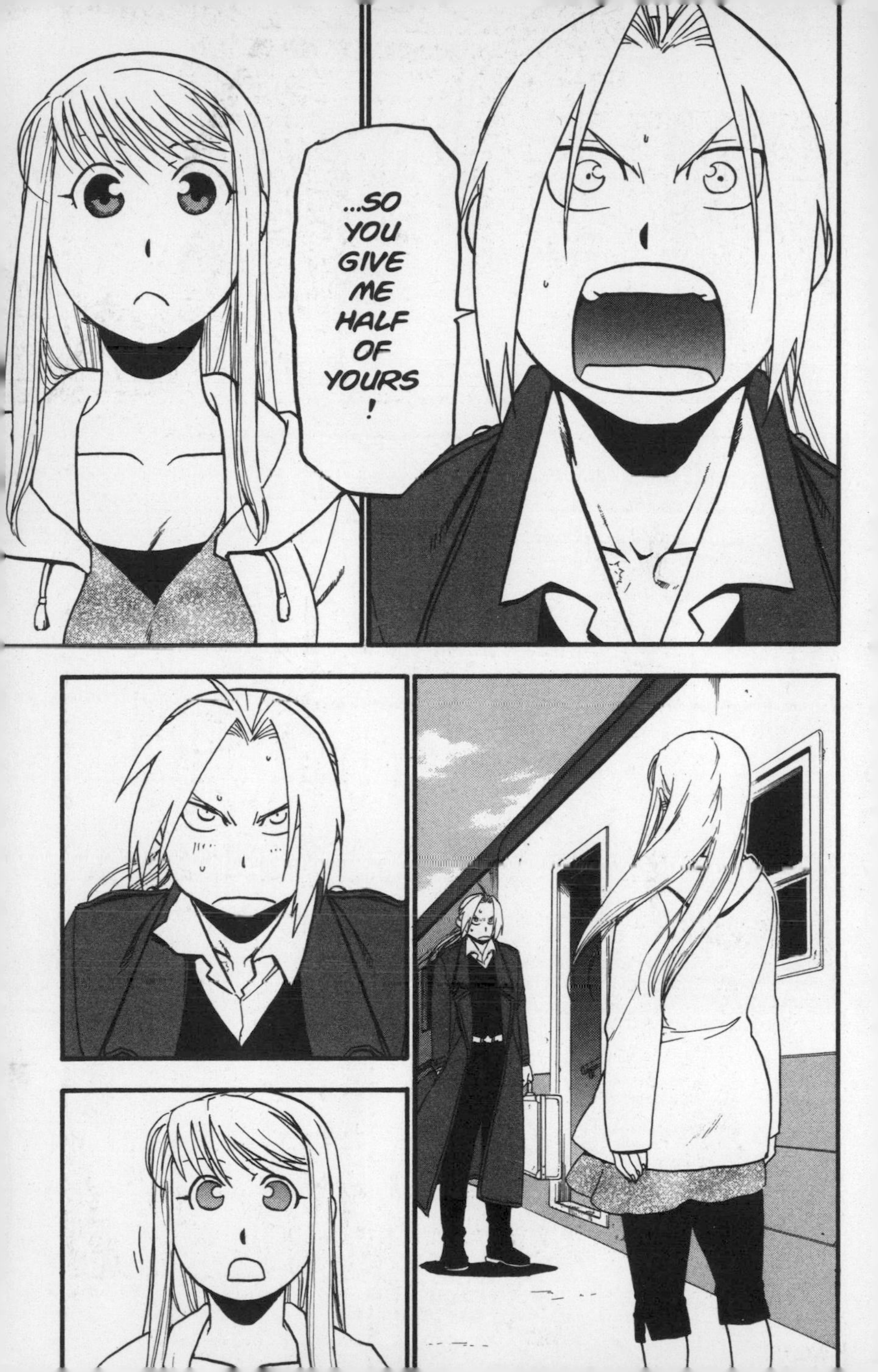
...SO YOU GIVE ME HALF OF YOURS!

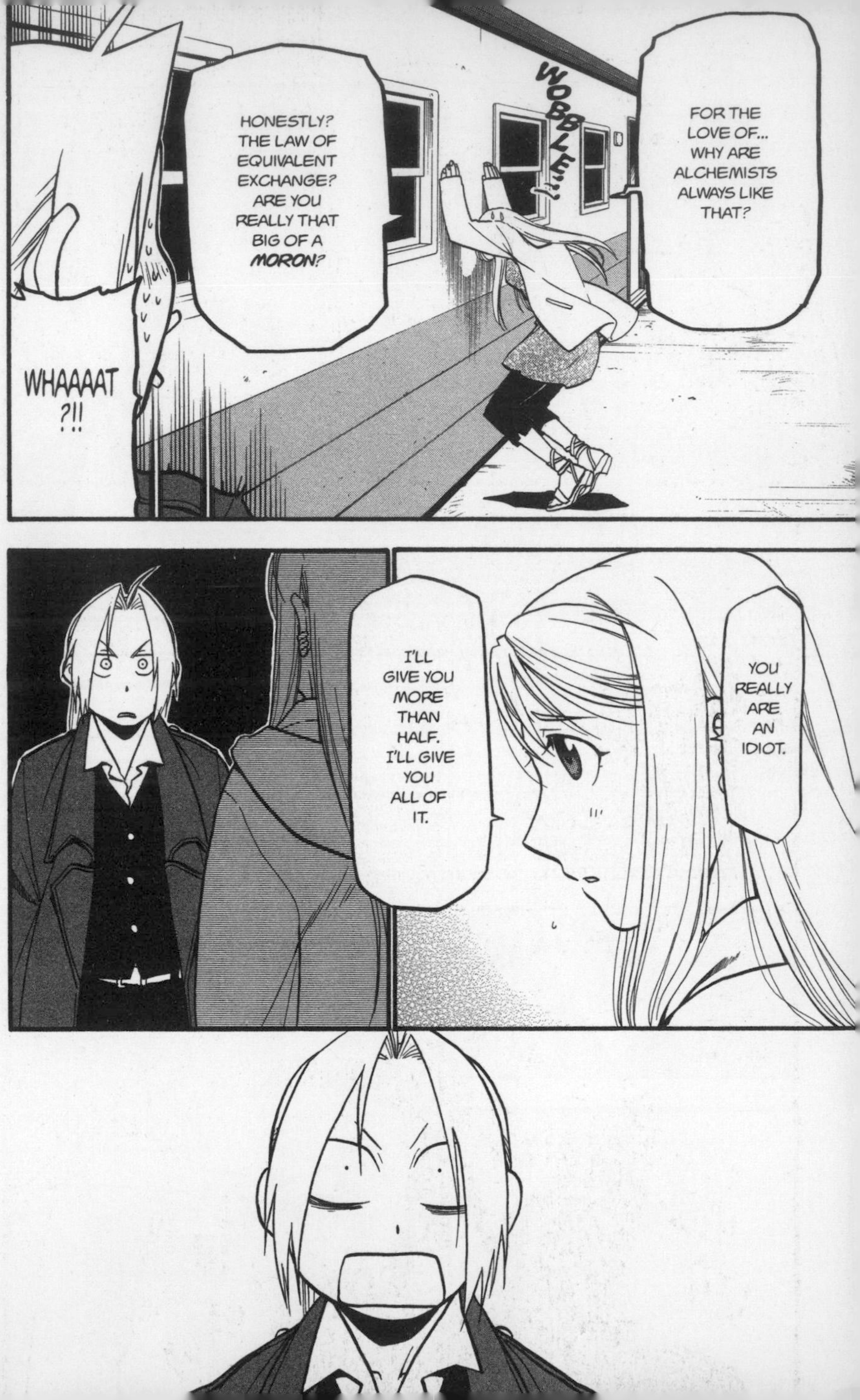
FOR THE LOVE OF... WHY ARE ALCHEMISTS ALWAYS LIKE THAT?
WOBBLE...
HONESTLY? THE LAW OF EQUIVALENT EXCHANGE? ARE YOU REALLY THAT BIG OF A *MORON*?
WHAAAAT?!!
YOU REALLY ARE AN IDIOT.
I'LL GIVE YOU MORE THAN HALF. I'LL GIVE YOU ALL OF IT.

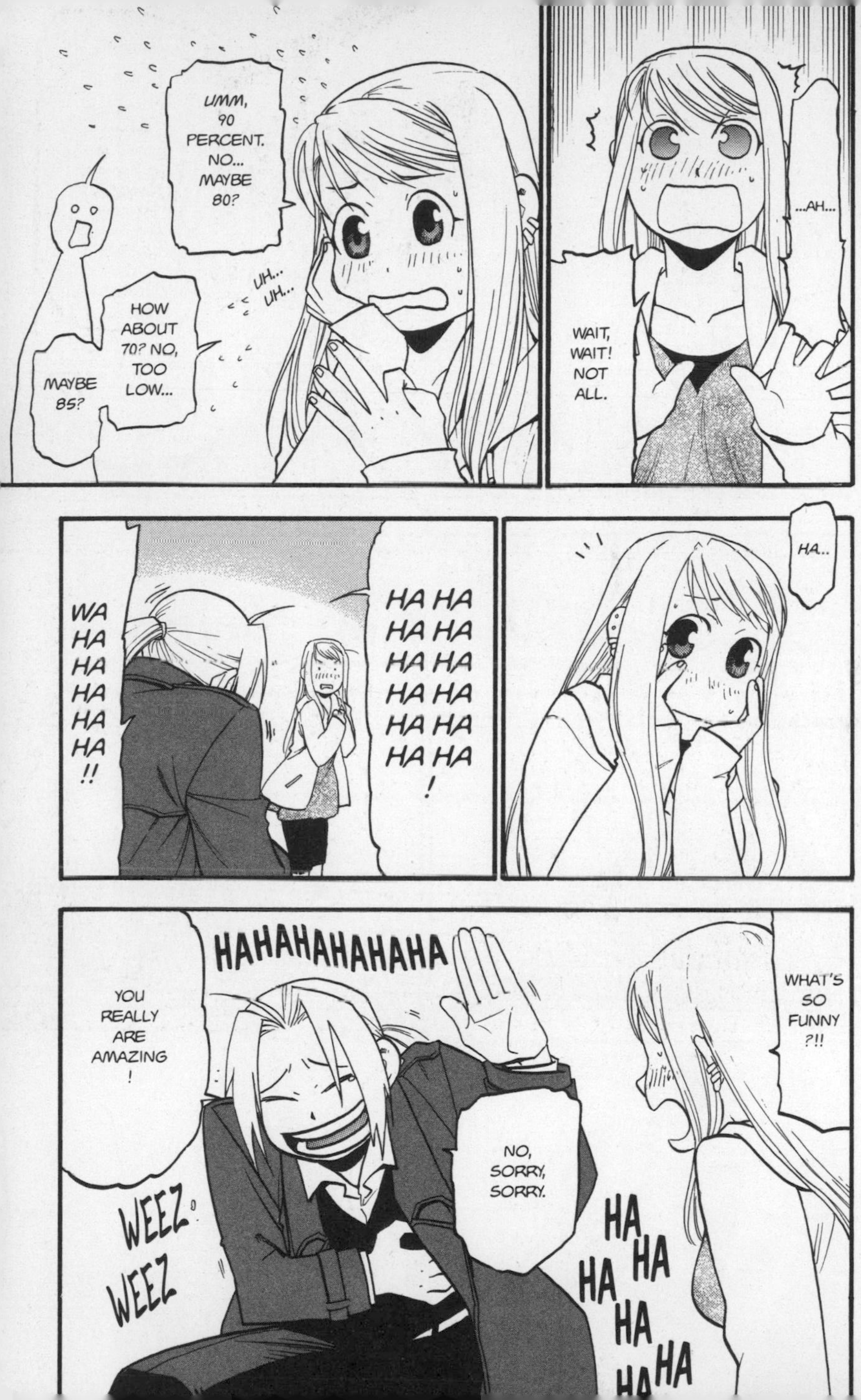
...AH...
WAIT, WAIT! NOT ALL.
UMM, 90 PERCENT. NO... MAYBE 80?
UH... UH...
HOW ABOUT 70? NO, TOO LOW...
MAYBE 85?
HA...
HA HA HA HA HA HA HA HA HA HA HA HA!
WA HA HA HA HA HA!!
WHAT'S SO FUNNY?!!
HAHAHAHAHAHA
YOU REALLY ARE AMAZING!
NO, SORRY, SORRY.
HA HA HA HA HA HA HA
WEEZ WEEZ

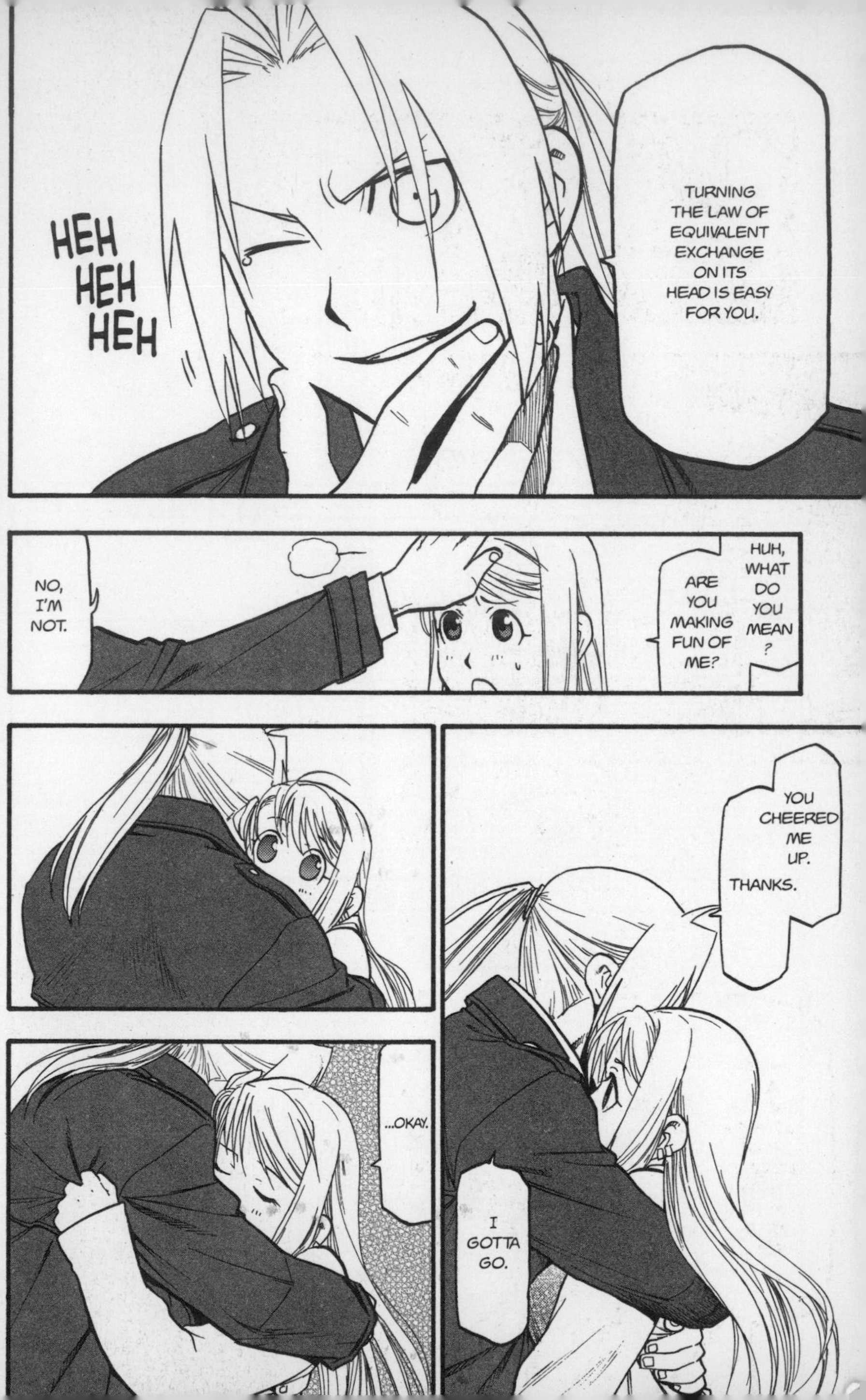
TURNING THE LAW OF EQUIVALENT EXCHANGE ON ITS HEAD IS EASY FOR YOU.
HEH HEH HEH
HUH, WHAT DO YOU MEAN?
ARE YOU MAKING FUN OF ME?
NO, I'M NOT.
YOU CHEERED ME UP.
THANKS.
I GOTTA GO.
...OKAY.

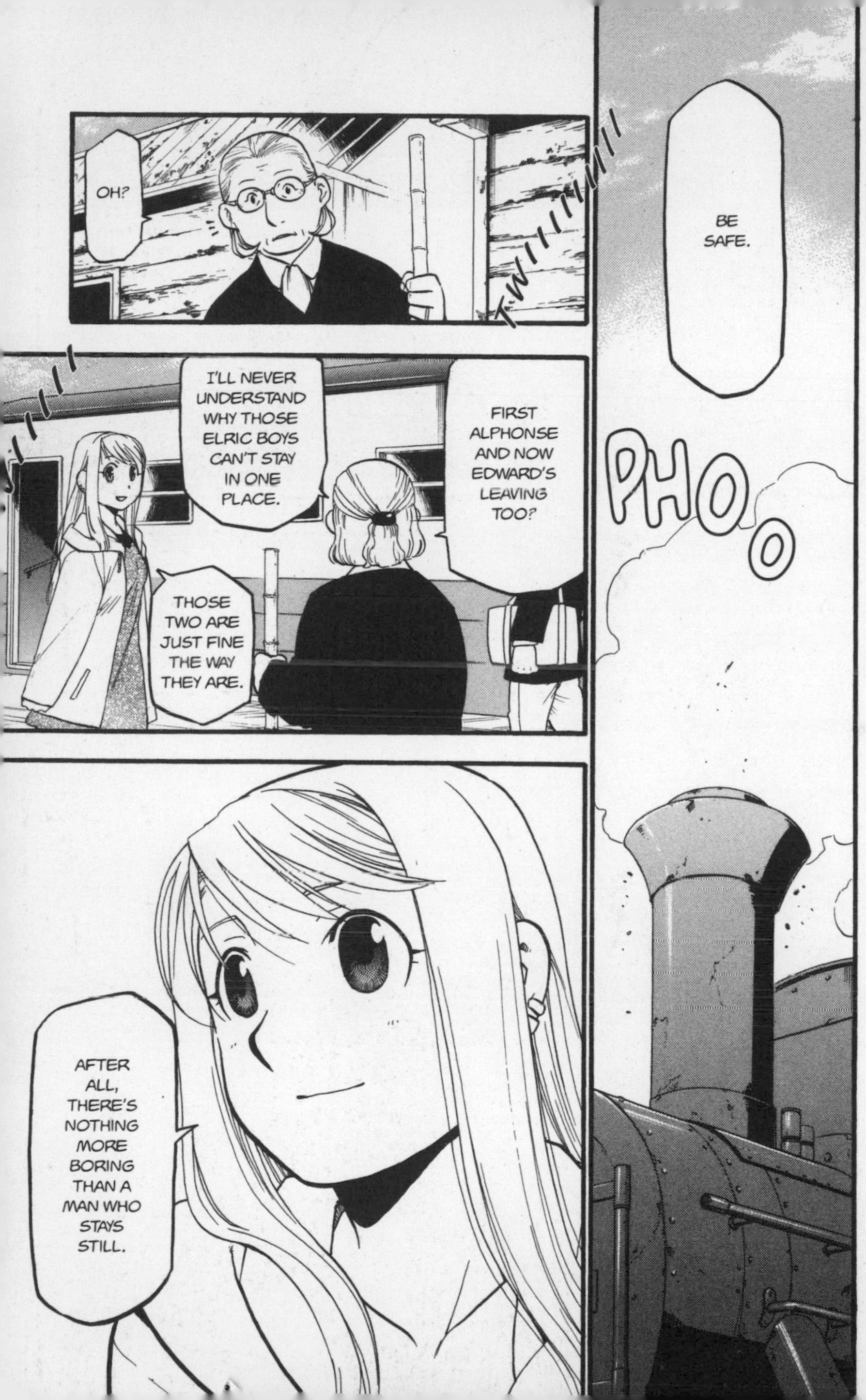
BE SAFE.
PHOOO
OH?
TWIIIIIIII
FIRST ALPHONSE AND NOW EDWARD'S LEAVING TOO?
I'LL NEVER UNDERSTAND WHY THOSE ELRIC BOYS CAN'T STAY IN ONE PLACE.
THOSE TWO ARE JUST FINE THE WAY THEY ARE.
AFTER ALL, THERE'S NOTHING MORE BORING THAN A MAN WHO STAYS STILL.

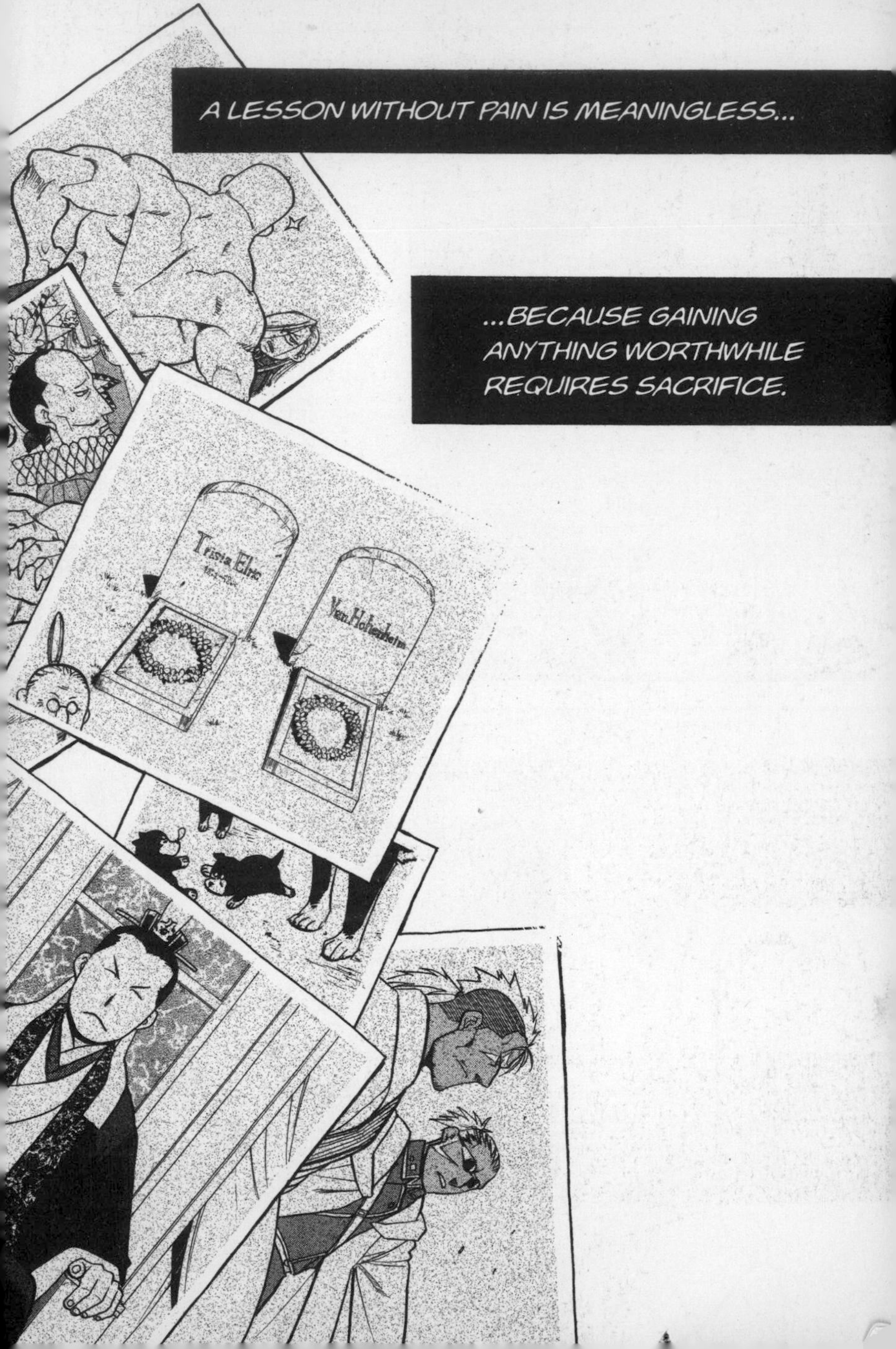
A LESSON WITHOUT PAIN IS MEANINGLESS...
...BECAUSE GAINING ANYTHING WORTHWHILE REQUIRES SACRIFICE.
Trisha Elric
Van Hohenheim

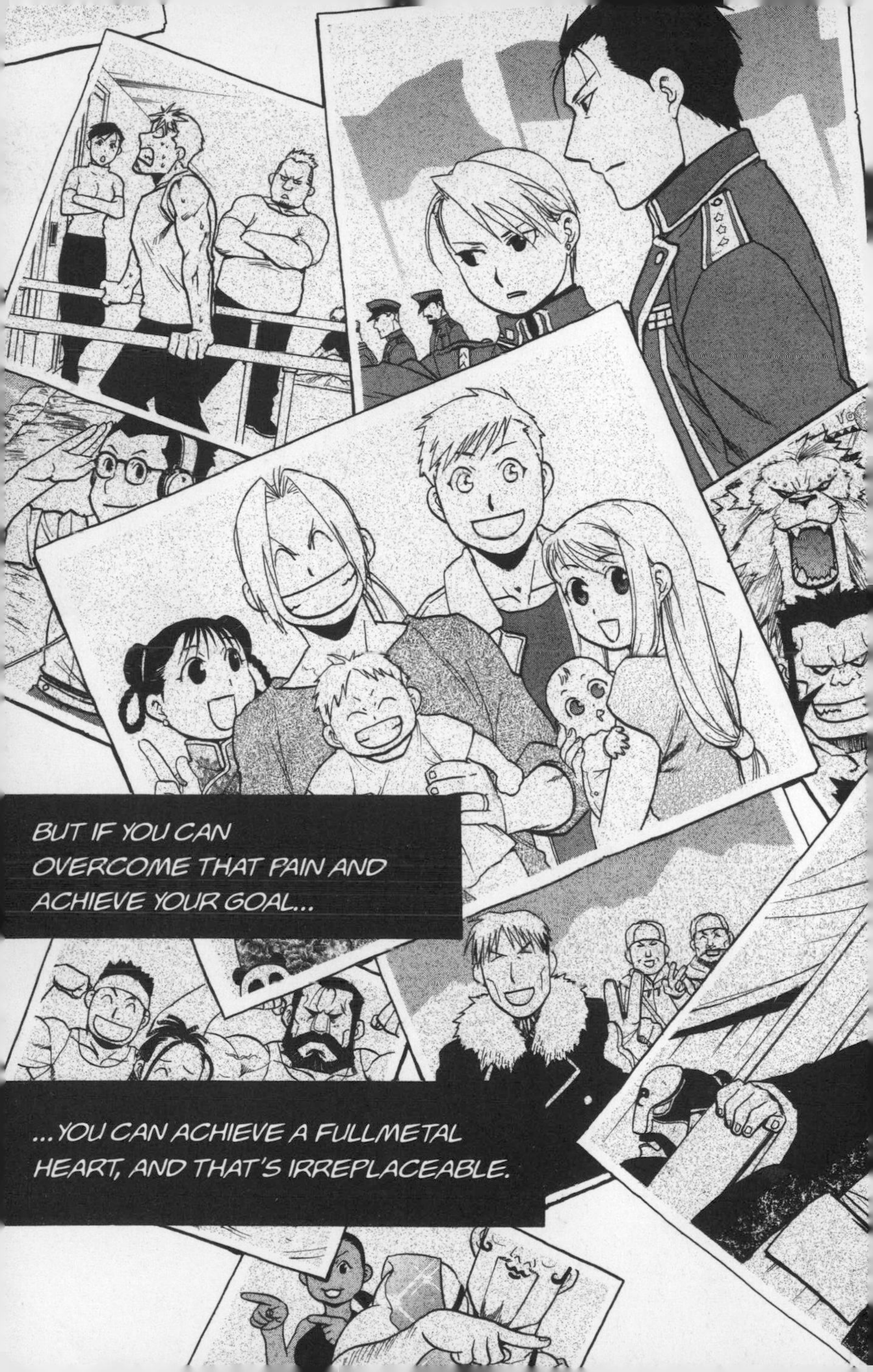
BUT IF YOU CAN OVERCOME THAT PAIN AND ACHIEVE YOUR GOAL...
...YOU CAN ACHIEVE A FULLMETAL HEART, AND THAT'S IRREPLACEABLE.

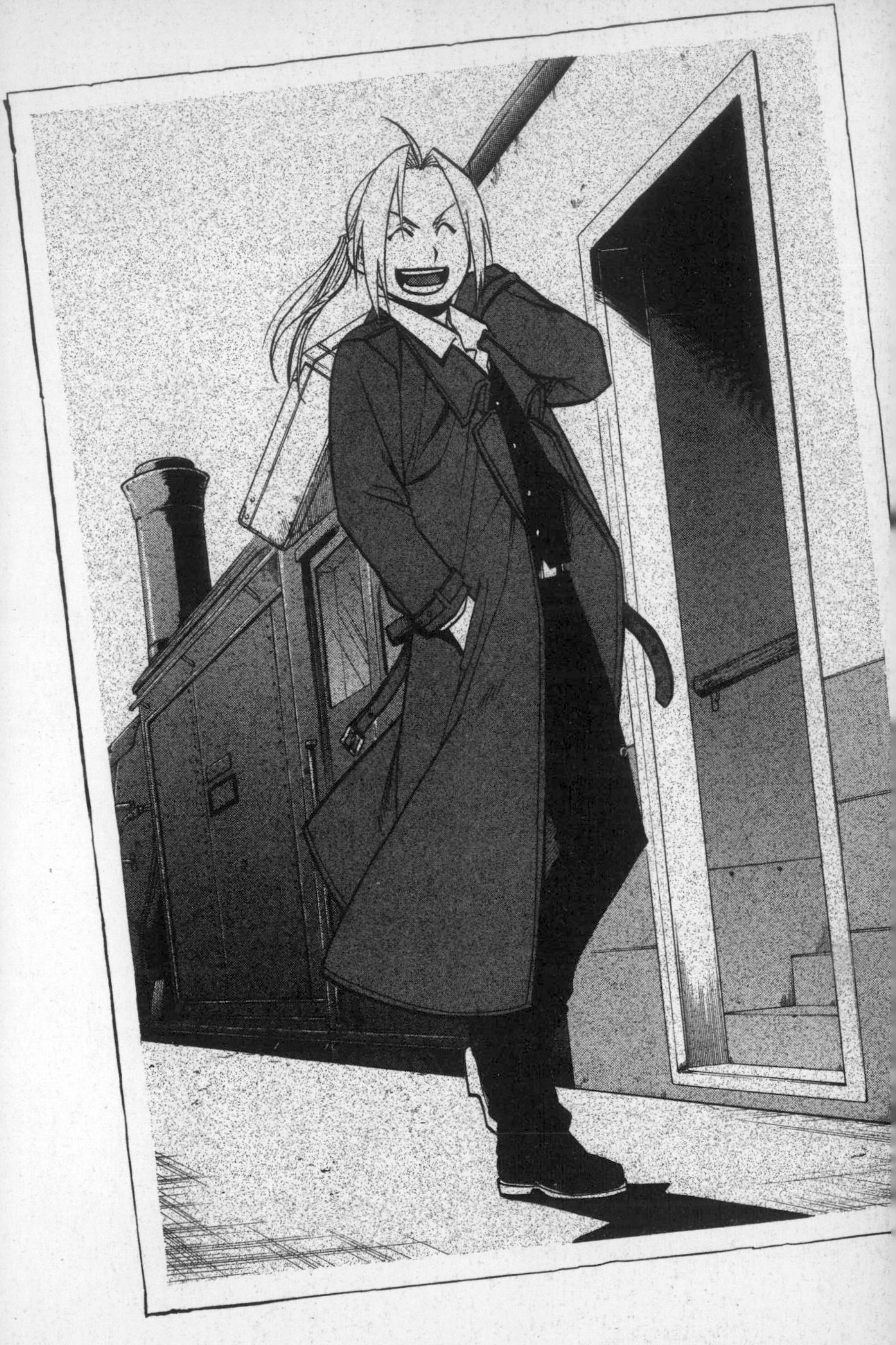

FULLMETAL
ALCHEMIST

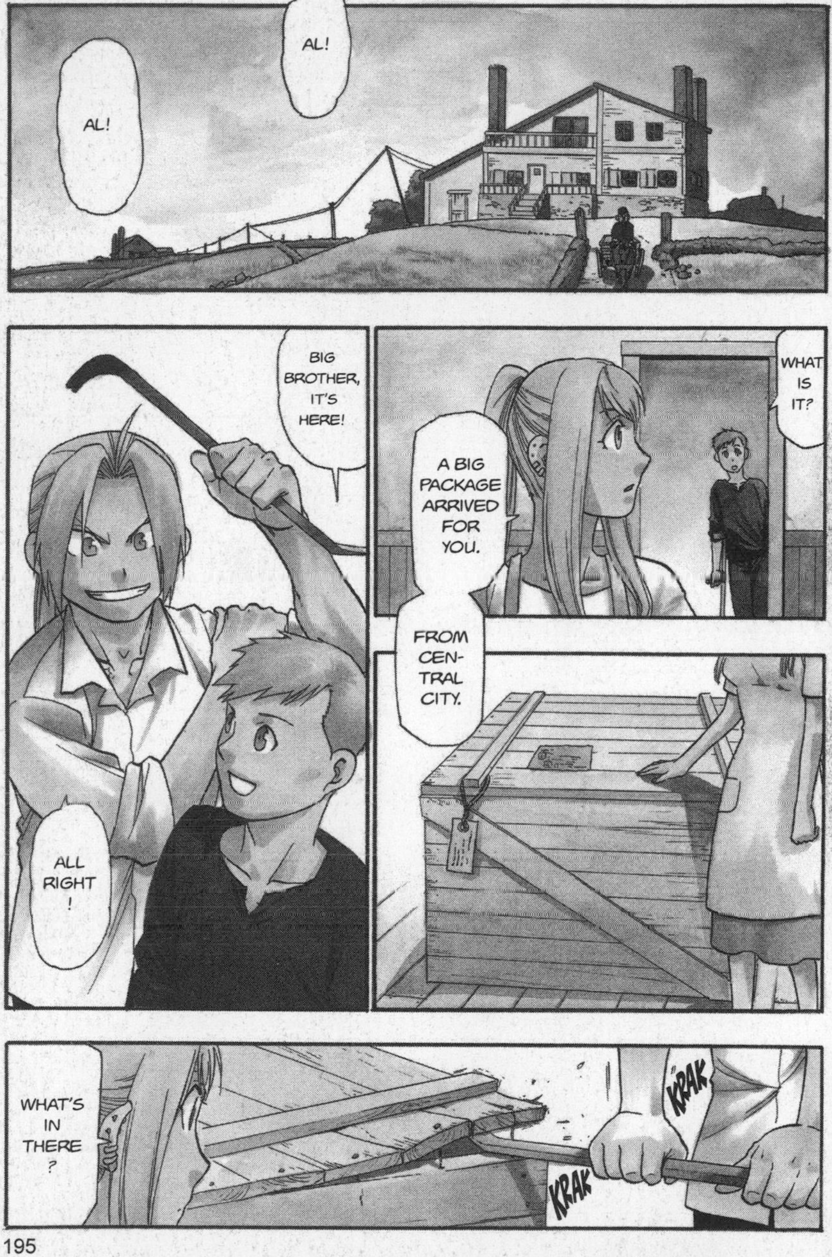
AL!
AL!
WHAT IS IT?
A BIG PACKAGE ARRIVED FOR YOU.
FROM CEN-TRAL CITY.
BIG BROTHER, IT'S HERE!
ALL RIGHT!
KRAK
WHAT'S IN THERE?
KRAK

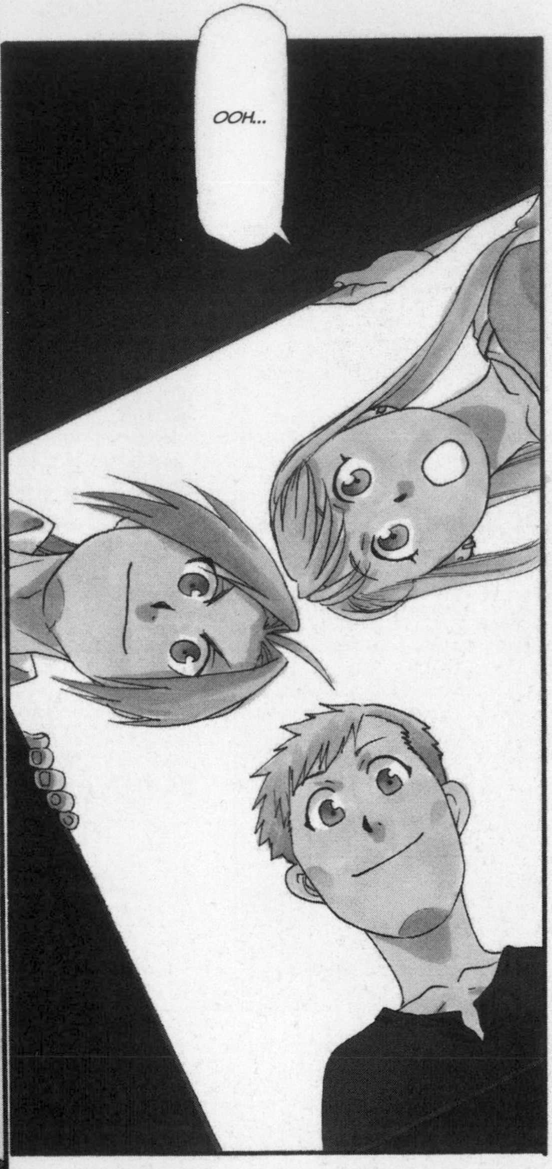
OOH...
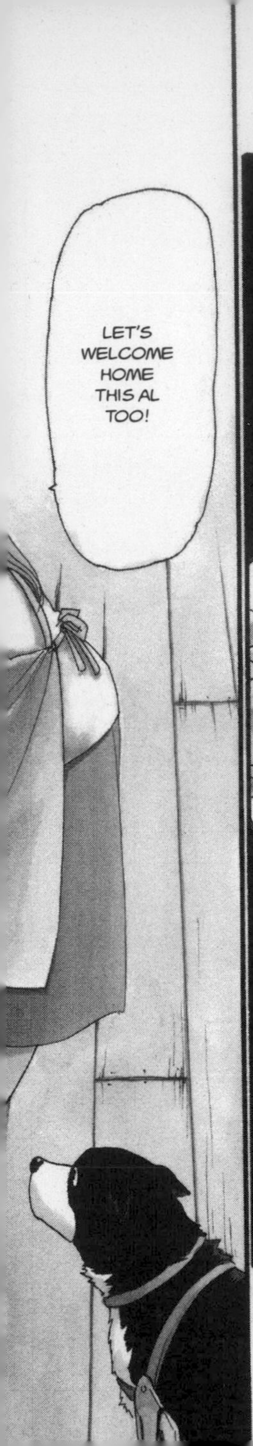
LET'S WELCOME HOME THIS AL TOO!

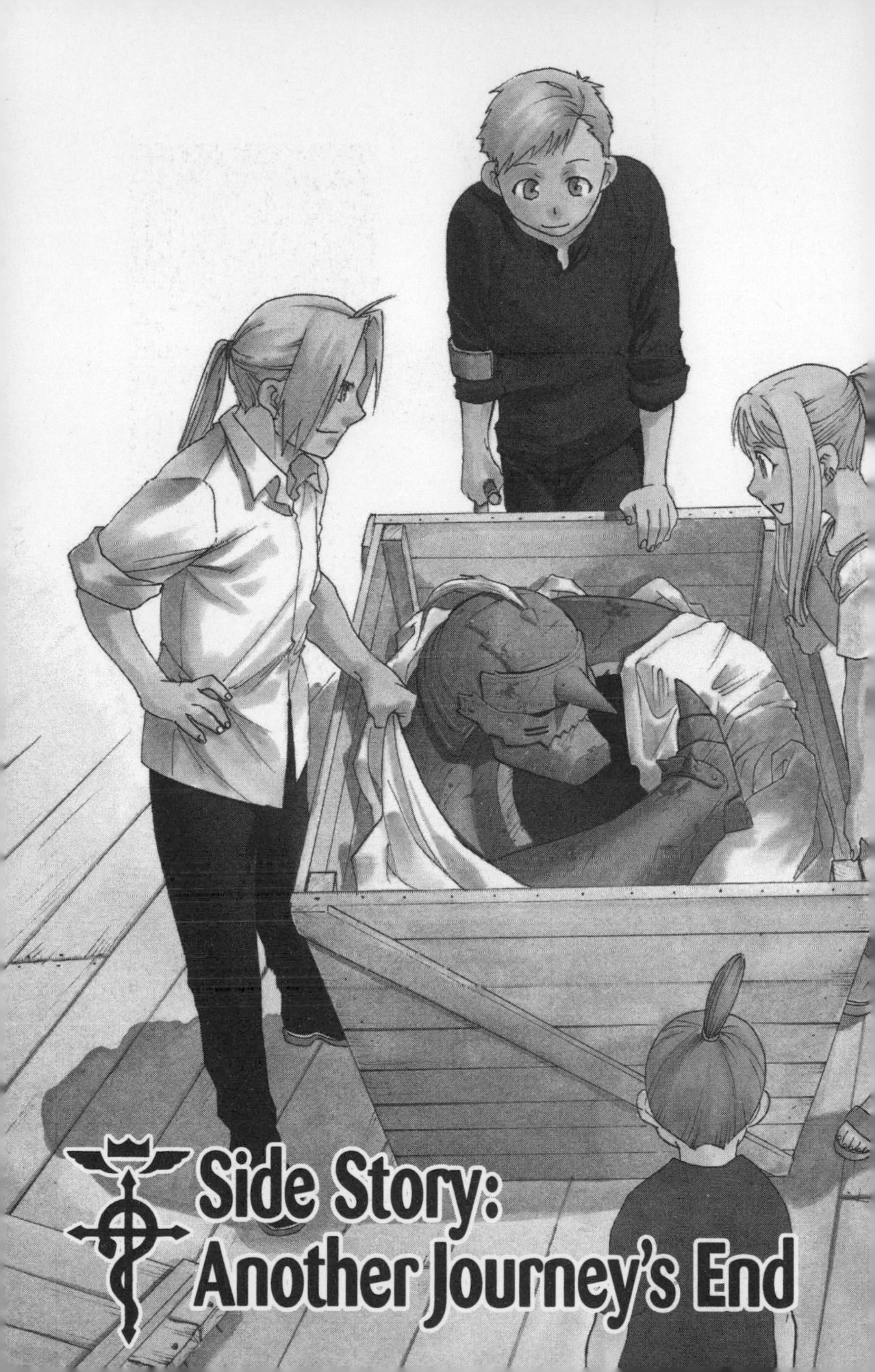
Side Story:
Another Journey's End

FULLMETAL
ALCHEMIST

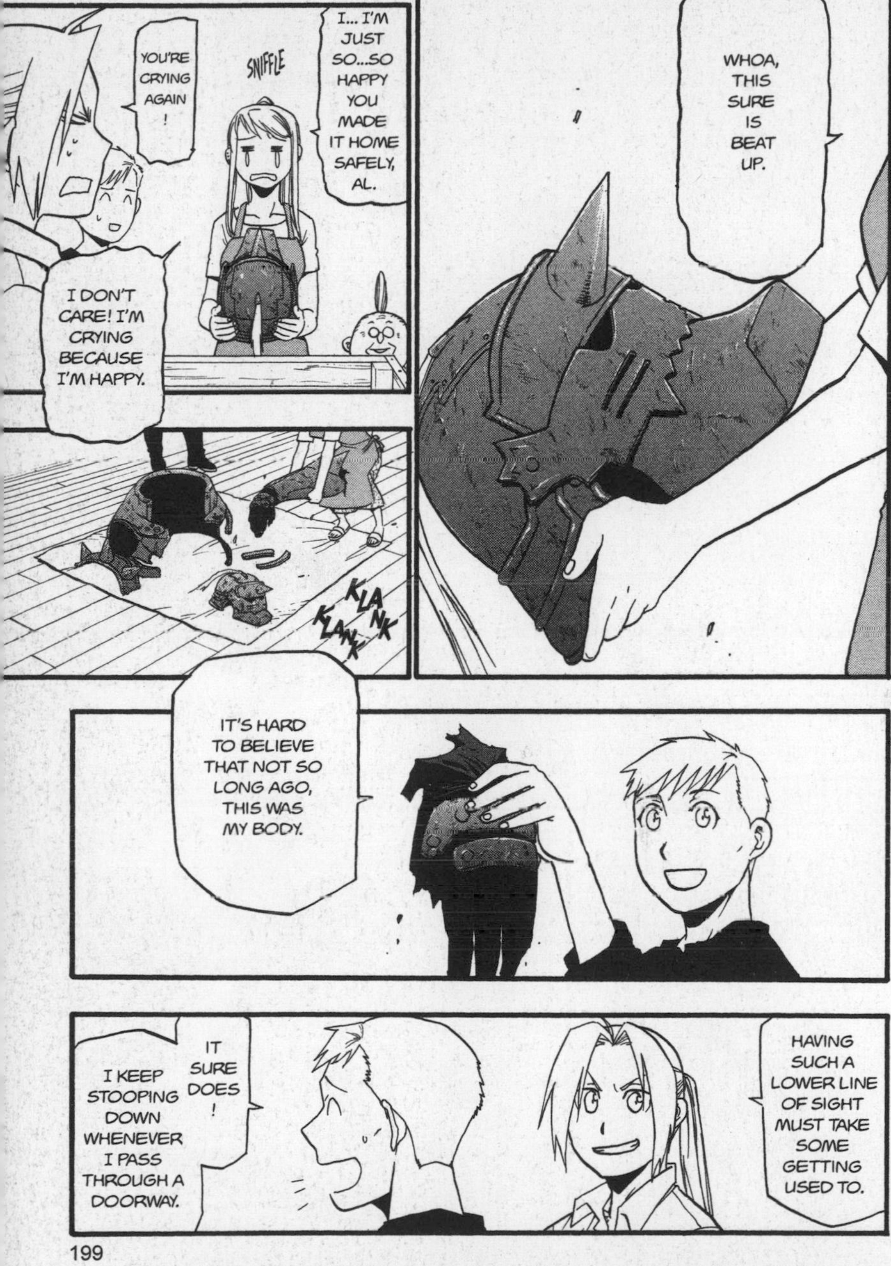
WHOA, THIS SURE IS BEAT UP.
I... I'M JUST SO...SO HAPPY YOU MADE IT HOME SAFELY, AL.
SNIFFLE
YOU'RE CRYING AGAIN!
I DON'T CARE! I'M CRYING BECAUSE I'M HAPPY.
KLANK KLANK
IT'S HARD TO BELIEVE THAT NOT SO LONG AGO, THIS WAS MY BODY.
HAVING SUCH A LOWER LINE OF SIGHT MUST TAKE SOME GETTING USED TO.
IT SURE DOES!
I KEEP STOOPING DOWN WHENEVER I PASS THROUGH A DOORWAY.

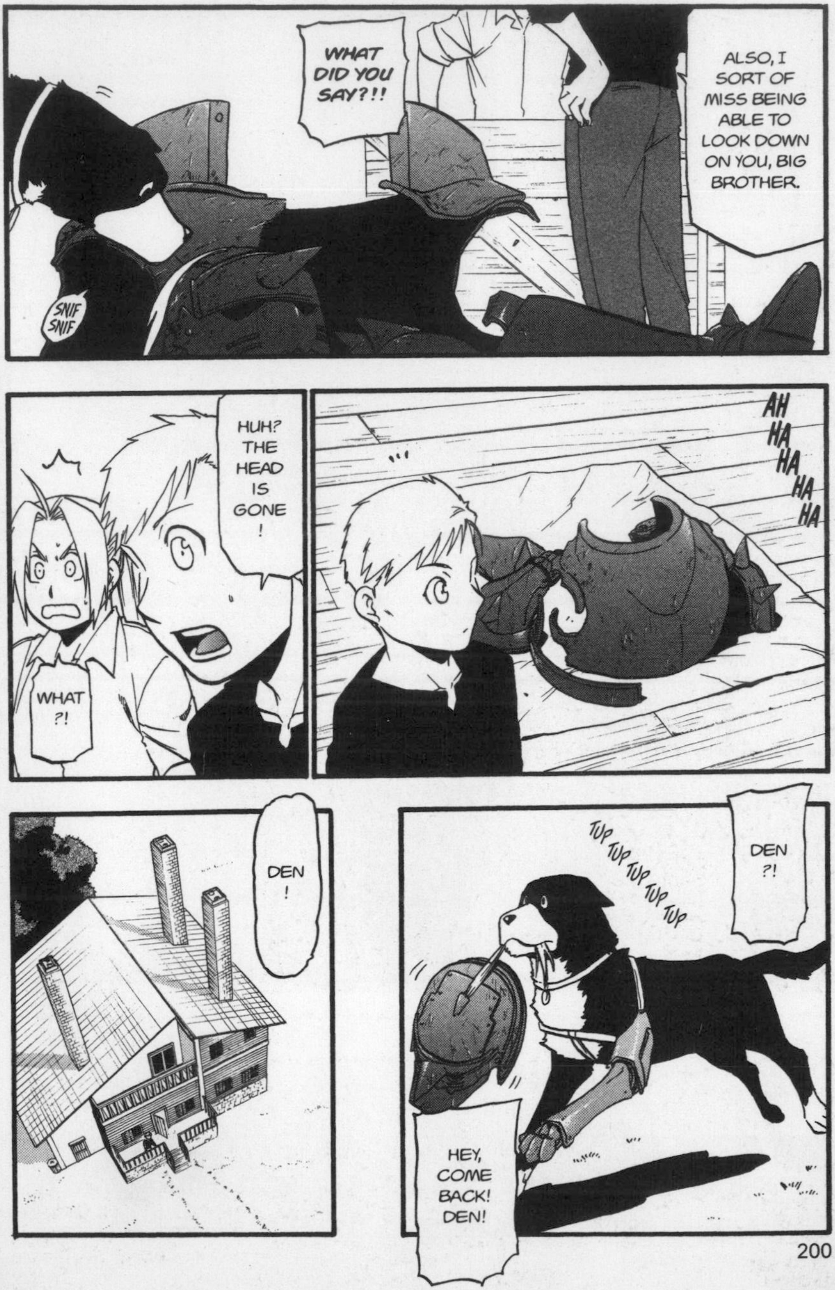
ALSO, I SORT OF MISS BEING ABLE TO LOOK DOWN ON YOU, BIG BROTHER.
WHAT DID YOU SAY?!!
SNIF SNIF
AH HA HA HA HA HA
HUH? THE HEAD IS GONE!
WHAT?!
DEN?!
TUP TUP TUP TUP TUP
HEY, COME BACK! DEN!
DEN!

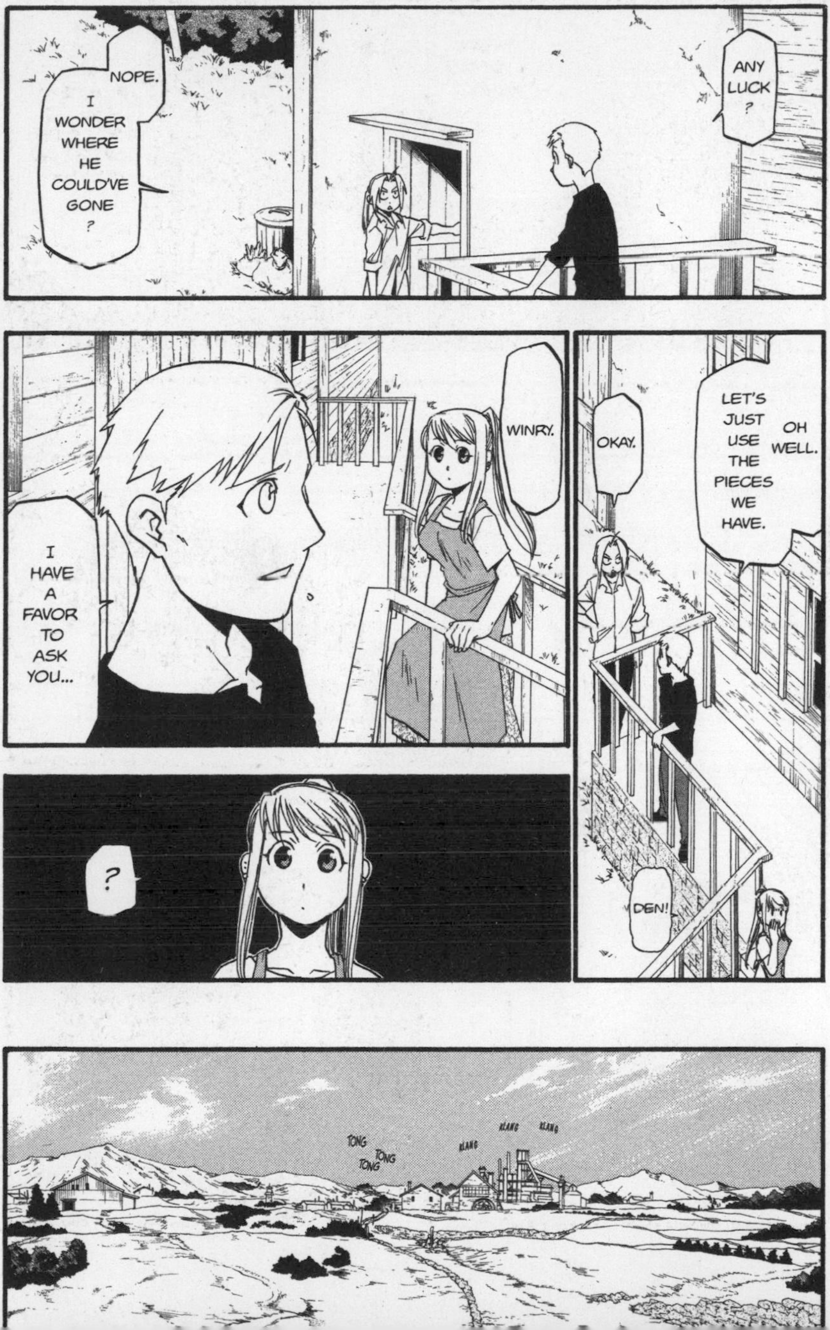
ANY LUCK?
NOPE. I WONDER WHERE HE COULD'VE GONE?
OH WELL.
LET'S JUST USE THE PIECES WE HAVE.
OKAY.
DEN!
WINRY.
I HAVE A FAVOR TO ASK YOU...
?
KLANG
KLANG
KLANG
TONG
TONG
TONG

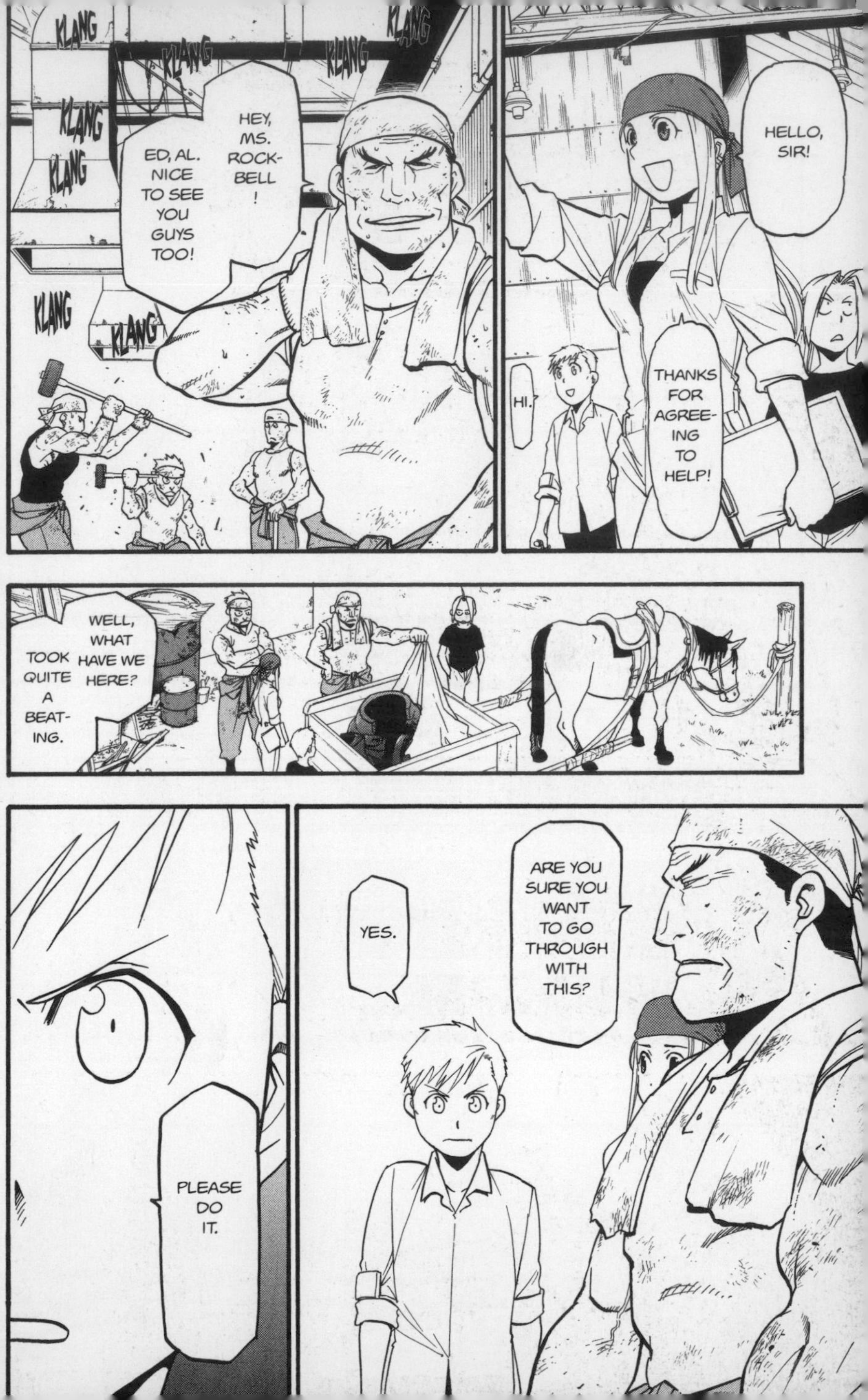
HELLO, SIR!
THANKS FOR AGREEING TO HELP!
HI.
KLANG KLANG KLANG KLANG
HEY, MS. ROCKBELL!
ED, AL. NICE TO SEE YOU GUYS TOO!
KLANG KLANG KLANG KLANG
WELL, WHAT HAVE WE HERE?
TOOK QUITE A BEATING.
ARE YOU SURE YOU WANT TO GO THROUGH WITH THIS?
YES.
PLEASE DO IT.

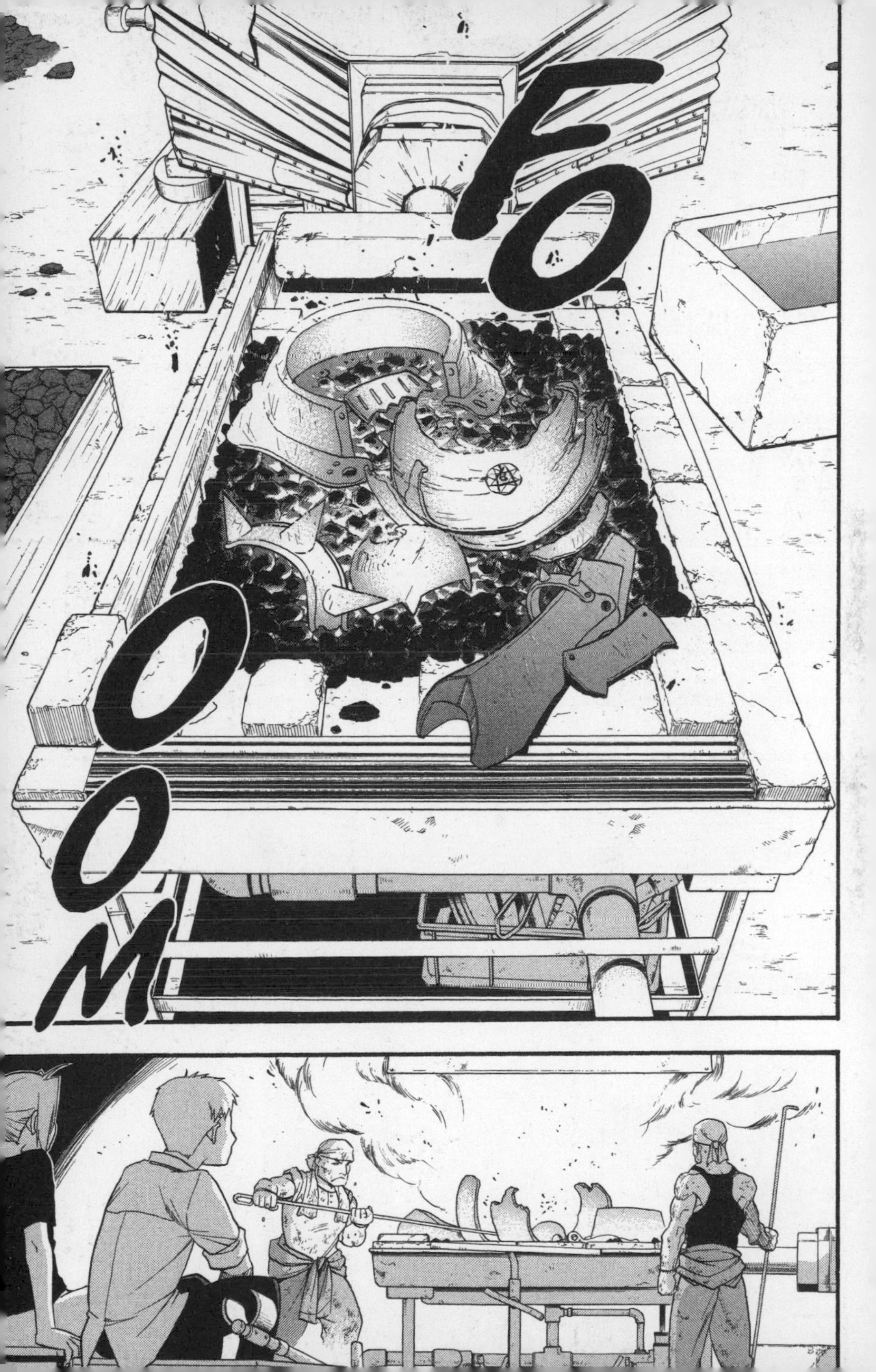
FOOOM

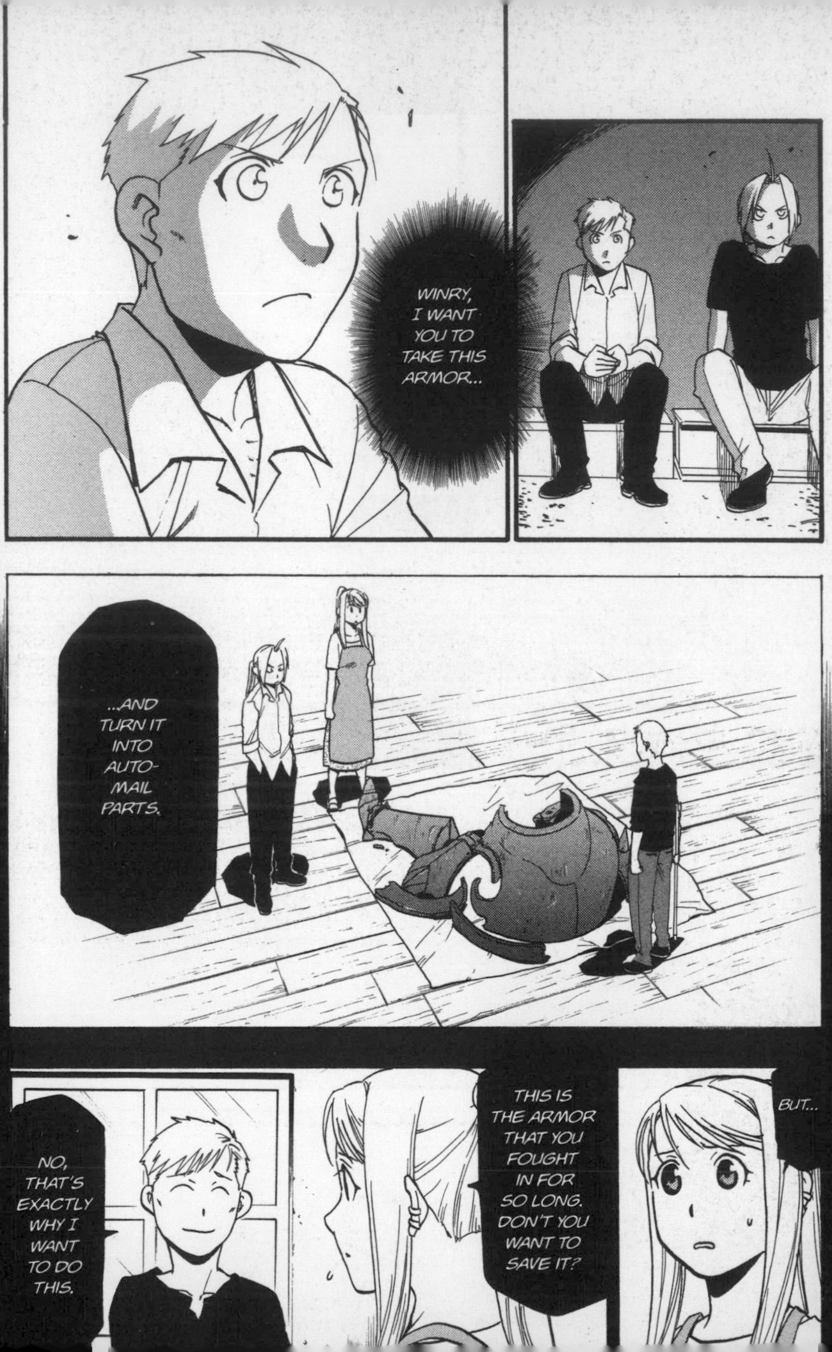
WINRY, I WANT YOU TO TAKE THIS ARMOR...
...AND TURN IT INTO AUTO-MAIL PARTS.
BUT...
THIS IS THE ARMOR THAT YOU FOUGHT IN FOR SO LONG. DON'T YOU WANT TO SAVE IT?
NO, THAT'S EXACTLY WHY I WANT TO DO THIS.

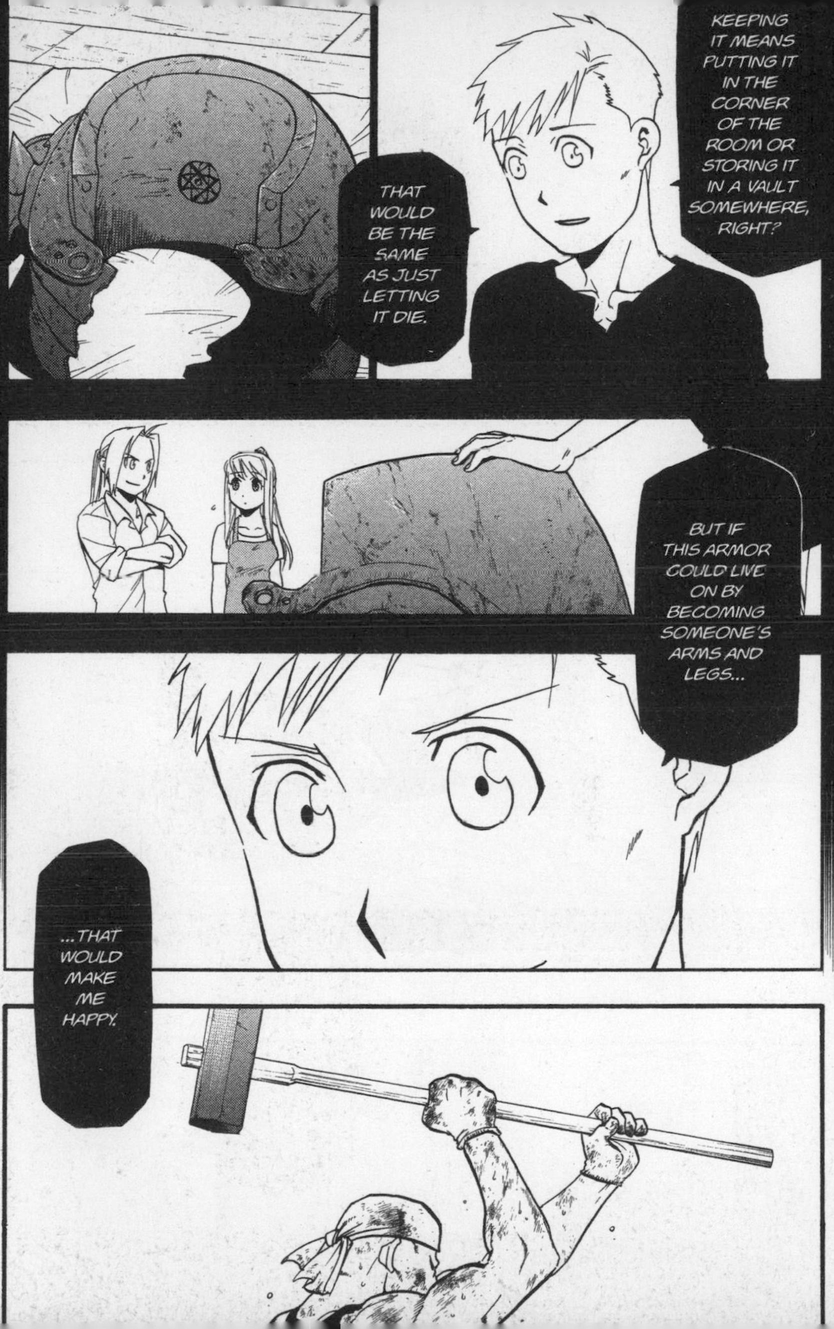
KEEPING IT MEANS PUTTING IT IN THE CORNER OF THE ROOM OR STORING IT IN A VAULT SOMEWHERE, RIGHT?
THAT WOULD BE THE SAME AS JUST LETTING IT DIE.
BUT IF THIS ARMOR COULD LIVE ON BY BECOMING SOMEONE'S ARMS AND LEGS...
...THAT WOULD MAKE ME HAPPY.

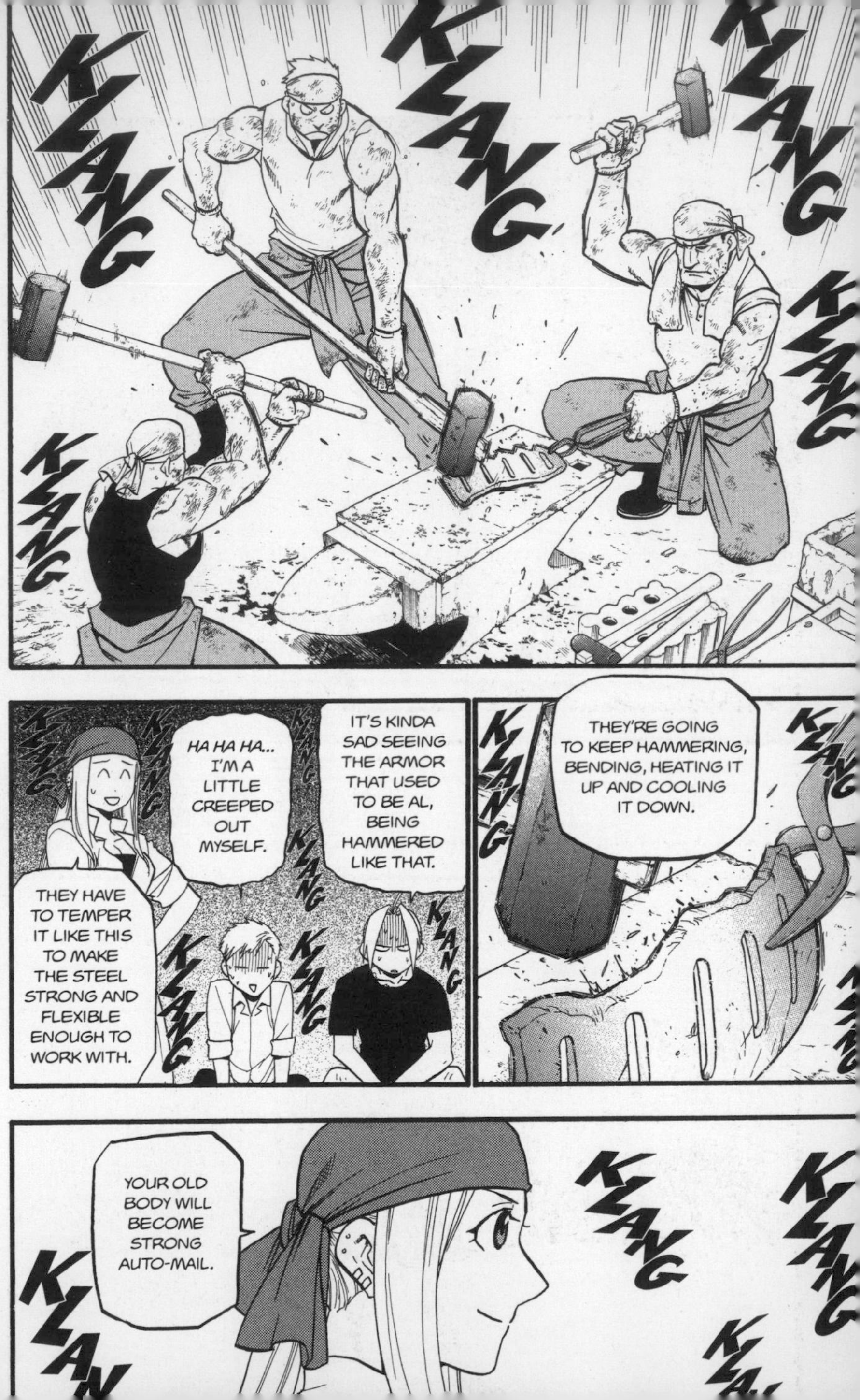
KLANG
KLANG
KLANG
KLANG
KLANG
KLANG
THEY'RE GOING TO KEEP HAMMERING, BENDING, HEATING IT UP AND COOLING IT DOWN.
KLANG
KLANG
IT'S KINDA SAD SEEING THE ARMOR THAT USED TO BE AL, BEING HAMMERED LIKE THAT.
HA HA HA... I'M A LITTLE CREEPED OUT MYSELF.
KLANG
KLANG
KLANG
THEY HAVE TO TEMPER IT LIKE THIS TO MAKE THE STEEL STRONG AND FLEXIBLE ENOUGH TO WORK WITH.
KLANG
KLANG
KLANG
YOUR OLD BODY WILL BECOME STRONG AUTO-MAIL.
KLAN

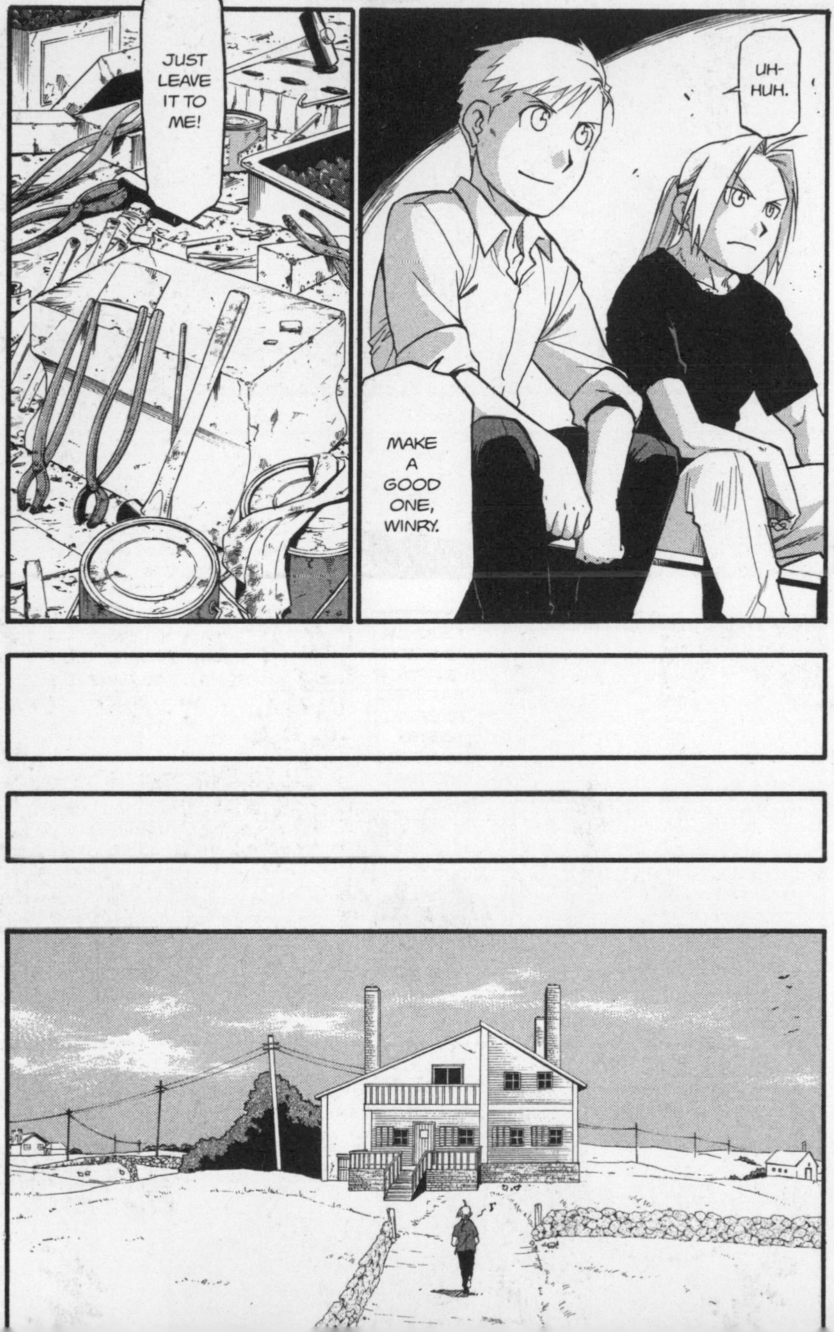
UH-HUH.
MAKE A GOOD ONE, WINRY.
JUST LEAVE IT TO ME!

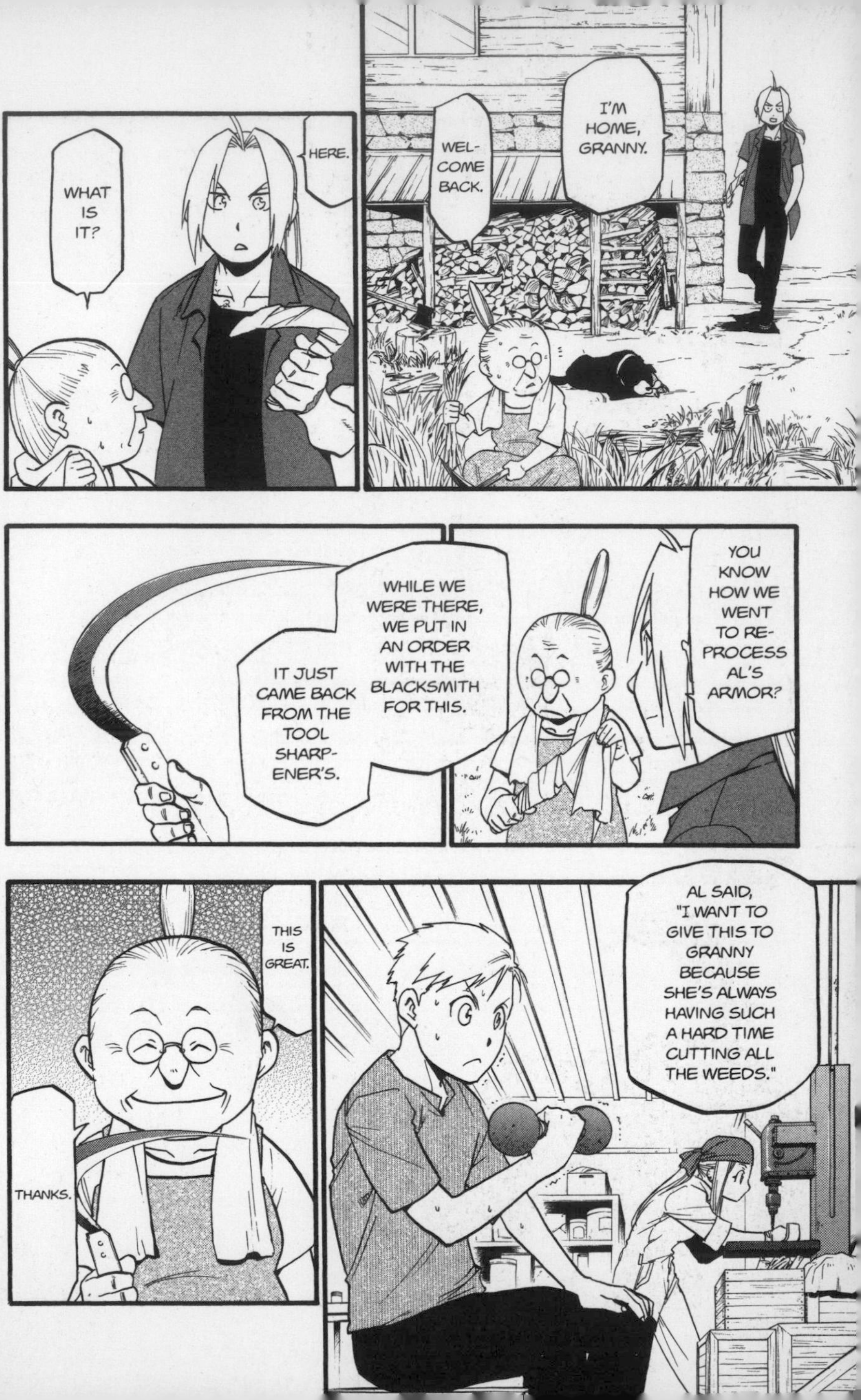
I'M HOME, GRANNY.
WEL-COME BACK.
HERE.
WHAT IS IT?
YOU KNOW HOW WE WENT TO RE-PROCESS AL'S ARMOR?
WHILE WE WERE THERE, WE PUT IN AN ORDER WITH THE BLACKSMITH FOR THIS.
IT JUST CAME BACK FROM THE TOOL SHARP-ENER'S.
AL SAID, "I WANT TO GIVE THIS TO GRANNY BECAUSE SHE'S ALWAYS HAVING SUCH A HARD TIME CUTTING ALL THE WEEDS."
THIS IS GREAT.
THANKS.

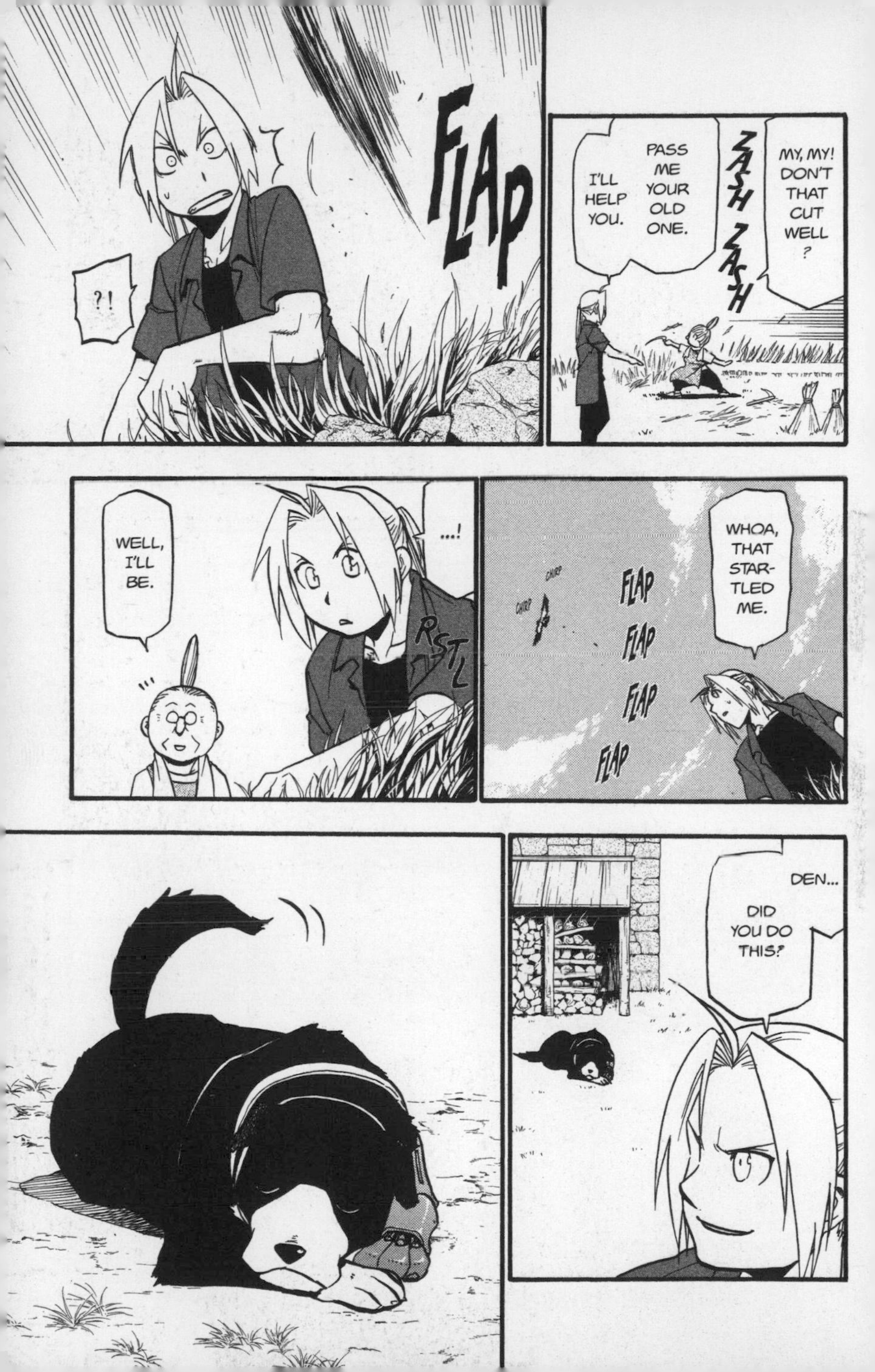
MY, MY! DON'T THAT CUT WELL?
ZASH ZASH
I'LL HELP YOU. PASS ME YOUR OLD ONE.
FLAP
?!
WHOA, THAT STAR-TLED ME.
CHIRP
CHIRP
FLAP
FLAP
FLAP
FLAP
...!
RSTL
WELL, I'LL BE.
DEN...
DID YOU DO THIS?

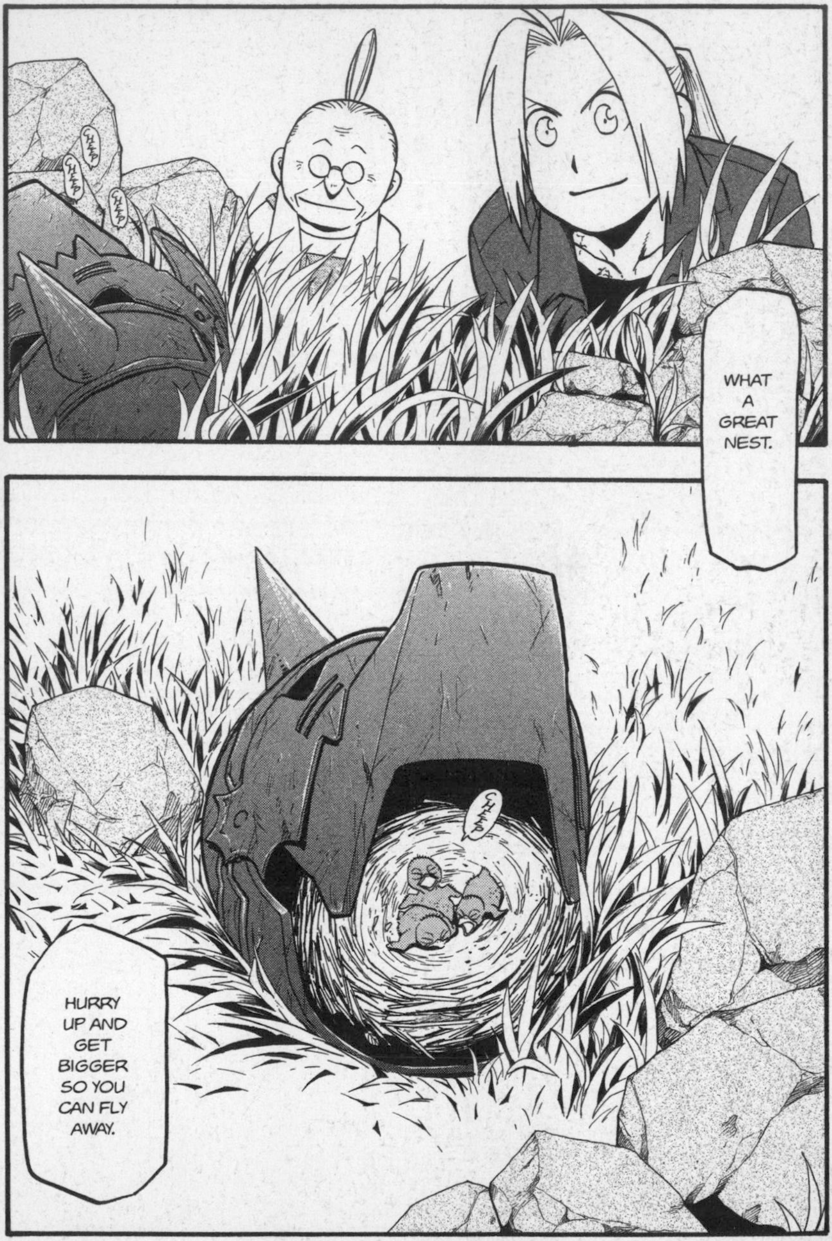
CHEEP
CHEEP
CHEEP
WHAT A GREAT NEST.
CHEEP
HURRY UP AND GET BIGGER SO YOU CAN FLY AWAY.

FULLMETAL ALCHEMIST 27 END

FULLMETAL
ALCHEMIST

EXTRAS

✳A REJECTED FINAL CHAPTER PIC.

From Scratch

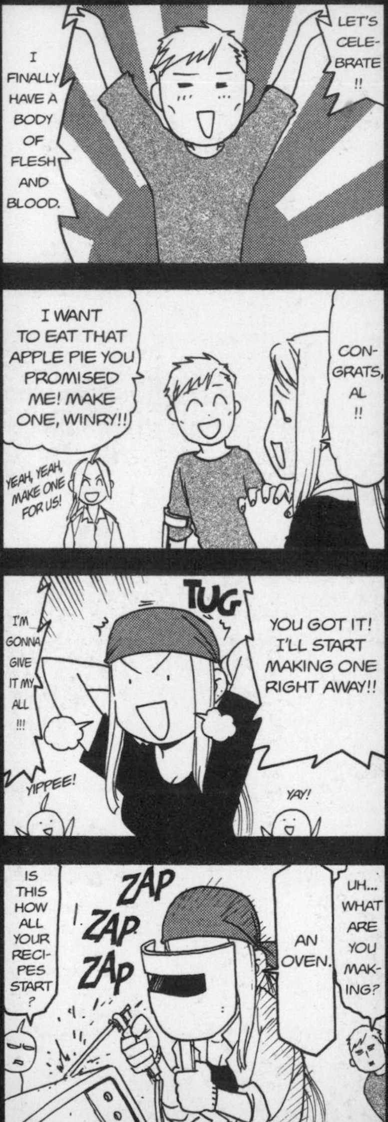

LET'S CELEBRATE!!
I FINALLY HAVE A BODY OF FLESH AND BLOOD.
CONGRATS, AL!!
I WANT TO EAT THAT APPLE PIE YOU PROMISED ME! MAKE ONE, WINRY!!
YEAH, YEAH, MAKE ONE FOR US!
TUG
YOU GOT IT! I'LL START MAKING ONE RIGHT AWAY!!
I'M GONNA GIVE IT MY ALL!!!
YAY!
YIPPEE!
UH... WHAT ARE YOU MAKING?
AN OVEN.
ZAP ZAP ZAP
IS THIS HOW ALL YOUR RECIPES START?

The Law

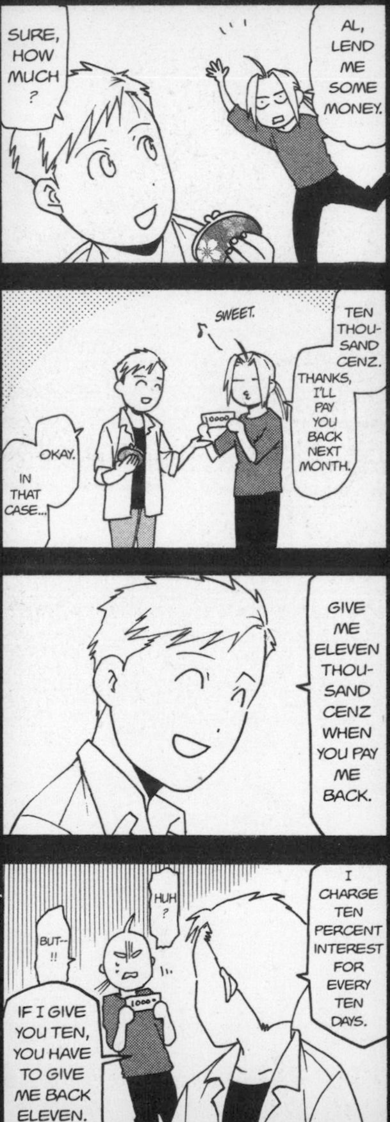

AL, LEND ME SOME MONEY.
SURE, HOW MUCH?
TEN THOUSAND CENZ.
SWEET.
THANKS, I'LL PAY YOU BACK NEXT MONTH.
OKAY. IN THAT CASE...
GIVE ME ELEVEN THOUSAND CENZ WHEN YOU PAY ME BACK.
I CHARGE TEN PERCENT INTEREST FOR EVERY TEN DAYS.
HUH?
BUT--!!
IF I GIVE YOU TEN, YOU HAVE TO GIVE ME BACK ELEVEN.

♀

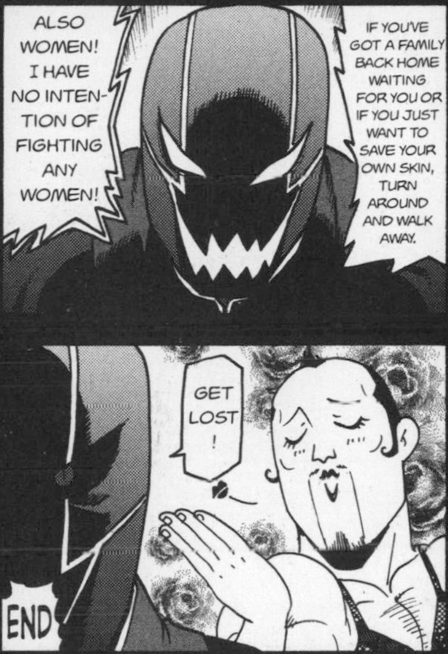
IF YOU'VE GOT A FAMILY BACK HOME WAITING FOR YOU OR IF YOU JUST WANT TO SAVE YOUR OWN SKIN, TURN AROUND AND WALK AWAY.
ALSO WOMEN! I HAVE NO INTEN-TION OF FIGHTING ANY WOMEN!
GET LOST!
END

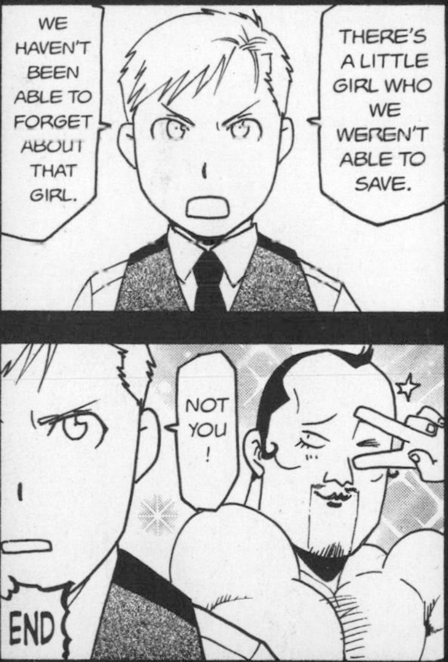
THERE'S A LITTLE GIRL WHO WE WEREN'T ABLE TO SAVE.
WE HAVEN'T BEEN ABLE TO FORGET ABOUT THAT GIRL.
NOT YOU!
END

The Pythagoras Switch

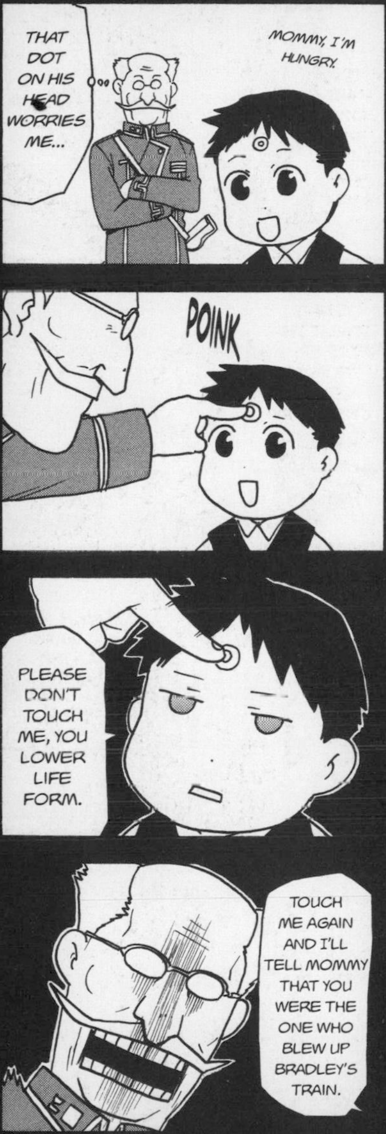
MOMMY, I'M HUNGRY.
THAT DOT ON HIS HEAD WORRIES ME...
POINK
PLEASE DON'T TOUCH ME, YOU LOWER LIFE FORM.
TOUCH ME AGAIN AND I'LL TELL MOMMY THAT YOU WERE THE ONE WHO BLEW UP BRADLEY'S TRAIN.

Unexpected Results

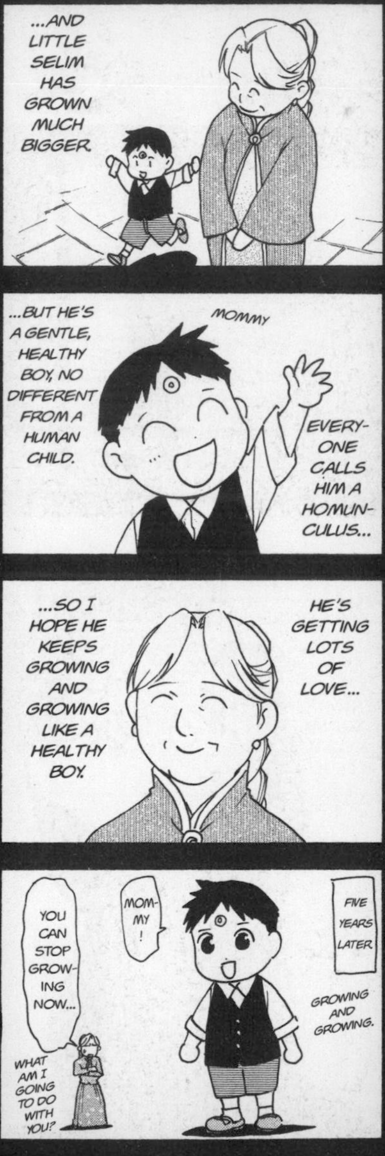
...AND LITTLE SELIM HAS GROWN MUCH BIGGER.
MOMMY
EVERY-ONE CALLS HIM A HOMUN-CULUS...
...BUT HE'S A GENTLE, HEALTHY BOY, NO DIFFERENT FROM A HUMAN CHILD.
HE'S GETTING LOTS OF LOVE...
...SO I HOPE HE KEEPS GROWING AND GROWING LIKE A HEALTHY BOY.
FIVE YEARS LATER
GROWING AND GROWING.
MOM-MY!
YOU CAN STOP GROW-ING NOW...
WHAT AM I GOING TO DO WITH YOU?

The Embarrassing Protagonist

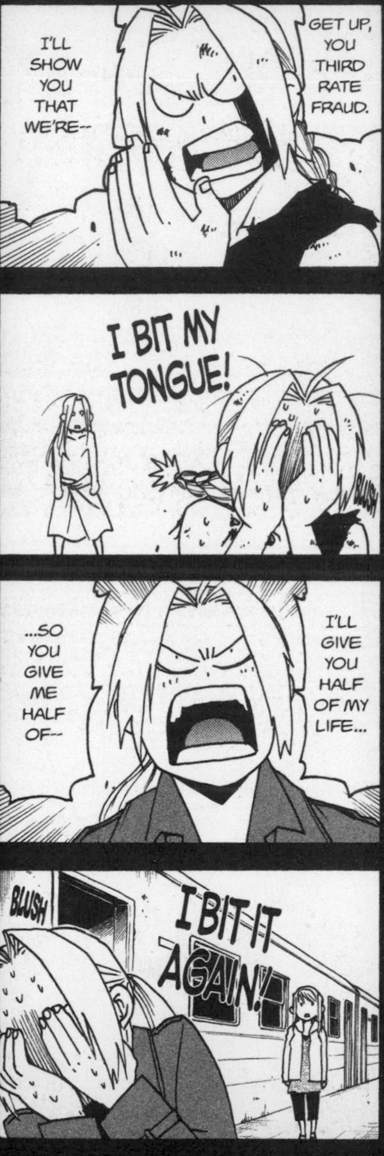
GET UP, YOU THIRD RATE FRAUD.
I'LL SHOW YOU THAT WE'RE--
I BIT MY TONGUE!
BLUSH
I'LL GIVE YOU HALF OF MY LIFE...
...SO YOU GIVE ME HALF OF--
I BIT IT AGAIN!
BLUSH

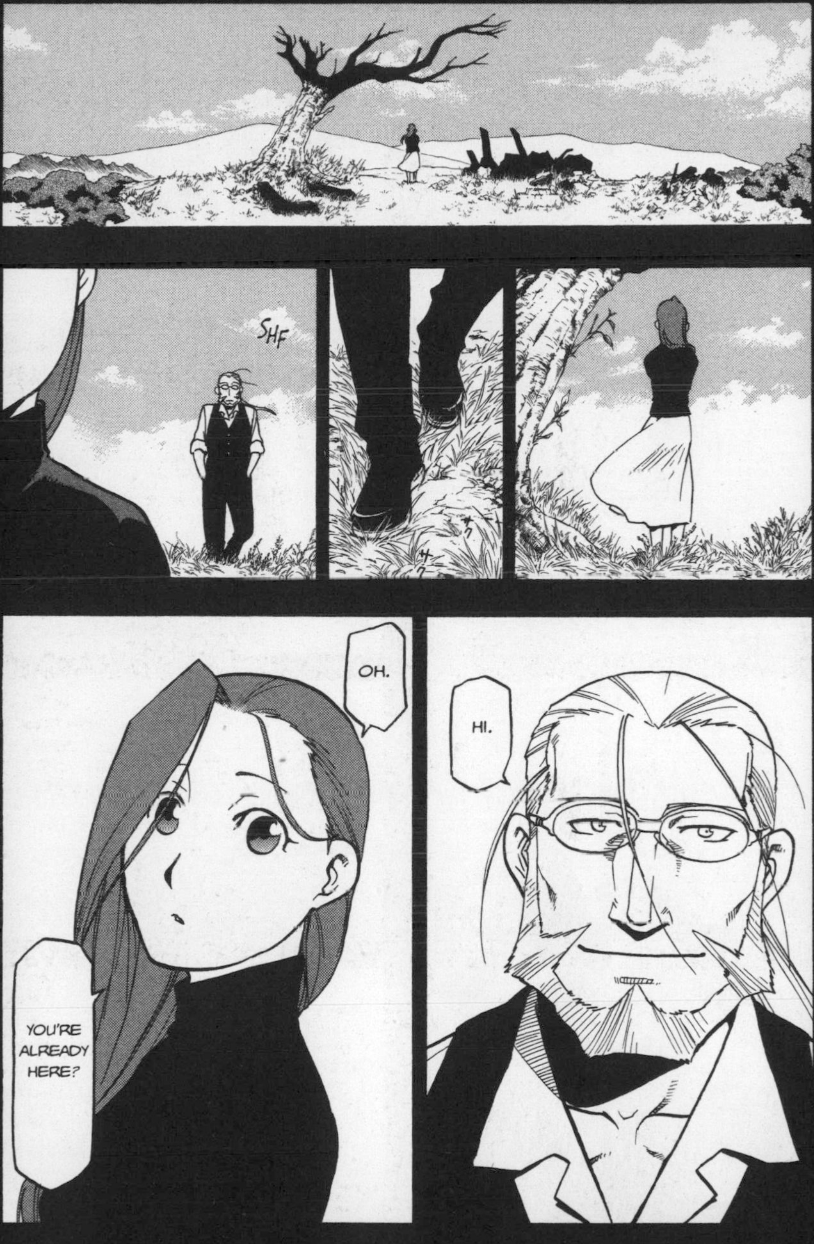
SHF
HI.
OH.
YOU'RE ALREADY HERE?

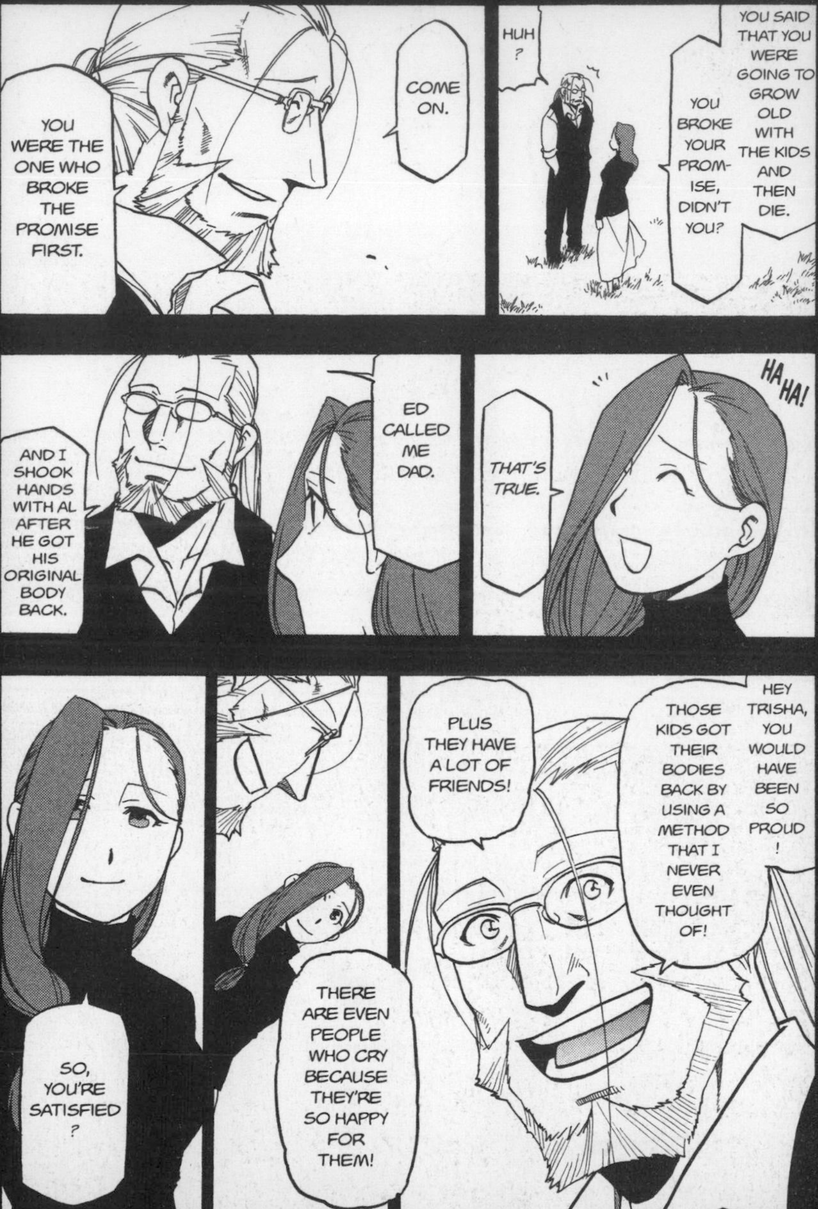

YOU SAID THAT YOU WERE GOING TO GROW OLD WITH THE KIDS AND THEN DIE.
YOU BROKE YOUR PROMISE, DIDN'T YOU?
HUH ?
COME ON.
YOU WERE THE ONE WHO BROKE THE PROMISE FIRST.
HA HA!
THAT'S TRUE.
ED CALLED ME DAD.
AND I SHOOK HANDS WITH AL AFTER HE GOT HIS ORIGINAL BODY BACK.
HEY TRISHA, YOU WOULD HAVE BEEN SO PROUD!
THOSE KIDS GOT THEIR BODIES BACK BY USING A METHOD THAT I NEVER EVEN THOUGHT OF!
PLUS THEY HAVE A LOT OF FRIENDS!
THERE ARE EVEN PEOPLE WHO CRY BECAUSE THEY'RE SO HAPPY FOR THEM!
SO, YOU'RE SATISFIED ?

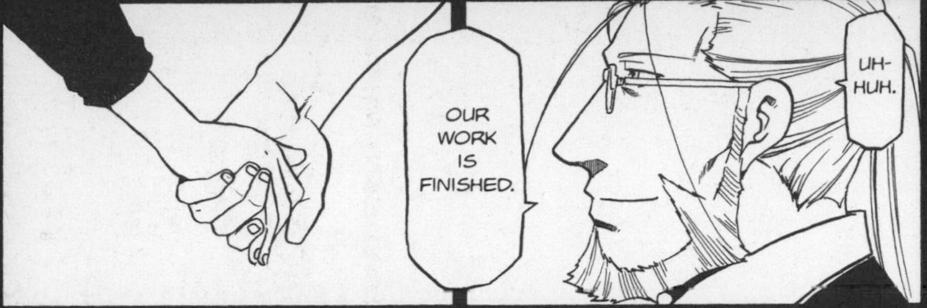
UH-HUH.
OUR WORK IS FINISHED.

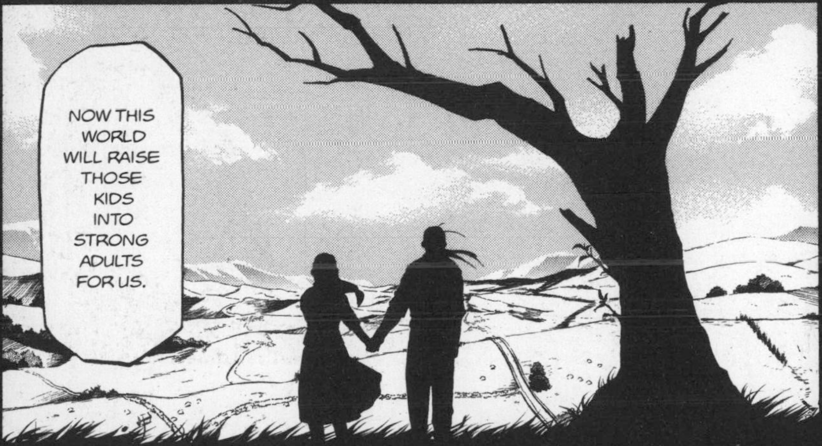
NOW THIS WORLD WILL RAISE THOSE KIDS INTO STRONG ADULTS FOR US.

FULLMETAL ALCHEMIST 27

THANKS TO:

KAZUFUMI KANEKO
MANATSU SAKURA
NORIKO TSUBOTA
JUNSHI BABA
MASANARI YUZUKA

YOICHI KAMITONO
KORI SAKANO
KEISUI TAKAEDA
NONO
MASASHI MIZUTANI

AIYABALL
MR. COUPON
MICHIKO SHISHIDO
JUN TOHKO
SANKICHI HINODEYA

MY EDITOR, YUICHI SHIMOMURA

AND YOU!!!

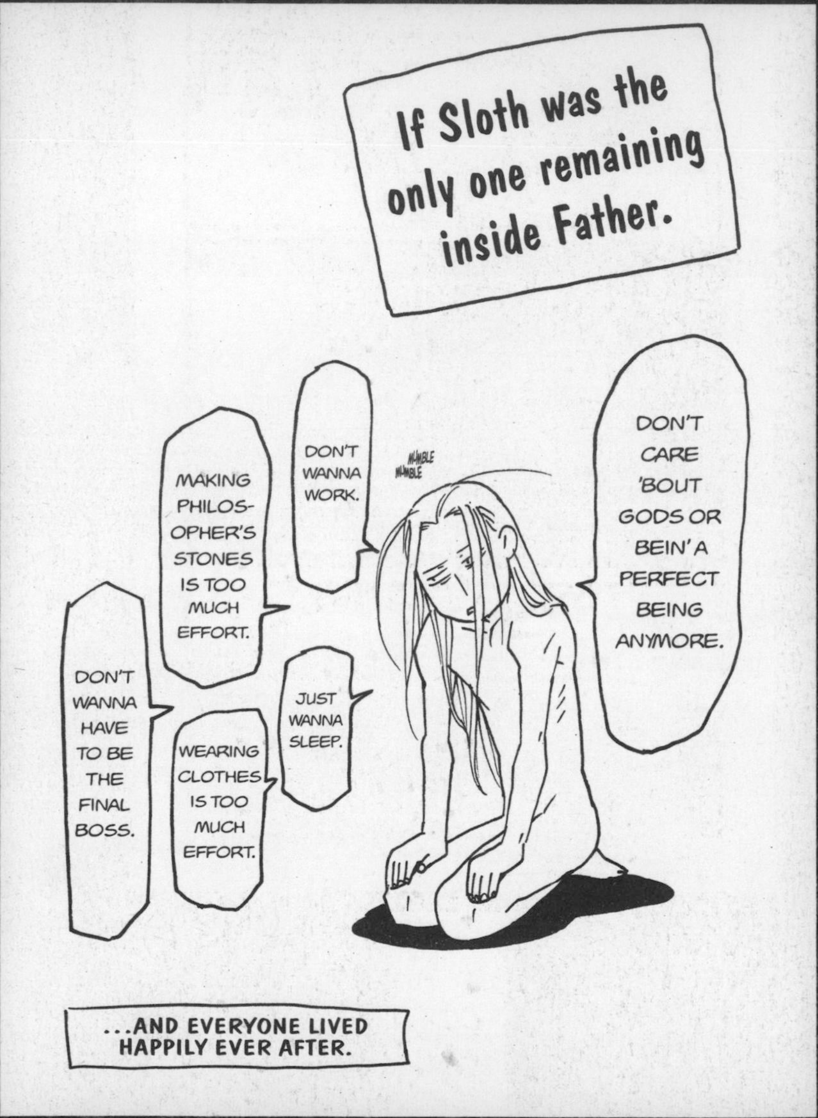
If Sloth was the only one remaining inside Father.
DON'T CARE 'BOUT GODS OR BEIN' A PERFECT BEING ANYMORE.
MUMBLE MUMBLE
DON'T WANNA WORK.
MAKING PHILOSOPHER'S STONES IS TOO MUCH EFFORT.
JUST WANNA SLEEP.
WEARING CLOTHES IS TOO MUCH EFFORT.
DON'T WANNA HAVE TO BE THE FINAL BOSS.
...AND EVERYONE LIVED HAPPILY EVER AFTER.

CONTINUED FROM THE PREVIOUS VOLUME.

GWOOM
ZOOOOSH
VOOP
1.
HUH?
THIS PROVES THE EARTH IS ROUND!!
And that's how Fullmetal Alchemist came to an end!!

Spoiler prevention is in effect for the final volume.

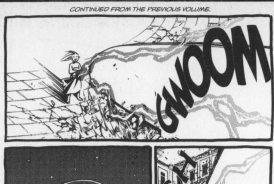

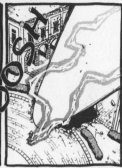

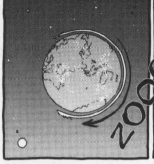

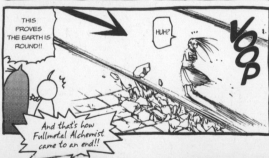

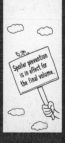

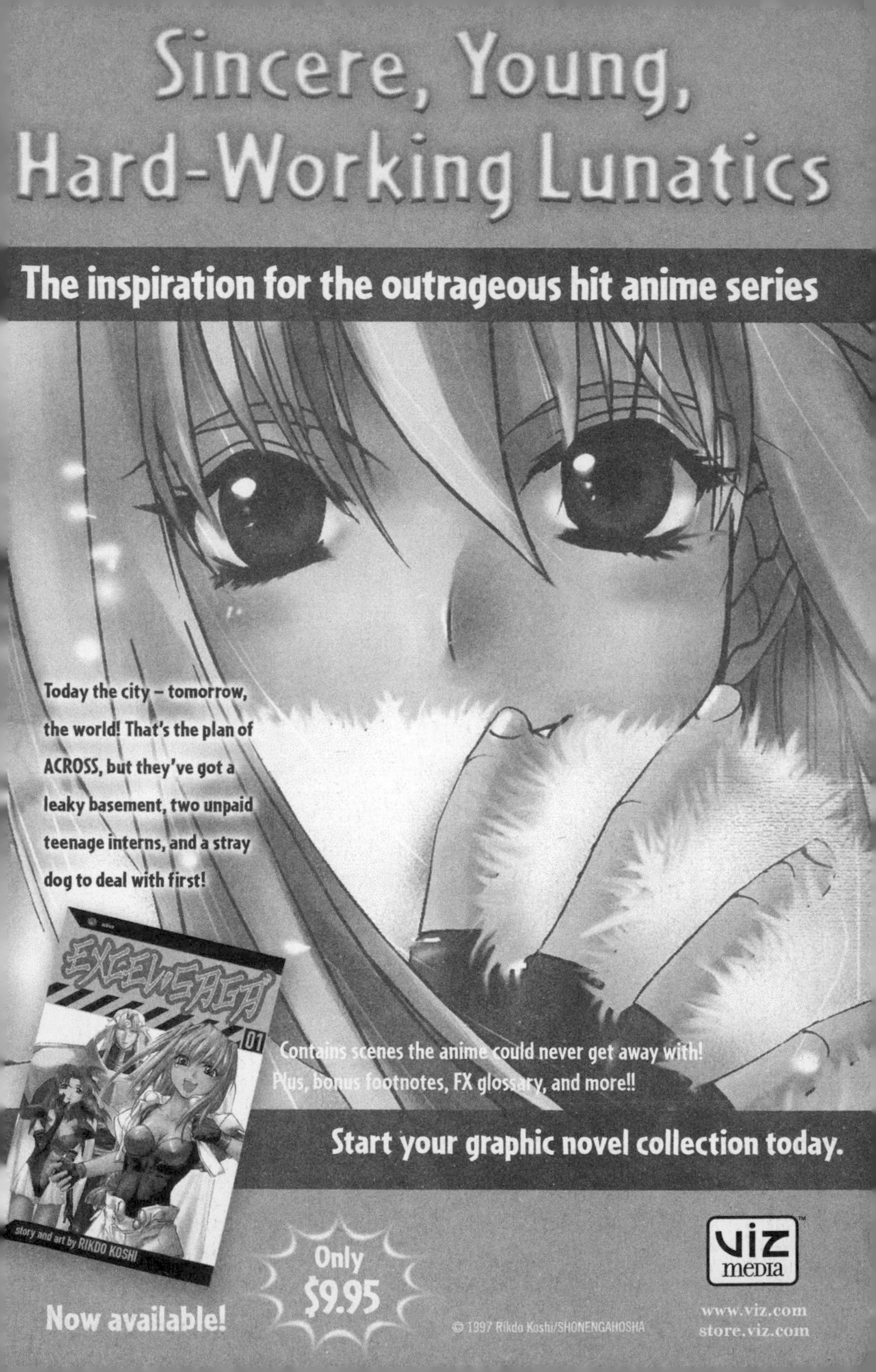

Sincere, Young, Hard-Working Lunatics
The inspiration for the outrageous hit anime series
Today the city – tomorrow, the world! That's the plan of ACROSS, but they've got a leaky basement, two unpaid teenage interns, and a stray dog to deal with first!
EXCEL SAGA
01
story and art by RIKDO KOSHI
Contains scenes the anime could never get away with! Plus, bonus footnotes, FX glossary, and more!!
Start your graphic novel collection today.
Only $9.95
Now available!
© 1997 Rikdo Koshi/SHONENGAHOSHA
VIZ media
www.viz.com
store.viz.com

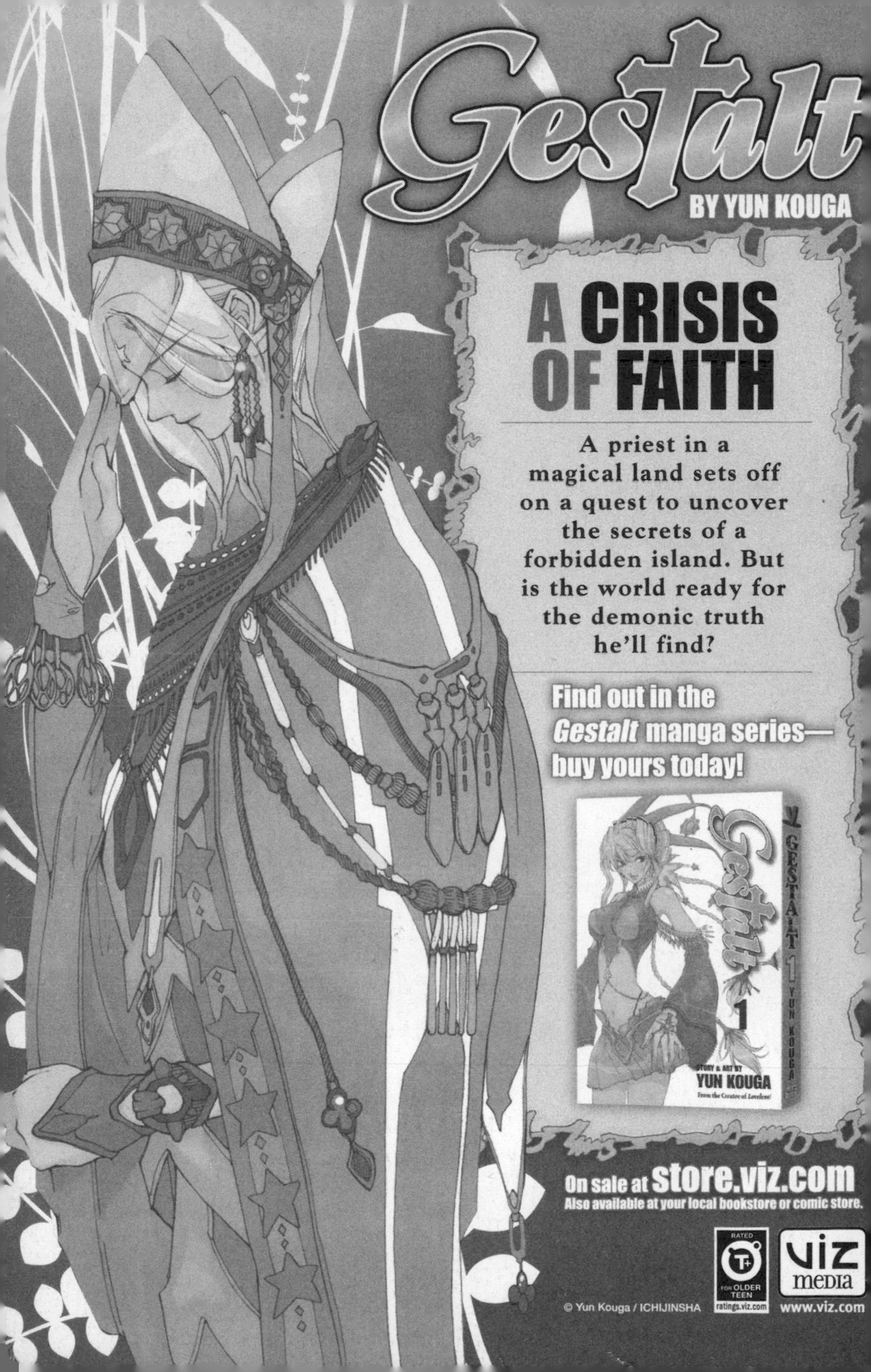
Gestalt
BY YUN KOUGA
A CRISIS OF FAITH
A priest in a magical land sets off on a quest to uncover the secrets of a forbidden island. But is the world ready for the demonic truth he'll find?
Find out in the *Gestalt* manga series—buy yours today!
Gestalt
GESTALT 1 YUN KOUGA
1
STORY & ART BY
YUN KOUGA
From the Creator of Loveless!
On sale at store.viz.com
Also available at your local bookstore or comic store.
RATED
T+
FOR OLDER TEEN
ratings.viz.com
VIZ media
www.viz.com
© Yun Kouga / ICHIJINSHA

ANIME ON

hulu™

Watch Your Favorites.
Anytime. For Free.

www.hulu.com

BLEACH © Tite Kubo / Shueisha, TV TOKYO, dentsu, Pierrot
SHONEN JUMP and BLEACH are trademarks of
Shueisha, Inc. in the United States and/or other countries.

NARUTO © 2002 MASASHI KISHIMOTO
SHONEN JUMP and NARUTO are trademarks of
Shueisha, Inc. in the U.S. and other countries.

DEATH NOTE © Tsugumi Ohba, Takeshi Obata/Shueisha
© DNDP, VAP, Shueisha, Madhouse
SHONEN JUMP and DEATH NOTE are trademarks of
Shueisha, Inc. in the United States and other countries.